GREEK TRAGIC WOMEN ON SHAKESPEAREAN STAGES

Greek Tragic Women on Shakespearean Stages

TANYA POLLARD

OXFORD
UNIVERSITY PRESS

OXFORD
UNIVERSITY PRESS

Great Clarendon Street, Oxford, OX2 6DP,
United Kingdom

Oxford University Press is a department of the University of Oxford.
It furthers the University's objective of excellence in research, scholarship,
and education by publishing worldwide. Oxford is a registered trade mark of
Oxford University Press in the UK and in certain other countries

First Edition published in 2017
Impression: 1

Published in the United States of America by Oxford University Press
198 Madison Avenue, New York, NY 10016, United States of America

British Library Cataloguing in Publication Data
Data available

Library of Congress Control Number: 2017932558

ISBN 978–0–19–879311–3

Printed and bound by
CPI Group (UK) Ltd, Croydon, CR0 4YY

Acknowledgments

This book has developed over many years, and with the support of many people and institutions. I am grateful for support from the National Endowment for the Humanities, the Whiting Foundation, Brooklyn College, the CUNY Graduate Center, Oxford Brookes University, Montclair State University, the Columbia Shakespeare Seminar, and PSC-CUNY Awards, jointly funded by The Professional Staff Congress and The City University of New York. I am also grateful for opportunities to present material from this book to audiences at Brooklyn College, Cambridge University, Columbia University, the CUNY Graduate Center, Oxford Brookes University, Oxford University, New York University, Université Paul-Valéry Montpellier, and Yale University, as well as at conferences including the Shakespeare Association of America and the Renaissance Society of America. An earlier version of Chapter Three was published as "What's Hecuba to Shakespeare?" in *Renaissance Quarterly* 65:4 (2012), 1060–93; I am grateful for permission to reproduce that material here. For help with special collections of early printed Greek books, I would like to thank the staff at the Bodleian Library and Columbia University's Rare Book and Manuscript Library. For turning this material into a book, I am grateful to everyone who has contributed to its production at Oxford University Press, including Jacqueline Baker, Eleanor Collins, Aimee Wright, Lakshmanan Sethuraman, my copy-editor Helen Belgian, and the external readers.

On a more personal front, while writing this book I have benefited enormously from the warm support of colleagues and friends. At CUNY I am grateful for the support of my Brooklyn College Department Chair, Ellen Tremper, and Deputy Chair, Elaine Brooks, as well as the head of my Graduate Center Department, Mario DiGangi, and colleagues including Liv Yarrow, Rich McCoy, Marty Elsky, Clare Carroll, Steve Monte, Tanya Agathacleous, Talia Schaffer, Helen Phillips, Marie Rutkoski, Corinne Amato, Nancy Silverman, and Kathy Koutsis. I am very grateful for research support at the Graduate Center from Jennifer Alberghini, Dan Jacobson, Patrick James, Ja Young Jeon, Melina Moore, Yeree Shim, and Rose Tomassi, and at Brooklyn College from Leigh Stein and Alex Hajjar; I am also grateful to the wonderful librarians at Brooklyn College and the Graduate Center for their help in supplying me with books, chapters, and articles. For conversations, questions, and suggestions at various stages in this project, I would like to thank scholars and friends including Chimene Bateman, Gordon Braden, Stefanie Buchenau, Charlotte Coffin, Allison Deutermann, Helene Foley, Jesse Gale, Clare Hutton, Andras Kisery, Naomi Conn Liebler, Fiona Macintosh, Laurie Maguire, Justine McConnell, Yves Peyré, Tiffany Stern, Oliver Taplin, Janice Valls-Russell, and Susanne Wofford. For community and moral support, I am grateful to local Brooklyn friends and neighbors, especially Kim Bernhardt, Suzanne Blezard, Sharon Herbstman, Gilly Nadel, Nicole Rice, and Ramona Sekulovic. For inspiration and collaboration I would like to thank Beatrice Bradley, with whom I co-authored an article on Shakespeare and Plautus while writing this book. I owe special thanks to Tania Demetriou, with whom I've worked closely co-organizing, co-editing, and co-writing on Greek in early modern England, for both intellectual insights and warm conversations across sprawling topics and international settings.

For insights into the world of theatrical performance, I am grateful to everyone at Theatre for a New Audience, especially Jeffrey Horowitz and all my colleagues on the Council of Scholars. I would also like to thank Michael Sexton and Ann McDonald at the Shakespeare Society, Jesse Berger and George Mayer at the Red Bull Theater, and the many wonderful actors and directors I've spoken with, for ongoing conversations about Shakespeare and early modern plays. For keeping me aloft, I am grateful to the aerial circus world of Om Factory—especially to Kristina Cubrillo, Jan Manke, Kat Schamens, and Fran Sperling, who have exhorted me to slow down, make each move count, and make it beautiful; and advised me, if the view isn't good, to flip it.

I owe special debts to the generosity of friends who have regularly read, advised, and offered support. This book is in many ways a collaborative product of my writing group—Pamela Allen Brown, Bianca Calabresi, Julie Crawford, Natasha Korda, Bella Mirabella, and Nancy Selleck—who have read rigorously, challenged fiercely, debated, and guided the project over many years, and who have reminded me of what I wanted to say when I lost sight. Katharine Craik has continued a long and happy tradition of sharing work and friendship, offering questions, suggestions, support, and inspiration. Lucy Munro heroically read the entire book—some of it multiple times—without ever losing her warmth, diplomacy, and skill at tactfully reining in some of my more reckless instincts. Cristiana Sogno has read, listened, taken satisfyingly firm stances when decisions were necessary, and crucially contributed to my sanity with many happy escapes from work.

My biggest debts, as ever, are to my family. My in-laws, Robin and Lis Stenhouse; my father, Robert Pollard; and especially my mother,

Vicki Pollard, have all contributed to my ability to write this book. My husband, Will Stenhouse, has done more than anyone to support me with writing, and with everything else. I am deeply grateful for all that he has contributed to this project, and for all the other ways he makes my life better. My daughters, Bella and Lucy Stenhouse, have shaped this book at every stage. The book is dedicated to them.

Table of Contents

Introduction

Recovering Greek Tragic Women

A young man of literary interests takes up study in 1570s Oxford amid heady conversations about exploring the long-hidden realm of Greek language and literature. Caught up in the excitement of this avant-garde milieu, he earns admiration by translating an electrifying Greek play about a father's wartime sacrifice of his daughter, which spurs her mother's grief and rage. The play is a tragedy, but it has a happy ending of sorts: after stepping up bravely to be killed, the daughter is miraculously spirited away by a goddess. Yet this apparent relief is shadowed by the knowledge, hinted at in the play, that the girl's devastated mother will nonetheless later murder her husband in revenge. The play's warm reception encourages the young man to write a long poem about another raging mother whose daughter is also sacrificed for the same war, then a play about the man whose adulterous passion led to their deaths. After these works lead him into a successful career writing marketable plays for London's recently established commercial theaters, the man joins forces with a rising younger playwright to write a tragedy exploring sacrifice, grief, and rage, with self-conscious allusions to the tragic women who had captured his imagination in Oxford. Not long after this collaborative venture, the older playwright suffers an untimely death, but the younger playwright continues exploring the same figures, patterns, and allusions in other plays, which attract audiences and spark competitive emulation from his contemporaries. Centuries after his death, this younger playwright remains a theatrical sensation and a household name.

This story may be unfamiliar, but it is not apocryphal. George Peele spent the 1570s in Oxford, where the study of Greek was rapidly becoming not simply widespread but inescapable.[1] He flourished within its Hellenized literary coteries, winning praise from playwright and translator William Gager for his English translation of Euripides' *Iphigenia*, in which Agamemnon's decision to sacrifice his daughter for the Trojan War incurs the grief and fury of his wife Clytemnestra.[2] Peele went on to explore the grief and rage of Hecuba, Troy's fallen queen, in the epyllion *A Tale of Troy* (*c.*1580), and returned to Troy in the pastoral comedy *The Arraignment of Paris* (*c.*1581), which depicts the origins of the Trojan War. After settling in London, Peele made a name for himself as a commercial playwright, joining writers such as John Lyly, Thomas Lodge, Christopher Marlowe, Robert Greene, and Thomas Nashe, who had been similarly immersed in Greek study. He brought his Greek dramatic training to a collaboration with the younger writer William Shakespeare on *Titus Andronicus* (*c.*1592), a play that frames its depictions of loss, grief, and rage with self-conscious allusions to Hecuba, the period's most prominent representative of Greek tragedy.[3] Peele died young, reportedly of syphilis contracted in a life described as drunken and dissolute, but Shakespeare's literary career was just beginning. *Titus* was his first tragedy, and he revisited its exploration of loss, grief, and rage in plays including *Hamlet*, in which meditations on the sympathetic emotions inspired by the theater lead its protagonist to wonder, "What's Hecuba to him, or he to Hecuba,/ That he should weep for her?"[4]

This book argues that rediscovered ancient Greek plays exerted a powerful and uncharted influence on sixteenth-century England's dramatic landscape, not only in academic and aristocratic settings, but also at the heart of the developing commercial theaters. Beginning with their appearance in print near the turn of the sixteenth century, these plays reached early modern readers and audiences not only in Greek, and in Latin and vernacular translations, but also in mediated forms including adaptations and imitations.[5] The Greek plays most popular in the period were tragedies—especially tragedies by Euripides featuring grieving and raging female protagonists—but their partial restorations of loss, such as Iphigenia's rescue from sacrifice, suggested tragicomic possibilities. These tragedies attracted praise for their emotional power, widely linked with both the sympathetic pull of their protagonists and the unexpected swerves of their generically unstable plots. Identified with the origins of theatrical performance, and represented especially by passionate female figures, these newly visible Greek plays challenged early modern writers to reimagine the affective possibilities of tragedy, comedy, and the emerging hybrid genre of tragicomedy. Because tragedy in particular was firmly linked with its Greek origin and etymology, iconic figures such as Hecuba and Iphigenia acquired a privileged status as synecdoches for the tragic theater, and especially for the sympathetic transmission of emotion between bodies with which it was linked. These figures haunt the early modern stage both directly, as when Hecuba captures Hamlet's thoughts, and indirectly, when bereaved mothers and sacrificial virgins in

Greek-inflected settings irrupt into dramatic scenes at charged moments. Redirecting sympathies both onstage and off, these Greek dramatic icons destabilize their plays' affective trajectories, and generate unexpectedly potent consequences.

Greek tragic women on early modern stages represent not only the affective transmission of the theater, but also complex processes of literary transmission. Surfacing in both explicit and subtle allusions, they suggest uncanny and capacious forms of literary influence, challenging traditional intertextual models.[6] As Tania Demetriou has shown of Renaissance encounters with Homer, Greek texts were intimately associated with the layers of literary adaptation through which they were typically first encountered.[7] Beyond their newly visible plays, Greek tragic women reached early modern readers and audiences through Latin writers such as Ovid, Seneca, and Virgil, as well as through other Greek writers including Aristophanes, Heliodorus, and Plutarch. Latin literary responses to Euripides' lamenting female figures played crucial roles in transmitting their affective power to Shakespeare and his contemporaries, yet the emerging realm of Greek offered newly intimate forms of access.[8] Euripides' contemporary Aristophanes parodied Euripidean figures in his comedies, offering later playwrights such as Ben Jonson a model for simultaneously mocking and profiting from their theatrical power.[9] Later Greek prose fictions such as Heliodorus' *Aethiopica*, exceptionally popular in the early modern period, not only imitated Euripidean figures and plots but also quoted his heroines verbatim.[10] Shakespeare's most intimately consulted Greek source, Plutarch, who looked back to ancient Greek drama as a subject of the Roman Empire, offered a particularly potent channel for conveying tragic material.[11] As Gordon Braden has observed, Plutarch quoted Greek tragedies 547 times in his *Moralia* and 61 times in the *Lives*, so that in reading him, "Shakespeare was learning from the Greek tragedians whether he realized it or not."[12] By reproducing and refracting Greek tragedy in different forms, Greek comedies, prose fiction, and non-fiction, along with Latin plays and poems, all served as carriers transporting and redefining Euripides' passionate female figures to early modern readers. Tracing these figures across time and genres shows both persistent traits and telling variations, suggesting unrecognized ways in which Renaissance playwrights collaborated with literary pasts. Exploring versions of Greek tragic women first in English translations of Greek plays, and subsequently in new plays by Kyd, Peele, Jonson, and especially Shakespeare, I argue that playwrights' explorations of these privileged tragic icons offer an explicitly theatrical model for intertextual engagement, with implications not only for classical reception but also for emerging ideas of dramatic collaboration.

Although a number of early modern playwrights responded to the female figures who represented Greek drama's legacy, Shakespeare's self-conscious engagement with them makes him this study's central figure. Scholars often depict Shakespeare's sources as valuable primarily for highlighting his departures from them: Catherine Belsey has argued, "It's what he changes that throws into relief what makes him Shakespeare."[13] Yet tracing what he seeks and borrows from other writers may be even more telling. At a moment when the newly visible realm of Greek tragedy inspired reflections on the eloquent, suffering women who represented the theater's origins, Shakespeare's explicit and recurring interest in these figures stood out, as his contemporaries noticed. In 1598 Francis Meres identified him with "these Tragicke Poets [who] flourished in Greece, Aeschylus, Euripedes, Sophocles" [*sic*]; in 1646 the poet Samuel Sheppard referred to Shakespeare as "him whose Tragick Sceans *Euripides*/ Doth equal"; in 1648 the pseudonymous "Mercurius Melancholicus" called for the return of "the whole crowd of Poets, Seneca/ Sophocles, Shakspeare, Iohnson now in clay/ Evripides"; and Ben Jonson memorably wrote that he would "call forth thundering Aeschylus/ Euripides, and Sophocles" into Shakespeare's company.[14] I suggest that in imagining Shakespeare among a cohort of ancient Greek playwrights, these authors respond to Shakespeare's own active pursuit of their legacy. Through his uses of Greek tragic icons, he presents himself as heir to the Greek dramatic tradition.

NEW GENRES, GREEK GENRES

Newly revived as dramatic genres in the sixteenth century, tragedy and comedy were widely identified with their origins in Greek plays, which had begun circulating in the west after the fall of Byzantium.[15] This claim may seem counterintuitive: scholars have typically explained the formal development of early modern English plays through tracing debts to the earlier liturgical dramas, mystery cycles, and morality plays that they replaced, and to Latin plays by Seneca, Terence, and Plautus.[16] Yet Latin tragedies and comedies imitated earlier Greek originals, as the emergence of Greek plays in print reminded sixteenth-century readers and audiences. As these plays became increasingly visible, writers increasingly turned to Greek words to describe theatrical performances. Frederick Boas has noted that records of Oxford and Cambridge colleges' dramatic productions shifted from the Latin terms "ludus" or "interlude" to the Greek terms "comedia" and "tragedia" in the 1530s, and records of commercial plays show a similar shift on the public stage.[17] In discussions of these genres, literary treatises in both England and continental Europe employed an explicitly Greek vocabulary—chorus, prologue, epilogue, protasis, epitasis, catastrophe—to discuss their forms and conventions, frequently printing these terms in Greek letters, and self-consciously attending to their etymologies.[18] Sixteenth-century printings of the treatise *De Tragoedia et Comoedia*, which conflated Donatus' *De Comoedia* with Evanthius' *De Fabula*, consistently departed from their usual Latin to present the etymological origin of tragedy as "ἀπό τοῦ τράγου," from *tragos* (goat), and of comedy as "ἀπό τοῦ κωμάζειν," from *komazein* (to revel), as did influential literary critics such as Julius Caesar Scaliger.[19] Vernacular English treatises followed suit. Describing "the Tragedy writers" in 1586, the critic William Webbe began with "*Euripides*, and *Sophocles*," and claimed, "Tragedies had their inuention by one *Thespis*," citing the ancient Greek actor whose name led to the word thespian.[20] In his 1589 *Art of English Poesie*, George Puttenham wrote that "forasmuch as a goate in Greeke is called Tragos, therfore these stately playes were called Tragedies"; and in his 1599 *Model of Poesy*, William Scott similarly referred to "*tragedy* so named because the reward was a goat."[21]

Although we typically assume that English commercial playwrights lacked interest in Greek, many of them also self-consciously linked these genres with their Greek origins. In his 1579 defense of the theater, Thomas Lodge attributed "the name of tragedy . . . to his original of *tragos, hircus*, et *ode, cantus*, so called for that the actors thereof had in reward for their labor a goat's skin filled with wine."[22] Similarly, to defend "Actors and Their Ancient Dignity" in 1612, Thomas Heywood emphasized the theater's illustrious Greek origins, citing the familiar etymologies that "[t]he word *Tragedy*, is derived from the Greeke word τραγος," and "*Comedy* is derived from the Greeke word κομος a street, and οδη, *Cantus*, a song, a streetsong" [*sic*].[23] In his 1601 *Poetaster*, Ben Jonson singles out a Greek genre and playwright to evoke theater's power, asking, "If all the salt in the old comedy/ Should be so censured . . . / What age could then compare with those for buffoons?/ What should be said of Aristophanes?"[24] In their attention to iconic Greek words, genres, and authors, these writers reflect a widespread identification of the new dramatic forms with their Greek roots. Widely perceived by early modern writers as keys unlocking a lost realm of theatrical origins and authority, Greek plays and their commentaries shaped conversations about the nature of dramatic forms and their effects on audiences. As such, they inspired playwrights' approaches to the newly revived Greek genres of tragedy and comedy.

In the context of these genres' pervasive identification with the Greek dramatic tradition, sixteenth-century ideas about Greek theater have significant consequences for the development of early modern tragedy and comedy. Scholars have explored early modern responses to Ovid, Virgil, Seneca, and Plautus, but no one has yet collated and analyzed the evidence regarding the reception of Greek plays—through printed editions, translations, performance records, and commentaries.[25] In undertaking this task, I focus especially on Greek plays' impact within England, but because excavating Greek texts was a transnational enterprise, I also attend to continental editions, which circulated in England, and continental performances, accounts of which similarly crossed national borders.[26] Tracing these various forms of reception not only shows that Greek plays were far more visible than scholars have previously claimed, but also illuminates specific patterns.[27] Roman playwrights were more influential in the realm of comedy, widely understood as the secondary dramatic genre and derivative from tragedy, but early moderns seem to have linked the prestigious genre of tragedy especially closely with its Greek origins.[28] Reflecting their higher numbers among extant plays overall, Greek tragedies dramatically outnumber Greek comedies among editions and performances before 1600. More surprisingly, in the popular realms of vernacular translations and performances, Greek tragedies seem also to slightly outnumber those of Seneca.[29] Contrary to popular opinion, then, the scholar Roger Ascham may not have been a minority in his view that, "In Tragedies, (the goodliest Argument of all . . .) the Grecians Sophocles and Euripides far ouer match our *Seneca* in *Latin.*"[30]

Within the prestigious realm of tragedy's Greek originals, early modern preferences focused overwhelmingly on women. 80 percent of the Greek tragedies printed in individual or partial editions before 1600 featured female protagonists—strikingly higher than their 51 percent ratio in the full canon of extant Greek tragedies—and in the more accessible realm of vernacular translations, the number is an even higher 94 percent.[31] The prominence of female protagonists in these editions is also strikingly higher than in the period's editions of Seneca, which in fact heavily favored male protagonists despite his evenly divided plays, suggesting not only that early modern selections actively intensified this association, but that it was specific to Greek plays.[32] In particular, the most popular of the extant Greek tragedies were Euripides' *Hecuba*, which appeared in at least 52 individual or partial editions, and *Iphigenia in Aulis*, with 39; most visible after these were the same playwright's *Medea* (19), *Alcestis* (13), and *The Phoenician Women* (12), and Sophocles' *Antigone* (12) and *Electra* (11).[33] These plays have acquired various meanings at different stages in their rich afterlives, but early modern responses emphasized their shared focus on bold female figures: especially raging, bereaved mothers, and sacrificial virgin daughters who respond heroically to death. Not only did these female-centered plays appear more often in print, but translators regularly expanded their protagonists' lines, and commentators singled them out for praise. Although we should not lean too heavily on quantitative data that is almost certainly incomplete, especially in the ephemeral field of performance records, consistency across the categories of print, translation, and performance supports these patterns, as do early modern translators of and commentators on the plays. Because early moderns understood the origins of drama, and especially the most prestigious dramatic genre—tragedy—as intrinsically Greek, they identified it with the fierce and proactive female figures who came to define their Greek canon.[34]

HECUBA AND THE THEATER OF SYMPATHY

Like *Hecuba*, their most visible representative, the Greek plays that attracted attention in this period are distinctive for their Euripidean authorship, their shared focus on bereaved mothers and sacrificial virgin daughters, and the ways these figures convert suffering into unexpected forms of vindication through appeals to sympathy.[35] Their heroines earn *kleos*, or fame, by drawing on affectively charged rhetorical power to attract allegiances and respond to threats. By eloquently enlisting support from her women and from Agamemnon, Hecuba achieves the satisfaction of bringing her son's murderer to justice. By nobly accepting her sacrifice, Iphigenia is praised for her heroism, and rescued from death by Artemis. Medea soars away triumphantly in the chariot of the sun god to a prearranged haven after successfully punishing her vow-breaking husband. Alcestis is brought back from voluntary death as a reward for her courage and generosity in sacrificing herself for her husband's life.

Throughout these plays, Euripides roots his heroines' theatrical power in their successful solicitation of their audiences' sympathies, which they achieve especially through moving performances of lament. Iphigenia wins the admiration of Achilles, as well as the rest of Greece; Medea carries out her plan by earning the loyalty and secrecy of her chorus of Corinthian women, and the Athenian ruler Aegeus; Hecuba persuades Agamemnon to permit her retribution, and her women to collaborate with her in carrying it out. These figures attract sympathy through their expressions of potent emotion, which they link explicitly with a receptive permeability widely attributed to both virginal and maternal bodies in a range of Greek texts.[36] Accounts of these bodies suggest a privileged capacity to absorb and transmit; one not yet entered, the other emptied after inhabitation by another body, both serve as conductors for a kind of affective electricity. Encountering these models amid growing interest in Greek medical depictions of the body's openness, early modern authors took a particular interest in the theatrical possibilities of these iconic female tragic figures.[37] Crucially, early modern writers identified them not only with affective intensity, but also with the sympathetic transfer of emotions between bodies: the ability to make listeners share their feelings. Their shadowy presences, accordingly, acquired particular significance onstage as emerging literary conversations increasingly prized tragedy and comedy for their ability to conjure forceful emotions in audiences.[38]

These associations are especially pronounced in responses to Euripides' *Hecuba*, which stands out conspicuously as the most prominent Greek play in the period: the first tragedy to be translated (into Latin, by Erasmus, 1503) and performed (1506–1514); the most frequently printed and translated in the sixteenth century; and the object of praise from critics including Philip Sidney, Julius Caesar Scaliger, and Antonio Minturno.[39] Gasparus Stiblinus, the translator and editor of a 1562 Greek–Latin volume of Euripides' complete works that became especially influential because of its extensive commentaries on the plays, pronounced *Hecuba* first among the tragedies, and especially praised the affective power of Hecuba's suffering. "Whom," he asks, "would she not move?" ("quem non commoueret?").[40] *Movere*, to move, was part of the affective triad of *docere*, *delectare*, and *movere* (to teach, delight, and move) described by Cicero in *De Oratore*, but Stiblinus's compound verb *commovere* suggests a distinctively interpersonal capacity to move with, alongside, in response to.[41] Sidney similarly, if less directly, cited Euripides' *Hecuba* as an example of "how much [tragedy] can move," in retelling Plutarch's account of the play's impact on "the abominable tyrant Alexander Pheraeus, from whose eyes a tragedy well made and represented drew abundance of tears."[42]

The effects attributed in the period to Euripides' protagonist resonate with contemporary depictions of Hecuba's impact on audiences. Thomas Norton and Thomas Sackville's *Gorboduc* (1561) refers to Hecuba as "the wofullest wretch/ That euer liued to make a myrour of," suggesting a capacity not simply to reflect but also to shape others' emotions.[43] Their language implicitly invoked the influential *Mirror for Magistrates* (1559), and the tradition of counsel literature that it inspired; as Jessica Winston has observed, Jasper Heywood's 1559 translation of Seneca's *Troas*, dedicated to Elizabeth I, added the lines, "Hecuba that wayleth now in care,/ That was so late, of high estate a queene/ A Mirrour is, to teache you what you are."[44] Other references to Hecuba similarly emphasized her mirroring functions. Hamlet remarks specifically on her power to reproduce her own grief in others: "What's Hecuba to him . . . that he should weep for her?" (2.2.536–7). Similarly, when Lucrece struggles to articulate her suffering to herself, she lacks a model, "Till she despairing Hecuba beheld," at which point she "shapes her sorrow to the beldame's woes."[45]

Here and elsewhere, Shakespeare presents Hecuba's ability to shape audiences in her own image as a synecdoche for the mysterious workings of the tragic theater.[46] Like Falstaff, who claims, "I am not only witty in myself, but the cause that wit is in other men," Hecuba represents not simply her own tragic passions, but also the possibility of conjuring tragic passions in others.[47] And just as Hecuba embodies both the tragic stage and its sympathetic transmission of emotion, her Greek literary roots remind us that sympathy, like tragedy, is a Greek word and concept; linked to the reciprocal influence of bodies and spirits, it first entered English in the sixteenth century through responses to newly accessible Greek texts.[48]

As early modern critics observed, Euripides links Hecuba's powers of affective transmission to her rhetorical force, and roots both in the experience of motherhood. Her most powerful and efficacious laments emphasize the affective and physiological power of her maternal bond. Pleading with the Greeks not to sacrifice her daughter Polyxena, she explains, "In her I rejoice, and forget my sorrows; she is my consolation for many losses, my city, nurse, staff, and guide on the path."[49] Influential early Latin translations, such as Erasmus (1503) and Stiblinus (1562), followed Euripides' Greek closely in these lines.[50] Through his use of "*sortis…gravis*" (heavy fate) to translate Euripides' *kakōn* (sorrows, evils, sufferings), Erasmus even implicitly heightens the centrality of motherhood; "*gravis*" means not only serious, painful, and burdensome, but also pregnant. The influential Italian translator and playwright, Lodovico Dolce—whose 1549 *Giocasta*, a version of Euripides' *Phoenician Women*, inspired Gascoigne and Kinwelmersh's 1566 English *Jocasta*—expands these lines dramatically, more than doubling both the lament in which they appear (to 92 lines, from Euripides' 45), and this section (to 8 lines, from 3), underscoring their perceived significance.[51] When Polyxena insists on accepting the sacrifice to which she has been condemned, Hecuba again emphasizes the scope of her maternal loss—"I, myself, am deprived of all my fifty children"[52]—and her resulting devastation: "Do not leave me childless."[53] When she later discovers the corpse of her son Polydorus, she wails, "Oh child, child of a miserable mother!"[54] When she successfully persuades Agamemnon of her right to a violent revenge, she does so by emphasizing the physical tie binding her to her child: "He was my son; I carried him in my womb."[55] Nicole Loraux has demonstrated that Euripides repeatedly and insistently links the physiological experience of childbirth with privileged access to extreme emotion, and Greek medical writings similarly attributed greater openness and receptivity to bodies that had experienced childbirth.[56] Depicted as both physically and affectively intertwined with the fifty bodies that have previously inhabited her womb, Hecuba offers an iconic symbol of profoundly interpersonal connectivity.

Although Polydorus' corpse proves the immediate catalyst to Hecuba's retribution, her laments focus especially on her daughter Polyxena, whose sacrifice recalls the period's other most popular Greek play, *Iphigenia in Aulis*. Described repeatedly by Euripides as *parthenos* (virgin) and *korē* (maiden), Polyxena is singled out for sacrifice precisely because of her purity, which Achilles' ghost, like a god, requires for his tribute: his son offers to appease his spirit with "the dark blood of a pure maiden" (*melan korēs akraiphnes haima*).[57] As feminist scholars have discussed, her sacrifice becomes a kind of marriage: Hecuba describes her daughter paradoxically as "unmarried bride and devirginated virgin" [*nymphēn t'anymphon parthenon t'aparthenon*].[58] The virginity central to Polyxena's aptness for this rite offers a paradoxical parallel to her mother's insistently maternal body. Giulia Sissa has observed that virginity was required for priestesses such as the Pythia (Delphic Oracle) precisely because a virgin's empty, uninhabited body was uniquely receptive to the god, whose *pneuma*— vapors, fumes, spirits—entered the priestess's body through her genitals as she sat on a tripod.[59] The model of virgin priestesses would have resonated with early moderns from Roman accounts of vestal virgins, and Plutarch discussed the Delphic oracle's virginity in his *Moralia*, widely translated and circulated in the early modern period. Plutarch explained "that the said *Pythias* keepeth her bodie pure and cleane from the company of man, and forbidden she is to converse or have commerce al her life time with any stranger," adding that "it is knowen unto the God, when her bodie is prepared and disposed to receive (without danger of her person) this Enthusiasme."[60] Literally referring to possession by a god within one's body, this "enthusiasm" resulted in a metaphysical pregnancy; in his treatise *On the Sublime*, which also began circulating in Europe in the sixteenth century, Longinus wrote that, "by divine power set down in this way, [the Pythia] is impregnated, and delivers oracles through this inspiration."[61] Like its maternal counterpart, then, the virginal body offers an exceptionally effective conductor for absorbing and transmitting spirits.

This openness to other selves proves far from passive. Like her mother, Polyxena uses this embodied power towards proactive ends. Offering herself willingly and proudly to death, like Iphigenia, Alcestis, and Antigone, Polyxena incurs praise from the messenger Talthybius as *aristē*, the best, and from the chorus for her *deinos charactēr*: strange, wonderful, and terrifying nature.[62] Feminist scholars have questioned whether these sacrifices are heroic or simply misogynistic, but early modern readers shared Talthybius' account of this willingness to die as a sign of a bold, proud spirit: like Achilles, to whom both Iphigenia and Polyxena are offered in marriage, these virgins choose to earn *kleos*, or fame, in a short and heroic life rather than peaceful obscurity. In 1554, Giraldi Cinthio wrote "it was very appropriate in Euripides' Hecuba that Polixena, having lost her father, brothers, and her kingdom, and left without any hope of happiness, should boldly embrace death . . . It was worthy of her royal spirit to deem death less vile than submitting shamefully to a slavish yoke [*seruil giogo*]."[63] His language closely mirrors that of Iphigenia, who tells the Greeks to leave her free (Euripides' ἐλευθέραν, Erasmus's *liberam*), and that she will offer her neck with a brave heart (Euripides' εὐκαρδίως, Erasmus's *intrepida*).[64] For both figures, embracing sacrifice does not signify passive surrender to suffering, but an active insistence on achieving glory through a heroic death.

Early modern commentators identified the tragic efficacy of Euripides' *Hecuba* especially with the emotional charge located in and between Hecuba and Polyxena. Describing their poignant farewell, Stiblinus wrote, "the miraculous force of empathy and ethopoeia is expressed in this matter. The bitter separation of the only daughter and the aged mother burns to such an extent with emotions [*affectibus*]."[65] Strikingly, in these lines he departs from his usual Latin to frame the key rhetorical terms *empatheia* and *ethopoeia*—ἐμπάθεια and ἠθοποιΐα—in Greek letters, underscoring their distinctively Greek roots. Giraldi similarly wrote,

> Hecuba most marvelously observes her character as a mother when she bewails the wretchedness of her daughter and wishes to die instead of her, or at least to end her wretched days with her—most fitting conduct in view of the motherly pity and the magnitude of grief which she was experiencing.[66]

As his praise suggests, while maternal and virginal receptivity indicate vulnerability, they equally signal generativity. Famous for dreaming, while pregnant with Paris, of giving birth to a firebrand, Hecuba produced the child who destroyed her city: she is the mother of Troy's fall, the original catastrophe identified with the origins of the Greek literary tradition.[67] The sacrifice of Polyxena to Achilles' ghost, meanwhile, offers a corollary to this myth of origin, not only by signaling the Trojan War's end, but also by recalling Iphigenia's death, which (also presented as a marriage to Achilles) allowed the Greeks to sail and the war to begin. Rooted in Homeric authority, and extensively imitated both within and beyond antiquity, these figures evoke literary as well as physical reproduction.

Euripides emphasizes Hecuba's resourcefulness in translating her bereavement into purposeful and effective action. Unlike Seneca's Hecuba, whose appearance in *Troades* more closely approximates her smaller role in Euripides' *Trojan Women*, she does not lament passively; her grief mobilizes her to enact justice for her son Polydorus' wrongful death by punishing his murderer, Polymestor.[68] When Polymestor asks her, "Do you take pleasure in abusing me, you evil-doer?," she replies, "Why should I not take pleasure in taking revenge on you?"[69] Euripides' verb *chaireis*—to take pleasure, rejoice—identifies Hecuba's response not simply with relief, but with joy: an emotion that echoes in Erasmus's 1503 Latin *gaudes*, also used by Aemilius Portus in his 1597 translation, as well as in Dolce's 1543 Italian "*allegri*."[70] And despite the moral ambivalence of this pleasure, Euripides presents Hecuba's violence against Polymestor as more heroic than monstrous. Her actions are carefully planned, successfully orchestrated, publicly upheld as both triumphant and just, and even portrayed as a civic duty: Agamemnon tells her that "this is for the common good, for both the individual and the state (*polis*), that the bad person should be punished and the good one succeed."[71]

Although for much of the play Hecuba evokes pathos, here she points to another model of tragedy: the triumph of action, and in particular of revenge. Her delight in her victim's suffering evokes Euripides' Medea, who similarly conjoins cruelty with sympathetic grief, and looks ahead to the charismatic monstrosity of Seneca's hero-villains, especially Medea and Atreus, who played a crucial role in mediating Greek tragic material to Renaissance readers and audiences.[72] Perhaps more surprisingly, her blinding of Polymestor, as Froma Zeitlin has noted, echoes Odysseus' blinding of the Cyclops Polyphemos, an action widely identified by Renaissance writers not only with cleverness, but also with the origins of tragicomedy.[73] In debates about whether classical writers condoned generic mixing, early moderns cited both Homer's *Odyssey* and Euripides' *Cyclops* as authoritative examples that they did.[74]

For some sixteenth-century theorists of tragedy, Hecuba's triumph represented not only an ethical problem but also an aesthetic failing, because it jarred with their conceptions of the genre. Despite his praise for the play's structure, Scaliger objected that her revenge provided too upbeat an ending: "since the issue of tragedy should be unhappy, and *Hecuba* is a tragedy, Hecuba ought to have been made more miserable at the end than at the beginning; this is certainly not done, for the end furnishes some scant relief to her misery."[75] Yet despite this critique, Seneca's Roman tragedies of proud atrocity were strikingly popular in the sixteenth century, and other contemporary critics relished the triumphant endings that audiences clearly enjoyed. And this move towards an apparently pleasurable success resonates with a broader opening up of generic boundaries at this time. Giraldi Cinthio contributed to the rise of tragicomedy when he justified writing "tragedies with happy endings [*tragedie di fin felice*]" by explaining that he found it wrong "to displease those for whose pleasure the play is put on the stage [*dispiacere a coloro, per piacere de quali la fauola si conduce in Scena*]."[76] In his attention to spectators' pleasure, he followed not only Castelvetro, who argued that "poetry was invented for the sole purpose of providing pleasure," but arguably also Aristotle, who established the idea of tragedy with a happy ending in his *Poetics*, and identified audience pleasure as central to theatrical success.[77] In her power to solicit audience sympathies, and her unsettling juxtaposition of grief with pleasure, Hecuba offers a potent prototype not simply for the tragic theater but for the affectively disorienting generic hybridity that would come to define the early modern stage more broadly.

Early modern literary interest in Hecuba has attracted thoughtful readings. Critics including Amy Cook, Marina Warner, Mary Jo Kietzman, and Lizette Westney have explored her identification with sorrow and empathy, and Marguerite Tassi and Judith Weil have noted the symbolic power of her fury.[78] Katharine Goodland has observed that her associations with maternal grief evoked another iconic mourning mother, the Virgin Mary, whose affective meanings were especially charged in Reformation England.[79] Lynn Enterline has examined Hecuba's influential Ovidian incarnation, and Heather James has explored the similarly potent associations of Virgil's Dido, another classical female model evoking literary sympathies.[80] The literary and cultural reverberations of Roman and Christian suffering women contributed to Hecuba's meanings and prestige, but new access to Euripides' play showed a crucially theatrical prehistory that anchored and authorized later versions. Although Hecuba's literary origins ultimately lie in Homeric epic, the popularity of Euripides' *Hecuba* in the context of tragedy's rediscovery underscored the performative capacity of her passionate and proactive laments to instill emotions in her audiences, both onstage and off. Theater, as Marvin Carlson and Joseph Roach have argued, invokes and recreates the ghosts of the past, and Greek theater, rooted in personages from myth and legend, relies especially self-consciously on familiar legends.[81] Hecuba's curiously double status as a Homeric ghost reconstituted on the Euripidean stage heightens her identification with theatrical reiteration. Discussing Hamlet and Lucrece's invocations of Hecuba, Enterline observes that both implicitly ask, "How is it possible for anyone to imitate Troy's grieving mother?"[82] Yet Hecuba's iconic status as an original source of textual and affective reproduction makes her almost compulsively prone to further imitation. In the wake of new European interest in theater's affective impact on audiences—which Matthew Steggle has shown was identified with dramatic success in early modern plays and commentaries, and which Nicholas Cronk has traced to the influence of newly visible Greek literary thought by Aristotle and Longinus—Hecuba, along with other popular Euripidean heroines, becomes a symbol of theatrical power.[83]

A dramatic tradition epitomized by Hecuba offers a surprising point of origin for the apparently male-centered plays typically identified with the early modern tragic canon. Yet the period's drama features potent and often overlooked tragic mother–daughter dyads, such as Isabella and Bel-Imperia in *The Spanish Tragedy*, Tamora and Lavinia in *Titus Andronicus*, Gertrude and Ophelia in *Hamlet*, and Hermione and Perdita in *The Winter's Tale*. Not only do these figures' mobilizing passions play a crucial role in shaping their plays, but the plays' male protagonists themselves imitate and ventriloquize Greek tragic heroines, becoming textual transvestites.[84] Tragic female voices, meanwhile, acquire surprising new prominence in comedy and tragicomedy. Plays such as *The Comedy of Errors* and *Twelfth Night* depart from their Plautine models with Greek-inflected settings, allusions to Greek prose fictions (such as Heliodorus' *Aethiopica*), and lamenting female figures who complicate plots by eliciting sympathies. In *Much Ado about Nothing*, *Pericles*, and *The Winter's Tale*, suffering female figures evoke Alcestis by reviving triumphantly after apparent death, drawing on self-consciously Greek female institutions such as the Delphic oracle and the temple of Diana at Ephesus. As recognizable tropes for Shakespearean tragicomic redemption, these figures also became targets for affectionate mockery from Ben Jonson, who parodies them in his self-conscious reflections on Shakespeare's plays in *Bartholomew Fair*. The proactive passions of Greek dramatic heroines, rooted in plays identified with the authority of tragic origins, mobilized playwrights' interests in the theater's capacity for soliciting emotion, both within tragedy and beyond it.

RETHINKING RECEPTION

In taking seriously early modern attractions to Greek tragic heroines, this book not only argues for the importance of Greek models in shaping the development of tragedy and comedy in England, but also challenges influential models of classical reception in this period. The western literary tradition is often imagined as a parade of male heroes following in each other's footsteps, from Achilles to Odysseus, Aeneas, Hamlet, Leopold Bloom, and beyond. Prominent models of intertextuality, such as Harold Bloom's theory of the anxiety of influence, have followed Freud in looking to Sophocles' Oedipus as a model for strong masculine figures usurping their forerunners' sovereignty.[85] Yet amid the early modern period's fierce preoccupations with the literary past, the parricidal Oedipus was a relatively marginal figure.[86] Bloom's Oedipal model of literary reception is itself rooted in a strong misreading, overlooking the widespread sixteenth-century preference for Euripides' fertile female figures over Sophocles' isolated men in a genre that we have come to identify with the heart of the period's literary achievement. In fact, early moderns would have seen Oedipus' Greek origins primarily in Euripides' *Phoenician Women* and Sophocles' *Antigone*, which focus on his wife/mother Jocasta and daughter/sister Antigone.[87] Depicted as possessing a privileged access to passionate emotion, which mobilizes them to unexpected triumphs, Greek tragic heroines embody a distinctive literary authority. Their sixteenth-century surge in visibility, together with the conversations about dramatic genre that they sparked, provided English writers not only with dramatic resources, but also with a model of literary reception and production identified more with procreation than usurpation.

Why have we not yet recognized the substantial legacy of Greek plays and their passionate heroines in this period? Despite some notable challenges, scholars have long held that early modern English playwrights, especially Shakespeare, could not have been familiar with Greek drama.[88] A longstanding tradition of English exceptionalism has presented the British Isles as isolated from the Greek learning of continental Europe, and the popular realm of England's commercial theater as the epitome of England's presumed anti-classicism.[89] Just as many have viewed England's literary culture as productively liberated from the classical past, the lack of attention to Greek in this period has also resulted from a New Historicist tendency to prioritize the new at the expense of the old, accompanying a broad shift from the use of the backward-looking term "Renaissance" to the forward-looking "early modern" to describe the period.[90] Yet alongside these assumptions, some critics have observed echoes of Greek drama in Shakespeare and his contemporaries, which they have struggled to explain. "[N]ot by conscious imitation," Boas wrote more than a century ago, "but by instinctive affinity of method, [Kyd] reproduces something of that Sophoclean dramatic irony which is among the crowning glories of the Attic stage."[91] More recently, Michael Silk similarly argued that, "Against all the odds, perhaps, there is a real affinity between Greek and Shakespearean tragedy. What there is not is any 'reception' in the ordinary sense," and A. D. Nuttall proposed recognizing a "response in Shakespeare to the Greeks of a kind... which is unscholarly, irresponsible—and aesthetically alert."[92] In dismissing the possibility of historically grounded reception behind apparent engagement with Greek precedents, these scholars have gestured towards an oddly mystical notion of shared aesthetic spirit, lacking logical causation.

In contrast to these claims of a literary metempsychosis, this book argues that similarities between early modern English dramatic genres and their Greek originals do not result from coincidence, affinity, or simply from Latin intermediaries.[93] Rather, they have specific historical and material causes, which can be traced to the surge of interest in printing, translating, performing, and theorizing the newly accessible Greek plays in this period. Recent transnational studies have expanded our understanding of the extensive traffic between drama in England and continental Europe, problematizing the distinction between a classical, intellectual continental dramatic culture and its popular, natural English corollary.[94] Similarly, scholarship on the collaborative nature of early modern playwriting has undermined a notion of Shakespeare as isolated from the classical learning of his more highly educated contemporaries.[95] New approaches to English literary negotiations with the past, such as Lucy Munro's work on archaisms, and explorations of Latin legacies by scholars including Heather James, Lynn Enterline, Colin Burrow, Jonathan Bate, and Robert Miola, have expanded and complicated our understandings of the period's temporal engagements.[96] Simultaneously, renewed interest in both book history and performance history has prompted more attention to records of print and performance, expanding access to evidence of how early modern English writers read, published, translated, staged, and discussed Greek plays.[97]

Alongside these developments, both early modern scholars and classicists have made important contributions to rethinking the availability and influence of Greek plays in early modern England. Emrys Jones made a persuasive case for the influence of Euripides' *Hecuba* on *Titus Andronicus*; Louise Schleiner argued for Shakespeare's exposure to Greek plays about Orestes in Latin translations; Laurie Maguire has traced routes through which Euripides reached England in order to argue for the likelihood of Shakespeare's familiarity with him; and a number of scholars have suggested the influence of Euripides' *Alcestis* on *The Winter's Tale*.[98] Proponents for the Earl of Oxford as author of Shakespeare's plays have combed through Greek references to support claims that the plays were written by an educated aristocrat, rather than the glove-maker's son from Stratford.[99] Looking beyond Shakespeare, Matthew Steggle has shown the influence of Aristophanes on Ben Jonson and the so-called war of the theaters.[100] New work on classical and neoclassical drama has led to discussions of Greek plays in performance, especially at the universities and Inns of Court.[101] At the same time, a growing body of scholarship on classical reception has offered new theoretical horizons and vocabularies for exploring the active processes by which later periods reread and rewrote the past.[102] Tracing and theorizing the reception of ancient drama has become an important branch of classical study, and scholars including Edith Hall, Fiona Macintosh, Lorna Hardwick, and Helene Foley have demonstrated the importance of exploring Greek plays' afterlives in order to illuminate interpretations, effects, and ongoing transformations of the plays.[103] Scholarship on early modern reception of nondramatic Greek texts has also contributed to our understanding of the complex standing of Greek literary influence in the period.[104]

This book argues that the sixteenth-century emergence of Greek plays had substantial literary consequences, not only in yoking the authority of tragedy's origins with the potent effects of female eloquence, but also in expanding notions of literary reception and collaborative authorship. Scholars of early modern reception frequently use the umbrella term "classical" to refer only to Latin literature, while ignoring Greek.[105] Yet newly available Greek texts constituted a radically different realm than the familiar Latin canon, and prompted different kinds of responses. Greek texts occupied an unstable and uncanny temporal position: they were simultaneously familiar and unknown, authoritative and avant-garde, prior and belated, offering a corrective response to Roman models as well as a point of origin for them.[106] The Latin literary tradition itself emphasized the primacy of Greek literature: as Erich Segal has commented, "Conscious emulation of Greek models was the tradition in Rome from the very beginning."[107] Ascham depicted all post-Greek literature as drawing on idealized Greek origins:

> Now, let Italian, and Latin it self, Spanishe, French, Douch, and Englishe
> bring forth their lerning and recite their Authors, *Cicero* onelie excepted, and
> one or two moe in Latin, they be all patched cloutes and ragges, in comparison
> of faire wouen broade clothes. And trewelie, if there be any good in them, it
> is either lerned, borowed, or stolne, from some one of those worthie wittes
> of *Athens*.[108]

Latin literature, in Ascham's account, models the belated forms of imitation that he prescribes for his contemporaries; Latins are to Greeks as Elizabethans are to the ancients.

The period's central proponent of Greek study, Erasmus, similarly identified with Latin imitators of Greek. "For whereas we Latins have but a few small streams, a few muddy pools," Erasmus wrote, "the Greeks possess crystal-clear springs and rivers that run with gold."[109] Writing in Latin, Erasmus labels not only himself but also his contemporaries ("we Latins") as Roman, implicitly underscoring the strange novelty of Greek models by contrast. He similarly likened his own versions of Greek plays to those of Seneca in order to justify taking liberties with meter: "After all, Horace did not strive to reproduce the great freedom in prosody and variety of metres shown by the lyric poets, nor Seneca those of the tragedians, although each of them was merely imitating the Greeks, not translating them as well."[110] His reference to Seneca as an early imitator of

Greek tragedy points to an especially complex site of layered tragic transmission. Some of the attractions linked with Greek tragic figures reached early modern readers through Seneca's versions of these figures, but new access to Greek texts underscored crucial differences. Seneca portrays only the grieving Hecuba of Euripides' *Trojan Women*, rather than the conversion from grief to triumph emphasized in *Hecuba*, and his Medea is defined primarily by turbulent passions, rather than the resourceful wit and careful solicitation of audience sympathies of Euripides' version.[111] Perhaps most important, Seneca did not dramatize Iphigenia, Polyxena, or Alcestis, the heroic sacrificial figures central to early modern admiration for Euripides' tragic women. Despite Seneca's conspicuous influence, then, new access to tragedy's mythic originals offered distinct and theatrically potent meanings.

The imagined realm of Greek literary origins held its own hierarchy of originality, and early moderns followed an established path in identifying Homer as the ultimate point of literary origin. Among the already belated Attic tragedians, Euripides is the most belated: his plays, which self-consciously respond not only to Homer but also to Aeschylus and Sophocles, were defined by intertextual conversations even before their imitations and adaptations by Roman authors. Greek writers themselves reflected actively on literary imitation, reception, and response; Aristophanes staged a contest between Aeschylus and Euripides in his *Frogs*, and in a phrase widely circulated in the sixteenth century, Aeschylus reportedly claimed that all of his tragedies were "slices from the great banquets of Homer."[112] In his account of literary inspiration, Longinus likened the Delphic oracle's workings to "the imitation (*mimēsis*) and emulation of previous great poets and writers."[113] "In the same way," he went on, "from the great natures of earlier men, to the souls of those who emulate them, as from sacred fissures, are carried along what we might call outpourings, so even those who seem little likely to be possessed, become inspired [*epipneomenoi*] with them, and become possessed [*sunenthousiōsi*] by others' greatness."[114] Longinus' account imagines poetic outpourings as a form of the divine *pneuma* (spirits, fumes) that emanates from caves at sacred sites such as Delphi. This *pneuma* penetrates the souls of poets just as it does the body of the Pythia, and in response writers become possessed—*sunenthousiōsi*, literally enthused, absorbing an internal divinity, by or with it. Merging ideas of divine possession, pregnancy, and poetic inspiration, Longinus identifies literary influence and creativity with a Euripidean model of the female body's potent receptivity.

Euripides, by Longinus' model, conceived his plays through absorbing the inspiration of Homer, Aeschylus, and Sophocles before him. By the time the plays reached early modern readers, they were simultaneously original models and secondary copies—sources and variants, first and second generations—not unlike the mother–daughter dyads who came both to represent his dramatic canon and to pass it on to later periods. Because early moderns understood the new dramatic genres of tragedy and comedy as Greek, they identified them with the literary imitation, physical reproduction, and sympathetic transfer of emotions that they represented.

In keeping with these associations, responses to these newly visible plays prompted new models for literary production. Recent work on the early modern theater industry has emphasized the collective nature of playing companies, collaborative playwriting, and the crucial contributions of other forms of labor to dramatic productions.[115] Early modern accounts of translation suggest that Greek playwrights, especially Euripides, became members of a diachronic collaborative community that facilitated new literary modes. As Belén Bistué and Deborah Uman have demonstrated, early modern writers understood translation to be both a form of authorship and a collaborative practice.[116] Just as Machiavelli famously described talking with the ancients, English translators entered into conversation with Greek tragedians and their protagonists.[117] In his praise of George Peele's translation of Euripides' *Iphigenia*, Oxford scholar and playwright William Gager imagined a warm fellowship linking author, translator, and character: "If Euripides lived, he would consider himself indebted to you, and Iphigenia herself would give you thanks."[118] Similarly, in a dedicatory letter opening his Latin translation of *Antigone*, Thomas Watson positions himself in direct conversation not only with Sophocles but with Antigone herself. "I took up Sophocles," he writes, "I taught his Muses to grow gentle. . . . I taught Antigone how to speak Latin. . . . Now, coming back to life and escorted by Latin Muses, she approaches, fearing to tarry. She will bear you wondrous things."[119] Both Gager and Watson imagine translating Greek drama as engaging with its Greek female protagonists, who become figurative participants in an ongoing literary production. And if Peele became a living proxy for both Euripides and Iphigenia, his collaborative contributions to *Titus Andronicus*—Shakespeare's first tragedy—expand this mingling of voices further, bringing Greek playwright and protagonist into the joint production of the period's new versions of tragedy. Inevitably involving borrowing and adaptation, translation offered a crucially flexible version of authorship for contemporary playwrights, modeling their own active exchange of types, tropes, plots, and phrases.[120]

The collaborative nature of translation, combined with Euripides' reputation for distinctive and powerful female voices, attracted a striking degree of female interest in these plays. The first documented vernacular English translation of a Greek play, *c.*1557, was the *Iphigenia* of Jane, Lady Lumley. In keeping with women's substantial contributions to translation and closet drama more broadly, Elizabeth I also translated a play by Euripides; sadly, we do not know which one.[121] Other Euripides translations emphasized female patronage: Matteo Bandello dedicated his 1539 translation of Euripides' *Hecuba* to Marguerite de Navarre, and in a brief afterword to their 1566 *Jocasta*, Gascoigne and Kinwelmersh attribute their commentary to a woman's curiosity: "I did begin these notes at request of a gentlewoman who vnderstode not poetycall words or termes."[122] In their work on collaborative translation, Bistué and Uman argue that the collaborative space of translation offered an unusually accessible site "for women to play with preconceived notions of authority and to raise questions about their relationship to the written word, the public sphere, and the role of the author."[123] Euripides' fertile female protagonists, I suggest, opened up new possibilities for authorship by inspiring models for engaging collaboratively with the past, rather than along adversarially Oedipal lines.

In identifying translation and reception as forms of collaboration, this book intervenes in a larger conversation about intertextuality. Studies of classical afterlives have shifted away from terms such as "influence" or "transmission," which attribute agency to earlier authors, and toward "reception," underscoring the creative agency of the later authors who read and interpret these texts.[124] Yet although this shift has revitalized readings, emphasizing the active roles of receiving and responding can elide the new elements that earlier authors and texts bring to these conversations. My collaborative model is indebted to Bruce Smith's creative term "confluence," an alternative to "influence" that suggests a reciprocal conversation between literary authors and periods.[125] I suggest that early modern English playwrights developed new forms of theatrical power, identified especially with affectively potent female voices, through imagined conversations and collaborations with newly visible Greek plays.

ENCOUNTERING AND ENGLISHING
GREEK PLAYS

The chapters that follow explore English responses, both direct and mediated, to the iconic figures who came to represent the Greek dramatic tradition. Their case studies move roughly chronologically, beginning in the middle of the sixteenth century with English translations of Greek tragedies, and continuing on to commercial tragedies, comedies, and tragicomedies in the late sixteenth and early seventeenth centuries. Chapter 1, "Greek Plays in England," examines the textual, curricular, and performative contexts through which Greek plays reached English readers, audiences, and playwrights. Tracing the emergence of England's traditions of Greek study, printing, and translation, the chapter examines the two earliest English translations of Greek plays: Lumley's *Iphigenia* (*c.*1557) and Gascoigne and Kinwelmersh's *Jocasta* (1566). Unlike *Hecuba*, with its focus on a daughter's death and a bereaved mother's vindication, these plays explore the transmission of fierce passions from grieving queens to their daughters, who absorb and enact their mothers' authority. Modeling forms of female counsel and succession, they implicitly link debates about female monarchs and virginity with questions about the transmission of literary authority. Situating these plays within the development of English traditions of teaching and performing Greek texts, the chapter closes by surveying exposure to Greek among playwrights who wrote for the commercial stage, establishing a foundation for subsequent chapters' readings of new English plays. In the context of the evidence for both the circulation of Greek plays and the education of English playwrights, I argue that familiarity with the most popular of these Greek plays would have been the rule rather than the exception. I propose, accordingly, that English dramatic references to Greek tragic women have important and unrecognized meanings that alter our understandings of the plays in which they appear.

Chapter 2, "Imitating the Queen of Troy," examines the afterlives of iconic Greek mother–daughter dyads in early popular English tragedies. I argue that Kyd's *The Spanish Tragedy* (*c.*1587) and Shakespeare and Peele's *Titus Andronicus* (*c.*1592) explore tragedy's power for engaging sympathies by calling upon the ghosts of Greek tragic mothers and daughters. *The Spanish Tragedy* opens and closes with the sacrificial virgin Proserpine, whose pity for the slain Andrea sets the play's revenge in motion. Her specter haunts the passionate Bel-Imperia, who, along with Horatio's bereaved mother Isabella, engenders the rage and grief that eventually animate Hieronimo's revenge, which he carries out, notably, by performing a tragedy in which he speaks his lines in Greek. While critics have observed *Titus Andronicus*'s many echoes of *The Spanish Tragedy*, they have not recognized the plays' shared emphasis on suffering women who inspire the protagonist's grief and violence, nor connected this pairing to *Titus*'s two invocations of Hecuba. Both of these plays suggest Greek literary debts; Kyd studied Greek at the Merchant Taylors' School under the Cambridge-educated scholar Richard Mulcaster, and Peele studied Greek at Oxford, where he translated Euripides. Attending to these plays' engagement with the ghosts of Greek tragic women illuminates the connection they establish between female grief and tragedy's power to engage sympathies. These two foundational English popular tragedies, I argue, build a crucial bridge between newly visible Greek tragic women and the conventions of early modern English tragedy.

Chapter 3, "'What's Hecuba to Him?," explores Shakespeare's reac-
tions to Greek tragedy's legacy in *Hamlet* (*c*.1600), his most sustained
and self-conscious reflection on the genre. Revisiting many of the structural conventions of *The Spanish Tragedy* and *Titus Andronicus*, the play
deepens their engagement with Greek tragic female figures. Inquiring
into tragedy's effects on audiences, Hamlet implicitly competes with
Hecuba, the period's reigning icon of Greek tragedy, underscoring the
gap between his own "unpregnant" reticence towards action and the
triumphant vindication rooted in her physiological and literary fertility.
Ambivalent about undertaking tragic action, Hamlet reflects on the
bereaved mothers and sacrificial virgins who constitute the genre's traditional center. The chapter argues that Shakespeare's interest in Greek tragic
women, spurred partly by working with Peele, shapes this play's challenges
to the revenge tragedy tradition. Shakespeare self-consciously constructs his
male tragic protagonist in negotiation with a female-centered Greek tradition, in which Hecuba represents the genre's power to move audiences.

Chapter 4, "Iphigenia in Illyria: Greek Tragic Women on Comic
Stages," explores the surprising prominence of female tragic figures in
Shakespeare's comedies. Although Shakespeare took his comic plots most
conspicuously from Latin and Italian models, he alters these models with
Greek settings and allusions that establish the characteristically tragic
undertones of his comic worlds. In *The Comedy of Errors* (*c*.1594) and
Twelfth Night (*c*.1600–1), Shakespeare departs from the shipwrecked
twins of Plautus' *Menaechmi* by drawing on the Greek prose fictions
Apollonius of Tyre and Heliodorus' *Aethiopica*, respectively. These texts'
tragic backdrops, suffering women, and culminating scenes of recognition
and reunion played a crucial role in mediating Greek tragic figures and
plots to early modern audiences. In *The Comedy of Errors*, Ephesus'
associations with Artemis and Amazons, along with the play's allusions
to Circe and sirens, offer important backdrops for the prominence of the
lamenting Adriana, and the unexpected emergence of the twins' mother.
Written after Hamlet's confrontation with Hecuba, and a new surge of
Greek material on London stages, *Twelfth Night* goes even further in drawing
on Greek tragic models, explicitly identifying Viola with a near-sacrificial
virgin from *The Aethiopica* to deepen Shakespeare's challenges to comedy's
generic boundaries.

Chapter 5, "Bringing Back the Dead: Shakespeare's Alcestis," revisits
Shakespeare's transformation of tragedy into comedy by tracing a structural
trope that recurs throughout his plays: a grieving husband's acceptance of
a veiled woman who turns out to be his apparently dead wife. Exploring
the figures of Hero in *Much Ado About Nothing* (1599), Thaisa and Marina
in *Pericles* (1608), and Hermione and Perdita in *The Winter's Tale* (1611),
the chapter argues that these plays alter their immediate romance sources

through summoning the ghost of Euripides' *Alcestis*. Tracing Greek debts and allusions in the plays, I explore the development of Shakespeare's versions of Alcestis, from suffering bride in *Much Ado*, to both dying mother and suffering virgin in *Pericles*. Finally, *The Winter's Tale* highlights the passionate maternal affect at the heart of reigning Greek tragic icons by portraying Hermione's grief-stricken collapse and miraculous return as deliberate responses to the death of her son, and the return of her daughter, respectively. By giving these women triumphant agency and voice in their returns, Shakespeare crucially rewrites Alcestis' ambivalent ending, suggesting a particular investment in redeeming female suffering. I suggest that the trope of retrieving and reanimating apparently dead women takes inspiration not only from Euripides' tragedies of loss restored, but also from a broader, and related, fascination with the theater's necromantic power to bring back the dead.

The sixth and last chapter, "Parodying Shakespeare's Euripides in *Bartholomew Fair*," turns to Ben Jonson's reflections on the affectively charged dramatic models that Shakespeare took from Euripides. Just as Jonson praised Aristophanes for parodying Euripides, he adopted similar strategies for both reviving and mocking Shakespeare's Euripidean figures in *Bartholomew Fair* (1614). The play presents the women of the fair as caricatures of Greek tragic figures, "Ceres selling her daughter's picture" (2.5.8) and "Mother o'the Furies" (2.5.56). It also portrays mothers and daughters moving audiences to sympathy and action through mock-laments; wives disappearing to a mock-underworld before returning to astonished recognition and reunion; and, most strikingly, the restoration of losses during a performance of *Hero and Leander*, whose story was identified in the period with tragedy and Greek origins.[126] I argue that in a playful homage to Shakespeare's just-ended career, Jonson not only acknowledges the pleasures of Shakespeare's Greek-inflected plots, but also discovers ways he can profit from them himself.

In these plays and many others, Greek tragic women play crucial roles in prompting the sympathetic transmission of emotions at the heart of the theater. By calling on potent earlier models of tragic affect, they produce theatrical electricity, moving audiences both within their plays and beyond. Marked by both direct and indirect allusions, these figures highlight increasingly elastic models of imitation, contributing to a new model of creative collaboration with the literary past. Just as the theater offers a privileged site for reanimating ghosts of the past, some ghosts offer privileged sites for animating the theater. The early modern afterlives of Hecuba, Iphigenia, Alcestis, and their kin offer some of the most potent of these sites. I suggest that by exploring their theatrical itineraries, we can better understand the reanimation of tragedy, comedy, and tragicomedy on Shakespearean stages.

NOTES

1. Queen's College, Oxford established regular Greek lectures in 1563/4, followed by Merton in 1565, Balliol in 1571, and Brasenose in 1572; in 1576, statutes specified that if an undergraduate "heare not everye Day the Greeke Reader, [he] shall forfaite for everye fault iiijd." See Micha Lazarus, "Greek Literacy in Sixteenth Century England," *Renaissance Studies* 20:3 (2015), 433–58, 450, and Strickland Gibson, ed., *Statuta Antiqua Universitatis Oxoniensis* (Oxford: Clarendon Press, 1931), 408.

2. On Peele's schooling, translation, and praise from Gager, see *The Life and Works of George Peele*, vol. 1, ed. David H. Horne (Yale University Press, 1952). Gager does not specify which of Euripides' *Iphigenia* plays Peele translated, but the widespread popularity of *Iphigenia in Aulis* in the period, combined with the near-invisibility of *Iphigenia in Tauris*, argues persuasively for the former.

3. Although still a subject of critical debate, the question of Peele's contributions to *Titus Andronicus* has achieved considerable scholarly consensus; see especially Brian Vickers, *Shakespeare, Co-Author: A Historical Study of Five Collaborative Plays* (Oxford: Oxford University Press, 2002); and Macdonald P. Jackson, "Stage Directions and Speech Headings in Act 1 of *Titus Andronicus* Q (1594): Shakespeare or Peele?," *Studies in Bibliography*, 49 (1996), 134–48. Jonathan Bate, who edited the play for the Arden Shakespeare, argued in that edition for Shakespeare's sole authorship, but later conceded Vickers's claims; see Bate, "In the Script Factory," *TLS* (15 April 2003), 3–4.

4. William Shakespeare, *Hamlet*, ed. Ann Thompson and Neil Taylor, Arden Shakespeare (London: Thompson Learning, 2006), 2.2.494–5; see Pollard, "What's Hecuba to Shakespeare?," *Renaissance Quarterly* 65:4 (2012), 1060–93.

5. The first printed edition of Greek plays was *Tragoediae quattuor*, ed. J. Lascaris (Florence: Alopa, 1495), featuring Euripides' *Medea, Hippolytus, Andromache*, and *Alcestis*; see Appendices for further details.

6. On notions of haunting and indirect memory as productive ways of tracing complex literary engagement with the past, see especially Laurie Maguire and Emma Smith, "What Is A Source? Or, How Shakespeare Read His Marlowe," *Shakespeare Survey* 68 (2015), 15–31.

7. "The discovery of Homer was first a 'rediscovery backwards' of the Homer already known—referred to, quoted and imitated by other authors and completely 'assimilated' by Virgil . . . In discovering Homer it is the known that is first rediscovered." See Tania Demetriou, "'Strange Appearance': The Reception of Homer in Renaissance England" (PhD diss., University of Cambridge, 2008), 33–4.

8. On Latin literary debts to Euripides, see *Beyond the Fifth Century: Interactions with Greek Tragedy from the Fourth Century BCE to the Middle Ages*, ed. Ingo Gildenhard and Martin Revermann (Berlin and New York: de Gruyter, 2010); Clifford Weber, "The Dionysus in Aeneas," *Classical Philology* 97:4 (2002),

322–43; Dan Curley, *Tragedy in Ovid: Theater, Metatheater, and the Transformation of a Genre* (Cambridge: Cambridge University Press, 2013); and David Larmour, "Tragic *Contaminatio* in Ovid's *Metamorphoses*," *ICS* 15:1 (1990), 131–41.

9. On Aristophanes' stagings of Euripides, see especially Helene Foley, "Generic Boundaries in Late Fifth-century Athens," in *Performance, Iconography, Reception: Studies in Honour of Oliver Taplin*, ed. Martin Revermann and Peter Wilson (Oxford: Oxford University Press, 2008), 15–36, esp. 17–27, and Rosemary Harriott, "Aristophanes' Audience and the plays of Euripides," *Bulletin of the Institute of Classical Studies* 9:1 (1962), 1–8.

10. Heliodorus' exact dates are uncertain, but scholars typically situate him in either the third or fourth century of the common era. On Euripidean elements in Greek romances, see Silvia Montiglio, "The Call of Blood: Greek Origins of a Motif, From Euripides To Heliodorus," *Syllecta Classica* 22 (2011), 113–29; Montiglio, *Love and Providence: Recognition in the Ancient Novel* (Oxford: Oxford University Press, 2013); James Pletcher, "Euripides in Heliodorus' *Aethiopiaka* 7–8," *GCN* 9 (1998), 17–27; Anna Lefteratou, "Myth and Narrative in the Greek novel" (Oxford D. Phil, 2010); and Lefteratou, "Iphigenia revisited: Heliodorus' *Aethiopica* and the 'Der Tod und das Mädchen' pattern," in *Intende, Lector—Echoes of Myth, Religion and Ritual in the Ancient Novel*, ed. Marília P. Futre Pinheiro, Anton Bierl, and Roger Beck (Berlin: de Gruyter, 2013), 200–22.

11. Plutarch lived *c.*46–120 CE, and was a Roman citizen.

12. See Gordon Braden, "Classical Greek Drama and the English Renaissance Theater," in *Homer and Greek Tragedy in Early Modern England's Theatres*, ed. Tania Demetriou and Tanya Pollard, special issue of *Classical Receptions Journal* 9:1 (2017), 103–19; also Leah Whittington, "Shakespeare and the Greeks: Theatricality and Performance from Plutarch's *Lives* to *Coriolanus*," in *Homer and Greek Tragedy in Early Modern England's Theatres*, 120–43; Christopher Pelling, "The Shaping of *Coriolanus*: Dionysius, Plutarch, and Shakespeare," *Poetica* 48 (1997), 3–32; and Pelling, "Seeing a Roman Tragedy through Greek Eyes: Shakespeare's *Julius Caesar*," in *Sophocles and the Greek Tragic Tradition*, ed. Simon Goldhill and Edith Hall (Cambridge: Cambridge University Press, 2009), 264–88.

13. See Catherine Belsey, "The Elephants' Graveyard Revisited: Shakespeare at Work in *Antony and Cleopatra*, *Romeo and Juliet* and *All's Well That Ends Well*," *Shakespeare Survey* 68 (2015), 62–72.

14. Francis Meres, *Palladis Tamia* (London: Cuthbert Burbie, 1598), 283r. Elsewhere, he similarly writes "As the Greeke tongue is made famous and eloquent by Homer, Hesiod, Euripedes, Aeschylus, Sophocles, . . . so the English tongue is mightily enriched and gorgeously inuested in rare ornaments and resplendent abiliments by Sir Philip Sydney, Spencer, Daniel, Drayton, Warner, Shakespeare, Marlow, and Chapman" (Meres, 280r). Samuel Sheppard, *The Times Displayed in Six Sestyads* (London: J. P., 1646), 23; Mercurius Melancholicus, *The Second Part of Crafty Crvmwell* (London:

1648), A2r; Ben Jonson, "To the Memory of My Beloved, the Author, Mr. William Shakespeare," in *Mr. William Shakespeares Comedies, Histories, & Tragedies* (London: Jaggard and Blount, 1623), A4r–A4v.

15. Prior to the sixteenth century, European usage of these terms typically referred to narrative rather than dramatic structures. On the emerging sense of tragedy as a staged genre rather than an unhappy tale, see Timothy Reiss, "Renaissance Theatre and the Theory of Tragedy," *The Cambridge History of Literary Criticism*, vol. 3: *The Renaissance*, ed. Glyn Norton (Cambridge: Cambridge University Press, 1999), 229–47; and Tanya Hagen, "An English Renaissance Understanding of the Word 'Tragedy,'" *Early Modern Literary Studies* 1 (1997), 5.1–30 http://purl.oclc.org/emls/si-01/si-01hagen.html, accessed September 1, 2014.

16. On native traditions, see Willard Farnham, *The Medieval Heritage of Elizabethan Tragedy* (Berkeley: University of California Press, 1936); David Bevington, *From Mankind to Marlowe* (Cambridge, MA: Harvard University Press, 1962); and Peter Happe, *English Drama before Shakespeare* (London: Longman, 1999). On Latin influence, see Robert S. Miola, *Shakespeare and Classical Comedy: The Influence of Plautus and Terence* (Oxford: Clarendon Press, 1994); Miola, *Shakespeare and Classical Tragedy: The Influence of Seneca* (Oxford: Clarendon Press, 1992); Wolfgang Riehle, *Shakespeare, Plautus, and the Humanist Tradition* (Cambridge: Boydell and Brewer, 1990); Gordon Braden, *Renaissance Tragedy and the Senecan Tradition* (New Haven, CT: Yale University Press, 1985); John W. Cunliffe, *The Influence of Seneca on Elizabethan Tragedy* (New York: G. E. Stechert & Co: 1925); Howard Norland, *Neoclassical Tragedy in Elizabethan England* (Newark: University of Delaware Press, 2009); and Jessica Winston, "Seneca in Early Elizabethan England," *Renaissance Quarterly* 59:1 (2006), 29–58.

17. See Frederick S. Boas, *University Drama in the Tudor Age* (Oxford: Clarendon Press, 1914), 11–12, and Alfred Harbage, ed. *Annals of English Drama, 975–1700*, revised. S. Schoenbaum, 3rd edition, revised by Sylvia Stoler Wagonheim (London and New York: Routledge, 1989).

18. See Benedictus Philologus, "De Tragoedia," in *Senecæ Tragoediae*, ed. Benedictus Philologus (Florence, 1506), aiiiir; Jacobus Micyllus, "De Tragoedia et Eivs Partibus προλεγομενα," in *Evripides Poeta Tragicorum princeps* (Basel: Ioannes Oporinus, 1562), 671–9, 672; and Nicodemus Frischlinus, "De Veteri Comoedia Eiusque Partibus," in *Aristophanes Veteris Comoediae Princeps* (Frankfurt: Johann Spiess, 1586), 16r. On these and similar paratexts, see Pollard, "Greek Playbooks and Dramatic Forms in Early Modern England," in *Forms of Early Modern Writing*, ed. Allison Deutermann and Andras Kisery (Manchester: Manchester University Press, 2013), 99–123.

19. See "De tragoedia et comoedia," *Tragoediae selectae AESCHYLI, SOPHOCLIS, EURIPIDIS* (Geneva: Henricus Stephanus, 1567), 118–28, 118. In 1561 Julius Caesar Scaliger similarly explained, "The name tragedy is derived from *tragos*, the he-goat" ["nomen traxit ab hircu"]; see Scaliger, *Select Translations from Scaliger's Poetics*, ed. and trans. Frederick Morgan Padelford

(New York: Henry Holt, 1905), I.6, 39; Scaliger, *Poetices libri septem*, ed. Luc Deitz (Stuttgart: Frommann-Holzboog, 1994), vol. 1, I.6, 130.

20. William Webbe, *A Discourse of English Poetrie* (London: John Charlewood, 1586), C1r. Other references to Thespis as originator of tragedy include Thomas Heywood, *Apology for Actors* (London: Nicholas Okes, 1612), D1v and D2r, and John Rainolds, *Th'Overthrow of Stage Plays* (Middleburg: Richard Schilders, 1599), 20.

21. George Puttenham, *The Art of English Poesy* (London: Richard Field, 1589), 27; William Scott, *The Model of Poesy*, ed. Gavin Alexander (Cambridge: Cambridge University Press, 2013), 23.

22. Thomas Lodge, *A Reply to Stephen Gosson's School of Abuse, in Defence of Poetry, Music, and Stage Plays* (London: 1579), 35.

23. Heywood, *Apology for Actors*, D1v, D2r.

24. Jonson, *Poetaster*, "To the Reader: Apologetical Dialogue," 173–7, in *The Cambridge Edition of the Works of Ben Jonson*, ed. David Bevington, Martin Butler, and Ian Donaldson, vol. 2: *1601–1606* (Cambridge: Cambridge University Press, 2012), 1–181.

25. My appendices are indebted especially to Rudolf Hirsch, "The Printing Tradition of Aeschylus, Euripides, Sophocles and Aristophanes," *Gutenberg Jahrbuch* 39 (1964), 138–46, and R. R. Bolgar, *The Classical Heritage and its Beneficiaries* (Cambridge: Cambridge University Press, 1954). Records of performances draw especially on the Performance Database of the Archive of Performances of Greek and Roman Drama (APGRD), http://www.apgrd. ox.ac.uk/research-collections/performance-database/productions.

26. On English access to foreign books, see Alan B. Farmer, "Cosmopolitanism and Foreign Books in Early Modern England," *Shakespeare Studies* 35 (2007), 58–65; James Raven, "Selling Books Across Europe, c. 1450–1800: An Overview," *Publishing History* 34 (1993), 5–19; and Elizabeth Armstrong, "English Purchases of Printed Books from the Continent, 1465–1526," *English Historical Review* 94 (1979), 268–90. Leedham-Green lists 122 Greek, Latin, or parallel-text editions of Greek plays in inventories from sixteenth-century Cambridge (56 by Euripides, 36 by Sophocles, 29 by Aristophanes, 4 by Aeschylus, and 2 collections of tragedies); see Elisabeth Leedham-Green, *Books in Cambridge Inventories* (Cambridge: Cambridge University Press, 1986). Robert Fehrenbach and Leedham-Green show 48 editions in inventories from sixteenth-century Oxford: 19 Euripides, 15 Sophocles, 14 Aristophanes and 2 Aeschylus; see Robert J. Fehrenbach and Leedham-Green, *Private Libraries in Renaissance England* (Binghamton, N.Y.: Medieval & Renaissance Texts & Studies, 1992–2004). On the transnational impact of European theatrical performances, see *Transnational Exchange in Early Modern Theater*, ed. Robert Henke and Eric Nicholson (Aldershot, Ashgate, 2008), and *Transnational Mobilities in Early Modern Theater*, ed. Robert Henke and Eric Nicholson (Aldershot, Ashgate, 2014).

27. As recently as 2010, Adrian Poole wrote that a small handful of plays represented Greek tragedy "until the end of the 18th century, when, like

Sophocles' and Aeschylus', [Euripides'] plays first became available to the Greekless reader in their entirety," although all of Euripides' plays were available in Latin by 1541, all of Sophocles by 1543, and all of Aeschylus by 1555. See Adrian Poole, "Euripides," in *The Classical Tradition*, ed. Anthony Grafton, Glenn W. Most, and Salvatore Settis (Cambridge, MA: Harvard University Press, 2010), 346–7. Deborah Shuger has similarly claimed that only five Greek tragedies were translated before 1560; see Shuger, *The Renaissance Bible: Scholarship, Sacrifice, and Subjectivity* (Berkeley: University of California Press, 1998), 129.

28. On the perceived superiority of tragedy, see George Puttenham on its "higher and more loftie" nature (*The Arte of English Poesie*, Fiiir), and Philip Sidney's praise for "the high and excellent *Tragedie*" (*Defence of Poesie* [London: 1595], F3v). The 6 editions of Aristophanes in vernacular translation before 1600 lag far behind the 65 vernacular translations of Latin comedy (39 Terence, and 26 Plautus), and the 11 documented productions of Aristophanes' plays before 1600 similarly lag behind the 177 of Latin comedy (123 of Plautus and 54 of Terence).

29. Although records may well be incomplete, they suggest that the period before 1600 saw 57 editions of Greek tragedians in vernacular translation, as opposed to 24 of Seneca; see Appendices. Euripides alone, with 38 editions of vernacular translations, outpaces Seneca. Seneca was more frequently read in Latin, and the 33 extant Greek tragedies outweigh his 10, but the disparity is nonetheless striking given typical assessments of Seneca's larger influence. (For vernacular translations I am equating individually published volumes of translations regardless of whether they include single, multiple, or complete works.) Similarly, in the realm of performance, the 33 documented productions of Greek tragedies again outpace the 26 of Seneca. These figures are tenuous, given how little information we have about the productions: many are adaptations, and some titles (*Medea, Hippolytus, Oedipus, Agamemnon*) could refer to either Greek or Roman tragedies. Yet more of these plays could only be Greek (*Philoctetes, Antigone, Electra, Ajax, Iphigenia, Alcestis, Jocasta, Persians*) than could only be Senecan (*Thyestes*); see Appendices for further details.

30. See Roger Ascham, *The Scholemaster* (London: John Day, 1570), 52v.

31. See Appendices. Twelve out of 19 (63%) of the extant plays attributed to Euripides in the period were titled for female protagonists, as were 2 out of 7 (29%) of the plays attributed to Aeschylus, and 3 of the 7 (43%) plays attributed to Sophocles, for a total of 17 out of 33, or 51%. For these purposes, I define a play's protagonist(s) by the person(s) named in the play's title. My calculations about the popularity of individual plays exclude printed editions of playwrights' complete works, which do not show processes of selection. On the prominence of women in Greek tragedy, see especially Helene P. Foley, *Female Acts in Greek Tragedy* (Princeton, NJ: Princeton University Press, 2001); for an overview of critical approaches to women's roles on the ancient stage, see Victoria Wohl, "Tragedy and Feminism," in

A Companion to Tragedy, ed. Rebecca Bushnell (Oxford: Blackwell Publishing, 2009), 145–60.

32. Vernacular translations of Seneca's tragedies before 1600 feature almost four times as many plays with male protagonists (19) as with female (5), although his ten tragedies feature five male and five female protagonists. *Agamemnon* and *Thyestes* were by far the most popular of his plays in this period; see Appendices for additional details.

33. These numbers combine printed editions in Greek and Latin with vernacular translations; see Appendices for additional details.

34. See Diane Purkiss, "Introduction," *Three Tragedies by Renaissance Women* (London and New York: Penguin, 1998); Naomi Liebler, ed., *The Female Tragic Hero in English Renaissance Drama* (Basingstoke: Palgrave, 2002); and Blair Hoxby, "The Doleful Airs of Euripides: The Origins of Opera and the Spirit of Tragedy Reconsidered," *Cambridge Opera Journal* 17:3 (2005), 253–69.

35. On generic hybridity in Greek plays, see Bernard Knox, "Euripidean Comedy," in *The Rarer Action: Essays in Honor of Francis Fergusson*, ed. Alan Cheuse and Richard Koffler (New Brunswick, NJ: Rutgers University Press, 1970), 68–96; Oliver Taplin, "Fifth-Century Tragedy and Comedy: A Synkrisis," *Journal of Hellenic Studies* 106 (1986), 163–74; C. John Herington, *Aeschylus* (New Haven, CT: Yale University Press, 1986); Justina Gregory, "Comic Elements in Euripides," *Illinois Classical Studies* 24–5 (1999–2000), 59–74; and Elizabeth Watson Scharffenberger, "Euripidean 'Paracomedy': A Reconsideration of the *Antiope*," *Text and Presentation* 17 (1996), 65–72.

36. On Greek accounts of female physiological receptivity, see especially Ruth Padel, "Women: Model for Possession by Greek Daemons," in *Images of Women in Antiquity*, ed. Averil Cameron and Amélie Kuhrt (London: Routledge, 1983), 3–19; Nicole Loraux, *Tragic Ways of Killing a Woman*, trans. Anthony Forster (Cambridge, MA: Harvard University Press, 1987); Loraux, *Mothers in Mourning*, trans. Corinne Pache (Ithaca, NY: Cornell University Press, 1998); and Giulia Sissa, *Greek Virginity*, trans. Arthur Goldhammer (Cambridge, MA: Harvard University Press, 1990).

37. On early modern literary interest in Greek medicine, see especially Gail Kern Paster, *The Body Embarrassed: Drama and the Disciplines of Shame in Early Modern England* (Ithaca, NY: Cornell University Press, 1993); Paster, *Humoring the Body: Emotions and the Shakespearean Stage* (Chicago, IL: University of Chicago Press, 2004); and Michael Schoenfeldt, *Bodies and Selves in Early Modern England: Physiology and Inwardness in Spenser, Shakespeare, Herbert, and Milton* (Cambridge: Cambridge University Press, 1999).

38. See Matthew Steggle, *Laughing and Weeping in Early Modern Theatres* (Aldershot: Ashgate, 2007); Nicholas Cronk, "Aristotle, Horace, and Longinus: the Conception of Reader Response," *The Cambridge History of Literary Criticism*, vol. 3, 199–204; Katharine Craik and Tanya Pollard, eds, *Shakespearean Sensations: Experiencing Literature in Early Modern England* (Cambridge: Cambridge University Press, 2013); and Pollard, "Audience

Reception," in *The Oxford Handbook to Shakespeare*, ed. Arthur Kinney (Oxford: Oxford University Press, 2011), 452–67.

39. On Hecuba's exceptional status, see Malcolm Heath, "'Jure principem locum tenet': Euripides' *Hecuba*," in *Bulletin of the Institute of Classical Studies* 34 (1987), 40–68; Judith Mossman, *Wild Justice: A Study of Euripides'* Hecuba (Oxford: Clarendon Press, 1995); and Helene Foley, *Euripides'* Hecuba (London: Bloomsbury, 2014). *Hecuba* also inspired the first partial Latin translations of Greek drama, by the Calabrian Greek scholar Leontius Pilatus (1362), Francesco Filelfo (1398–1481) and Pietro da Montagnana (fl. 1432–78); see Robert Garland, *Surviving Tragedy* (London: Duckworth, 2004), 96–7.

40. Gasparus Stiblinus, "In Hecabam Euripidis Praefatio," in *Evripides Poeta Tragicorum Princeps* (Basel: Johannes Oporinus, 1562), 38. English translations of Stiblinus are indebted to the translations in Donald Mastronarde's "Stiblinus' Prefaces and Arguments on Euripides (1562)," http://ucbclassics.dreamhosters. com/djm/stiblinus/stiblinusMain.html, accessed August 7, 2015.

41. See Marcus Tullius Cicero, *De Oratore*, ed. E. W. Sutton and H. Rackham (Cambridge, MA: Harvard University Press, 1942, 1976–77), 2 vols, vol. 1, bk 2; and Quintilian, *Institutio Oratoria*, ed. Donald Russell (Cambridge, MA: Harvard University Press, 2002), 5 vols, vol. 3, bk 6. On responses to classical rhetorical models of affect, see Katharine Craik, *Reading Sensations in Early Modern England* (Basingstoke: Palgrave, 2007). On interpersonal models of selfhood, see Nancy Selleck, *The Interpersonal Idiom in Shakespeare, Donne and Early Modern Culture* (London: Palgrave MacMillan, 2008).

42. Sidney, *Defence*, F4r. Plutarch cited this anecdote in two essays, but Sidney's language echoes Amyot's translation of *On the fortune or virtue of Alexander the Great* (see "mollify his hardened heart," vs. "qu'il l'avoit amolly comme du fer"), which refers to *Hecuba*; see Pollard, "What's Hecuba to Shakespeare?," 1072–3.

43. Thomas Norton and Thomas Sackville, *Gorboduc* (1561), in *Early English Classical Tragedies*, ed. John W. Cunliffe (Oxford: Clarendon Press, 1912), 3.1.14–15.

44. Seneca, *Troas*, trans. Jasper Heywood (London, 1560), B3v; see Winston, 41.

45. William Shakespeare, *The Rape of Lucrece*, in *Shakespeare, The Poems*, ed. John Roe (Cambridge: Cambridge University Press, 1992, 2006), ll. 1447, 1458.

46. See Pollard, "Hecuba," in *A Dictionary of Shakespeare's Classical Mythology*, ed. Yves Peyré (2009–), http://www.shakmyth.org/myth/107/ hecuba/analysis.

47. William Shakespeare, *Henry IV Part Two*, ed. James Bulman, Arden Shakespeare (London: Bloomsbury, 2016), 1.2.9–11.

48. The OED's first cited use of the term, "a SYMPATHIA or equalitie of frendshipp," appears in Matteo Bandello, *Certaine Tragicall Discourses*,

trans. Fenton (London: Thomas Marshe, 1567), 40; Bandello taught Greek, and translated Euripides' *Hecuba* (1539). In 1574, the physician John Jones wrote, discussing the Greek physician Galen, "Of the good effectes, *Simpathia*, vnity, agreements of the spirites, humors and members, health is...preserued" (*A Briefe, Excellent, and Profitable Discourse* (London: William Iones, 1574), 29). Jones similarly cited a Greek philosopher in defining the word, writing in 1579, "Divine Plato also testifieth suche a *sympathia* to be betweene the body and the soule"; Jones, *The Arte and Science of Preseruing Bodie and Soule* (London: Henrie Bynneman, 1579), aivv. See "sympathy," *OED* online. On early modern conceptions of sympathies and antipathies as physical forces operating between bodies, see Mary Floyd-Wilson, *Occult Knowledge, Science, and Gender on the Shakespearean Stage* (Cambridge: Cambridge University Press, 2013); for an alternative reading of sympathy as a poetic rather than physical force, see Richard Meek, "'O, what a sympathy of woe is this': Passionate Sympathy in *Titus Andronicus*," *Shakespeare Survey* 66 (2013), 287–97.

49. "ταύτῃ γέγηθα κἀπιλήθομαι κακῶν:/ἥδ' ἀντὶ πολλῶν ἐστί μοι παραψυχή,/ πόλις, τιθήνη, βάκτρον, ἡγεμὼν ὁδοῦ." Euripides, *Hecuba*, in *Euripidis Fabulae*, ed. James Diggle (Oxford: Oxford University Press, 1984), vol. 1, ll. 279–81. All translations are my own unless otherwise specified.

50. Erasmus has, "Oblecto in hac me, sortis oblita gravis:/ Solamen haec est, una pro multis mihi,/ Urbs, atq; nutrix, scipio rector gradus" [I delight myself in her, forgetful of my heavy fate: she is my one solace for many (sorrows), city and nurse, scepter, director of my step]; *HECUBA, & Iphigenia in Aulide Euripidis tragoediae in Latinum tralatae Erasmo* (Venice: Aldus, 1507), aiiiiiir. Stiblinus, similarly, writes "Illa me oblecto, & obliuiscor malorum:/ Illa pro multis unicum est mihi solatium,/ Vrbs, atq: nutrix, scipio, rectrix gradus." Stiblinus, *Evripides Poeta Tragicorum*, 19.

51. "In lei giusto Signor: Signor in lei/ E quel poco di gioia & di contento,/ Ch'io prender posso in questa vita trista:/ Per lei la sorte mia m'esce di mente;/ Ne sento il peso e le mie spalle greue./ Ella in cambio di molti è il mio conforto,/ Mia città, mia nutrice, appoggio, & guida/ De passi miei, che senza lei non vanno." *La Hecuba Tragedia di M. Lodovico Dolce, Tratta da Euripide* (Venetia: Gabriel Gioli di Ferrari, 1543), 16r.

52. "ἡμεῖς δὲ πεντήκοντά γ' ἄμμοροι τέκνων," Euripides, 421; "At ego orba quinquies decem iam liberis," Erasmus, *Hecuba*, aiiiiiiiiv; "At nos sumus orbae quinquaginta liberis," Stiblinus, *Evripides Poeta Tragicorum*, 22; "Et me spingera morte/ Di Cinquanta figliuoli orbata & priva," Dolce, 21v. Euripides' reference to fifty children expands significantly on the nineteen children attributed to Hecuba by Homer, suggesting an especially acute interest in Hecuba's prolific maternity.

53. "μὴ λίπῃς μ' ἄπαιδ'," Euripides, 440; "Da ne relinquas orbam," Erasmus, bir; "Da: ne relinquas orbam," Stiblinus, 22; "Non mi lasciar senza di te figliuola," Dolce, 22v.

54. ὦ τέκνον τέκνον ταλαίνας ματρός," Euripides, 694; Erasmus has "Heu gnate gnate matris infaustissimae," Erasmus, biiiiir. Stiblinus assigns these lines to Hecuba's chorus: "O fili, fili miserae/ Matris," 27. Dolce expands these lines considerably, but also adapts them very freely; see Dolce, 31v–32r.

55. "τοῦτόν ποτ᾽ ἔτεκον κἄφερον ζώνης ὕπο," Euripides, 762. Erasmus has "Peperi ego hunc olim, ac ventre gestavi meo" [I once gave birth to him; I carried him in my womb], Erasmus, biiiiiir. Stiblinus has the same words; Stiblinus, 28. Dolce has the very similar "Fu mio parte: e'l portai nel ventre mio," Dolce, 33v.

56. Loraux writes that "a mother owes her pre-eminent position alongside the dead to the unconditional privilege given once and for all by the bond of childbirth. A bond that is without mediation, exacting, painful, and that Euripides' choruses sometimes describe as 'terrible': terribly tender, terribly strong, simply *terrible*" (*Mothers in Mourning*, 38). For accounts of pregnancy in the Hippocratic corpus, see especially "Diseases of Women 1," trans. Ann Ellis Hanson, *Signs* 1:2 (1975), 567–84, 570; on pregnancy and tragedy, see Pollard, "Conceiving Tragedy," in Craik and Pollard, eds, *Shakespearean Sensations*, 85–100.

57. See, for example, *Hecuba* 151, 355, 612 (*parthenos*), and 22, 536 (*kore*); "μέλαν κόρης ἀκραιφνὲς αἷμ᾽," 536–7. On the prominence of virgins in Greek gods' demands for human sacrifices, see Dennis D. Hughes, *Human Sacrifice in Ancient Greece* (London: Routledge, 1991), esp. 61–89.

58. "νύμφην τ᾽ ἄνυμφον παρθένον τ᾽ ἀπάρθενον," *Hecuba*, 612. See Helene Foley, "Marriage and Sacrifice in Euripides' *Iphigeneia in Aulis*," *Arethusa* 15:1/2 (1982), 159–80, and Diane Purkiss, "Blood, Sacrifice, Marriage and Death: Why Iphigenia and Mariam have to die," *Women and Writing* 6:1 (1999), 27–45.

59. Sissa writes, "The virginity of the prophetess is not merely an accessory quality... it is that which makes reception of the god possible"; Sissa, *Greek Virginity*, 4.

60. Plutarch, "Of The Oracles That Have Ceased To Give Answere," in *The philosophie, commonlie called, the morals vvritten by the learned philosopher Plutarch of Chaeronea*, trans. Philemon Holland (London: Arnold Hatfield, 1603), 1350.

61. "αὐτόθεν ἐγκύμονα τῆς δαιμονίου καθισταμένην δυνάμεως παραυτίκα χρησμῳδεῖν κατ᾽ ἐπίπνοιαν." Longinus, *On the Sublime*, ed. William Rhys Roberts (Cambridge: Cambridge University Press, 1907), 13:2. On early editions and translations of Longinus in this period, see Bernard Weinberg, "Translations and Commentaries of Longinus, *On the Sublime*, to 1600: A Bibliography" in *Modern Philology* 47 (1950), 145–51; I am grateful to Katharine Craik for this reference, and for sharing unpublished work on responses to Longinus.

62. "ἀρίστη," *Hecuba*, 580; "δεινὸς χαρακτὴρ," *Hecuba*, 379. Erasmus translates the former as "summo," the greatest, and the latter as "mira... nota," a

strange and wonderful sign; see *HECUBA, & Iphigenia in Aulide Euripidis tragoediae*, XVv and Ciiv.

63. Giovan Battista Giraldi Cinthio, *Discourse or Letter on the Composition of Comedies and Tragedies*, trans. Daniel Javitch, *Renaissance Drama* 39 (2011), 207–55, 242. Giraldi's Italian reads, "fu molto conueneuole nel l'Hecuba di Euripide, che Polissena priua del padre, dei fratelli, del regno, & rimasa senza alcuna speranza di bene, andasse animosamente alla morte . . . E fu cosa degna del real animo di Polissena giudicar men male il morire, che star sempre uituperosamente col collo sopposto al seruil giogo"; see *Discorsi di M. Giovambattista Giraldi Cinthio* (Ferrarra, 1554), 262. On Giraldi's criticism, see especially Daniel Javitch, "Introduction to Giovan Battista Giraldi Cinthio's *Discourse or Letter on The Composition of Comedies and Tragedies*," *Renaissance Drama* 39 (2011), 197–206.

64. Euripides, *Hecuba*, 549 and 550; Erasmus, *Hecuba*, XVr.

65. "in qua re mira vis exprimitur ἐμπαθείας καὶ ἠθοποιίας. Tam ardet affectibus unicae filiae et grandaevae matris acerba divulsio." Stiblinus, "Argumentum Actus Secundi," *Evripides Poeta Tragicorum Princeps*, 40.

66. Giraldi Cinthio, *Discourse*, 242. The original reads "serua marauigliosamente, in quanto madre, il costume, che le conuiene, la Regina Hecuba, nel dolersi della infelicita della sua figliuola di bramare di morire per lei, o almeno di finire con lei gli infelici suoi giorni; cosa conueneuolissima e alla pieta materna, & alla grandezza del dolore, nel quale si trouaua la misera madre" (*Discorsi*, 262).

67. Hecuba's firebrand dream features in multiple classical texts and commentaries, including Euripides' *Trojan Women*, Virgil's *Aeneid*, Apollodorus' *Library*, Ovid's *Heroides*, and Conti's *Mythologia*; see Pollard, "Hecuba."

68. This pattern appears in many of Seneca's influential plays, which responded to Euripides; see R. J. Tarrant, "Senecan Drama and its Antecedents," *Harvard Studies in Classical Philology* 82 (1978), 213–63.

69. "χαίρεις ὑβρίζουσ' εἰς ἔμ', ὦ πανοῦργε σύ;/ οὐ γάρ με χαίρειν χρή σε τιμωρουμένην;" (*Hecuba*, 1257–8).

70. Erasmus translates, "Malefica gaudes, me quod afficias malis?/ Quid enim, ulta te, non gaudeam iure optimum?" (*Evripidis tragoediae dvae, Hercuba & Iphigenia in Aulide,* trans. Erasmus [Basel: Joannes Froben, 1524]; underlining in Columbia University's copy, Shelfmark Gonzalez Lodge 1524 Eu73). Aemilius Portus offers a slightly different formulation, but the same key verb: "Gaudes insultans mihi o malitiosa tu?/ Non enim me gaudere oportet te quae vlta sum?" (*Euripides Tragoediae XIX*, trans. Aemilius Portus (Heidelberg: Commelinus, 1597)). Dolce has "Tu t'allegri crudel d'havermi ucciso./ Non mi debbo allegrar di tal vendetta?" See Dolce, *Hecuba*, 46v.

71. "πᾶσι γὰρ κοινὸν τόδε,/ ἰδίᾳ θ' ἑκάστῳ καὶ πόλει, τὸν μὲν κακὸν/ κακόν τι πάσχειν, τὸν δὲ χρηστὸν εὐτυχεῖν." Euripides, *Hecuba*, 902–4. See Billing, "Lament and Revenge in the *Hekabe* of Euripides," *New Theatre Quarterly* 23:1 (2007), 49–57.

72. When Jason learns of her murder of his children, Euripides' Medea flaunts her successful punishment of him: "For I, as necessary, have attacked your heart in return" [τῆς σῆς γὰρ ὡς χρῆν καρδίας ἀνθηψάμην], *Medea*, in *Euripidis Fabulae*, 1360. Discussing Hieronimo's account of his revenge in *The Spanish Tragedy*, Gordon Braden identifies his pride with "the recognition to which Seneca's Medea and Atreus aspire in their last scenes" (Braden, *Renaissance Tragedy and the Senecan Tradition*, 211); I suggest that this pride reflects Seneca's debts to Euripides.

73. See Froma Zeitlin, *Playing the Other: Gender and Society in Classical Greek Literature* (Chicago: University of Chicago Press, 1996), 194–8; I am grateful to David Quint for calling this to my attention.

74. On Renaissance identification of the *Odyssey* with the origins of tragicomedy, see Sarah Dewar-Watson, "Shakespeare's Dramatic Odysseys: Homer as a Tragicomic Model in *Pericles* and *The Tempest*," *Classical and Modern Literature* 25:1 (2005), 23–40; on Euripides' *Cyclops*, see Marvin T. Herrick, *Tragicomedy: Its Origin and Development in Italy, France, and England* (Urbana: University of Illinois Press, 1955); and on classical authority for tragicomedy more broadly, see Pollard, "Tragicomedy," in *The Oxford History of Classical Reception in English Literature*, vol. 2: *The Renaissance*, eds. Patrick Cheney and Philip Hardie (Oxford: Oxford University Press, 2015), 419–32.

75. Scaliger, *Select Translations*, III.97, 61. "Quare Hecuba dicitur illa Euripidae, quia ab initio ad calcem ubique est. Verum cum tragoediae sit infelix exitus et tragoedia sit Hecuba, oportuit Hecubam in fine quam in principio maestiorem. Id autem nequaquam fit; ultione enim paulo minus tristis." Scaliger, *Poetices libri septem* (1995), vol. 3, III.96, 30–2.

76. Giraldi, trans. Javitch, 218; *Discorsi*, 220, 221.

77. Lodovico Castelvetro, *Castelvetro on the Art of Poetry*, ed. and trans. Andrew Bongiorno (Binghamton, NY: Medieval and Renaissance Texts & Studies, 1984), 19. On Aristotle and tragedy with a happy ending, see Sarah Dewar-Watson, "Aristotle and Tragicomedy," *Early Modern Tragicomedy*, ed. Subha Mukherji and Raphael Lyne (Suffolk: Boydell and Brewer, 2007), 15–27, and Pollard, "Tragicomedy."

78. See Amy Cook, "For Hecuba or for Hamlet: Rethinking Emotion and Empathy in the Theatre," *Journal of Dramatic Theory and Criticism* 25:2 (2011), 71–87; Marina Warner, "'Come to Hecuba': Theatrical Empathy and Memories of Troy," *The Shakespearean International Yearbook* 11 (2011), 61–87; Mary Jo Kietzman, "'What Is Hecuba to Him or [S]he to Hecuba?' Lucrece's Complaint and Shakespearean Poetic Agency," *Modern Philology* 97:1 (1999), 21–45; Lizette Westney, "Hecuba in Sixteenth-Century English Literature," *College Language Association Journal* 27:4 (1984), 436–9; Judith Weil, "Visible Hecubas," *The Female Tragic Hero in English Renaissance Drama*, 51–69; and Marguerite Tassi, *Women and Revenge in Shakespeare* (Selinsgrove, PA: Susquehanna University Press, 2011).

79. See Katharine Goodland, *Female Mourning in Medieval and Renaissance English Drama: From the Raising of Lazarus to King Lear* (Aldershot: Ashgate, 2006).

80. See Lynn Enterline, *Shakespeare's Schoolroom: Rhetoric, Discipline, Emotion* (Philadelphia: University of Pennsylvania Press, 2011), and Heather James, "Dido's Ear: Tragedy and the Politics of Response," *Shakespeare Quarterly* 52:3 (2001), 360–82.

81. Marvin Carlson describes "the physical theater, as...among the most haunted of human cultural structures," and "a cultural activity deeply involved with memory and haunted by repetition"; Carlson, *The Haunted Stage: The Theatre as Memory Machine* (Ann Arbor: University of Michigan Press, 2001, 2003), 2, 11. Joseph Roach similarly describes theater as a series of surrogates, "the doomed search for origins by continually auditioning stand-ins"; see *Cities of the Dead: Circum-Atlantic Performance* (New York: Columbia University Press, 1996), 3.

82. Enterline, *Shakespeare's Schoolroom*, 123.

83. See Steggle, *Laughing and Weeping in Early Modern Theatres*; Cronk, "Aristotle, Horace, and Longinus"; and Craik and Pollard, eds, *Shakespearean Sensations*.

84. See Elizabeth D. Harvey, *Ventriloquized Voices: Feminist Theory and English Renaissance Texts* (London: Routledge, 1992); also Enterline, *Shakespeare's Schoolroom*. Whereas Harvey and Enterline explore male authors adopting female voices, I examine male characters echoing earlier female models.

85. Bloom defines his focus as "Battle between strong equals, father and son as mighty opposites, Oedipus and Laius at the crossroads"; see Harold Bloom, *The Anxiety of Influence: A Theory of Poetry* (Oxford: Oxford University Press, 1973, 1997), 11.

86. Scholarship on early modern imitation of the classics includes Thomas M. Greene, *The Light in Troy: Imitation and Discovery in Renaissance Poetry* (New Haven, CT: Yale University Press, 1982); David Quint, *Origin and Originality in Renaissance Literature* (New Haven, CT: Yale University Press, 1983); and G. W. Pigman, "Versions of Imitation in the Renaissance," *Renaissance Quarterly* 33:1 (1980), 1–32.

87. Including Latin and vernacular translations as well as Greek texts, the sixteenth century saw twelve editions of *The Phoenician Women*, twelve editions of *Antigone*, and six editions of *Oedipus Rex*; see Appendices.

88. Gordon Braden has held that "the generally insufficient knowledge of or even interest in Greek tragedy on the part of Renaissance dramatists is hard to deny" (Braden, *Renaissance Tragedy and the Senecan Tradition*, 1); Robert Miola has claimed, "Though Elizabethan schools emphasized the study of Greek, no Greek text has appeared behind Shakespeare's works" (Miola, *Shakespeare's Reading* [Oxford: Oxford University Press, 2000], 166); and A. D. Nuttall has conceded, "That Shakespeare was cut off from Greek poetry and drama is probably a bleak truth we should accept" (Nuttall,

"Action at a Distance: Shakespeare and the Greeks," in *Shakespeare and the Classics*, ed. Charles Martindale and A. B. Taylor [Cambridge: Cambridge University Press, 2004], 209–22, 210).

89. G. K. Hunter presented English drama as "a commercial and pragmatic enterprise," in contrast with continental Europe's scholarly classicism (G. K. Hunter, "Elizabethan Theatrical Genres and Literary Theory," *The Cambridge History of Literary Criticism*, vol. 3, 248–58, 248), and Martin Mueller similarly argued, "Elizabethan tragedy proudly measures its distance from ancient models" (*Children of Oedipus and Other Essays on the Imitation of Greek Tragedy 1550–1800* [Toronto: University of Toronto Press, 1980], xiv). On English exceptionalism and the classics, see Richard Jenkyns, "United Kingdom," in *A Companion to the Classical Tradition*, ed. Craig W. Kallendorf (Oxford: Blackwell, 2007), 265–78.

90. New Historicist interest in contemporary settings discouraged studying authors' responses to earlier models, most notably with Stephen Greenblatt's description of source study as "the elephant's graveyard of literary history"; see "Shakespeare and the Exorcists," in *Shakespeare and the Question of Theory*, ed. Patricia Parker and Geoffrey Hartman (New York: Methuen, 1985), 163–87, 163. On tensions between diachronic and synchronic approaches to early modern literary study, see Heather James, "Shakespeare, the Classics, and the forms of Authorship," *Shakespeare Studies* 36 (2008), 80–9.

91. *The Works of Thomas Kyd*, ed. Frederick S. Boas (Oxford: Clarendon Press, 1901, repr 1962), xxxvii. Lane Cooper similarly wrote that Shakespeare, "though more Roman than Greek in his dramatic origins, is nearer . . . to Aristotle and the spirit of Greek tragedy"; *The Poetics of Aristotle* (Ithaca, NY: Cornell University Press, 1923), 134.

92. Michael Silk, "Shakespeare and Greek tragedy: Strange Relationship," in *Shakespeare and the Classics*, 241–57, 241; Nuttall, "Action at a Distance," 212. Newman similarly identified Shakespeare's link with Greek literary thought as instinctive: "he knew something about dramatic poetry which was also known to Aristotle." See Newman, "Small Latine and Lesse Greeke? Shakespeare and the Classical Tradition," in *Literae Humaniores: Classical Themes in Renaissance Guise*, ed. J. K. Newman (*Illinois Classical Studies* 9:2 [1984], 309–30, 310).

93. In 1598, Francis Meres suggested the model of reincarnation in his famous claim that "the sweet witty soul of Ovid lives in mellifluous and honey-tongued Shakespeare"; see Meres, *Palladis Tamia*, 281v.

94. See, for instance, Louise Clubb, *Italian Drama in Shakespeare's Time* (New Haven, CT: Yale University Press, 1989); Robert Henke, *Pastoral Transformations: Italian Tragicomedy and Shakespeare's Late Plays* (Newark: University of Delaware Press, 1997); Michele Marrapodi, ed., *Italian Culture in the Drama of Shakespeare and His Contemporaries* (Aldershot: Ashgate, 2007); Henke and Nicholson, eds, *Transnational Exchange in Early Modern Theater*.

95. On Shakespeare's literariness, see Lukas Erne, *Shakespeare as Literary Dramatist* (Cambridge: Cambridge University Press, 2003); on relations with fellow

dramatists, see James Shapiro, *Rival Playwrights: Marlowe, Jonson, Shakespeare* (New York: Columbia University Press, 1991); Martin Wiggins, *Shakespeare and the Drama of his Time* (Oxford: Oxford University Press, 2000); Heather Hirschfeld, *Joint Enterprises: Collaborative Drama and the Institutionalization of the English Renaissance Theater* (Amherst: University of Massachusetts Press, 2004); and Ton Hoenselaars, ed., *The Cambridge Companion to Shakespeare and Contemporary Dramatists* (Cambridge: Cambridge University Press, 2012).

96. On literary archaism and anachronism in the period, see especially Lucy Munro, *Archaic Style in English Literature, 1590–1674* (Cambridge: Cambridge University Press, 2013). Studies of Latin literary influences on the period's drama include Miola, *Shakespeare and Classical Comedy* and *Shakespeare and Classical Tragedy*; Enterline, *The Rhetoric of the Body from Ovid to Shakespeare* (Cambridge: Cambridge University Press 2002) and *Shakespeare's Schoolroom*; Heather James, *Shakespeare's Troy* (Cambridge: Cambridge University Press, 1997); Colin Burrow, *Shakespeare and Classical Antiquity* (Oxford: Oxford University Press, 2013); and Jonathan Bate, *Shakespeare's Ovid* (Cambridge: Cambridge University Press, 1994).

97. Some of these include REED, Records of Early English Drama, http://reed. utoronto.ca; DEEP, Database of Early English Playbooks, http://deep.sas. upenn.edu; the Lost Plays Database, http://www.lostplays.org; and the APGRD.

98. See Emrys Jones, *The Origins of Shakespeare* (Oxford: Clarendon Press, 1977); Louise Schleiner, "Latinized Greek Drama in Shakespeare's Writing of *Hamlet*," *Shakespeare Quarterly* 41:1 (1990), 29–48; and Laurie Maguire, *Shakespeare's Names* (Oxford: Oxford University Press, 2007), 97–104. On *Alcestis* and *The Winter's Tale*, see Tom F. Driver, "Release and Reconciliation: The *Alcestis* and *The Winter's Tale*," in *The Sense of History in Greek and Shakespearean Drama* (New York: Columbia University Press, 1960), 168–98; Douglas B. Wilson, "Euripides' *Alcestis* and the Ending of Shakespeare's *The Winter's Tale*," *Iowa State Journal of Research* 58 (1984), 345–55; Sarah Dewar-Watson, "The *Alcestis* and the Statue Scene in *The Winter's Tale*," *Shakespeare Quarterly* 60:1 (2009), 73–80; Bruce Louden, "Reading through The *Alcestis* to *The Winter's Tale*," *Classical and Modern Literature* 27:2 (2007), 7–30; and Shakespeare, *The Winter's Tale*, ed. Israel Gollancz (London: J. M. Dent, 1894), viii.

99. See Andrew Werth, "Shakespeare's 'Lesse Greek,'" *The Oxfordian: The Annual Journal of the Shakespeare Oxford Society* 5 (2002) 11–29; Earl Showerman, "Orestes and Hamlet: From Myth to Masterpiece, Part I," *The Oxfordian* 7 (2004), 89–114; Showerman, "'Look Down and See What Death Is Doing': Gods and Greeks in *The Winter's Tale*," *The Oxfordian* 10 (2007), 55–74; and Showerman, "Shakespeare's Many Much Ado's: *Alcestis*, Hercules, and *Love's Labour's Wonne*," *Brief Chronicles* I (2009), 109–40. I disagree with these articles' claims about authorship but appreciate their observations about Greek allusions.

100. See Matthew Steggle, "Aristophanes in Early Modern England," in *Aristophanes in Performance, 421 BC–AD 2007: Peace, Birds and Frogs*, ed. Edith Hall and Amanda Wrigley (Oxford: Legenda, 2007), 52–65; Steggle, *Wars of the Theatres: The Poetics of Personation in the Age of Jonson* (Victoria: English Literary Studies, 1998).

101. See Bruce R. Smith, *Ancient Scripts and Modern Experience on the English Stage 1500–1700* (Princeton, NJ: Princeton University Press, 1988); Jonathan Walker and Paul D. Streufert, eds, *Early Modern Academic Drama* (Burlington: Ashgate, 2008); Sarah Dewar-Watson, "Jocasta: 'A Tragedie Written in Greek'," *International Journal of the Classical Tradition* 17:1 (2010), 22–32; Sarah Knight, "'Goodlie anticke apparrell?': Sophocles' *Ajax* at Early Modern Oxford and Cambridge," *Shakespeare Studies* 38 (2009), 25–42; Robert S. Miola, "Euripides at Gray's Inn: Gascoigne and Kinwelmersh's *Jocasta*," in *The Female Tragic Hero in English Renaissance Drama*, 33–50; Inga-Stina Ewbank, "'Striking too short at Greeks': The Transmission of *Agamemnon* on the English Renaissance Stage," in *Agamemnon in Performance: 458 BC to AD 2004*, ed. Fiona Macintosh, Pantelis Michelakis, Edith Hall, and Oliver Taplin (Oxford: Oxford University Press, 2005), 37–52; Diane Purkiss, "Medea in the English Renaissance," in *Medea in Performance, 1500–2000*, ed. Edith Hall, Fiona Macintosh, and Oliver Taplin (Oxford: Legenda, 2000), 32–48.

102. On reception studies, see Hans Jauss, *Toward an Aesthetic of Reception*, trans. Timothy Bahti (Minneapolis: University of Minnesota Press, 1982); Charles Martindale, *Redeeming the Text: Latin Poetry and the Hermeneutics of Reception* (Cambridge: Cambridge University Press, 1993); Martindale and Richard Thomas, eds, *Classics and the Uses of Reception* (Oxford: Blackwell, 2006), and Lorna Hardwick and Christopher Stray, eds, *A Companion to Classical Reception*s (Oxford: Blackwell, 2008).

103. See Helene P. Foley, *Reimagining Greek Tragedy on the American Stage* (Berkeley: University of California Press, 2012); Fiona Macintosh, "Performance Histories," in *A Companion to Classical Receptions*, 247–58; Edith Hall, "Towards a Theory of Performance Reception," *Arion* 12:1 (2004), 51–89; Hall, "Greek Tragedy and the British Stage, 1566–1997," *Cahiers du Gita*, 12 (1999), 113–34; Macintosh and Hall, *Greek Tragedy and the British Theatre, 1660–1914* (Oxford: Oxford University Press 2005); Hall and Stephe Harrop, eds, *Theorising Performance: Greek Drama, Cultural History, and Critical Practice* (London: Duckworth, 2010); Hall, Macintosh, and Amanda Wrigley, eds, *Dionysus Since 69: Greek Tragedy at the Dawn of the Third Millenium* (Oxford: Oxford University Press, 2004); and Macintosh, *Dying Acts: Death in Ancient Greek and Modern Irish Tragic Drama* (Cork: Cork University Press, 1994). Although she emphasizes Latin rather than Greek sources, Katherine Heavey traces Medea's afterlife in *The Early Modern Medea* (London: Palgrave 2014).

104. See Neil Rhodes, "Marlowe and the Greeks," *Renaissance Studies* 27:2 (2013), 199–218; Jane Grogan, "'Headless Rome' and Hungry Goths: Herodotus and *Titus Andronicus*," *English Literary Renaissance* (2013), 30–60; Victor

Skretkowicz, *European Erotic Romance: Philhellene Protestantism, Renaissance Translation and English Literary Politics* (Manchester: Manchester University Press, 2010); Steven Mentz, *Romance for Sale in Early Modern England: The Rise of Prose Fiction* (Aldershot: Ashgate, 2006); Demetriou, "'Strange Appearance'"; Demetriou, "Chapman's *Odysses* (1614–1615): Translation and Allegory," in *Homère à la Renaissance: Le Mythe et Ses Transfigurations*, ed. Luisa Capodieci and Philip Ford (Rome: Somogy/Académie de France à Rome, 2011), 245–60; and Demetriou, "'Essentially Circe': Spenser, Homer and the Homeric Tradition," *Translation and Literature* 15:2 (2006), 151–76.

105. Miola, in *Shakespeare and Classical Comedy* and *Shakespeare and Classical Tragedy*, explores only Roman literary models, as does James in *Shakespeare's Troy*. In *Shakespeare and Classical Antiquity*, the only Greek author Colin Burrow discusses is Plutarch, whose belatedness and Roman citizenship align him in many ways with Latin authors.

106. On uncanny temporalities, see Lucy Munro, "Shakespeare and the Uses of the Past: Critical Approaches and Current Debates," *Shakespeare* 7:1 (2011), 102–25, and *Archaic Style in English Literature*.

107. Erich Segal, *Roman Laughter: The Comedy of Plautus* (Oxford: Oxford University Press, 1968), 5. For a recent argument that Latin literature developed out of a culture of translating Greek, see Denis Feeney, *Beyond Greek: The Beginnings of Latin Literature* (Cambridge MA: Harvard University Press, 2016).

108. Ascham, *Scholemaster*, 17v.

109. Erasmus, Ep. 149, in *Collected Works of Erasmus* (hereafter *CWE*), vol. 2, trans. Roger Aubrey Baskerville Mynors and Douglas Ferguson Scott Thomson (Toronto: University of Toronto Press, 1975), 24–7, 25.

110. Erasmus, Ep. 208, "To William Warham" (1507), in *CWE*, vol. 2, 133.

111. On Seneca's responses to Euripides, see Tarrant, "Senecan Drama and its Antecedents"; Vassiliki Panoussi, "Polis and Empire: Greek Tragedy in Rome," in *A Companion to Greek Tragedy*, ed. Justina Gregory (Oxford: Blackwell, 2005), 413–27; and Gildenhard and Revermann, *Beyond the Fifth Century*. See also Phillip John Usher, "Tragedy and Translation," *A Companion to Translation Studies*, ed. Sandra Bermann and Catherine Porter (Oxford: Wiley-Blackwell, 2014) 467–78, esp. 471–2.

112. "λαμπροῦ Αἰσχύλου, ὃς τὰς αὐτοῦ τραγῳδίας τεμάχη εἶναι ἔλεγεν τῶν Ὁμήρου μεγάλων δείπνων." Athenaeus, *The Deipnosophists*, ed. Charles Burton Gulick (London: William Heinemann, 1930), 7 vols, vol 4, 74–5 (8.347e). I am grateful to Tania Demetriou for calling this quotation to my attention.

113. "ἡ τῶν ἔμπροσθεν μεγάλων συγγραφέων καὶ ποιητῶν μίμησίς τε καὶ ζήλωσις." Longinus, *On the Sublime*, 13.2.

114. "οὕτως ἀπὸ τῆς τῶν ἀρχαίων μεγαλοφυΐας εἰς τὰς τῶν ζηλούντων ἐκείνους ψυχὰς ὡς ἀπὸ ἱερῶν στομίων ἀπόρροιαί τινες φέρονται, ὑφ' ὧν ἐπιπνεόμενοι καὶ οἱ μὴ λίαν φοιβαστικοὶ τῷ ἑτέρων συνενθουσιῶσι μεγέθει." Longinus, *On the Sublime*, 13.2.

115. On repertory companies, see Lucy Munro, *Children of the Queen's Revels: A Jacobean Theatre Repertory* (Cambridge: Cambridge University Press, 2005), and Bart van Es, *Shakespeare in Company* (Oxford: Oxford University Press, 2013). On invisible offstage theatrical labor, see Natasha Korda, *Labors Lost: Women's Work and the Early Modern English Stage* (Philadelphia: University of Pennsylvania Press, 2011).

116. See Belén Bistué, *Collaborative Translation and Multi-Version Texts in Early Modern Europe* (Aldershot: Ashgate, 2013), and Deborah Uman and Belén Bistué, "Translation as Collaborative Authorship: Margaret Tyler's *The Mirrour of Princely Deedes and Knighthood*," *Comparative Literature Studies* 44:3 (2007), 298–323.

117. "Fitted out appropriately, I step inside the venerable courts of the ancients, where, solicitously received by them, I nourish myself on that food that *alone* is mine and for which I was borne; where I am unashamed to converse with them and to question them about the motives for their actions, and they, out of their human kindness, answer me." "Niccolo Machiavelli To Francesco Vettori, Florence, December 10, 1513," in *Machiavelli and His Friends: Their Personal Correspondence*, trans. James B. Atkinson and David Sices (DeKalb: Northern Illinois University Press, 1996), 262–5, 264.

118. "Viueret Euripides, tibi se debere putaret,/ Ipsa tibi grates Iphigenia daret"; William Gager, "In Iphigenia[m] Georgij Peeli Anglicanis Versibus Reddita[m]," in *The Life and Works of George Peele*, vol. 1, 43. The poem is assumed to date from the late 1570s, when Peele studied at Oxford.

119. "Arripui Sophoclem, docui Musas,... Antigonen docui verba/ Latina loqui. . . . / Iamque reviviscens, et Musis ducta Latinis/ Huc venit, et Thoebis amplius esse timet./ Mira tibi referet." Thomas Watson, dedicatory epistle, *Sophoclis Antigone* (London: John Wolf, 1581), 6; English translation by Dana Sutton, *Sophocles' Antigone,* http://www.philological.bham.ac.uk/watson/antigone/act1eng.html, accessed August 15, 2014.

120. On playwrights' engagement with contemporary dramatists in this period, see Janet Clare, *Shakespeare's Stage Traffic* (Cambridge: Cambridge University Press, 2014).

121. Citing a secretary of state under James I, William Chetwood wrote of Elizabeth I that, "Sir Robert Naunton and others inform us, that she translated for her own Amusement, one of the Tragedies of *Euripides*." See Chetwood, *The British Theater* (London: R. Baldwin, 1752), 3. On early modern women's contributions to closet drama and translation, see Straznicky, *Privacy, Playreading.*

122. See "A La Cristianissima Prencipessa Margarita di Francia," in *Ecuba: Tragedia di Euripide, Tradotta in verso Toscano da Matteo Bandello* (1539; published Rome: Nella stamperia De Romanis, 1813), 11–15; George Gascoigne and Francis Kinwelmersh, *Jocasta*, in *Early English Classical Tragedies*, 159. Geoffrey Fenton dedicated his 1567 English translation of Bandello's *Tragical Discourses*—in which he quoted Euripides—to Mary Sidney; see Fenton, "To the righte honorable and vertuous *Ladie, the Ladye*

Marye Sydney," in Bandello, *Certaine Tragicall Discourses,* trans. Fenton (London: Thomas Marshe, 1567), *iir–v. On patronage as a form of agency through which women contributed to literary production, see Julie Crawford, *Mediatrix: Women, Politics, and Literary Production in Early Modern England* (Oxford: Oxford University Press, 2014); on women's dramatic patronage, see Clare McManus, *Women on the Renaissance Stage: Anna of Denmark and Female Masquing in the Stuart Court (1590–1619)* (Manchester: Manchester University Press, 2002).

123. Uman and Bistué, "Translation as Collaborative Authorship," 303; see also Marie-Alice Belle, "Locating Early Modern Women's Translations: Critical and Historiographical Issues," *Women's Translations in Early Modern England and France* (special issue of *Renaissance & Reformation/Renaissance et Réforme* 34:5), ed. Marie-Alice Belle (2012), 5–23.

124. See especially Jauss, *Toward an Aesthetic of Reception*; Martindale, *Redeeming the Text*; Martindale and Thomas, *Classics and the Uses of Reception*.

125. See Smith, *Ancient Scripts and Modern Experience*, 6.

126. See Ben Jonson, *Bartholomew Fair*, ed. John Creaser, in *The Cambridge Edition of the Works of Ben Jonson*, ed. David Bevington, Martin Butler, and Ian Donaldson, vol. 4: *1611–1616* (Cambridge: Cambridge University Press, 2012), 271–428.

1

Greek Plays in England

Although studies of Greek plays' sixteenth-century reception have largely overlooked England's contributions, the English played a crucial role in new transnational conversations about these rediscovered texts.[1] The first full translations of Greek tragedies—Erasmus's Latin versions of Euripides' *Hecuba* (1503) and *Iphigenia in Aulis* (1506)—were crucially indebted to English support, and their shared focus on grieving but triumphant women shaped responses to Greek drama through both England and continental Europe. Situating these translations in the context of England's early engagement with newly visible Greek texts, this chapter traces the ensuing development of Greek plays' circulation in England, with a focus on the two earliest translations of Greek plays into English: Lumley's *Iphigeneia* (*c.*1557) and Gascoigne and Kinwelmersh's *Jocasta* (1566). Like *Hecuba*, these plays feature mourning mothers and self-sacrificing virgins, but whereas *Hecuba* features a bereaved mother's partial vindication after her daughter's death, the suffering queens of *Iphigeneia* and *Jocasta* transmit their fierce passions to their daughters, who achieve measures of triumph despite their mothers' defeats. In each of these plays, queens earn praise for their political acumen, which the plays present as rooted in the authority of their maternal experience, and which their daughters in turn acquire from them. Modeling forms of female counsel and succession, both plays implicitly intervene in debates about not only female monarchs, but also the transmission of literary authority to a younger generation. I argue that these translations, along with the literary developments they represented, established important foundations for the Greek tragic icons who went on to haunt England's commercial theaters.

Although Greek plays began to appear in print in Florence and Venice at the turn of the sixteenth century, their broader dissemination began with Erasmus's Latin *Hecuba*, which he dedicated to William Warham, Archbishop of Canterbury, and *Iphigenia*, which he not only dedicated to Warham but translated in London, with support from English patrons.[2] Erasmus's selections shaped the surge of interest in Greek drama that followed, because of their new accessibility in Latin and his fervent promotion of their pedagogical value.[3] One of the period's primary proponents of Greek, and a crucial architect of humanist education, Erasmus argued that "almost all knowledge of things is to be sought in the Greek authors"; in his recommendations for school and university curricula, he named Euripides the third most important Greek poet, after Aristophanes and Homer.[4] Erasmus insisted that his warm reception among England's classical scholars made his translations possible.[5] In 1505 he wrote, "There are indeed five or six men in London profoundly versed in Latin and Greek, and I doubt if Italy itself contains such good ones at the moment"; in 1506 he similarly observed, "there is no land on earth which, even over its whole extent, has brought me so many friends, or such true, scholarly, helpful, and distinguished ones, graced by every kind of good quality, as the single city of London."[6] When he sent his translations of Euripides to Aldus Manutius in 1507, he cited these scholars' authority to justify his projects. "I am sending you my translations of two tragedies," he wrote;

> It was audacious to attempt them, of course, but it is for you to decide for yourself whether I have translated them properly. Thomas Linacre, William Grocyn, William Latimer, and Cuthbert Tunstall, who are your friends as well as mine, had a very high opinion of them. You are aware that these men are too scholarly to be at sea in their judgment, and too honest to be ready to flatter a friend, unless they are sometimes blinded by personal affection for me.[7]

Erasmus's frequent references to the crucial support of his English friends and colleagues suggest that these English-sponsored Latin translations by an itinerant cosmopolite count among England's contributions to Greek reception. They have a central place, accordingly, in the history of English engagement with Greek plays. They also suggest early distinctions between Euripides' plays. Erasmus translated *Hecuba*, the earlier play, with strict attention to literal equivalence, "striving to render verse for verse and almost word for word"; he noted, "I do not fully share the freedom in translating authors that Cicero both allows others and (I should almost say excessively) practices himself."[8] Of *Iphigenia*, however—one of Euripides' later plays— Erasmus wrote that he "detected a different flavor in the language, and another style of poetry; for, if I am not mistaken, it has somewhat more naturalness and its style is more flowing."[9] In response to this sense of the play's style, he wrote, "I have decided to relax my former strictness somewhat...Accordingly I have translated the *Iphigenia* a little more freely and also a little more expansively."[10]

While the earlier and stricter *Hecuba* dominated sixteenth-century continental European discussions of Greek plays, the later and freer *Iphigenia in Aulis* proved a particularly rich source of inspiration to

English translators and neoclassical dramatists. It not only became the first play translated into English—by Jane, Lady Lumley, around 1557—but was translated again by George Peele in the 1570s, and performed by St. Paul's boys in London in the same decade.[11] The play also provided the template for both John Christopherson's *Jephthah*, the first English tragedy written in Greek (*c.*1544), and Scottish scholar George Buchanan's Latin tragedy *Jephthes, Sive Votum* (*Jephtha, or the Vow*; written 1540s, printed 1554)—which underscored the link by naming Jeptha's sacrificial daughter "Iphis."[12] Another self-sacrificing Greek virgin, Antigone, appeared both in George Gascoigne and Francis Kinwelmersh's 1566 *Jocasta* (an English translation of Euripides' *Phoenician Women*, by way of Lodovico Dolce's 1549 *Giocasta*), and in Thomas Watson's 1581 Latin translation of Sophocles' *Antigone*, which was subsequently performed in St. John's College, Cambridge, in 1583. As observed in the Introduction, the young Elizabeth I translated a Euripides play—sadly, we do not know which—and Buchanan produced Latin versions of *Medea* and *Alcestis* (staged in Bordeaux in 1539 and 1542, and printed with Erasmus's *Hecuba* and *Iphigenia* in 1544); London publisher John Day also produced a 1575 Greek edition of Euripides' *Trojan Women*.[13] With the particular focus on Iphigenia and similar sacrificial figures, these translations, editions, and adaptations collectively represent the newly unearthed realm of Greek tragedy especially with bold young women seeking justice, as well as the bereaved mothers. While scholars and translators from Catholic countries emphasized the powerful agencies unleashed by grieving mothers, tacitly reinforcing the cultural primacy of the Virgin Mary, English attention to virgin daughters who voluntarily accepted death to benefit others offered tragic female analogues for the biblical figure of Isaac, and for Christ himself.[14] Their precarious ascendance over their grieving mothers suggests a shift of power from an older generation to a younger, implicitly modeling a shift in authority from classical literary sources to their modern descendants.[15]

In the context of the period's pervasive association between Greek tragedy and mobilizing female figures, it is striking both that England's formal Greek study owed crucial debts to a powerful female patron, Lady Margaret Beaufort, and that England was the only country in which women are known to have translated Greek plays in the sixteenth century. Lumley produced her *Iphigeneia* in the mid/late-1550s, and Elizabeth I's unknown Euripides translation probably dated from the late 1540s, when she studied Greek with Roger Ascham. Religious, political, and humanist developments all contributed to interest in Greek virgin daughters and their regal mothers, but playwrights seem to have taken a particular interest in these figures' theatrical power. Identified with the authority of the Greek tragic tradition and the affective receptivity attributed to virginal and maternal bodies, these figures acquired an iconic force that went on to animate the English commercial stage. By linking acts of transmission with mother–daughter dyads, they offered a model of literary imitation that suggested both intimate exchange and the possibility of a triumphant afterlife for the younger follower.

ERASMUS, MARGARET BEAUFORT, AND ENGLAND'S GREEK

England's primary promoter of Greek, Erasmus, played a crucial role in coordinating early transnational efforts to recover access to the language and its texts. Largely lost from the west by about 600 CE, Greek had attracted glimmerings of interest among European scholars during the twelfth and thirteenth centuries, and gained momentum when fourteenth-century poets such as Petrarch and Boccaccio struggled to learn the language in order to gain access to lost literary texts.[16] Beginning with Manuel Chrysoloras' 1397 arrival in Florence from Constantinople, and intensifying with the escalating migration of Greek refugees and manuscripts to Italian cities after the 1453 fall of the Byzantine Empire, scholars from all over Europe—including England—flocked to Italy to study Greek. By the start of the sixteenth century, studying and printing Greek lay at the heart of the humanist project, extolled especially by Erasmus. The language, for him, promised both religious authority and intoxicating access to lost and hidden literary realms. "I have turned my entire attention to Greek," he wrote in 1500; "The first thing I shall do, as soon as the money arrives, is to buy some Greek authors; after that, I shall buy clothes."[17] His prioritization of Greek over basic essentials casts the language as fulfilling an elemental need, an emphasis he echoed elsewhere; in 1504, he wrote, "my experience teaches me this, at any rate, that we can do nothing in any field of literature without a knowledge of Greek."[18] In the context of Erasmus's well-established transnational networks, his glowing reports of early English Greek scholars—including William Grocyn, Thomas Linacre, William Lily, and John Colet—evoked an intimate and avant-garde coterie with the enormous task of reframing England's intellectual underpinnings.

These men played crucial roles in shaping the development of English humanist education. Yet, like Aldus Manutius, the primary figure in Italy's Greek publication revival, who dedicated his *Musarum Panegyris* (Praise of the Muses) to Caterina Pio, and Matteo Bandello, who dedi- cated his translation of Euripides' *Hecuba* to Marguerite de Navarre,

Erasmus found important support in learned women.[19] In keeping with the female patronage behind so many early translations of Greek plays, the development of Greek study in England received crucial support from Lady Margaret Beaufort (1443–1509), the mother of Henry VII and an accomplished translator in her own right.[20] A powerful and wealthy patron, as well as a scholar, Lady Margaret consolidated Erasmus's English base by establishing the Greek-centered Cambridge professorship—the Lady Margaret Professor of Divinity—that he held from 1511 to 1514. She went on to found St. John's College, Cambridge, the country's first prestigious center of Greek scholarship and home to its most prominent Hellenists, including Richard Croke, John Cheke, and Roger Ascham.[21] This crucial female patronage prefigured later support for Greek by England's most famous maternal virgin queen, Elizabeth I, who, as noted, studied the language with Ascham. The Cambridge circle created by Erasmus and Lady Margaret served for some time as the uncontested center of England's Greek scholarship, but as the intellectual appeal of Greek grew, competition did as well. When Richard Fox founded Oxford's Corpus Christi College in 1517 to exemplify the new humanist learning, its statutes specified a daily public lecture in Greek, and other colleges followed suit.[22]

Associated with unmediated access to God's word—a key factor in its glittering appeal—Greek attracted controversy, especially after Erasmus published his Greek New Testament in 1516, setting into motion the theological inquiries that led to Luther's 1522 German Bible and the start of the Reformation.[23] Greek study rapidly disappeared in Catholic countries, and in England it incurred hostility; in 1518 Thomas More complained about an Oxford group calling themselves the Trojans, who violently protested against the study of the language. "Things have come to such a pass," More wrote, "that no-one can admit in public or in private that he enjoys Greek without being subjected to the jeers of these ludicrous 'Trojans.'"[24] In keeping with his grandmother's Greek patronage and his own move towards Protestantism, however, King Henry VIII himself intervened to protect Greek scholarship, which became an increasingly fierce arena of competition between the universities. In 1520, Cambridge scholar Richard Croke warned his students, "The Oxford men, whom you have up till now vanquished in every branch of knowledge, have now betaken themselves to Greek learning. They watch by night, they go hungry, they suffer heat and cold, there is nothing they do not do to make it their own."[25] As interest escalated, both opportunities and mandates acquired increased urgency. In 1535 Thomas Cromwell required the wealthier colleges at both universities to provide daily public lectures in Greek, which students from poorer colleges were required to attend, under penalty of not being fed; he also established the King Henry VIII lectures, public readerships in Greek or Hebrew at both universities, which in 1540 became the Regius Professorships.[26] Again, royal patronage, extending Lady Margaret Beaufort's early support, played a crucial role in preserving the language's fortunes.

By the early 1540s, England's achievements in Greek were well established. Cheke, the first Regius Professor of Greek, at St. John's College, Cambridge, acquired an international reputation for philological achievement. In 1542 Ascham, who had studied with Cheke in the 1530s and went on to join him in teaching at St. John's, wrote to a friend,

> Aristotle and Plato are read by the young men in the original, but that has been done among us at St. John's for the last five years. Sophocles and Euripides are here better known than Plautus used to be when you were up. Herodotus, Thucydides, Xenophon, are more on the lips and in the hands of all now than Livy was then. What you used to hear about Cicero you now hear about Demosthenes. There are more copies of Isocrates in the hands of young men than there were of Terence then.[27]

Ascham depicts a thriving philhellenic literary community, in which Greek authors mingle intimately with English scholars, "on the lips and in the hands of all." Later historians have joined him in promoting Cheke's legacy, which has been described as a high point of Renaissance Greek study: R. R. Bolgar claimed that "Cheke and his fellows were the real heirs of Italy."[28] Cheke was a famously charismatic lecturer, especially evangelical on the power and significance of Greek, and generations of graduates entered the world convinced of its intellectual primacy. And while no women attended Cambridge or Oxford in this period, educating young women in Greek became a hallmark of aristocratic elites, in keeping with a new emphasis on companionate marriage encouraged by Erasmus and Sir Thomas More.[29] More's daughter Mary Roper (née More) studied Greek, and taught it to her daughter, Mary Clarke Bassett (née Roper), who translated Eusebius's *Ecclesiastical History* from Greek and dedicated it to Mary Tudor. Lady Jane Grey studied Greek with John Aylmer, a Cambridge graduate, who also taught the language to his daughter Judith Aylmer. Mildred Cecil, Lady Burghley, was known for her expertise in the Greek Church fathers and Hesiod, and wrote verse in Greek, as did her sister, Elizabeth Hoby Russell. Literary correlations between Greek texts and strong female figures found a literal corollary in rising levels of female Greek scholarship.

THE DAUGHTER ALSO RISES: LUMLEY'S
IPHIGENEIA

The growing excitement of England's mid-century achievements in Greek, along with their expanding outreach into female education, offers important context for the first English translation of a Greek play, Lumley's *The Tragedie of Euripides called Iphigeneia*, written in about 1557.[30] Lumley's father Henry Fitzalan, Earl of Arundel, godson and page of Henry VIII, was among the aristocrats who believed in providing an elite education to his daughters; Jane translated Greek texts by Isocrates as well as Euripides, and her sister Mary translated Greek *sententiae* into English and Latin.[31] Lumley's Greek prowess benefited not only from her father, but probably also from her husband (John, Baron Lumley) and her brother (Henry Fitzalan, Baron Maltravers), who both studied at Queens' College, Cambridge in the Greek-steeped late 1540s. The sisters had both an unusually rigorous education and an unusually prominent place in their household: their mother died when they were young, and their brother predeceased them in 1557, before Mary died later that year; when their father died in 1580, the family title passed to Mary's son, Philip Howard.[32] Lumley's Euripides translation grew out of both emerging Greek pursuits and the changing roles of female aristocrats, among heated debates about succession and female monarchy.

As the first extant English play by a female writer, as well as the first English translation of a Greek play, Lumley's *Iphigeneia* has attracted attention especially from scholars interested in early modern women's writing.[33] The play dramatizes Agamemnon's ambivalence over his decision to sacrifice his daughter Iphigenia as an offering to Artemis, in response to a decree from the prophet Calchas that the Greek army will not be able to sail to Troy to begin the war until she is killed. Critics have observed the Christ-like imagery linked with Iphigenia's voluntary sacrifice,[34] and the complex stakes of Lumley's critiquing a male aristocrat's politically motivated sacrifice of his daughter, especially in the context of her dedication of the play to her father, who had played a key role in the recent death of Lady Jane Grey, his niece and Lumley's cousin, after her brief coronation.[35] Situating the play in the context of contemporary approaches to Euripides' mother–daughter dyads expands these conversations by highlighting Lumley's attention to the transmission of both tragic passions and heroic agency from mother to daughter. Critics have focused primarily on the figure of Iphigenia, but Lumley's notable interventions include expanding Clytemnestra's role to 280 lines, considerably outweighing Iphigenia's 192 lines and intensifying the importance already accorded to her by Euripides; despite the title's emphasis on Iphigenia, the original play gives nearly equal attention to Clytemnestra, with 205 lines, as to Iphigenia, with 207.[36] Attending to Lumley's sympathetic presentation of Clytemnestra also illuminates her depiction of Iphigenia, whose boldness and insight have roots in her mother's emotional and rhetorical power. Lumley shows the potent affect unleashed by maternity as mobilizing not only mothers themselves, but also their audiences, especially the intimate audiences of their own kin. In her portrait of Iphigenia's decisive claim to glory, Lumley implicitly argues for the redemptive heroism not only of women, but also of a new generation, in repairing and reviving a trouble-torn older world.

Clytemnestra may at first seem peripheral to the play's action: she is shut out from both Agamemnon's initial decision to sacrifice their daughter and Iphigenia's eventual decision to offer herself voluntarily for this sacrifice. Yet the powerful, vengeful Clytemnestra of Aeschylus' earlier *Agamemnon* haunts Euripides' play, and Lumley's version channels her ghost in framing defiant challenges to male authority, even more assertively than in Euripides' Greek.[37] As the play begins, Agamemnon regrets having sent for his wife and daughter under the pretense of marrying Iphigenia to Achilles, but he has again resigned himself to the terrible necessity of her sacrifice by the time they arrive. From her first appearance, however, Clytemnestra makes it clear that her daughter's affairs are hers to manage, not his. When he attempts to send her away, insisting that "it doth not become you to be amongste suche a companye of men" (693–5), she refuses, explaining "yet the mother ought to be at the mariage of the daughter" (696–8), and ultimately insisting, "I will not goo home yet, for you oughte to do sacrafice onlie: but I muste see all thinges made redie for the marriage" (702–4).[38] No match for her stubbornness, Agamemnon gives up the argument, confessing in an aside, "I haue labored in vayne: for althoughe I haue used deceite and crafte, yea unto my dearest frindes: yet I can not fulfill my purpose" (705–8). In the face of his wife's firmness, he acknowledges to himself both that he is in the wrong, and that she will not be dissuaded. Rooting her authority in her maternal privilege, Clytemnestra emerges from this first round the victor.

Clytemnestra is similarly forceful upon encountering and greeting Achilles, who wonders at her boldness: "Who are you I pray you, that you beinge a woman dare come amongst suche a companie of men?" (727–9).[39] Achilles' words closely echo Agamemnon's earlier reproach that she should not be "amongste suche a companye of men" (694–5), yet again Clytemnestra neither apologizes nor backs down from her assertive public role in a company of men. On the contrary, she resolutely maintains that it is her place to oversee all matters and decisions connected to the child she bore, and upon learning that Achilles knows nothing of his supposed upcoming marriage to Iphigenia, she determines, "I will nowe goo, and knowe the truthe of all this matter" (763–4). When a servant reveals Agamemnon's terrible plan, Clytemnestra wastes no time confronting her husband directly: "I heare saie that you goo aboute to sleye your owne childe" (933–4).[40] In response to his evasions, she insists on her right to know and decide matters involving her own child, stating, "I have not enquired of any thinge that dothe not become me" (943–4).[41] In her insistence on arguing with her husband about matters of both family and military policy, she presents herself as possessing an authority at least equal to his own, if not superior. Other voices in the play concur with her claims: the female chorus advises Agamemnon, "you shulde folowe your wives councell. for it is not lawfull that a father shulde destroy his childe" (1023–6).[42] As Allyna Ward has observed, the word "counsel" occurs twenty times in the play, especially in conjunction with Clytemnestra and Iphigenia.[43] Reading the play in the context of Lumley's other Greek translations, of Isocrates' political orations, Goodrich suggests that Lumley "presents Clytemnestra as a potential political counsellor with a solid grasp of commonwealth theory."[44] Although her counsel fails to sway Agamemnon, the play upholds her authority over the domestic sphere.

Lumley's attention to Clytemnestra's personal and political authority complements an equally heightened emphasis on the pathos of her grief. When Iphigenia and Clytemnestra learn of Agamemnon's plan, both of them lament, but the prospect of mourning a daughter's death is more painful than that of dying.[45] "Alas," Clytemnestra tells Iphigenia, "I wretched creature have greate cause to mourne" (847). In response to her daughter's attempts to persuade her not to grieve, she rejoins, "How can I do otherwise, seinge I shall loose you?" (850). When Iphigenia announces her intention to embrace her sacrifice, Clytemnestra is stricken: "I pray you daughter tarie, and do not forsake me now" (889–90). Her simple and homely words directly evoke the pity and fear identified with tragedy's affective power: Hodgson-Wright observes, "The ripping of the bond between mother and daughter is given primary importance in Lumley's text."[46] Similarly, in words that both plead and threaten, Clytemnestra asks Agamemnon,

> if you kille my daughter, what lamentacion must I nedes make, Whan I shall goo home, and wante the companie of her? Considering that she was slaine bi the hands of her owne father: Wherfore if you will not be moued with pitie, take hede leste you compelle me to speke thos thinges, that do not become a good wife: yea and you your selfe do thos thinges that a good man ought not. (986–97)

In her portrait of a bereaved future, Clytemnestra represents the terrible loss at the tragedy's heart. The specter of Aeschylus' vengeful Clytemnestra, who not only speaks but carries out those things that do not become a good wife, looms behind her insistence that Agamemnon should be moved not simply by pity but also by fear: incurring his wife's righteous fury will not be in his own interest. Lumley here condenses Euripides' passage, in which Clytemnestra goes on to answer her rhetorical questions by rehearsing the lamentations she will make: "Oh child, the father that begot you has destroyed you himself, no one else, nor by another's hand, leaving this sort of a return to his home."[47] Instead, she moves quickly to her threat: if Agamemnon insists on doing what he should not, he will force her to do what she should not. Her future vengeance looms as an inevitable consequence of his wrongful action.

Clytemnestra's reflections on the mobilizing power of maternal grief are echoed and supported by her female chorus. After learning that Iphigenia will be sacrificed, they lament the pain that her death will bring to her mother. "Truly," they note, "it is a uerie troblesome thinge to haue children: for we are euen by nature compelled to be sorie for their mishappes" (831–3). Although Lumley's language is characteristically simple, her rendition emphasizes the negative aspects of ambiguous Greek terms, and in this respect she comes closer to Euripides than to Erasmus's translation, which she owned.[48] Euripides' chorus says, "Giving birth carries a strange and terrible [*deinon*] spell, and suffering [*hyperkamnein*] for their children is shared by all women."[49] Euripides' Greek uses the word *deinon*—strange, terrible, marvelous, dangerous—to frame the emotional impact of maternity as ambivalent, and *hyperkamnein* denotes excessive suffering. Erasmus, on the other hand, omits the metaphor of a drug or spell (*philtron*), with its implications of powerlessness, and instead emphasizes strength: "Res efficax peperisse, uimque maximam/ Amoris adfert omnibus communiter,/ Vti pro suis summe adlaborent liberis" [It is a powerful thing to have given birth, and it brings the greatest force of love to all in common, so that they expend the greatest amount of effort for their children].[50] "Efficax," "vim," and "adlaborent" suggest power, force, and effort, rather than the strange marvels and suffering of the Greek and English versions. Demers describes these lines of Lumley's translation as "pallid and prosaic," but their emphasis on the terrible passions intrinsic in maternity is strikingly Euripidean.[51] And although Lumley's choices are in keeping with other vernacular translators' approaches to Euripides' plays, in the light of her emphasis it is poignant to note that her own three children all died in infancy.[52]

Yet if Lumley presents maternity as a source of terrible grief, the association hardly renders Clytemnestra weak and vulnerable. On the contrary, Lumley shows this grief to be the mobilizing force behind Clytemnestra's boldness, which in turn implicitly shapes Iphigenia's own turn from fear to assertive heroism. Some classicists have charged Euripides with inconsistency in his portrait of Iphigenia, who at first pleads to avoid death, but later chooses to embrace it.[53] Others, however, have identified her decision to confront death as part of a "new heroism" that Euripides located in apparently marginal figures, including women, children, and slaves.[54] Lumley's version supports this positive interpretation. From her first appearance, Lumley emphasizes Iphigenia's intelligence. "Trulye daughter," Agamemnon tells her, "the more wittely you speake, the more you troble me," and when she playfully offers "to seme more folisshe," he acknowledges his pride in her cleverness: "Suerly I am constrained to praise gretlye your witte, for I do delite moche in it" (608–14). Like her mother, Lumley's Iphigenia shows both interest in and mastery of political strategy.[55] As Deborah Uman has noted, Lumley omits a passage in which Euripides presents Iphigenia as resorting to tears rather than words, pointedly refusing to convey her as even temporarily lacking verbal power.[56] Yet Lumley's Iphigenia is not simply clever. Equally important, she uses her intelligence not to deceive, or to persuade others to ease her predicament—as do other clever Euripidean women, most infamously Medea—but instead to recognize the glory that she will personally earn in actively choosing, and embracing, a heroic death.

In explaining her decision, Lumley's Iphigenia draws on a Greek political model of citizenship, underpinned with Christian notions of sacrifice. "Remember," she tells her mother,

> how I was not borne for your sake onlie, but rather for the commodite of my countrie, thinke you therefore that it is mete, that suche a companie of men beinge gathered together to revenge the great iniurie, whiche all grece hathe suffered shoulde be let of their journey for my cause. (808–13)

She similarly comforts her father, while insisting on a public death:

> O father, I am come hether to offer my bodie willinglie for the wellthe of my countrie: Wherfore seinge that I shall be sacrificed for the commodite of all grece, I do desier you, that none of the grecians may slaaie me previlie: for I will make no resistance ageinste you. (926–30)

In her translation of Erasmus's prefatory argument, Lumley explains that

> Iphigenia her selfe changed hir minde, and perswadethe hir mother, that it is better for her to dye a glorious deathe, then that for the safegarde only of hir life, either so many noblemen shoulde fall out within them selves, or else such a noble enterprise, being taken in hande, shulde shamefullye againe be let slippe. (47–52)

In the Greek text, Euripides repeatedly emphasizes Iphigenia's *kleos*, or fame, and describes her as *aristē*, the best.[57] As noted in the Introduction, her determination to die for glory evokes the famous choice of Achilles, whose admiration she earns in the play, to earn fame in a life that is short but glorious rather than long but unremembered.[58]

Just as Clytemnestra's affective power, like that of Hecuba, is rooted in her maternity, Iphigenia's has roots in her virginity, which Lumley emphasizes especially in references to her sacrifice. Lumley's translation of Erasmus's prefatory argument refers to Agamemnon's unsent letter asking Clytemnestra not to "sende the uirgine hir daughter unto Aulyda," and refers to "Menelaus waitinge afore daye for the cominge of the uirgine" (Argument, 30–1, 37–8). Menelaus subsequently tries "to perswade him not to sley the uirgine for his sake" (49–50) and Achilles becomes angry that the host had "determined the deathe of the uirgine" and "required the uirgine" (67–8, 74). Lumley's extensive repetition of the word "virgin" considerably exceeds that of her source; some of these references translate Erasmus's "virgine," but others translate "puella" (girl).[59] Similarly, within the play, when Agamemnon bids Iphigenia to prepare for the sacrifice, Lumley translates his line as "make you redie withe the other uirgins" (650–1), and when Iphigenia makes her final exit at the end of the play, the chorus announce, "Beholde yonder goethe the uirgine to be sacrificed" (1319–20). When the messenger describes the miracle of Iphigenia's rescue by the goddess, he reports the wish of the host that the goddess would "accepte the sacrifice of the uirgins blode" (1358–9). As discussed in this book's Introduction, the virginity requisite for both sacrificial offerings and transmitting oracles signals the purity and receptivity necessary for divine possession, an inhabited bodily state parallel to that of pregnancy. Lumley's attention to the play's portrayal of a virgin sacrificed to a virgin goddess underscores Euripides' emphasis on Iphigenia's distinctively female brand of heroism, with its particular conversion of threat to triumph.

Lumley's emphasis on Iphigenia's virginity also offers suggestive resonances with recent research on the play's likely performance, setting, and audiences. Although Lumley's play has typically been seen as a closet drama, written to be read rather than performed, recent scholarship by Marion Wynne-Davies, Alison Findlay, and Gweno Williams has argued for the likelihood that it was performed privately for an aristocratic audience, which may well have included the newly crowned Elizabeth I.[60] Lumley's condensed, informal prose style lends itself to oral presentation; her manuscript refers to "the names of the spekers," rather than the characters; and specific changes from the Greek—such as turning a lamp into a candle, a scroll into a letter, a forest into a garden, and Artemis to Diana—suggest Lumley's banqueting house in Nonsuch, acquired in 1554, which featured an altar to Diana, and where Lumley and her father were documented as having staged theatrical performances.[61]

Noting these details, as well as the cutting of long rhetorical passages less engaging for public entertainment, Wynne-Davies suggests, "The first scene is therefore not so much a translation as a reworking of a Greek play to answer the necessities of an early modern banqueting house performance."[62] In 1559, Lumley entertained Elizabeth I at Nonsuch with an unknown play by the Children of St. Paul's, who went on to perform a play titled *Iphigeneia* at court in 1571.[63] Although the evidence is circumstantial and speculative, Wynne-Davies argues persuasively that, "the time, place and nature of the textual emendations affirm that Jane Lumley's *Iphigeneia* was most probably prepared for a performance at the Nonsuch banqueting house, even if that performance never took place."[64] If Lumley translated the play for a live performance directed especially at the newly crowned virgin queen, its presentation of the heroic powers linked with both virginity and maternity take on even more pointed political undertones. Lumley, a young Greek-educated aristocrat, emphasizes her commonality with the young Greek-educated queen in a celebration of female political counsel, presented as rooted in the receptive power of women's bodies and minds.

In amplifying Iphigenia's embodied heroism, and implicitly offering her as a model for politically astute English female aristocrats, Lumley links her boldness to Clytemnestra's similarly embodied vehemence and intelligence, and to the mobilizing force of her grief. Goodrich argues persuasively that Lumley presents Iphigenia and Clytemnestra as exemplars of heroic female power: "In portraying these characters as counsellors with knowledge of commonwealth theory, Lumley implies that aristocratic women could transform the domestic sphere into an arena for limited political action."[65] I argue in addition that by exploring and heightening the terrible grief that leads to this heroism, Lumley gives both mother and daughter a distinctively affective and theatrical power to communicate their suffering to others, which she presents as linked to their rhetorical and political astuteness. Iphigenia's glory leads onlookers in Lumley's play to feel more admiration than pity towards her: witnessing her heroic resolve and eloquence, they are "wonderfullye astonied at the stoutenes of her minde" (932).[66] In embracing her sacrificial status, Iphigenia complicates her play's genre, turning it towards tragicomic hybridity as she becomes triumphant agent rather than victim. Some feminist scholars have criticized Lumley's depiction of Iphigenia's willingness to die in the place of men: Purkiss describes Lumley as "more misogynistic than Euripides," and Demers suggests that "an ambivalence about the value or disposability of a woman's life is at the heart of this tragedy."[67] Yet Lumley insists on Iphigenia's intelligence and courage, and, most importantly, on the fact that her sacrifice and resulting glory are her own, rather than her father's. When Iphigenia reminds her mother that she is actively volunteering for sacrifice, she tells her mother, "I shall get you moche honor by my deathe," and Lumley presents Clytemnestra—usurping a line that Euripides had given to the chorus—as similarly observing, "In dede by this meanes you shall get your selfe a perpetuall renowne for euer" (1312–13).[68]

As Hodgson-Wright points out, by claiming "sole responsibility for the ensuing victory," Iphigenia asserts her primacy: her "decision to die is expressed in terms which effectively erase Agamemnon from the scenario."[69] "What the play dramatizes," she suggests, "is not whether this sacrifice is right or wrong, but who has the right to demand it of whom," and it demonstrates that this right—along with the credit for it—is Iphigenia's alone.[70] Similarly, Uman argues that "Iphigenia's belief that she will be made glorious not just by her action but by her decision to go willingly suggests that she is concerned with her own reputation, and not just that of her father or of the Greek men."[71] The play insists not only on women's capacity for moral and rhetorical greatness, but also on their right to claim the glory that this capacity can confer.

Lumley's translation emphasizes Iphigenia's genre-crossing glory and its roots in her mother's boldness, and she finds support for both in Euripides. Discussing the play, Purkiss argues that classical tragic traditions offered English writers "a noble, heroic role for the female protagonist of tragedy, one both firmly gendered and equal to the significantly masculine roles of the heroes of chronicle plays and other political tragedies."[72] Although Iphigenia's closing courage might seem to contrast with the final scenes of a weeping bereaved Clytemnestra, the juxtaposition of the two figures shows Iphigenia steeling herself to this courage precisely through her experience of loss and grief. In response to Clytemnestra's last words to her—"I pray you daughter tarie, and do not forsake me nowe"—Iphigenia replies, "Suerlye I will goo hence Mother, for if I did tarie, I shulde moue you to more lamentation" (1293–7). Although her death defies her mother's wishes, she models her decision on the authority of her mother's political counsel. The play implicitly criticizes Agamemnon's warning to Iphigenia—"Leaue to enquier of suche thinges, for it is not lawfull that women shulde knowe them" (636–9)—by demonstrating the value of female counsel and capacity for heroic action, and attributing them to an authority acquired through women's affective experience.

ENGLAND'S GREEK AFTER MID-CENTURY

Lumley's *Iphigeneia* testifies both to an emerging identification of Greek drama with powerful mother–daughter dyads, and to England's Greek achievements by the middle of the sixteenth century. Most scholarly accounts have held that Greek scholarship in England declined sharply after this moment, suffering from hostility to Greek during Mary's reign, when many Protestant Greek scholars left England for the continent after threats and/or imprisonment.[73] In 1894, Ingram Bywater, the Regius Professor of Greek at Oxford, claimed, "The Elizabethan age is almost a blank in the history of Greek learning in England," and scholars since then have largely concurred.[74] As Micha Lazarus has recently demonstrated, however, the widely shared belief in the decline of England's Greek studies is wrong: in fact, Greek study actually escalated after this point.[75] This misinterpretation stems largely from the absence in later decades of the avidly documented early discussions among evangelizing pioneers such as Erasmus, More, and their circle: as Greek study in schools and universities became increasingly commonplace, it received less attention.[76]

The curricular principles designed by these and other early scholars bore fruit slowly. Inspired by Erasmus's *De Ratione Studii* (1511), early humanist writings on education, such as Thomas Elyot's *The Book of the Governour* (1531) and Juan Luis Vives' *De Tradendis Disciplinis* (1531), had recommended studying Greek and Latin concurrently. Over the course of the sixteenth century their recommendations gradually came to reshape school curricula, echoed by later texts such as Richard Mulcaster's *Positions* (1581), influenced by the author's Cambridge training with Cheke.[77] Required daily Greek lectures that stood out as noteworthy in 1517 attracted less attention in college statutes from the 1550s, 1560s, 1570s, and 1580s, although Greek requirements steadily increased during these decades.[78] By the 1570s, St. John's College, Cambridge, offered three levels of Greek classes, and 1576 Oxford statutes decreed that each university bachelor, "if he heare not everye Day the Greeke Reader, shall forfaite for everye fault iiijd"; records of book ownership and students' notes similarly document increasingly widespread Greek teaching during these decades, demonstrating that not only did Greek show no signs of decline during the second half of the sixteenth century, but in fact it sharply escalated.[79] As Lazarus has shown, critiques of England's Greek have looked for scholarly and philological contributions, rather than evidence of the teaching and reading of Greek, but England's Erasmian approach focused on the acquisition of Greek as a necessity for reading Greek texts, especially Scriptures; the language was increasingly a means to an end, especially medical and religious study, rather than as a scholarly end in itself.[80] "The history of Greek *literacy* in England," Lazarus observes,

> in short, overlaps but is not the same as the history of Greek *scholarship*, and while we require the former meaningfully to estimate access to classical texts

among English readers, only the latter is provided by the standard historical accounts on which literary scholarship predominantly draws.[81]

We have not recognized the level of Greek knowledge in England, then, because we have not actually been looking for it.

Assessing the state of Greek literacy requires attending not only to the steadily increasing opportunities and requirements for learning Greek at the universities, but especially to the rising standard of Greek study in the grammar schools, which were far more widely attended. The new humanism was most forcefully enacted in St. Paul's School, refounded by Colet in conversation with Erasmus from 1508–10. Its statutes, which were copied by Merchant Taylors' School in 1561, required that the master be "lernyd in the good and clene laten litterature and also in greke yf suyche may be gotten," and its first headmaster, William Lily (who taught from 1510–22), like Colet, was part of the small circle of early Greek scholars counted as Erasmus's dearest friends.[82] Even earlier, William Horman had taught Greek first as headmaster at Eton (1485–94) and then Winchester (1494–1502); his 1519 grammar, *Vulgaria*, contained samples from Greek plays.[83] Westminster School also strongly emphasized Greek, which Alexander Nowell (who later became Dean at St. Paul's) began teaching upon becoming master in 1543; later headmaster Edward Grant wrote a Greek–Latin grammar (*Graecae Linguae Spicilegium*, 1575), as did later headmaster William Camden (*Institutio Graecae Grammatices Compendaria*, 1597).[84] Merchant Taylors' School was modeled after St. Paul's, and was run for a time by the Cambridge-educated Mulcaster.[85] Greek was ordained in the statutes of Bury St. Edmund's (1550), and with reference to specific Greek authors at East Retford (1552).[86] After the 1550s, grammar schools rapidly began requiring regular Greek teaching: Eton and Westminster established Greek classes in 1560, followed by Merchant Taylors' School (1561), Shrewsbury (1561–2), St. Saviour's (1562), Norwich (1566), Bangor (1569), Rivington (c.1570), Thame (1574), Ruthin (1574), Sandwich (1580), St. Bees, Cumberland (1583), Hawkshead school, Lancashire (1588), Harrow (1591), and more. Grammar school achievement in Greek became increasingly important for university study; in 1570 Pembroke College, Cambridge, established seven Greek scholarships, for which Merchant Taylors' boys competed, and Mulcaster's boys at St. Paul's were examined in Greek for entry to St. John's College, Oxford.[87] Bolgar calculates that students at strong grammar schools in the 1570s would have read between 135 and 165 pages of Greek, at 25 lines/page—more than most undergraduate students of classics today.[88] The ability to read Greek plays, then, would certainly not have been limited to those with university education, nor to a small handful of elite schools.

Knowledge of Greek did not necessarily mean knowledge of Greek plays, but, as noted earlier, they were among the texts advocated by Erasmus and emerging humanist theories of education.[89] Because of Greek's prominent theological and political implications, the most commonly recommended texts for Greek study in England were the New Testament and orators such as Isocrates and Demosthenes, but Greek poets and playwrights also entered curricula.[90] Erasmus particularly recommended Euripides and Aristophanes, and his advocacy introduced Greek plays into curricula at Oxford, Cambridge, and many grammar schools.[91] Cambridge's 1549 statutes, written by Cheke for both universities, specify that the "professor of the Greek language shall lecture in Homer, Demosthenes, Isocrates, Euripides, or some other of the more ancient authors, and at the same time shall teach the art, together with the properties of the tongue."[92] Beyond curricular references to Greek authors, inventories point to specific texts; records of books bought for St. Paul's School in 1582–3 cite "Euripides graeco-latin. Cum annotate. Stiblini et Brodaei," indicating Oporinus's 1562 edition of Euripides with commentaries by Gasparus Stiblinus.[93]

Schools and universities introduced Greek not only in curricula, but also in performances.[94] Although continental European productions of Greek plays appeared in a range of venues, English performances of Greek plays seem to have taken place almost exclusively in academic settings.[95] School performances were not limited to full productions of plays: prevailing practices of memorizing and reciting texts ensured a central place for oral performances.[96] But official productions became pervasive, and even mandatory. The 1545 statutes of St. John's College, Cambridge (as noted, Erasmus's primary English legacy) required annual performances of comedies and tragedies, and other colleges, as well as grammar schools, soon followed suit.[97] Although records show more performances of Latin plays than Greek, statutes typically required both: in 1554 Christ Church College, Oxford, required four annual plays, "of the which fower playes there shall be a Comedy in Lattin & a Comedy in Greek and a Tragedie in Lattin and a Tragedy in Greek."[98] In the arena of print, England's engagement with Greek drama lags behind that of the continent, but England's recorded performances of Greek or Greek-inspired plays during the sixteenth century outpace those of any other European country, suggesting both that performance was an important medium for English encounters with Greek plays, and that the educational institutions that typically produced them had an especially important shaping role.[99] Because these performances were open to the public as well as members of schools and university communities, and some were staged in Latin or English translation, they could also reach wider audiences than printed editions.

The earliest documented English performances of Greek plays were comedies by Aristophanes, performed at Cambridge: *Plutus* (St. John's College, 1536), *Peace* (Trinity College, 1546, produced by John Dee), and later *Plutus* (college unknown, 1588), and an adaptation, *Plutophthalmia* (Trinity College, 1616; adapted by Thomas Randolph, who became a commercial playwright and later turned the play into a city comedy called called *Hey for Honesty!*).[100] Boas has attributed comedy's prominence to lower staging costs; it may also reflect Erasmus's particular interest in Aristophanes, which continued to bear fruit in Cambridge's later development of vernacular comedies "akin in spirit and method to the Old Comedy of Aristophanes."[101] Although university and school statutes typically required performances of both genres, records show nearly twice as many comedies as tragedies in academic settings in sixteenth-century England, and, among classical plays, nearly three times more performances of comedies than tragedies.[102] Yet as with printed editions and European performances, classical comedy seems to have been primarily identified with Rome: among recorded English sixteenth-century performances, Latin comedies outweighed Aristophanes by forty-two to three, and the Aristophanes play most frequently performed (*Plutus*) was a late play close in spirit to New Comedy.[103]

The same was not true of tragedy. Across Europe (England and the continent), the forty-three documented performances of tragedies identified with Euripides, Sophocles, and/or Aeschylus before 1600 outnumber the twenty-six identified with Seneca.[104] These figures are tenuous, given how little information we have about the productions: many are adaptations with uncertain relationships to their sources, and some titles (*Medea, Hippolytus, Oedipus, Agamemnon*) could refer to either Greek or Roman tragedies. Yet more of these plays could only be Greek (*Philoctetes, Antigone, Electra, Ajax, Iphigenia, Alcestis, Jocasta, Persians*) than could only be Senecan (*Thyestes*). Whatever the precise numbers, scholars took pride in their Greek theatricals. In 1575, William Soone wrote from Cambridge,

> In the months of January, February and March, to beguile the long evenings, they amuse themselves with exhibiting public plays, which they perform with so much elegance . . . that if Plautus, Terence, or Seneca were to come to life again, they would admire their own pieces . . . and Euripides, Sophocles, and Aristophanes would be disgusted at the performances of their own citizens.[105]

Soone specifies that while Roman playwrights would be simply pleased by the plays, Greek authors would be taken aback by English superiority to their own theaters, suggesting a particularly pointed theatrical competition: onstage, the Greeks were the ones to beat.

FROM MARGINS TO CENTER: GASCOIGNE
AND KINWELMERSH'S *JOCASTA*

The rising Greek tide of the century's middle decades offers an important context for the second English translation of a Greek play, which echoes' *Iphigenia*'s juxtaposition of a bereaved mother and a heroic virgin daughter. Unlike Lumley, a privately taught aristocrat whose translation seems to have been intended for an intimate household audience, George Gascoigne and Francis Kinwelmersh were established poets and members of the Inns of Court, an institution spanning private and public realms.[106] Their *Jocasta*, a translation of Euripides' *Phoenician Women*, was performed in 1566 at Gray's Inn, becoming the first English translation of a Greek play with a documented public performance.[107] *The Phoenician Women* depicts Thebes' bloody civil war after Jocasta's failed attempt to reconcile her warring sons Polyneices and Eteocles, culminating with their killing each other in battle, and Jocasta's suicide. Critics have traditionally distanced *Jocasta* from Euripides, presenting it as a translation only of Lodovico Dolce's 1549 *Giocasta*, and an unrecognizably Christian, moralizing echo of Euripides' fiercer tragic vision.[108] Recent scholarship, however, has complicated these assumptions. Howard B. Norland has demonstrated that the play expands its female roles even beyond Dolce's own expansions, and Sarah Dewar-Watson has pointed out the translators' use of Rudolphus Collinus' 1541 Latin translation of Euripides' play, based on details that do not appear in Dolce.[109] Although their sources were eclectic, its translators clearly understood the play to be, as they titled it, *A Tragedie Written in Greke by Euripides*.[110]

   Situating the play in the context of other early modern representations of Euripides, I suggest that Gascoigne and Kinwelmersh follow Lumley in presenting a distinctively Greek model of tragedy rooted in a mother–daughter dyad. In their version of Thebes' siege, Gascoigne and Kinwelmersh pair the demise of a politically engaged female monarch with the coming-of-age story of a bold youthful virgin. Mirroring criticism of Lumley's *Iphigeneia*, attention to the title character has often obscured the play's presentation of Jocasta's daughter Antigone, whose role intersects crucially both with her mother's and with her own very different persona in Sophocles' *Antigone*, which Thomas Watson went on to translate into Latin in 1581. Arlene W. Saxonhouse has shown that *The Phoenician Women*, the later play, self-consciously dramatizes a prehistory of Sophocles' famously defiant Antigone: "Whereas Sophocles' Antigone appears on stage ready to confront Creon with her appeal to the universal unwritten laws of the gods and later dissolves into the female lamenting a lost womanhood, Euripides' Antigone experiences almost the opposite journey."[111] The pairing of Jocasta and Antigone explicitly explores the nature of succession, linking *Jocasta* with *Gorboduc* (1561), another Inns of Court neoclassical tragedy exploring succession anxieties provoked by Elizabeth I's virginity, but *Jocasta* diverges from the earlier play in dramatizing affective and political power passed down specifically from mother to daughter.[112]

The Phoenician Women might seem a curious choice for the second Greek tragedy to be translated into English. Unlike *Hecuba* and *Iphigenia*, the play was not one of the earliest to be translated into Latin; it similarly lacked the authority of Erasmus's imprimatur, or the Trojan saga widely linked to Britain's own history. Yet with twelve individual or partial editions before 1600, five of which were vernacular translations, it was among the period's most prominent Greek tragedies.[113] The play's visibility had roots in its earlier popularity; with *Hecuba* and *Orestes*, it formed part of Euripides' Byzantine triad, featured prominently in classical educational curricula, and was imitated in texts by Plutarch, Seneca, and Statius that circulated in the early modern period.[114] One of Euripides' later plays, from between 411–409 BCE, it draws self-consciously on an intertextual web of previous plays and poems about Thebes' tragic past, including Aeschylus' *Seven Against Thebes* (467), Sophocles' *Antigone* (*c.*441) and *Oedipus the King* (*c.*427), and Euripides' *Suppliant Women* (423).[115] The play also draws implicitly on Trojan prestige by alluding to the other exceptionally popular classical story of a city's tragic siege; Antigone's viewing of soldiers from the Theban walls self-consciously echoes Helen's viewing of soldiers from Troy's walls in *The Iliad*.[116] Yet beyond the fascination of these familiar stories of riven cities, early modern responses suggest that the play's attraction lay especially in its affective intensity; Gasparus Stiblinus remarked, "The play is exceedingly tragic and full of vehement emotions."[117] And as we have seen elsewhere, these vehement emotions are identified especially with the play's grieving but proactive mother and daughter.

Gascoigne and Kinwelmersh follow Dolce in expanding the role of the play's suffering mother. Replacing the original title's emphasis on its chorus of Phoenician women, they describe the play as "the wofull tragedie of Iocasta" (Aiv). The play opens with Jocasta, and lengthens her laments even beyond Dolce's already considerable expansion of them. Following Dolce's *Giocasta*, Kinwelmersh changed the queen's opening soliloquy into a conversation with a servant, emphasizing the queen's intrinsically dialogic approach to setting the scene.[118] "O Faithfull seruaunt of mine auncient sire," she opens the play,

Though vnto thée, sufficiently be knowen
The whole discourse of my recurelesse griefe
By seing me from Princes royall state
Thus basely brought into so great contempt,
As mine owne sonnes repine to heare my plaint,
Now of a Quéene but barely bearing name,
Seyng this towne, seyng my fleshe and bloude,
Against it selfe to leuie threatning armes,
(Wherof to talke my heart it rendes in twaine)
Yet once againe, I must to thée recompte
The wailefull thing that is alredy spred,
Bycause I know, that pitie will compell
Thy tender hart, more than my naturall childe,
With ruthfull teares to mone my mourning case. (75)

Jocasta implicitly compares her servant, to whom she must "recompte/ The wailefull thing that is already spred," favorably to her "owne sonnes," who "repine to heare my plaint." While her sons will neither listen nor respond, her servant will both hear and empathize; "pitie will compel/ [His] tender hart. . . / With ruthful teares to mone." This interpolated sympathetic auditor, an invented addition to Euripides' text, comes to stand in for the play's audience, who are similarly enjoined to listen and feel for Jocasta as she details the play's terrible backstory: how she married Laius, bore Oedipus, and unwittingly entered an incestuous union that produced four children, and how Oedipus' curse on Polyneices and Eteocles has brought Thebes to civil war. Her children are destroying the city, each other, and Jocasta herself: "this towne" is her "fleshe and bloude," now fragmented and fighting against itself. Felicity Dunworth writes of this passage that the translators shift "from a focus upon the mother as an emblem of the state towards a reading of the mother as a material embodiment of the nation, her physical person a microcosmic version of the nation that is threatened."[119] Describing her heart as broken in two, Jocasta gives bodily form to her splintered emotions, city, and family. She is the heart of Thebes, as well as the heart of the tragedy.

Gascoigne and Kinwelmersh follow Euripides, as well as Dolce, in attributing the intensity of Jocasta's suffering to her motherhood. "There is no love," their Chorus insists, "may be comparde to that,/ The tender mother beares unto hir chyld:/ For even so muche the more it doth encrease,/ As their griefe growes, or contentations cease" (94). Euripides' text reads "The children of their labor pangs are wondrous and terrible [*deinon*] to women, and the whole female race is somehow attached to their children [*philoteknon*]."[120] These lines recall the similar passage in *Iphigenia* discussed earlier, in which Euripides' chorus holds, "Giving birth carries a strange and terrible [*deinon*] spell, and suffering [*hyperkamnein*] for their children is shared by all women."[121] As in that couplet, Jocasta's chorus uses the Greek word *deinon*—strange, terrible, marvelous, dangerous—to frame the emotional impact of maternity as ambivalent, carrying the same generically hybrid mixed emotions as these tragic plays themselves. Also like the lines in *Iphigenia*, printed commonplace marks suggest that these were singled out as a *sententia* in Gascoigne and Kinwelmersh's text, which echoes Dolce's translation closely in expanding the two lines of Euripides that it recreates.[122] The translators' Latin edition rendered these lines (also in printed commonplace marks) as "Preciosa res mulieribus per dolores fiunt geni/ Et amans liberorum est quodammodo muliebre genus" (To give birth through pains is a precious thing to women, and the female race is somehow affectionate to their children).[123] Intriguingly, and contrary to typical claims, both the English and Italian vernacular versions are, as in Lumley's *Iphigeneia*, closer here to the emotional spirit of the Greek original than is the more academic, and technically correct, Latin. Their suggestion that grief is inherent in maternity acknowledges the ambivalent overtones of the Greek *deinon*—terrible, dangerous, marvelous—in stark contrast to the straightforwardly positive *preciosa* as a modifier for the effects of giving birth. The expansion of these and other lines on motherhood suggests that to these translators, maternal suffering was central to the tragedy's power.

Although Jocasta opens the play, and occupies its affective center, she does not survive to encompass it fully. In the play's last act a messenger reports that the queen, overcome by the horror of her sons' mutual slaughter, has thrust Polyneices' dagger in her own throat.[124] Before surrendering to death, however, she summons forth Antigone—in the one scene that the two characters share onstage—to join her efforts at diplomatic mediation:

> *Antigone* my swete daughter, come forth
> Out of this house, that nought but woe retaines,
> Come forth I say, not for to sing or daunce,
> But to preuent (if in our powers it lie)
> That thy malicious brethren (swolne with ire)
> And I alas, their miserable mother,
> Be not destroide by stroke of dreadfull death.   (135)

Inviting Antigone out of the house, Jocasta summons her from her private offstage chambers into the public space of Thebes and battle. It might appear that Jocasta fails in her hope that Antigone will "prevent" her brothers' malice and her mother's death: each of these terrible events goes on to take place shortly after her speech. Yet the primary early modern sense of "prevent" drew on the word's Latin roots, meaning to come before, rather than to stop.[125] In this sense, Antigone succeeds at preventing all of these events: she arrives onstage and in public before they take place, managing both to serve as witness and to take over her mother's role as the play's central authority.

Jocasta's words of counsel may not achieve all of their desired effects, but she succeeds in passing on her sovereignty, as well as her affective power, to her female heir before dying. Thalia Papadopoulou has observed of the ending of Euripides' play that "Antigone resembles her mother, in a way which suggests that after her mother's death the burdens of the family are to be carried by her."[126] Ancient scholiasts claimed that the same actor who played Jocasta—technically the protagonist, or first actor—would have played Antigone as well, with another masked actor stepping in as Antigone for their one brief shared scene.[127] This literal overlap in their staged identities resonates both with the play's depiction of a daughter's development into her mother's role, and with its insistent reminders of Antigone's muddled generational status. "O Gentle daughter of King *Oedipus*," Bailo greets her first entrance, "O sister deare to that vnhappie wight" (82). As the product of an incestuous union, and the sister of her own father, Antigone is Jocasta's sister-in-law as well as her daughter, merging the hierarchy of their positions and further intertwining their identities.

Just as Iphigenia absorbs both Clytemnestra's grief and her capacity for political counsel, Antigone echoes Jocasta's voice on both familial and civic matters. After Jocasta's lengthy opening discussion of her family's travails, Antigone's first words emphasize fraternal concern: in reply to Bailo's question of why she has left her maiden chambers, she tells him, "The loue I beare to my swéete *Polynice*,/ My deare brother, is onely cause hereof" (82). Also like Iphigenia, she imagines resolving the crisis through heroic self-sacrifice. When Bailo asks, "Why daughter, knowst thou any remedie/ How to defend thy fathers citie here/ From that outrage and fierce repyning wrathe,/ Which he against it, iustly hath conceiued?," she answers, "might this my faultlesse bloude/ Suffise to stay my brethrens dyre debate,/ With glad consent I coulde afford my life/ Betwixt them both to plant a perfect peace" (82). And as with Iphigenia's similar vision, this idea seems to have been of particular interest to the play's English translators. Norland has observed that Antigone's discussion with Bailo, along with Jocasta's laments, contains Gascoigne and Kinwelmersh's most substantial expansions of Dolce's play, which had already expanded these sections considerably from Euripides.[128]

As witness to the terrible death of her mother and brothers, Antigone absorbs the grief and self-sacrifice earlier embodied by Jocasta. "[W]hat could be more miserable," Stiblinus asked rhetorically of the play, "than the fact that Antigone beholds her twin brothers with their mother lying in their mingled blood and struggling with death?"[129] Like the family's merging and conflating of generations, this literal mingling of blood suggests a fusion of identities, which crucially enables Antigone's succession to her mother's status as regal bearer of family memory and grief. Yet rather than incapacitating her, as it ultimately does her mother, this grief mobilizes a new boldness in Antigone. As she assumes her mother's role, Antigone transforms from the tentative onlooker of the play's start to the defiant figure depicted by Sophocles. She opposes Creon in her insistence on looking after her father and burying her brother, showing a filial and sisterly devotion that won praise from early modern commentators: Stiblinus approved of the play's "outstanding example of piety in Antigone, who cared less for a royal marriage, wealth, power, and showy honors than for her despised and needy father."[130] Similarly, in 1599 Anthony Gibson wrote,

> The constancy of Antigone, described by Antimachus and Euripides, is of such merite, as all men together cannot boast of any thing to come neere it: her piety is of such commendation, as the most religious of our Atheistical age haue iust cause to complaine, that Christianity as yet neuer conceiued the like.[131]

These accolades to her feminine piety either overlook or justify her closing ferocity. When she refuses to marry Creon's son, Haemon, Creon insists—"Against thy will then must I thée constraine"—to which Antigone responds with an even more defiant threat: "If thou me force, I sweare thou shalt repent." When pressed for details, she claims she will murder Haemon: "This hardie hand shall soone dispatche his life." Creon's astonishment— "O simple foole, and darst thou be so bolde?"—meets with firmness: "Why should I dread to doe so doughtie deed?" (158–9). Like Clytemnestra, who warns Agamemnon of dark consequences if he sacrifices Iphigenia, and like Hecuba and Medea, who boast of triumph after bringing about the punishment they understand as justice, Antigone understands violence as a necessary and even heroic means of carrying out her moral duty.[132]

Although Euripides' Antigone seems to have been slightly more visible than that of Sophocles, both plays were popular in the period, and Gascoigne and Kinwelmersh's Antigone was followed fifteen years later by Thomas Watson's 1581 Latin translation of Sophocles' *Antigone*. In Sophocles' version, Jocasta is dead before the play begins, and Antigone is forceful and defiant from the start.[133] Watson's *Antigone* lacks the explicit focus on maternal affect of Lumley's, Gascoigne's, and Kinwelmersh's plays, but its emphasis on the heroism of a sacrificial daughter resonates with these earlier plays. Although Sophocles' play was written first, Euripides positions his story as a prequel, so Watson's translation accordingly offers a kind of sequel to *Jocasta*. Having already seen the development of Antigone's boldness in the wake of her mother's and brothers' deaths, and her mother's proactive role in attempting to intervene in Theban policy, readers and audiences of Watson's play would encounter the next phase of this feud, in which Antigone's defiance leads to her burial of her brother, and ultimately to her own death.

Robert Miola has argued that Antigone was received in this period with ambivalence at best: "Most early modern commentators and translators betray a deep unease with Sophocles' female hero: some accord Antigone faint and qualified praise; some overlook or ignore her entirely; some domesticate her into a pious family supporter or a doomed romantic; and, finally, some simply dismiss her as a vicious sinner."[134] Yet Gascoigne and Kinwelmersh present Antigone as mobilized by grief and her mother's influence into a righteously bold political actor, and this figure earned praise. Watson, whom Miola reads as critical of Sophocles' Antigone, also presents her with considerable complexity. "[M]y Antigone craves to become dearer to you," he writes in a prefatory letter to his translation:

> she craves to become dearer than she was to Creon, more beloved than she was to her native soil. Now, coming back to life and escorted by Latin Muses, she approaches, fearing to tarry at Thebes. She will bear you wondrous things, if you wish to learn wonderments; she would make you pious, were you not such beforehand ... These things and more Antigone will set before your eyes, taught to teach by my effort.[135]

Watson imagines translating Greek as an encounter with a heroic virgin, who becomes a figurative participant in the joint literary production of wonder and piety. Unmoored from her perishable mother, she develops even greater strength over time, continuing a process of transmission in which she plays an integral part. Given a mandate by her mother to fulfill her role as representative of Thebes' painful memories, she survives in the realm of theater to enact her story again for sixteenth-century English readers and audiences.

ENGLAND'S GREEK DRAMATIC TRADITION

Watson's *Antigone*, Gascoigne and Kinwelmersh's *Jocasta*, and Lumley's *Iphigenia* draw on England's new traditions of Greek study to enter into a trans-European conversation about the theatrical and affective possibilities of Greek female tragic protagonists. As we have seen, their plays focus especially on the transmission of power between generations, with an emphasis on the future represented by idealistic virgins, who inherit their mothers' boldness and deploy it towards triumphant and socially lauded ends. Lumley, Gascoigne, Kinwelmersh, and Watson follow Erasmus's footsteps by highlighting the contributions of grieving mothers to their daughters' achievements, but they focus especially on heroic virgins. Strangely, scholars have not typically included these translators in accounts of the period's engagement with Greek drama. Despite Lumley's interest for feminist scholars, her *Iphigenia* has been widely ignored by histories of classical reception, partly because it circulated in manuscript rather than print, and partly because many have assumed that she relied on Erasmus, therefore offering only a mediated approach to the Greek text rather than a direct translation.[136] Gascoigne and Kinwelmersh are similarly often dismissed as having translated an indirect adaptation—Dolce's *Giocasta*— rather than grappling directly with Euripides' *Phoenissae*.[137] Watson has been excluded from accounts of English translations on the grounds that he translated into Latin rather than English. Another major British translator, Buchanan, has been taken as an honorary continental humanist: Scottish, living in France, and translating into Latin, he has been even more fully divorced from accounts of England's engagement with Greek, despite his status as an English-speaking humanist scholar who spent time living in London and York.[138] Similarly, Erasmus's Latin translations have not been linked with their English base and patronage.

Despite the substantial and surprisingly cohesive emphasis of this body of plays, then, critics of Greek dramatic reception continue to assert that "no English translations were printed before 1649," ignoring *Jocasta* (or denying it the status of translation), and excluding from relevance Lumley's manuscript (as well as Peele's) and the Latin editions of Watson and Buchanan.[139] Even when acknowledging these translations, more-over, scholars have identified them with a small, educated elite, reinforcing the assumption that English access to Greek was rarefied and restricted. Yet exploring the evidence of Greek study in England shows that readers and audiences had access to Greek plays even beyond these translations and the Latin editions that demonstrably circulated in England. Grammar schools and universities not only taught Greek to increasingly large numbers, but also sponsored performances of Greek plays that were open to the public as well as to students, teachers, and parents.

Because the English commercial theater is widely understood as a popular and hence anti-intellectual realm, scholars have typically positioned it as sharply removed from these academic worlds, but recent studies of academic drama have emphasized its considerable traffic with the commercial stage.[140] Just as authors including George Peele and Thomas Randolph both translated Greek plays and wrote commercial plays, some university plays appeared in commercial playing spaces and companies. The Inns of Court, commonly known as England's third university, staged *Jocasta* as well as commercial plays including Shakespeare's *Comedy of Errors* (Gray's Inn, 1594) and *Twelfth Night* (Middle Temple, 1602), and offered literary beginnings to commercial playwrights such as John Marston, Francis Beaumont, and Edward Sharpham.[141] Grammar schools not only shaped the rhetorical training of early modern playwrights, but also developed their own robust dramatic traditions, as did children's playing companies; in the later decades of the century they frequently performed for Queen Elizabeth and other notables, as well as local populations.[142] Given steadily rising levels of Greek knowledge; the plays' visibility in textual circulation, curricula, and public performances; and traffic between the academic and the commercial realms of performance; access to Greek and Greek-influenced plays was hardly a rarefied phenomenon. For the grammar school-trained boys who went on to write for the commercial theater, in fact, they would have been hard to miss.

Attending to specific sites of Greek study allows us to identify the Greek literacy of English commercial playwrights. The early Elizabethan playwrights known as the University Wits had extensive Greek training. John Lyly (1554–1606), grandson of Greek scholar William Lily, studied in the 1570s both at Magdalen College, Oxford, and at Cambridge, where Greek was required; William Ringler has identified Lyly's Euphuistic style with the influence of John Rainolds, Greek Reader at Corpus Christi College, Oxford, in the 1570s.[143] George Peele also studied at Oxford in the 1570s, and, as noted earlier, earned praise for his translation of Euripides' *Iphigenia*. Christopher Marlowe attended the academically rigorous King's School, Canterbury, in the 1570s under headmaster John Gresshop—who had studied at Oxford and owned an impressive collection of Greek books—and subsequently King's College, Cambridge, in the 1580s, where his Greek skill led him to intimate knowledge of texts by Lucan, Lucian, Musaeus, and Xenophon.[144] Robert Greene studied at St. John's, Cambridge—long England's most formidable center for Greek scholarship—in the late 1570s and early 1580s. Thomas Lodge, Thomas Kyd, and Lancelot Andrews studied at Merchant Taylors' under Cheke's student Mulcaster in the 1570s, when the school required intensive Greek; James Whitelocke, who studied there from the mid-1570s until 1588, recounted being "well instructed in the Hebrew, Greek, and Latin tongs."[145] Lodge also studied at Trinity College, Oxford, in the late 1570s, when Rainolds was presenting his Greek lectures. Thomas Watson, identified by Francis Meres in 1598 as among "our best for Tragedie," studied at Winchester College and Oxford, and translated Sophocles.[146] Among these early and widely imitated contributors to the commercial stage, then, we can reliably identify a high standard of Greek literacy, and in several cases (Peele, Marlowe, and Watson) direct experience of Greek literary translation.

Although the so-called University Wits might seem anomalous because of their extensive educations, later commercial playwrights show similar levels of Greek exposure and knowledge. Thomas Nashe studied at Cambridge with Cheke, whom he described as "the Exchequer of eloquence...supernaturally traded in all tongs."[147] Ben Jonson, who cited Greek plays in the original language in his writings, studied Greek at Westminster with William Camden, as did Thomas Randolph and Abraham Cowley.[148] We know little of George Chapman's education, but he learned enough Greek to translate Homer, and Greek literary references appear throughout his plays. We know similarly little of Thomas Heywood's education, but he quoted Greek in his 1616 *Apology for Actors*, and dramatized Greek epic and mythic material in his *Ages* plays, at one point bringing Homer himself onstage as a character.[149] John Webster studied at Merchant Taylors', and defended his pace of writing, in his preface to *The White Devil*, by comparing himself to Euripides.[150] John Marston studied at Brasenose College, Oxford, in the early 1590s, and Thomas Middleton studied at Queens College, Oxford, in the mid-1590s. John Fletcher attended the Cathedral School in Peterborough, and studied at Queens' College, Cambridge, in the 1600s.[151] Nathan Field studied at St. Paul's, the most Greek-centered of the period's grammar schools, where the close relationship between the school and the children's acting company formed of its choristers (who performed both *Iphigenia* and *Orestes* in the 1570s) gave its students an especially intimate relationship with London's emerging theater world.[152]

We know, then, that commercial playwrights including Lyly, Peele, Greene, Marlowe, Kyd, Nashe, Lodge, Watson, Jonson, Chapman, Field, Heywood, and Webster read Greek, and that Peele, Marlowe, Watson, and Chapman translated Greek literature. Influential nondramatic writers of the time, such as Philip Sidney, Fulke Greville, and Edmund Spenser, also demonstrably knew and used Greek.[153] Although it is difficult to trace details of Shakespeare's education with precision, his Stratford grammar school would almost certainly have taught some Greek: T. W. Baldwin has observed that "by Shakspere's day practically all grammar schools on regular foundations, as was that at Stratford, would at least hope to teach some Greek," and has identified Shakespeare's primary grammar school teacher as Thomas Jenkins, who studied both Greek and Latin at St. John's College, Oxford, in the late 1560s.[154] The collective and collaborative nature of the commercial theaters, moreover, meant that even without a documented Greek education, he, like other playwrights, would inevitably have absorbed the effects of Greek dramatic influence through contemporary friends, rivals, and colleagues including Marlowe, Peele, Jonson, and Chapman.

Tracing England's Greek suggests that early modern playwrights had many opportunities to read, watch, discuss, translate, and adapt the Greek plays that represented the theater's origins. It also suggests that the plays that most conspicuously represented this tradition shared a surprisingly consistent interest in the heroic powers of eloquent sacrificial virgins, mobilized by the affective intensity of their grieving mothers. This English canon of Greek plays overlaps significantly with a broader sixteenth-century European canon, yet England's apparent preference for bold sacrificial virgins such as Iphigenia and Antigone over raging mothers such as Hecuba suggests an important distinction. Recognizing these patterns suggests larger significance to allusions that might otherwise go unnoted or unexplored. When Marlowe's Barabas wryly notes, "I have no charge, nor many children,/ But one sole Daughter, whom I hold as deare/ As *Agamemnon* did his *Iphigen*," the specter of Euripidean sacrifice haunts *The Jew of Malta*'s black comedy.[155] When Chapman's Baligny refers to "the Princesse (sweet Antigone)/ In the graue Greeke Tragedian," a defiant virgin shadows the violent developments of *The Revenge of Bussy D'Ambois*.[156] Similarly, when Peele, writing collaboratively with Shakespeare, alludes twice to Hecuba in *Titus Andronicus*, Euripides' ghost hovers behind the invocations.[157] In the chapters that follow, I examine the shadows cast by these and other Greek tragic women on the period's commercial plays, and suggest that their ghosts exert unexpectedly potent effects across dramatic genres.

NOTES

1. See especially Tania Demetriou and Tanya Pollard, "Homer and Greek Tragedy in Early Modern English Theatres: An Introduction," in *Homer and Greek Tragedy in Early Modern English Theatres*, ed. Demetriou and Pollard, special issue of *Classical Receptions Journal* 9:1 (2017), 1–35; also, Kirsty Milne, "The Forgotten Greek Books of Elizabethan England," *Literature Compass* 4:3 (2007), 677–87. On early textual transmission of Greek, see Robert Garland, *Surviving Tragedy* (London: Duckworth, 2004); N. G. Wilson, *From Byzantium to Italy: Greek Studies in the Italian Renaissance* (Baltimore: Johns Hopkins University Press, 1992); L. D. Reynolds and N. G. Wilson, *Scribes and Scholars: A Guide to the Transmission of Greek and Latin Literature* (Oxford: Clarendon Press, 1968, rprt 1991); and Deno John Geanakoplos, *Greek Scholars in Venice* (Cambridge, MA: Harvard University Press, 1962). On printed editions, see especially Rudolf Hirsch, "The Printing Tradition of Aeschylus, Euripides, Sophocles and Aristophanes," *Gutenberg Jahrbuch*, 39 (1964), 138–46; R. R. Bolgar, *The Classical Heritage and its Beneficiaries* (Cambridge: Cambridge University Press, 1954); and Jean Christophe Saladin, "Euripide Luthérien?," in *Mélanges de l'Ecole Française de Rome* 108:1 (1996), 155–70.

2. See Erika Rummel, "Fertile Ground: Erasmus' Travels in England," in *Travel and Translation in the Early Modern Period*, ed. Carmine di Biase (Amsterdam: Rodopi, 2006), 45–52. On patronage as a form of literary agency and production, see Julie Crawford, *Mediatrix: Women, Politics, and Literary Production in Early Modern England* (Oxford: Oxford University Press, 2014).

3. On Erasmus's prominence in promoting Greek, see Erika Rummel, *Erasmus as a Translator of the Classics* (Toronto: University of Toronto Press, 1985), and Simon Goldhill, "Learning Greek is Heresy! Resisting Erasmus," in *Who Needs Greek?: Contests in the Cultural History of Hellenism* (Cambridge: Cambridge University Press, 2002), 14–59.

4. Erasmus awarded "first place to Aristophanes, second to Homer, third to Euripides." Erasmus, *De Ratione Studii* (1521), trans. Brian McGregor, in *Collected Works of Erasmus* (hereafter *CWE*), vol. 24, ed. Craig R. Thompson (Toronto: University of Toronto Press, 1978), 666–91, 669.

5. Greek was taught and studied in England prior to this time, but this moment marks an important turning point in its establishment; see especially Micha Lazarus, "Greek Literacy in Sixteenth Century England," *Renaissance Studies* 20:3 (2015), 433–58; also, Arthur Tilley, "Greek Studies in Early Sixteenth-Century England," *English Historical Review* 53 (1938): 221–39 & 438–56; M. L. Clarke, *Classical Education in Britain* (Cambridge: Cambridge University Press, 1959); Michael Van Cleave Alexander, *The Growth of English Education, 1348–1648: A Social and Cultural History* (University Park: Pennsylvania State University Press, 1990); and Kenneth Charlton, *Education in Renaissance England* (London: Routledge, 1965).

6. Erasmus, Epistle 185, "To Servatius Rogerus," and Epistle 195, "To John Colet," in *CWE*, vol. 2, trans. Roger Aubrey Baskerville Mynors and Douglas Ferguson Scott Thomson (Toronto: University of Toronto Press, 1975), 99 and 119. The men in question are typically assumed to be Linacre, Grocyn, Latimer, More, Lily, and Colet.

7. Erasmus, Ep. 207, "To Aldo Manuzio" (1507), in *CWE*, vol. 2, 131–2.

8. Erasmus, Ep. 188, "To William Warham" (1506), in *CWE*, vol. 2, 107–10, 109.

9. *Iphigenia in Aulis* was written between 408–406 BCE, just before Euripides' death in 406, and was produced posthumously in 405.

10. Erasmus, Ep. 208, "To William Warham" (1507), in *CWE*, vol. 2, 133–5, 133. *Iphigenia* dates from 408–406 BCE, nearly 20 years later than *Hecuba* (424 BCE) and at the end of Euripides' writing career.

11. On Peele's *Iphigenia*, see William Gager, "In Iphigenia[m] Georgij Peeli Anglicanis Versibus Reddita[m]," British Museum MS Add. 22, 583, fols 48–9, printed in *The Life and Works of George Peele*, ed. David H. Horne (New Haven, CT: Yale University Press, 1952), vol 1, 43. Gager does not specify which of Euripides' two Iphigenia plays Peele translated, but the prominence of *Iphigenia in Aulis* in the period, along with the near-invisibility of *Iphigenia in Tauris*, persuasively argues for the former. On the St. Paul's boys production, see the Archive of Performance of Greek

duction/3983, accessed April 22, 2015; also F. P. Wilson, *The English Drama, 1485–1585* (Oxford: Clarendon Press, 1968), 146.

12. See Paul Streufert, "Christopherson at Cambridge: Greco-Catholic Ethics in the Protestant University," in *Early Modern Academic Drama*, ed. Jonathan Walker and Paul Streufert (Burlington, VT: Ashgate, 2008), 45–63; Deborah Shuger, *The Renaissance Bible: Scholarship, Sacrifice, and Subjectivity* (Berkeley: University of California Press, 1998), 136.

13. In 1749 William Rufus Chetwood reported of Sir Robert Naunton (1563–1635), who chronicled Elizabeth's reign, "Sir Robert Naunton and others inform us, that she translated for her own Amusement, one of the Tragedies of *Euripides*"; see Chetwood, *A General History of the Stage: From Its Origin in Greece Down to the Present Time* (London: W. Owen, 1749), 15–16.

14. The fifty-two individual or partial editions of *Hecuba*, the most popular of Greek tragedy's mourning mothers, were all published and/or translated on the European continent; by contrast, England produced at least three versions of *Iphigenia*, and one of *Antigone*. On the resonances between Greek tragedy's mourning mothers and the Virgin Mary, see especially Katharine Goodland, *Female Mourning in Medieval and Renaissance English Drama: From the Raising of Lazarus to King Lear* (Aldershot: Ashgate, 2006).

15. Deborah Shuger has argued suggestively that sixteenth-century poetics and biblical commentaries construct "multiple links between tragedy and sacrifice," linking "patriotic expiation, female blood, and the scapegoat but also the Crucifixion," and highlighting the "beautiful transgressive creature who displaces the Son." See Shuger, *The Renaissance Bible*, 133, 166.

16. On the emergence of Greek, see Paul Botley, *Learning Greek in Western Europe, 1396–1529: Grammars, Lexica, and Classroom Texts* (Philadelphia: American Philosophical Society, 2010); Federica Ciccolella, *Donati Graeci: Learning Greek in the Renaissance* (Leiden: Brill, 2008); Geanakoplos, *Greek Scholars in Venice*; Wilson, *From Byzantium to Italy: Greek Studies in the Italian Renaissance*; and Filippomaria Pontani, "Ancient Greek," in *The Classical Tradition*, ed. Anthony Grafton, Glenn W. Most, and Salvatore Settis (Cambridge, MA: Harvard University Press, 2010), 405–9.

17. Erasmus, Ep. 124, "To Jacob Batt," 1500, in *CWE*, vol 1, trans. R. A. B. Mynors and D. F. S Thomson (Toronto: University of Toronto Press, 1974), 250–3, 252; in 1501, he similarly wrote that he was "spending all my time on studies, especially Greek.... If any new Greek books have come upon the scene, I would rather pawn my coat than fail to obtain them." See Ep. 160, "To Nikolaus Bensrott," 1501, in *CWE*, vol. 2, 46.

18. Epistle 181, "To John Colet," 1504, in *CWE*, vol. 2, 88.

19. Aldus dedicated his *Musarum Panegyris*, which Nicholas Barker has described as "something of a manifesto of Aldus's objectives for himself and for the future of Greek studies," to Caterina Pio of Carpi, the sister of Pico della Mirandola, whose sons Aldus tutored. See Aldus Manutius, "Epistolam ad Catherina Piam," in *Musarum Panegyris* (Venice: Baptista de Tortis,

1487–91), and Nicholas Barker, *Aldus Manutius and the Development of Greek Script Type in the Fifteenth Century* (New York: Fordham University Press, 1992), 44. I am grateful to Bianca Calabresi for calling this dedication to my attention. Matteo Bandello similarly dedicated his Italian translation of Euripides' Hecuba to Marguerite de Navarre; see Bandello, "A La Cristianissima Prencipessa Margarita di Francia, Sorella Unica del Christianissimo Re Francesco Serenissima Reina di Navarra," in *Ecuba: Tragedia di Euripide, Tradotta in Verso Toscano di Matteo Bandello* (1539; published Roma: Nella Stamperia di Romanis, 1813). On Erasmus's views regarding female education, see Erika Rummel, *Erasmus on Women* (Toronto: Toronto University Press, 1996).

20. See Michael K. Jones and Malcolm G. Underwood, *The King's Mother: Lady Margaret Beaufort, Countess of Richmond and Derby* (Cambridge: Cambridge University Press, 1993). On Lady Margaret as translator, see Patricia Demers, "'God may open more than man maye vnderstande': Lady Margaret Beaufort's Translation of the *De Imitatione Christi*," *Renaissance & Reformation/ Renaissance et Réforme* 35:4 (2012), 45–61.

21. Lady Margaret was no longer alive when St. John's College was founded, but she left explicit instructions, as well as funds, for it in her will; see Alexander, *The Growth of English Education, 1348–1648*, 71–9, and Jones and Underwood, *The King's Mother*.

22. See F. Donald Logan, "The Origins of the So-called Regius Professorships: An Aspect of the Renaissance in Oxford and Cambridge," in *Renaissance and Renewal in Christian History*, ed. Derek Baker (Oxford: Oxford University Press, 1977), 271–8, 277.

23. Erasmus's Greek New Testament, *Novum Instrumentum omne*, was printed in Basel by his friend Johann Froben, who also published numerous editions of Greek plays; in 1518 Aldus Manutius published a nearly identical version. On the excitement and scandals associated with Greek, see Pontani, "Ancient Greek," 407–8, and Goldhill, "Learning Greek is Heresy!" Erasmus's New Testament was an important source for Tyndale's English translation of the New Testament (Worms, 1526). On the literary implications of Greek's Protestant associations, see Victor Skretkowicz, *European Erotic Romance: Philhellene Protestantism, Renaissance Translation and English Literary Politics* (Manchester, Manchester University Press, 2010).

24. Sir Thomas More, "To Oxford University," in *Sir Thomas More: Selected Letters*, ed. Elizabeth Frances Rogers (New Haven, CT: Yale University Press, 1961), 94–103, 96.

25. Richard Croke, *Orationes* (Paris: Simon de Colines, 1520), cited in Tilley, "Greek Studies," 233. On the king's intervention on behalf of Greek study, see Erasmus, Ep. 948, "To Petrus Mosellanus," 1519, in *CWE*, vol. 6, 310–18, 316–17; also, Lazarus, "Greek Literacy," 442.

26. At Oxford, this requirement extended to Magdalen, New, Corpus Christi, and All Souls Colleges; at Cambridge, it included fourteen houses. See F. Donald Logan, "The First Royal Visitation of the English Universities,

1535," in *English Historical Review* 106 (1991), 861–88, 873, and Lazarus, "Greek Literacy," 443. On the King Henry VIII Lectures, see Logan, "The Origins of the So-called Regius Professorships," 274.

27. Ascham to Brandesby, in Roger Ascham, *The Whole Works of Roger Ascham*, ed. J. A. Giles, 3 vols, vol. 1 (London: J. R. Smith, 1864), 25–7, 26; English translation in *English Historical Documents, 1458–1558*, ed. C. H. Williams (Oxford: Oxford University Press, 1967), 1070–1.

28. Bolgar identified England's approach to Greek as practical, in contrast to the increasingly philological focus of France; see Bolgar, *The Classical Heritage and its Beneficiaries*, 365.

29. See Jane Stevenson, "Greek Learning and Women," *Encyclopedia of Women in the Renaissance: Italy, France, and England*, ed. Diana Maury Robin, Anne R. Larsen, and Carole Levin (Santa Barbara: ABC-Clio, 2007), 122–4.

30. Harold Child dates the play between 1550–3 ("Introduction," *Iphigenia in Aulis*, vi), as does Patricia Demers ("On First Looking into Lumley's Euripides," *Renaissance and Reformation/Renaissance et Réforme* 23:1 (1999), 25–42, 25–6), but Hodgson-Wright points out that Lumley's father, Arundel, only acquired a Greek–Latin edition of Euripides' *Iphigenia* after the 1553 arrest of Thomas Cranmer turned over Cranmer's library to Arundel; see Stephanie Hodgson-Wright, "Jane Lumley's *Iphigenia at Aulis: Multum in parvo*, or less is more," in *Readings in Renaissance Women's Drama: Criticism, History, and Performance 1594–1998*, ed. by S. P. Cerasano and Marion Wynne-Davies (London and New York: Routledge, 1998), 129–41, 131. I am persuaded by Hodgson-Wright and by Marion Wynne-Davies, who argues based on contextual writings and family events that Lumley made the translation in 1557; see Wynne-Davies, "The Good Lady Lumley's Desire: Iphigeneia and the Nonsuch Banqueting House," *Heroines of the Golden StAge: Women and Drama in Spain and England 1500–1700*, ed. Rina Walthaus and Marguérite Corporaal(Kassel: Reichenberger, 2008), 111–28, 117–21.

31. Depending on which system of numeration one uses, Henry Fitzalan was either the 12th or 19th Earl of Arundel; see *Burke's Peerage, Baronetage & Knightage*, 107th edition, ed. Charles Mosley (Wilmington, Delaware, Genealogical Books Ltd, 2003), 3 vols, 2:2915.

32. Philip Howard became the 13th/20th Earl of Arundel.

33. Diane Purkiss writes, "Women like Lady Lumley, Lady Pembroke and Elizabeth Cary were able to write tragedy because it was always potentially or partially dominated by female images"; Purkiss, "Introduction," *Three Tragedies by Renaissance Women*, ed. Purkiss (London and New York: Penguin, 1998), xxvii. See Ros Ballaster, "The First Female Dramatists," in *Women and Literature in Britain, 1500–1700*, ed. Helen Wilcox (Cambridge: Cambridge University Press, 1996), 267–73; Demers, "On First Looking into Lumley's Euripides"; Marta Straznicky, *Privacy, Playreading, and Women's Closet Drama, 1500–1700* (Cambridge: Cambridge University Press, 2004), 19–47; Deborah Uman, "Wonderfully Astonied at the Stoutenes of her Mind: Translating Rhetoric and Education in Jane Lumley's *The Tragedie of*

Iphigenia," in *Performing Pedagogy in Early Modern England: Gender, Instruction and Performance*, ed. Kathryn M. Moncrief, and Kathryn R. McPherson (Aldershot: Ashgate, 2011), 53–64; Uman, *Women as Translators in Early Modern England* (Newark: University of Delaware Press, 2012), 71–80; Jaime Goodrich, "Returning to Lady Lumley's Schoolroom: Euripides, Isocrates, and the Paradox of Women's Learning," *Renaissance & Reformation/ Renaissance et Réforme*, 35:4 (2012), 97–117; and Allyna Ward, *Women and Tudor Tragedy: Feminizing Counsel and Representing Genre* (Madison: Fairleigh Dickinson Press, 2013), 52–62.

34. On parallels between Iphigenia and Christ, see especially Shuger, "Iphigenia in Israel," in *The Renaissance Bible*, 128–66; Hodgson-Wright writes, "Iphigenia presents herself as an alternative female Christ" ("Jane Lumley's *Iphigenia*," 132), and Purkiss similarly holds, "Lumley understands Iphigenia as a Christ-figure" ("Blood, Sacrifice, Marriage and Death: Why Iphigeneia and Mariam have to Die," *Women and Writing*, 6:1 (1999), 27–45, 34).

35. On Arundel's role in the Lady Jane Grey controversy, see Ward, *Women and Tudor Tragedy*, 54.

36. Because Lumley's play is written in prose, line-counts will vary slightly by edition. I take my numbers from counting lines in Jane, Lady Lumley, *Iphigenia in Aulis*, ed. Harold Child (Malone Society Reprints, 1909); all citations refer to this edition.

37. In Aeschylus' *Agamemnon*, 458 BCE, Clytemnestra explains her murder of her husband by telling the chorus that "he sacrificed his own child, the dearest product of my labor pains, to charm the blasts of Thrace" [ἔθυσεν αὑτοῦ παῖδα, φιλτάτην ἐμοὶ/ὠδῖν᾽, ἐπῳδὸν Θρῃκίων ἀημάτων], 1417–18. Euripides wrote *Iphigenia in Aulis* approximately fifty years later, between 408–406 BCE.

38. Euripides' Clytemnestra says, "No, by the ruling Argive goddess! Go and manage things outdoors, but in the home I decide what is suitable for maidens' weddings" ("μὰ τὴν ἄνασσαν Ἀργείαν θεάν./ ἐλθὼν δὲ τἄξω πρᾶσσε, τὰν δόμοις δ᾽ ἐγώ,/ ἃ χρὴ παρεῖναι νυμφίοισι παρθένοις," 739–41). Erasmus translates, "No per numen Argiue dee/ Quin tu foris que sunt agas negocia/ Curas ego tracauero domesticas:/ Et quid puellis competat nubentibus:/ Id est mearum pensitare partium"; Erasmus, *Iphigenia in Aulide*, in *Hecuba et Iphigenia* (1506), Fo. LVIII v.

39. Euripides' Achilles lacks the emphatic "dare," asking more straightforwardly, "Who are you? Why have you come to the assembly of the Danaids, a woman to a fortified ring of men?" ("τίς δ᾽ εἶ; τί δ᾽ ἦλθες Δαναϊδῶν ἐς σύλλογον,/ γυνὴ πρὸς ἄνδρας ἀσπίσιν πεφραγμένους;" 825–6).

40. Euripides' Clytemnestra frames these lines as a question: "Do you intend to kill your child and mine?" (τὴν παῖδα τὴν σὴν τήν τ᾽ ἐμὴν μέλλεις κτενεῖν; 1131).

41. In response to Agamemnon's assertion that he doesn't have to answer this question, Euripides' Clytemnestra simply says, "I am not asking any other

questions; do not speak other answers to me" ("οὐκ ἀλλ' ἐρωτῶ, καὶ σὺ μὴ λέγ' ἄλλα μοι"; 1135).

42. Euripides' chorus tells him "πιθοῦ," be persuaded (1209).

43. See Ward, *Women and Tudor Tragedy*, 59.

44. Goodrich, "Returning to Lady Lumley's Schoolroom," 110. Ward similarly suggests that the play offers "a study on the place of women in the sixteenth-century political world"; *Women and Tudor Tragedy*, 59.

45. On classical tragedies' insistence that being forced to live is more painful than dying, see Emily Wilson, *Mocked with Death: Tragic Overliving from Sophocles to Milton* (Baltimore: Johns Hopkins Press, 2004).

46. She goes on to add that, "the familial bond becomes reconstructed as the exclusive bond between mother and child, a productive, life-giving, and mutually preserving bond" (Hodgson-Wright, "Jane Lumley's *Iphigenia*," 132).

47. "Ἀπώλεσέν σ', ὦ τέκνον, ὁ φυτεύσας πατήρ,/ αὐτὸς κτανών, οὐκ ἄλλος οὐδ' ἄλλη χερί,/ τοιόνδε νόστον καταλιπὼν πρὸς τοὺς δόμους" (1177–9).

48. Lumley had access to Erasmus's dual-language Greek–Latin edition, as well as a Greek edition of Euripides; see Sears Jayne and Francis R. Johnson, eds, *The Lumley Library: The Catalogue of 1609* (London: Trustees of the British Museum, 1956), nos.1736 & 1591a, cited in Straznicky, *Privacy, Playreading*, 33. I challenge the longstanding claim that Lumley worked directly from the Latin version and "shows no knowledge of Greek"; see Crane, "Euripides, Erasmus, and Lady Lumley," *The Classical Journal* 39:4 (1944), 223–8, 228.

49. "δεινὸν τὸ τίκτειν καὶ φέρει φίλτρον μέγα/ πᾶσίν τε κοινὸν ὥσθ' ὑπερκάμνειν τέκνων," 917–18.

50. See Εὐριπίδου Τραγωδίαι . . . *Evripidis tragoediae dvae, Hercuba & Iphigenia in Aulide*, trans. Erasmus (Basel: Johannes Froben, 1524), n6r; translation mine. Aemilius Portus later translated these lines "Res est vehemens parere, & advert ingens desiderium:/ Communeque omnibus est, vt laborent pro liberis," coming closer to Euripides' tone in portraying childbirth as violent, severe, and forceful. See *Evripidis Tragoediae XIX . . . Latinam interpretationem M. Aemilius Portus* (Heidelberg: Commelinus, 1597).

51. Demers, "On First Looking into Lumley's Euripides," 34.

52. As observed earlier, we do not know precisely when Lumley translated the play, but if it was around 1557, as growing consensus suggests, this would be around five years into her marriage.

53. For an overview and rebuttal of charges of Iphigenia's inconsistency, see Marianne McDonald, "Iphigenia's '*Philia*': Motivation in Euripides' *Iphigenia at Aulis*," *Quaderni Urbinati di Cultura Classica* 34: 1 (1990), 69–84, 69–70.

54. The term is Marianne McDonald's, from "Iphigenia's '*Philia*'," 70, and her "Cacoyannis and Euripides' *Iphigenia at Aulis*: A New Heroism," in *Euripides in Cinema: The Heart Made Visible* (Philadelphia: Centrum, 1983), 129–92. See also Mary R. Lefkowitz, *Women in Greek Myth* (Baltimore: Johns Hopkins University Press, 1986), 95; and Nicole Loraux, *Tragic Ways of Killing a Woman*, trans. Antony Foster (Cambridge: Cambridge University Press, 1987), 29.

55. On Lumley's depiction of Iphigenia as counselor, see Gweno Williams, "Translating the Self, Performing the Self," in *Women and Dramatic Production, 1550–1700*, ed. Alison Findlay and Stephanie Hodgson-Wright with Gweno Williams (London: Routledge, 2000), 15–41, 19.

56. Uman, *Women as Translators*, 79.

57. On Euripides' identification of Iphigenia with *kleos*, see McDonald, "Iphigenia's '*Philia*'," and Froma I. Zeitlin, "Art, Memory, and *Kleos* in Euripides' *Iphigenia in Aulis*," in *History, Tragedy, Theory: Dialogues on Athenian Drama*, ed. Barbara E. Goff (Austin: University of Texas Press, 1995), 174–201. Euripides uses the same terms to describe Alcestis' exceptional heroism; see Helene P. Foley, "*Anodos* Dramas: Euripides' *Alcestis* and *Helen*," *Female Acts in Greek Tragedy* (Princeton, NJ: Princeton University Press, 2001), 301–32; and Niall W. Slater, "Dead Again: (En)gendering Praise in Euripides' *Alcestis*," *Helios* 27:2 (2000), 105–21.

58. Achilles, Homer's iconic symbol of superhuman heroism, serves as analogue for other female protagonists popular in this period. Hecuba's daughter Polyxena, previously betrothed to him, is sacrificed as an offering to his spirit, and Medea's injured rage, along with her investment in the heroic code of helping friends and harming enemies, echoes his depiction in the *Iliad*; see Bernard Knox, "The *Medea* of Euripides," *Yale Classical Studies* 25 (1977), 197–202. Achilles' experience of being disguised as a girl by his mother to avoid fighting in the Trojan War offers a gender-crossing prehistory to these recurring literary alliances.

59. See *HECUBA, & Iphigenia in Aulide Euripidis tragoediae in Latinum tralatae Erasmo* (Venice: Aldus, 1507), fi–fii.

60. Findlay and Hodgson-Wright have argued, of early modern women's so-called closet drama, that a "script was written with a theatrical arena in mind, whether or not evidence of a production has survived in documentary form.... 'reading' and 'performance' were not mutually exclusive for early modern writers and readers." See Findlay and Hodgson-Wright, "Introduction," in *Women and Dramatic Production, 1550–1700*, 1–14, 2–3. For details about the proposed Lumley production, see Williams, "Translating the Self, Performing the Self," 16–23; Findlay, *Playing Spaces in Early Women's Drama* (Cambridge: Cambridge University Press, 2006), 74–8; and Wynne-Davies, "The Good Lady Lumley's Desire."

61. Wynne-Davies, "The Good Lady Lumley's Desire"; see also Williams, "Translating the Self, Performing the Self."

62. Wynne-Davies, "The Good Lady Lumley's Desire," 124.

63. On this play, which Chambers records as lost, see the APGRD, and E. K. Chambers, *The Elizabethan Stage* (Oxford: Clarendon Press, 1923), vol. 2, 14.

64. Wynne-Davies, "The Good Lady Lumley's Desire," 125.

65. Goodrich, "Returning to Lady Lumley's Schoolroom," 113. Ward similarly argues that "the distinct feminization of the rhetoric of counsel necessary for female regency in England ... opens the space for Iphigenia and Jocasta to be

considered suitable subjects for dramatic representation in the role of political counselor" (*Women and Tudor Tragedy*, 53).

66. See Uman, "Wonderfully Astonied at the Stoutenes of her Mind." Demers comments, "Lumley draws special attention to the fullness and tenacity of her heroine's intellect" (Demers, "On First Looking into Lumley's Euripides," 37).

67. Purkiss, *Three Tragedies*, 173; Demers, "On First Looking into Lumley's Euripides," 36. Purkiss develops this point further in "Blood, Sacrifice, Marriage and Death."

68. "κατ' ἐμὲ δ' εὐκλεὴς ἔσῃ," "you will be made famous [*eukleés*] by me" (1440); "κλέος γὰρ οὔ σε μὴ λίπῃ," "for fame [*kleos*] will never leave you" (1504).

69. Hodgson-Wright, "Jane Lumley's *Iphigenia*," 133. Findlay and Hodgson-Wright similarly observe, "we see women embracing the role of tragic sacrifice as an autonomous act, rather than passively accepting it as a victim"; Findlay and Hodgson-Wright, "Introduction," in *Women and Dramatic Production, 1550–1700*, 1–14, 4.

70. Hodgson-Wright, "Jane Lumley's *Iphigenia*," 133.

71. Uman, *Women as Translators*, 80.

72. Purkiss, *Three Tragedies*, xxx.

73. On the plight of Greek in Mary's reign (including Cheke's flight to the continent after his 1553 imprisonment by Mary), see Roger Ascham, *The Scholemaster* (London: John Day, 1570), 55–6.

74. Ingram Bywater, *Four Centuries of Greek Learning in England* (Oxford: Clarendon Press, 1919), 13. In his "Greek Studies in Early Sixteenth-Century England," Tilley stops tracing the period's teaching of Greek in 1540, which he sees as effectively its endpoint.

75. See Lazarus, "Greek Literacy."

76. See Lazarus, "Greek Literacy," 445–6. Clarke has given voice to the view that "The pioneering days of Croke and Cheke were over and inevitably something of the old enthusiasm was lost" (*Classical Education in Britain*, 32).

77. Elyot identified the ideal master as "excellently learned both in Greek and Latin"; Elyot, *Book of the Governor*, 28, cited in David Cressy, *Education in Tudor and Stuart England* (London: St. Martin's, 1976), 60. Mulcaster described the ideal schoolmaster as "able to teach the three learned tongues, the Latin, the Greek, the Hebrew"; Mulcaster, *Positions* (London, 1581), 238, cited in Cressy, 61. On the theatrical influence of Mulcaster, who became headmaster first of Merchant Taylors' School and then of St. Paul's, see Richard L. DeMolen, "Richard Mulcaster and the Elizabethan Theatre," *Theatre Survey* 13 (1972), 28–41.

78. See Lazarus, "Greek Literacy," 446–7, and James McConica, "The Rise of the Undergraduate College," in *The History of the University of Oxford*, vol. III, *The Collegiate University*, ed. James McConica (Oxford: Oxford University Press, 1986), 1–68, esp. 15, 57, 58, and 60.

79. On Greek classes at St. John's, see Clarke, *Classical Education*, 33; on 1576 Statutes, see Lazarus, "Greek Literacy," 450 and Strickland Gibson, ed., *Statuta Antiqua Universitatis Oxoniensis* (Oxford: Clarendon Press, 1931),

408. On details of Greek book ownership, see Lisa Jardine, "Humanism and the Sixteenth Century Cambridge Arts Course," *History of Education* 4:1 (1975), 16–31; *Private Libraries in Renaissance England*, ed. Robert J. Fehrenbach, E. S. Leedham-Green, and Joseph L. Black (Binghamton, Medieval & Renaissance Texts & Studies, 1992); and Strickland Gibson, *Abstracts from the Wills and Testamentary Documents of Binders, Printers, and Stationers of Oxford, from 1493 to 1638* (London, 1907), 11–14.

80. A large number of Greek scholars, including Linacre, Clements, Caius, Wotton, Fryer, Nicholas Carr, and William Turner, turned to medicine, many becoming presidents of the College of Physicians (Tilley, "Greek Studies," 454–5).

81. Lazarus, "Greek Literacy," 437.

82. See Donald Lemen Clark, *John Milton at St. Paul's School: A Study of Ancient Rhetoric in English Renaissance Education* (New York: Columbia University Press, 1954), 42; see also H. B. Wilson, *The History of Merchant-Taylors' School* (London, 1814), 11.

83. See Alexander, *The Growth of English Education*, 188.

84. Alexander Nowell claimed that every week he read from the New Testament "in greeke so well as I could, to such of my scholers as I had"; see T. W. Baldwin, *William Shakspere's Small Latine and Lesse Greeke*, 2 vols. (Urbana: University of Illinois Press, 1944), I. 171–9. Edward Grant studied Greek at Cambridge, and was a friend of Roger Ascham. On William Camden's classical scholarship, see Wyman H. Herendeen, *William Camden: A Life in Context* (Woodbridge: Boydell, 2007).

85. See F. W. M. Draper, *Four Centuries of Merchant Taylors' School, 1561–1961* (London: Oxford University Press, 1962).

86. Baldwin, *William Shakspere's Small Latine*, I. 296, II. 625.

87. Joan Simon, *Education and Society in Tudor England* (Cambridge: Cambridge University Press, 1979), 306; Wilson, *The History of Merchant-Taylors' School*, 37–40.

88. R. R. Bolgar, "Classical Reading in Renaissance Schools," *Durham Research Review* 6 (1955), 18–26, 22. See Lazarus, "Greek Literacy," 435–6, on the comparative impact of these numbers; I note that current U.K. and U.S. undergraduate expectations differ based on the more specialist approach of the U.K. system.

89. On humanist interest in literature at the heart of education, see Rebecca Bushnell, *A Culture of Teaching: Early Modern Humanism in Theory and Practice* (Ithaca, NY: Cornell University Press, 1996); Anthony Grafton and Lisa Jardine, *From Humanism to the Humanities: Education and the Liberal Arts in Fifteenth and Sixteenth-Century Europe* (London: Duckworth, 1986); and Jeff Dolven, *Scenes of Instruction in Renaissance Romance* (Chicago: University of Chicago Press, 2007).

90. Studies of the literary roots, and consequences, of sixteenth-century English schoolrooms include T. W. Baldwin, *William Shakspere's Small Latine*, and Clark, *John Milton at St. Paul's School*; see also Andrew Wallace, *Virgil's*

Schoolboys: The Poetics of Pedagogy in Renaissance England (Oxford: Oxford University Press, 2010).

91. See Erasmus, *De Ratione Studii*; for selections from early modern curricula that name Euripides and Aristophanes among core reading assignments, see Baldwin, *William Shakspere's Small Latine*, I. 89, 106, 107, 191, 262, 136, 348, 359–60, 417, 457, 539; II. 305 and 649.

92. *Collections of Statutes for the University and the Colleges of Cambridge* (London: William Clowes, 1840), 5–7, 290, cited in Rhodes, "Marlowe and the Greeks," 208.

93. Baldwin, *William Shakspere's Small Latine*, I. 648–9; Eric Glasgow, "Some Early Greek Scholars in England," and "Greek in the Elizabethan Renaissance," *Salzburg Studies in English Literature* 71:2 (1981), 3–17 and 18–31.

94. Public performances of comedies and tragedies in post-classical Europe had only begun shortly before Greek plays began appearing in print, starting with Plautus' *Asinaria* and Seneca's *Hippolytus*, both staged in Rome in the mid-1480s by students of Pomponius Laetus; see the APGRD database, and Bruce R. Smith, *Ancient Scripts and Modern Experience on the English Stage 1500–1700* (Princeton, NJ: Princeton University Press, 1988).

95. Records of documented performances are almost certainly incomplete, but the differences between English and continental documented performance traditions are suggestive; see Appendices.

96. See Lynn Enterline, *Shakespeare's Schoolroom: Rhetoric, Discipline, Emotion* (Philadelphia: University of Pennsylvania Press, 2012).

97. The 1545 St. John's statutes require "ceteras comoedias et tragoedias"; the 1546 Chapter 36 of Queens College, Cambridge, specifically required that these plays be performed in classical languages; and in 1560 the Chapter 24 Statutes of Trinity College, Cambridge, required five plays annually (see Frederick Boas, *University Drama in the Tudor Age*. Oxford: Clarendon Press, 1914, 16–17). A 1560 statute from Westminster School, titled, "As to Comedies and Plays to be Shown at Christmas," decreed, "That the youth may spend Christmas-tide with better result, and better become accustomed to proper action and pronunciation, we decree, that every year, within 12 days after Christmas day, or afterwards with the leave of the Dean, the Master and Usher together shall cause their pupils and the choristers to act, in private or public, a Latin comedy or tragedy in Hall, and the Choristers' Master an English one. And if they do not each do their part, the defaulter shall be fined 10 shillings." See Arthur F. Leach, *Educational Charters and Documents 598–1909* (Cambridge: Cambridge University Press, 1911), 518–19.

98. See Boas, *University Drama*, 17.

99. Identifying details of plays presented in performance is precarious, but extant records indicate considerably more Greek plays produced in England than elsewhere; see Appendix 4 for details.

100. The early productions adopted Cheke's controversial new rules for Greek pronunciation, taking part in heated contemporary debates about the

language; see Smith, *Ancient Scripts*, 169, and Boas, *University Drama*, 17. Dee described his production of *Peace* as "a Greeke Comedie of Aristophanes, named in Greek Eirene, in Latine Pax. with the p[er]formance of the Scarabeus his flying up to Jupiters Pallace, with a Man & his Basket of victualls on her Back" [*sic*]; printed in Alan H. Nelson, ed. *Records of Early English Drama: Cambridge*, (1989), s.v. 1546. For details on *Plutophthalmia*, see Smith, *Ancient Scripts*, 168–75, and Martin Butler, "The Auspices of Thomas Randolph's *Hey for Honesty, Down with Knavery*," *Notes and Queries*, n.s. 35 (1988), 491–2.

101. Boas, *University Drama*, 322, 347–8. On the Elizabethan tradition of vernacular satiric comedies at Cambridge, see Boas, *University Drama*, 322–49, and Darryll Grantley, *Wit's Pilgrimage: Drama and the Social Impact of Education in Early Modern England* (Aldershot: Ashgate, 2000).

102. See Appendices.

103. See Appendices.

104. The APGRD database lists 34 plays identified with Seneca before 1600, but 4 of these—*Progne* (1566), *La Famine, ou les Gabéonites* (1573), *Richardus Tertius* (1579), and Bernardino Stefonio's *Crispus* (1597)—can only be described as very distantly influenced by Seneca. Others, such as two productions of *Octavia* (1599, 1660), refer to plays no longer attributed to Seneca, though I include them as Senecan on the grounds that they were considered such in the period. See Appendices.

105. William Soone to George Braun, published in Braun and Hogenberg, ed., *Civitates Orbis Terrarum*, vol. 2 (Cologne, 1575), cited in Enid Porter, *Cambridgeshire Customs and Folklore* (London: Routledge & Kegan Paul, 1969), 245.

106. See Gillian Austen, *George Gascoigne* (Cambridge: D. S. Brewer, 2008). On the literary prominence of the Inns of Court, see A. Wigfall Green, *The Inns of Court and Early English Drama* (New Haven, CT: Yale University Press, 1931), and Jayne Archer, Elizabeth Goldring, and Sarah Knight, eds., *The Intellectual and Cultural World of the Early Modern Inns of Court* (Manchester: Manchester University Press, 2011).

107. See Robert S. Miola, "Euripides at Gray's Inn: Gascoigne and Kinwelmersh's *Jocasta*," in *The Female Tragic Hero*, ed. Naomi Liebler (New York: Palgrave, 2002), 33–50.

108. See J. P. Mahaffy, *Euripides* (London, 1879), 134–45; Max Th. W. Förster, "Gascoigne's Jocasta: A Translation from the Italian," *Modern Philology* 2:1 (1904), 147–50; J. W. Cunliffe, *Early English Classical Tragedies* (Oxford, 1912), 311; Miola, "Euripides at Gray's Inn"; and Austen, *George Gascoigne*, 53.

109. See Howard Norland, *Neoclassical Tragedy in Elizabethan England* (Newark: University of Delaware Press, 2009), 83–9, and Sarah Dewar-Watson, "*Jocasta*: 'A Tragedie Written in Greek,'" *International Journal of the Classical Tradition* 17:1 (2010), 22–32. The Latin edition that Dewar-Watson discusses is *Evripidis… Tragoediae XVIII… per Dorothevm Camillvm* (Basel: Robert Winter, 1541).

110. George Gascoigne and Francis Kinwelmersh, *Jocasta: A Tragedie vvritten in Greke by Euripides*, in Gascoigne, *A hundreth sundrie flowres bounde vp in one small poesie* (London: Henrie Bynneman, 1573), Aiv.

111. Arlene W. Saxonhouse, "Another Antigone: The Emergence of the Female Political Actor in Euripides' *Phoenician Women*," *Political Theory* 33:4 (2005), 472–94, 474. Others have challenged Saxonhouse's description of Sophocles' Antigone as weakening; see especially Bonnie Honig, *Antigone, Interrupted* (Cambridge: Cambridge University Press, 2013), who argues that Antigone's lament represents a form of political and ethical agency.

112. See especially Marie Axton, *The Queen's Two Bodies: Drama and the Elizabethan Succession* (London: Royal Historical Society, 1977); more recently, see Jessica Winston, "Expanding the Political Nation: *Gorboduc* at the Inns of Court and Succession Revisited," *Early Theatre* 8:1 (2005), 11–34.

113. The play was translated into Italian in 1532 by Guido Guidi before Dolce's 1549 translation and Gascoigne and Kinwelmersh's 1566 version; previous editions included a 1572 edition published in Wittenberg; a 1577 Latin translation by George Calaminus published in Strasbourg; a 1579 Latin translation by Albert Campius and Martin Norden, published in Rostock; inclusion in a three-play selection (*Phoenissae, Hippolytus,* and *Andromache*) translated into Latin by George Rataller and published by Christopher Plantins in 1580 and reprinted in 1581; and a 1592 Latin edition translated by Nicolaus Gablmann and published in Graz. See Appendices.

114. See Raffaella Cribiore, "The Grammarian's Choice: The Popularity of Euripides' *Phoenissae* in Hellenistic and Roman Education," in *Education in Greek and Roman Antiquity*, ed. Yun Lee Too (Leiden: Brill, 2001), 241–59, and J. M. Bremer, "The Popularity of Euripides' *Phoenissae* in Late Antiquity," in *Actes du VIIe Congrès de la Federation Internationale des Associations d'Études Classiques* 1 (1983), 281–8.

115. Sophocles' *Oedipus at Colonus* was written later, *c.*406; other tragedies about Thebes have survived in fragments, and many others are no longer extant. See Cribiore, "The Grammarian's Choice," 244–5, and Thalia Papadopolou, *Euripides: Phoenician Women* (London: Bloomsbury, 2014), 29. Elizabeth W. Scharffenberger has argued that the play also draws on the female-led scene of reconciliation in Aristophanes' *Lysistrata*; see Scharffenberger, "A Tragic Lysistrata? Jocasta in the 'Reconciliation Scene' of the *Phoenician Women*," *Rheinisches Museum für Philologie* 138:3/4 (1995), 312–36.

116. See Corinne Pache, "Theban Walls in Homeric Epic," *Trends in Classics* 6:2 (2014), 278–96; 288–90, and Papadopolou, *Euripides: Phoenician Women*, 29.

117. "Est autem admodum tragica ac plena uehementibus affectibus." See Gasparus Stiblinus, "Praefatio in *Phoenissas*," in *Evripides Poeta Tragicorum Princeps* (Basel: Johannes Oporinus, 1562), 124–6, 124.

118. According to their own notes in the play, Kinwelmersh translated Acts 1 and 4, while Gascoigne translated Acts 2, 3, and 5.

119. See Felicity Dunworth, *Mothers and Meaning on the Early Modern English Stage* (Manchester: Manchester University Press, 2010), 58.

120. "δεινὸν γυναιξὶν αἱ δι᾽ ὠδίνων γοναί,/ καὶ φιλότεκνόν πως πᾶν γυναικεῖον γένος." Euripides, *Phoenissae*, in *Euripidis Fabulae*, ed. Gilbert Murray (Oxford: Clarendon Press, 1913), vol. 3, ll. 355–6. In 1597, Aemilius Portus translated these lines as "Ac totum genus muliebre amans est liberorum./ Mater, bene & non bene cogitans, veni/ Ad viros inimicos, sed necesse est/ Omnes amare patriam" (with underlining, commonplace marks, and marginalia in the volume owned by Columbia University Library, shelfmark B88EI B97). Loraux writes of this and other Greek dramatic references to labor pains that in Greek thought, "a mother owes her pre-eminent position alongside the dead to the unconditional privilege given once and for all by the bond of childbirth. A bond that is without mediation, exacting, painful, and that Euripides' choruses sometimes describe as 'terrible': terribly tender, terribly strong, simply *terrible*....in order to designate the child as what is both the most precious and the most heart-rending possession of a mother, Euripidean tragedy readily calls it the *lôkheuma*, the product of childbirth" (*Mothers in Mourning*, 35–6).

121. "δεινὸν τὸ τίκτειν καὶ φέρει φίλτρον μέγα/ πᾶσίν τε κοινὸν ὥσθ᾽ ὑπερκάμνειν τέκνων." Euripides, *Iphigenia in Aulis*, 917–18.

122. Dolce's translation is very close: "Amor non è, che s'appareggia a quello,/ Che la pietosa madre a i figli porta:/ Ilqual tanto piu cresce, quanti in essi/ Scema il contento, & crescono gli affanni." Lodovico Dolce, *Giocasta* (Venice: Aldi Filii, 1549), 14v.

123. *Evripidis...Tragoediae XVIII*, 140. On Gascoigne and Kinwelmersh's access to this text, see Dewar-Watson, "*Jocasta*: 'A Tragedie Written in Greek.'"

124. "The mother thus beholding both hir sonnes/ Ydone to death, and ouercome with dolor,/ Drewe out the dagger of hir *Polinices,*/ From brothers brest, and gorde hir mothers throte" (151).

125. Early definitions for "prevent" in the *Oxford English Dictionary* are "I. To anticipate or act in advance...4.To act in anticipation of, or in preparation for...To come, appear, or act before the expected time"; www.oed.com, accessed August 6, 2015.

126. Papadopolou, *Euripides: Phoenician Women*, 70; see also Falkner, 1995, 208–9.

127. See Euripides, *Phoenissae*, ed. Donald J. Mastronarde (Cambridge: Cambridge University Press, 1994), 16; also Euripides, *Phoenician Women*, ed. E. M. Craik (Warminster: Aris & Phillips, 1988), 46; and Papadopolou, *Euripides: Phoenician Women*, 88–9.

128. See Norland, *Neoclassical Tragedy*, 85–6.

129. "Quid porro miserabilius quam Antigonen geminos fratres una cum matre confuso in sanguine se uolutantes ac cum morte luctantes aspicere?" Stiblinus, "Praefatio in *Phoenissas*," 124.

130. "Insigne pietatis exemplum est in Antigone, quae regias nuptias, opes, regnum, speciosos titulos, despecto et opis egenti parenti posthabuit." Stiblinus, "Praefatio in *Phoenissas*," 125.

131. Anthony Gibson, *A Womans Woorth, defended against all the men in the world* (London, 1599), 13. I am grateful to Tania Demetriou for calling this passage to my attention.

132. I disagree here with Miola's claim that "Gascoigne and Kinwelmersh recast Euripides' heroic and defiant Antigone into a more conventional mold: she appears as the good sister and dutiful daughter.... Throughout the scene, the translators tone down Antigone's ferocity" ("Euripides at Gray's Inn," 47). Instead, I suggest that the translators present Antigone's filial and sisterly devotion as consistent with a ferocious defiance, in keeping with other approaches to Greek plays in the period.

133. Sophocles' *Antigone* appeared in twelve individual or partial editions in the period, of which seven were vernacular translations, similar to the twelve editions of Euripides' *Phoenissae*.

134. Robert Miola, "Early Modern Antigones: Receptions, Refractions, Replays," *Classical Receptions Journal* 6:2 (2014), 221–44, 223.

135. "Et cupit Antigone charior esse tibi./ Charior esse tibi sperat, quam chara Creonti,/ Quam fuerit patrio vel peramata solo./ Iamque reviviscens, et Musis ducta Latinis/ Huc venit, et Thoebis amplius esse timet./ Mira tibi referet, si vis miracula nosse,/ Atque pium faceret, ni pius ante fores . . . Haec et plura tuis plane praefiget ocellis/ Antigone, studio docta docere meo." Watson, "Nobilissimo Proceri, Claroque Multis Nominibus Philippo Howardo Comiti Arundellae, Thomas Watsonus Solidam Foelicitatem Precatur," ll. 76–92, in *Antigone*, trans. Dana Sutton; see http://www.philo logical.bham.ac.uk/watson/antigone/act1eng.html, accessed August 15, 2014.

136. On the claim that Lumley worked directly from the Latin version and "shows no knowledge of Greek," see Crane, "Euripides, Erasmus, and Lady Lumley," 228.

137. Miola, among others, has argued that *Jocasta* was "three hands and three tongues removed from the original Greek"; see "Euripides at Gray's Inn: Gascoigne and Kinwelmersh's *Jocasta*," 33. For a counterargument, see Dewar-Watson, "*Jocasta*: 'A Tragedie Written in Greek'."

138. On Buchanan's background, scholarship, and translations, see D. M. Abbott, "Buchanan, George (1506–1582)," *Oxford Dictionary of National Biography* (Oxford University Press, 2004); online edn, May 2006: http://www. oxforddnb.com/view/article/3837, accessed August 18, 2016.

139. Rebecca Bushnell, "Tragedy and the Tragic," in *The Classical Tradition*, 942–7, 944. Discussing English translations, Neil Rhodes claims that there were "none of Greek tragedy and none of Homer until Hall's translation from the French in 1581," though he goes on to acknowledge in a footnote that, "in the case of Greek tragedy the only exceptions are Jane Lumley's unpublished *Iphigenia in Aulis* and George Gascoigne and Francis Kinwel- mersh's *Jocasta*, translated from Dolce's Italian version of Euripides' *Phoe- nissae*." Neil Rhodes, "Marlowe and the Greeks," *Renaissance Studies* 27:2 (2013), 199–218, 205.

140. See, for instance, Kent Cartwright, *Theatre and Humanism: English Drama in the Sixteenth Century* (Cambridge: Cambridge University Press, 1999); Robert S. Knapp, "The Academic Drama," in *A Companion to Renaissance Drama*, ed. Arthur F. Kinney (Oxford: Blackwell, 2002), 257–65; Jessica Winston, "Seneca in Early Elizabethan England," *Renaissance Quarterly*

59:1 (2006), 29–58; Norland, *Neoclassical Tragedy in Elizabethan England*; and Walker and Streufert, eds., *Early Modern Academic Drama*. Earlier, G. C. Moore Smith similarly observed that college drama gradually developed away from the more didactic aspect of its classical roots toward an emphasis on recreation, and on comedy, matching the focus in the commercial stage; see *College Plays Performed in the University of Cambridge* (Cambridge: Cambridge University Press, 1923), 11.

141. On Inns of Court drama, see Green, *The Inns of Court and Early English Drama*; the essays in *The Intellectual and Cultural World of the Early Modern Inns of Court*, esp. Alan H. Nelson, "New Light on Drama, Music, and Dancing at the Inns of Court to 1642," 302–14; and Alan H. Nelson, "The Universities and the Inns of Court," in *The Oxford Handbook to Early Modern Theatre*, ed. Richard Dutton (Oxford: Oxford University Press, 2009), 280–91.

142. On reading, rhetorical training, and the making of playwrights in early modern grammar schools, see Enterline, *Shakespeare's Schoolroom*. On school drama, see T. H. Vail Motter, *The School Drama in England* (London: Longmans, 1929); Draper, *Four Centuries of Merchant Taylors' School*; J. Howard Brown, *Elizabethan Schooldays* (Oxford: Blackwell, 1933). On the relationship between grammar schools and the playing companies that grew out of the choir schools, see Reavley Gair, *The Children of Paul's: The Story of a Theatre Company, 1553–1608* (Cambridge: Cambridge University Press, 1982), and Lucy Munro, *Children of the Queen's Revels: A Jacobean Theatre Repertory* (Cambridge: Cambridge University Press, 2005).

143. See William Ringler, "The Immediate Source of Euphuism," *PMLA* 53:3 (1938), 678–86. Ringler notes that Rainolds was "required to lecture on some Greek author to the whole University three times a week during term," and that "Contemporary comment indicates that he was at that time the most admired and the most popular lecturer at Oxford" (Ringler, 682), so Lyly would certainly have been familiar with his lectures.

144. See Rhodes, "Marlowe and the Greeks." Greek books in John Gresshop's library included Isocrates, Demosthenes, Aristotle's *Rhetoric*, Plato (though in Latin), Sophocles, Aristophanes Thucydides, two Greek New Testaments, various grammars and syntaxes, and Cheke and Smith's "De linguae graecae pronunciatione." See "The Inventory of John Gresshop," in William Urry, *Christopher Marlowe and Canterbury*, ed. Andrew Butcher (London: Faber and Faber, 1988), 108–22, cited in Rhodes, "Marlowe and the Greeks," 208.

145. See John Bruce, *Liber Famelicus of Sir James Whitelocke* (Camden Society, vol. LXX), 12, cited in Baldwin, *William Shakspere's Small Latine*, II. 420.

146. "As these Tragicke Poets flourished in Greece, *Aeschylus, Euripedes, Sophocles, Alexander Aetolus, Achaeus Erithriaeus, Astydamas Atheniensis, Apollodorus Tarsensis, Nicomachus Phrygius, Thespis Atticus,* and *Timon Apolloniates;* and these among the Latines, *Accius, M. Attilius, Pomponius Secundus* and *Seneca:* so these are our best for Tragedie, the Lorde *Buckhurst,* Doctor *Leg* of

Cambridge, Doctor *Edes* of Oxforde, maister *Edward Ferris,* the Authour of the *Mirrour for Magistrates, Marlow, Peele, Watson, Kid, Shakespeare, Drayton, Chapman, Decker,* and *Beniamin Iohnson*"; Francis Meres, *Palladis Tamia* (London 1598), 283. On Watson's educational background, see Chatterley, "Watson, Thomas (1555/6–1592)," *Oxford Dictionary of National Biography,* online edn., Jan 2008: http://www.oxforddnb.com/view/article/28866, accessed August 18, 2016.

147. *The Works of Thomas Nashe,* ed. R. B. McKerrow, rev. F. P. Wilson, 5 vols. (Oxford: Blackwell, 1958), III.31, cited in Rhodes, "Marlowe and the Greeks," 202.

148. Jonson cites ll. 850–2 of Aristophanes' *Plutus* in *The Devil is an Ass* (1616,) 5.8.112–14.

149. On Heywood's classical reading, see Yves Peyré, "Heywood's Library," in Thomas Heywood, *Troia Britanica,* ed. Peyré et al., in *Early English Mythological Texts Series,* http://www.shakmyth.org/page/Early+Modern +Mythological+Texts%3A+Troia+Britanica%2C+Library, accessed August 7, 2015; on Homer in the Ages plays, see Charlotte Coffin, "Heywood's *Ages* and Chapman's Homer: Nothing in Common?," 55–78, and Claire Kenward, "Sights to make an Alexander? Reading Homer on the Early Modern Stage," both in *Homer and Greek Tragedy in Early Modern English Theatres,* ed. Demetriou and Pollard, 79–102.

150. "To those who report I was a long time in finishing this Tragedy . . . I must answere them with that of Eurypides to Alcestides, a Tragicke Writer: Alcestides objecting that Eurypides had onely in three daies composed three verses, whereas himself had written three hundreth: Thou telst truth, (quoth he) but heres the difference, thine shall onely bee read for three daies, whereas mine shall continue three ages." Webster, "To the Reader," *The White Devil,* in *The Works of John Webster,* ed. David Gunby, David Carnegie, Antony Hammond, and Doreen DelVecchio (Cambridge: Cambridge University Press, 1995), vol. 1, 140.

151. On Fletcher's attendance at the Cathedral School, see *The Publications of the Northamptonshire Record Society,* ed. William Thomas Mellows, vol. 13 (1941), liv; on studying at Queens College, where he seems to have met Francis Beaumont and Nathan Field, see Hilton Kelliher, "Francis Beaumont and Nathan Field: New Records of their Early Years," *English Manuscript Studies 1100–1700,* 8 (2000), 1–42. I am grateful to Lucy Munro for sharing this information and these references.

152. Records show that St. Paul's choristers took classes together with the students of St. Paul's grammar school; some went on to become full-time grammar school students, while others went straight to the universities. See Gair, *The Children of Paul's,* esp. 35–43, and Michael McDonnell, *The Annals of St. Paul's School* (Cambridge: Cambridge University Press, 1959), 106–7, 158–61. Summarizing William Malym's record of school plays during his time at Eton, McDonnell has argued that Malym must have similarly "encourage[d] the acting by schoolboys of plays when he

became High Master of St. Paul's" in the 1570s, and goes on to speculate, "I have little doubt that the boys of Dean Colet's School participated with the choristers of the Cathedral in the production of these plays" (*The Annals of St. Paul's School*, 107). On Lyly's plays, and his debts to the earlier tragicomic children's plays of Richard Edwardes and the "courtly-philosophical version of tragi-comedy" that they represent, see especially Michael Pincombe, *The Plays of John Lyly: Eros and Eliza* (Manchester: Manchester University Press, 1996), 25.

153. Philip Sidney and Fulke Greville studied at Shrewsbury, where the head-master was Thomas Ashton, a former fellow of St. John's, Cambridge, alongside Ascham and Cheke. On Sidney's Greek, see Micha Lazarus, "Sidney's Greek Poetics," *Studies in Philology* 112:3 (2015), 504–36. Edmund Spenser studied at Merchant Taylors' with Mulcaster; continued on to Pembroke College, Cambridge; and translated the *Axiochus*, a Socratic dialogue attributed to Plato. On Spenser's Greek, see Tania Demetriou, "'Essentially Circe': Spenser, Homer and the Homeric Tradition," *Translation and Literature*, 15:2 (2006), 151–76.

154. See Baldwin, *William Shakspere's Small Latine*, II. 626, II. 468–79. In addition to tracing Jenkins' study at St. John's College, Oxford, Baldwin suggests that he probably also studied under Richard Mulcaster at Merchant Taylors' School; see I. 478–9.

155. Christopher Marlowe, *The Jew of Malta*, in *The Complete Works of Christopher Marlowe*, vol. 4, ed. Roma Gill (Oxford: Clarendon Press, 1995), 1.1.133–5.

156. Chapman, *The Revenge of Bussy D'Ambois*, ed. Robert J. Lordi, in *The Plays of George Chapman*, ed. Allan Holaday (Cambridge: D. S. Brewer, 1987), 2.1.113–14.

157. *Titus Andronicus* receives more discussion in Chapter 2.

2

Imitating the Queen of Troy

As we have seen, English translations of Greek tragedies emphasized the affective power of grieving mothers and bold sacrificial daughters, who move their audiences with both grief and unexpected forms of triumph. The titles of these translations—*Iphigenia, Jocasta, Antigone*—reflect the reigning sixteenth-century canon of Greek plays, which similarly highlight female protagonists. Yet our canon of prominent early modern tragedies—plays such as *Hamlet, Othello, Macbeth,* and *Lear*—features predominantly male names, reflecting an early seventeenth-century shift towards a growing focus on male protagonists.[1] How and why did English playwrights reimagine a genre widely identified with female grief as increasingly focused on male suffering? And given this shift, what forms do Greek dramatic icons take in this period's tragedies?

This chapter argues that Greek tragic women haunt two of the period's most popular and influential early commercial tragedies: Thomas Kyd's *Spanish Tragedy* (*c.*1587) and Shakespeare and George Peele's *Titus Andronicus* (*c.*1592). Early modern audiences identified the plays with their raging fathers, as well as with each other; Ben Jonson's *Bartholomew Fair* refers sardonically to popular taste for "*Jeronimo* or *Andronicus.*"[2] Yet both Hieronimo and Titus carry out revenge in response to the passionate exhortations of mourning mothers and sacrificial daughters, who reflect and revise the iconic types widely associated with tragedy's Greek origins. These figures are not the plays' only Greek tragic echoes: *The Spanish Tragedy*'s action is initiated by Proserpine, the archetypal sacrificial daughter of Greek myth, and *Titus* links both its suffering female figures with explicit allusions to Hecuba, the period's reigning symbol of Greek tragedy. These allusions and echoes reflect a broader identification of tragedy with its Greek literary origins: Titus and his fellow Romans turn to Troy's fall when reflecting on terrible loss, and when Hieronimo stages a tragedy, he insists on speaking his lines in Greek.

Tracing the legacies of Greek tragic women in two foundational commercial plays illuminates an unfamiliar genealogy of English tragedy. Long identified with the roots of male heroic tragedy, these plays are palimpsests calling on the unsettled ghosts of earlier literary models. Both include self-conscious allusions to Seneca and Ovid, but they also gesture to the Greek prototypes hovering behind these Roman poets.[3] In the context of Kyd's education at the Greek-steeped Merchant Taylors' School, and Peele's status as Euripidean translator, these plays suggest previously unrecognized lines of transmission between newly visible Greek tragic models and London's commercial theaters. They also suggest an evolution from implicit borrowings to more explicit debts. While Kyd's female figures invoke Greek models obliquely, and largely mediated through Latin, the self-conscious allusions to Hecuba in *Titus Andronicus* point to the increasingly specific Greek dramatic debts inspired by university-educated playwrights such as Peele, highlighting the growing traffic between Greek texts and the commercial stage. In the context of these plays' metatheatrical inquiries into the nature of tragedy, their attention to Greek legacies and tragic female icons establishes an important foundation for the genre's development in England.

MOBILIZING WOMEN IN
THE SPANISH TRAGEDY

One of the most influential plays of the early modern period, *The Spanish Tragedy* established the template for the enormously popular genre of revenge tragedy.[4] Critics have typically identified the play's consolidation of revenge conventions with its debts to Senecan drama, but the bereaved mother and sacrificial daughter who mobilize Hieronimo's revenge also suggest links with the Greek dramatic influences hovering behind Seneca's legacy. Female figures may seem unlikely focal points for a play whose structure and afterlife locate its affective power in the grieving, raging Hieronimo. As Clara Calvo and Jesús Tronch have observed, Hieronimo has by far the play's largest role, with 28 percent of the words; the two next largest roles belong to Lorenzo and the King.[5] Early modern texts routinely cited the play as "Jeronimo," and imitations and parodies focused on Hieronimo's grief and madness.[6] Yet just as Proserpine inspires the play's action, the grieving Isabella and determined Bel-Imperia together animate Hieronimo, inflaming him with their urgency, and modeling strategies for inciting audience sympathies. Complementing Pamela Allen Brown's argument that Bel-Imperia's centrality reflects the influential emerging figure of the Italian actress, I propose that Bel-Imperia, Isabella, and Proserpine together channel the potent theatrical legacy of Greek tragedy.[7] Just as these suffering female figures hint at Greek tragic ghosts, Hieronimo's decision to speak his lines in the play's culminating tragic performance "in Greek" (4.1.167) underscores the genre's literary roots. Our point of origin for an early modern genre identified with angry, grieving male revengers and insistent metatheatricality, the play is shaped by the shadowy afterlives of Greek tragic women.

The Spanish Tragedy's opening scene attributes the drama to a Greek tragic daughter. Killed in battle by Prince Balthazar, Andrea's ghost supplicates Pluto and Proserpine to learn his fate in the underworld. In response, Andrea's ghost reports, "the fair Proserpine began to smile,/ And begged that only she might give my doom" (1.1.78–9). The archetypal sacrificial virgin, Proserpine looms behind tragic female icons, whom she implicitly summons in her sympathy for Andrea.[8] "Forthwith, Revenge," Andrea recounts, "she rounded thee in th' ear,/ And bade thee lead me through the gates of horn" (1.1.81–2). By introducing and instructing Revenge, Proserpine quietly conveys her responsibility for the dream-like drama that will unfold. As patron and commissioner, she steers the play, hovering invisibly behind the strong-willed Bel-Imperia and Isabella. Revenge, her deputy, is typically staged as male, but in the context of the play's self-consciously classical setting (and the absence of gendered pronouns), the figure finds its closest correlates in the Greek Atē or Nemesis, both female deities. Together, Proserpine and Revenge establish the play's metatheatrical frame, directing audiences' attention to our own role as spectators of the tragedy that follows.[9]

As Proserpine's play begins, Andrea's beloved Bel-Imperia channels her authority. Revenge assures Andrea that she will enact the play's central triumph—"thou shalt see the author of thy death,/ Don Balthazar, the Prince of Portugal,/ Deprived of life by Bel-Imperia" (1.1.87–9)—and the first two acts bear out this centrality. After interrogating Andrea's friend Horatio on the murder of her beloved, and learning of his death at Balthazar's hands, Bel-Imperia immediately urges revenge: "Would thou hadst slain him that so slew my love!" (1.4.30). In the absence of a response, she devises a plan: "second love shall further my revenge./ I'll love Horatio, my Andrea's friend,/ The more to spite the Prince that wrought his end" (1.4.66–8). In punishing Balthazar, who seeks her love, by flaunting her attentions to Horatio, she spurs additional violence; Balthazar insists that, despite his affection for Horatio, "Yet must I take revenge or die myself,/ For love resisted grows impatient" (2.1.115–16). Despite Hieronimo's reputation as the play's central avenger, it is Bel-Imperia, moved by the desire to punish Andrea's murderer, who engineers the play's expanding cycle of retribution.

Bel-Imperia continues to mobilize the play's actions when Balthazar murders Horatio in the arbor where he and Bel-Imperia are enjoying a stolen tryst. While Horatio quickly surrenders to their attack, she responds with a heroic attempt at self-sacrifice: "Oh, save his life and let me die for him!" (2.4.55). Before Balthazar and Lorenzo carry her away, Bel-Imperia sounds the alarm that precipitates the play's remaining action: "Murder! Murder! Help, Hieronimo, help!" (2.4.61). Her words rouse the sleeping Hieronimo, and begin the transfer of the play's agency from her hands to his. "What outcries pluck me from my naked bed," Hieronimo wonders, "And chill my throbbing heart with trembling fear,/ Which never danger yet could daunt before?/ Who calls Hieronimo?" (2.5.1–4). These lines attracted contemporary attention and imitation; Jonson parodies them in *Poetaster* (1601), in which a request for "the rumbling player" prompts recitation of "Murder, murder!" and "Who calls out 'murder'? Lady, was it you?"[10] Similarly, the character of Burbage in *The Return from Parnassus* (1602) tells a would-be actor, "I think your voice would serve for Hieronimo, observe how I act it and then imitate me: 'who calls Hieronimo from his naked bed?'"[11] The scene's popularity suggests audiences' keen interest in the transmission of emotion from Bel-Imperia to Hieronimo. When he moves to the play's center, he does so in response to being directed—plucked, chilled, called—by another, "some woman [who] cried for help" (2.4.6). Even in Bel-Imperia's absence, her ghostly summons hovers behind Hieronimo's actions. As Hieronimo absorbs Horatio's death, he echoes the sense of wrenching loss that Bel-Imperia first voiced after Andrea's death. "Ay me, most wretched, that have lost my joy," he soliloquizes, "In leesing my Horatio, my sweet boy!" (2.5.32–3). As Bel-Imperia's grief becomes his own, his parental affections become increasingly central to his identity.

As Bel-Imperia recedes from the action, her grief and desire for revenge resurface not only in Hieronimo, but also in Isabella, Horatio's mother. Isabella appears in only three of the play's scenes, but her passionate laments for her dead son shape Hieronimo's response, and catalyze the play's climactic actions.[12] Unable to express his grief, Hieronimo turns to her for guidance. "Here, Isabella," he tells her, "help me to lament;/ For sighs are stopped, and all my tears are spent." In response, she gestures towards the conversion of mourning to revenge: "What world of grief— my son Horatio!/ Oh, where's the author of this endless woe?" (2.5.36–9). Isabella frames her response as a question, but her desire to know the author underscores her desire for revenge, which Hieronimo echoes: "To know the author were some ease of grief,/ For in revenge my heart would find relief" (2.5.40–1). His acknowledgment intensifies Isabella's frenzy:

> Then is he gone? And is my son gone too?
> Oh, gush out, tears, fountains and floods of tears!
> Blow, sighs, and raise an everlasting storm,
> For outrage fits our cursed wretchedness!   (2.5.42–5)

In voicing not simply lament but violent rage, Isabella furthers the movement towards revenge initiated by Bel-Imperia. Her language frames her suffering in material terms, as a force of nature with devastating consequences. Identifying her passions with violent liquid outpourings—"tears, fountains and floods of tears"—she imagines melting and moving others with her pain.

Isabella's liquid model of contagious emotion spills over into Hieronimo's language. "Seest thou this handkerchief besmeared with blood?" he asks rhetorically;

> It shall not from me till I take revenge.
> Seest thou those wounds that yet are bleeding fresh?
> I'll not entomb them till I have revenge.
> Then will I joy amidst my discontent.
> Till then my sorrow never shall be spent. (2.5.51–6)[13]

Contemplating the traces of Horatio's blood on the handkerchief dropped earlier by Bel-Imperia, Hieronimo implicitly translates this blood into the blood of his son's murderer; just as tears beget floods, blood begets more blood. But while Isabella imagines an everlasting storm, he imagines blood ending blood, joy replacing sorrow. His odd choice of "joy" evokes his earlier rhyming of joy with boy, linking his past joy in his son with his future joy in revenge: mingling emotions, the pleasure of retribution substitutes for the lost pleasure of Horatio himself. And although her stormy vision suggests less optimism, Isabella similarly prophesies the retribution that her husband craves. "The heavens are just," she insists; "murder cannot be hid./ Time is the author both of truth and right,/ And time will bring this treachery to light" (2.5.57–9). In her emphasis on revenge, she implicitly echoes both Bel-Imperia and Proserpine, and joins their efforts in steering the play towards its violent end.

Although Isabella seconds Bel-Imperia's efforts to stir Hieronimo to grief and revenge, Bel-Imperia has to intervene again when he proves slow to act. In the third act she reaches out from the tower where her brother Lorenzo has imprisoned her, by sending a letter written in blood. "For want of ink," she addresses Hieronimo in her letter,

> receive this bloody writ.
> Me hath my hapless brother hid from thee.
> Revenge thyself on Balthazar and him,
> For these were they that murdered thy son.
> Hieronimo, revenge Horatio's death,
> And better fare than Bel-Imperia doth. (3.2.26–31)

Partaking of Hieronimo's imagined economy, in which blood begets more blood, Bel-Imperia foreshadows her self-sacrifice by spilling her own blood in the cause of revenge. Writing with the contents of her own body, as Bianca Calabresi has observed, she highlights her authenticity as a witness.[14] Joining the bloody handkerchief, which had already merged Horatio's blood with her own bodily traces, her bloody letter brings about an intersubjective transfer that is both physiological and affective.[15] Conveyed from her body to Hieronimo, the blood on her letter gives material form to the transfer of passions that she urges. She similarly transfers the task of revenge from herself to Hieronimo with a profusion of the intimate pronouns "thee," "thyself," and "thy," assigning him a central role in a collaborative project.

As Hieronimo moves forward with Bel-Imperia's support, Isabella turns inward, to her garden. "So that you say this herb will purge the eye," she reflects in soliloquy, "And this the head,/ Ah, but none of them will purge the heart!" (3.8.1–3). Her wish for a medicine to purge grief suggests both the blood-letting through which Bel-Imperia writes her letter, and Hieronimo's belief that violent revenge will purge the pain of Horatio's death: as Lorenzo announces, "thus one ill another must expulse" (3.2.107).[16] Finding no remedy, however, Isabella instead pursues her own sacrifice. "Since neither piety nor pity moves/ The King to justice or compassion," she announces in soliloquy, "I will revenge myself upon this place/ Where thus they murdered my beloved son" (4.2.2–5). As with her ecological metaphor of the storm, Isabella imagines her garden as a version of herself.[17] "Fruitless for ever may this garden be," she curses, "Barren the earth, and blissless whosoever/ Imagines not to keep it unmanured" (4.2.14–16). Framed in the vocabulary of fruit and barrenness, Isabella's attack on her garden becomes an attack on her own maternal fertility. "And as I curse this tree from further fruit," she explains, "So shall my womb be cursed for his sake,/ And with this weapon will I wound the breast/ The hapless breast that gave Horatio suck" (4.2.35–7). Punishing her body for bearing her greatest pain, she similarly punishes her tree and garden for bearing Horatio's death.[18] Lines in the 1602 additions to the play, typically attributed to Ben Jonson but increasingly identified with Shakespeare, further identify the tree with fertility: Hieronimo describes planting it "of a kernel" and nurturing "the infant and the human sap" (3.12A.64, 66).[19] "At last it grew and grew, and bore and bore," he recalls, "Till at length/ It grew a gallows and did bear our son;/ It bore thy fruit and mine" (312A.69–71). Simultaneously child and parent, the tree offers an unsettling focal point for Isabella's passionate maternal grief.

Critics have described Isabella's suicide as a pale shadow of Hieronimo's revenge, but I suggest that her violent performance serves as crucial spur to the play's final actions.[20] When Bel-Imperia finally meets with Hieronimo, she echoes Isabella's botanical language in rebuking him. "Is this the love thou bear'st Horatio?" she asks; "Is this the kindness that thou counterfeits?/ Are these the fruits of thine incessant tears?" (4.1.1–3). Further developing the genealogical vocabulary of kindness and fruit, she compares his emotional investments unfavorably with maternal counterparts:

> Unhappy mothers of such children then!
> But monstrous fathers to forget so soon
> The death of those whom they, with care and cost,
> Have tendered so, thus careless should be lost! (4.1.17–20)

With her angry reference to unhappy mothers and monstrous fathers, Bel-Imperia accosts Hieronimo for failing both the child that he has tendered, and the wife whose maternal investment has been destroyed. Her sharp words finally succeed in rousing Hieronimo to action. Apologizing for his failings—"Pardon, oh pardon, Bel-Imperia" (4.1.38)—he promises to take revenge. "And here I vow," he tells her, " . . . I will ere long determine of their deaths/ That causeless thus have murdered my son" (4.1.42–5). In order to do so, he pleads for Bel-Imperia's support: "Whatsoever I devise/ Let me entreat you grace my practices" (4.1.49–50). Mobilized to action by bold and passionate female figures, Hieronimo learns from their ability to transfer their passions to others, and incorporates their lessons into his own plan for revenge.

Invited to entertain the rulers of Castile and Portugal—the fathers of his son's murders, Lorenzo and Balthazar—Hieronimo announces his plan to stage a tragedy. He introduces his performance as a revival, rooted in his literary education. "When in Toledo there I studied," he explains, "It was my chance to write a tragedy . . . Which, long forgot, I found this other day" (4.1.75–8). Hieronimo's tragedy, like those of Greece, has been "long forgot," but newly rediscovered. By linking the play with his own pedagogical history, he hints at the broader role of humanist study in recalling and reproducing the literary past. In devising a play as his vehicle for revenge, he also echoes the structure of the play he inhabits, presented by Proserpine as a show for Andrea's ghost. In his role as patron and commissioner, then, he replaces Bel-Imperia in channeling Proserpine, who devises and commands the larger show, implicitly picking up the mantle of female tragic authority and further enacting the play's transfer of agency from women to men. Hieronimo's dramatic strategy draws on his earlier association with the theater: in his first appearance, the King asks him to "grace our banquet with some pompous jest" (1.4.137), which he obliges with a dumb-show in which knights capture a king. The early show's violence hints at the direction to come, but Hieronimo's second performance follows Proserpine's by engaging collaborative participation. "I mean each one of you to play a part," he tells Balthazar and Lorenzo (4.1.79–81). More strikingly, he insists on the importance of Bel-Imperia's contribution: "For what's a play without a woman in it?" (4.1.94). His rhetorical question not only acknowledges Bel-Imperia's indispensability to his plan, but highlights female roles as crucial to tragedy's power. Like *The Spanish Tragedy*, Hieronimo's play *Soliman and Perseda* hinges on female grief and rage. After Perseda marries her beloved Erastus, her unrequited admirer—the Turkish Emperor, Soliman— confesses his feelings to a friend, who murders Erastus on Soliman's behalf. The grieving and angry Perseda, played by Bel-Imperia, kills her lover's murderer, and goes on to commit suicide. The play avenges its wrongs through female passions.

Just as the plot of Hieronimo's tragedy hinges on female agency, the performance—like the broader metatheatrical play introduced by Proserpine earlier—responds to the urging of a suffering daughter. In preparing for the show, moreover, Hieronimo attributes his renewed impetus to Isabella. "Bethink thyself, Hieronimo," he soliloquizes,

> Recall thy wits, recount thy former wrongs
> Thou hast received by murder of thy son,
> And lastly, not least, how Isabel,
> Once his mother and thy dearest wife,
> All woebegone for him, hath slain herself.
> Behoves thee then, Hieronimo, to be revenged.   (4.3.20–6)

Set into motion by a sacrificial daughter, inspired by the specter of a bereaved mother, and performed by the angry Bel-Imperia, *Soliman and Perseda* is crucially indebted to female affective force. Most strikingly, Bel-Imperia not only enacts Perseda's part, but carries out its violence literally: rather than simply pretending to murder Balthazar, she actually kills him. "But were she able," her character tells Balthazar's, "thus she would revenge/ Thy treacheries on thee, ignoble Prince (*Stabs him.*)" (4.3.64–5). After this action, she introduces her own variation on her role. Speaking the line, "And on herself she would be thus revenged," she concludes by stabbing herself, as Isabella did (4.3.66). Her death, which takes Hieronimo by surprise, evokes proud and defiant female figures such as Iphigenia and Polyxena, whom Giraldi Cinthio described as "boldly embrac[ing] death [rather] than submitting shamefully to a slavish yoke."[21] Implicitly echoing the heroic tragedies of other iconic young women who achieved fame through their glorious deaths, Bel-Imperia offers a new incarnation of the raging, grieving female roles identified with tragic power.

After the performance, Hieronimo directly links his tragedy to ancient Greek tradition. Addressing his audience, he explains that his play does not simply offer pleasurable fiction:

> Haply you think, but bootless are your thoughts,
> That this is fabulously counterfeit
> And that we do as all tragedians do,
> To die today—for fashioning our scene—
> The death of Ajax, or some Roman peer,
> And, in a minute starting up again,
> Revive to please tomorrow's audience.   (4.4.75–81)

In imagining his audiences' expectations, Hieronimo identifies the "fabulously counterfeit" nature of tragedy with a Greek figure—the maddened, suicidal Ajax—whose tragedy by Sophocles was both discussed and performed in England.[22] In linking Bel-Imperia's suicide with that of a male tragic hero, he implicitly emphasizes her distinctly gendered heroism. By singling out Ajax, in contrast with the unnamed Roman peer, he also underscores his decision to speak his own lines of the play in Greek, presenting his play as a version of Greek tragedy.

As Hieronimo points out, however, his tragedy differs from these legendary plays in unexpectedly literalizing their outcome: the deaths that result from his performance are real. "No, princes," Hieronimo continues:

> know I am Hieronimo,
> The hopeless father of a hapless son . . .
> Behold the reason urging me to this.
> *([Draws the curtain and] shows his dead son.)*
> See here my show, look on this spectacle.   (4.4.82–8)

Equating his murderous performance with his murdered son, Hieronimo describes his tragedy as a means to reproduce his own experience in his audiences. "And grieved I, think you, at this spectacle?" he asks; "Speak, Portuguese, whose loss resembles mine./ If thou canst weep upon thy Balthazar,/ 'Tis like I wailed for my Horatio" (4.4.112–15). Hieronimo aspires to make his audiences—Castile and Portugal, the fathers of Lorenzo and Balthazar—understand his loss through experiencing the parallel loss of their own sons. By making his audiences identify with his grief, Hieronimo remakes them in his own image, just as he has remade himself in the image of the female figures whose performances of grief have inspired his show.

Hieronimo's disquisition on theatrical sympathies ends with a return to a recurring term. "Here lay my hope," he tells his audience,

> and here my hope hath end;
> Here lay my heart, and here my heart was slain;

> Here lay my treasure, here my treasure lost;
> Here lay my bliss, and here my bliss bereft.
> But hope, heart, treasure, joy, and bliss,
> All fled, failed, died, yea, all decayed with this.   (4.4.89–94)

"Joy" is the one term from Hieronimo's final catalogue of nouns that does not appear in the anaphora of his previous four lines. A conspicuous outlier, it recalls instead his earlier twinning of joy with boy, gesturing towards the absent Horatio even as it emphasizes the finality of his disappearance. As such, the word enacts in miniature the passage's strategy of emphasizing absence through imagining its opposite, conjuring a pleasure to intensify its loss. In his elaborately patterned rhetoric, Hieronimo emphasizes the conversion of joy into grief that precedes the play's unsettling conversion, through revenge, of grief back to an alternate form of joy.

Hieronimo is not the only figure who finds a dark pleasure in his play's murderous success. After he tells his stricken onlookers that "my heart is satisfied" (4.4.128), his other onstage audience, Andrea's Ghost, similarly tells Revenge, "Ay, these were spectacles to please my soul" (4.5.12). "Now will I beg at lovely Proserpine," he continues,

> That by the virtue of her princely doom,
> I may consort my friends in pleasing sort,
> And on my foes work just and sharp revenge.   (4.5.13–16)

Andrea aspires to a classical heroic formula—the ability to help friends and harm enemies—rooted especially in Greek literary figures such as Homer's Achilles and Euripides' Medea.[23] Announcing that he will seek this satisfaction from Proserpine, he reminds the audience of her responsibility for the play's violence, again underscoring the female agency that lies behind Hieronimo's apparent triumph.

Indebted to female affective power and Greek tragic legends, Hieronimo's performance may be *The Spanish Tragedy*'s most influential dramatic innovation, as the first documented play within a play on the early modern commercial stage.[24] After its extraordinarily popular debut, the device became a central convention of early modern English revenge tragedy, in plays including *Hamlet* (c.1600), Thomas Middleton's *The Revenger's Tragedy* (1606), John Webster's *The Duchess of Malfi* (1614), and Philip Massinger's *The Roman Actor* (1626).[25] Offering a bridge between play and audience, the inset play invites reflection on the consequences of watching others' suffering. By depicting observers' responses to staged spectacles, moreover, it provides models for external audiences' responses, and identifies those responses as central to the drama.[26] The inset play's origins have never been explained, but the link between Hieronimo's tragedy and his earlier dumb-show recalls the prominence of the dumb-show in neoclassical plays and translations, such as *Jocasta* (1566), in which it joins and complements the Greek chorus. I propose that by presenting the responses of an onstage audience, the play within a play—like the dumb-show on which it builds— offers a version of the Greek chorus it replaces, which similarly mediates between play and audience.[27] Hieronimo's metatheatrical devices, that is, complement his turn to the Greek language and the Greek tragic Ajax, showing him revising Greek tragic conventions for sixteenth-century audiences.[28]

Just as Hieronimo's inset play adapts Greek tragic structures to explore the genre's capacity to move audiences, the broader play staged by Proserpine features the Greek tragic motifs of a mourning mother and sacrificial daughter, who mobilize the play's action with their grief and urgency. Kyd would have known these tragic icons through mediating textual and dramatic traditions: he translated Garnier's neoclassical female-centered tragedy *Cornélie* (1593–4), and Hieronimo both cites Seneca and refers to the pleasures of "Italian tragedians," while Lorenzo mentions "French tragedians" (4.1.157, 161), early responders to Greek plays.[29] Yet, as discussed in Chapter 1, Kyd also knew Greek texts directly, from studying at Merchant Taylors' School under Richard Mulcaster, who had studied with John Cheke at Cambridge.[30] Through his friendships with Thomas Watson and George Peele, moreover, Kyd would have known Watson's 1581 Latin translation of *Antigone* and Peele's earlier translation of *Iphigenia*; through his father's friendship with the printer Francis Coldock, he would also have known Heliodorus' *Aethiopica*, which Coldock published in Thomas Underdowne's English translation in 1569, 1577, and 1587, and which, as we will see in Chapter 4, imitated a Euripidean sacrificial virgin.[31] Kyd's access to Greek language and literature is well established, but we have not asked whether and how this literary background might have shaped his own plays. I suggest that *The Spanish Tragedy*'s powerful female figures, along with its use of Greek language and the Greek tragic Ajax, show Kyd's Greek training hovering behind his exploration of tragedy's moving power.

READING KYD THROUGH HECUBA: NEGOTIATING TRAGIC SYMPATHIES IN *TITUS ANDRONICUS*

Just as Proserpine, Bel-Imperia, and Isabella remake Hieronimo in their image in *The Spanish Tragedy*, the play itself spurred imitation from Kyd's contemporary playwrights. *Titus Andronicus*—Shakespeare's first tragedy, written in collaboration with George Peele—staged a conspicuous response.[32] Critics have observed the play's many echoes of *Spanish Tragedy*, yet we have not appreciated the way that *Titus* recreates Hieronimo's debts to a bereaved mother and sacrificial daughter, nor their links with Greek tragic women.[33] *Titus Andronicus*'s self-conscious classical allusions and setting have also inspired lively conversations about literary debts to Virgil, Seneca, Ovid, Herodian, and Herodotus.[34] Despite the Latin focus encouraged by the play's Roman setting, critics have also suggested affinities with Greek plays: Emrys Jones has described Titus as a male version of Euripides' Hecuba, recreating her grief, insanity, and revenge, and Penelope Meyers Usher juxtaposes the play's interest in sacrifice and supplication with *Iphigenia in Aulis*.[35] In joining these conversations, I argue that the play turns to Greek female tragic icons in order to reflect on the transmissions of sympathy at the heart of the tragic genre. The play's references to Hecuba mark the start of Shakespeare's reflections on her ability to inspire tragic grief and rage in audiences. With their specific details from Euripides' *Hecuba*, moreover, they reinforce the growing scholarly consensus that Euripidean translator George Peele contributed to the play, and suggest a likely channel from Euripides to Shakespeare.[36] While tragedy's power to shape audiences' sympathies attracts admiration in *The Spanish Tragedy*, however, in *Titus Andronicus* it raises ethical questions. I argue that the play complicates *The Spanish Tragedy*'s heroic model of revenge by challenging audiences' abilities to identify comfortably with any of the play's wronged revengers.

With his first words to the Romans, Titus indirectly conjures Hecuba's legacy by comparing his wartime losses with those of Troy: "Romans, of five-and-twenty valiant sons,/ Half the number that King Priam had,/ Behold the poor remains alive and dead!" (1.1.79–81).[37] Yet Titus quickly undermines sympathy for his bereavement by killing first the son of a supplicating queen, and then one of his own sons. "Stay, Roman brethren," Tamora interjects as Titus announces her son's sacrifice,

> Gracious conqueror,
> Victorious Titus, rue the tears I shed,
> A mother's tears in passion for her son;
> And if thy sons were ever dear to thee,
> O think my son to be as dear to me.   (1.1.104–8)

Tamora's plea emphasizes not only the moving power of a mother's tears, but also the idea of sympathetic identification based on shared parental feeling. Her appeal to resemblance recalls Hieronimo's equation of himself with Castile and Portugal, "whose loss resembles mine" (4.4.113). By underscoring parallels between themselves and their immediate audiences, Hieronimo and Tamora implicitly invoke the same parallel with their external audiences, appealing to their own experiences of loss as grounds for eliciting compassion. Yet Titus not only rejects her demands, insisting that Roman losses "ask a sacrifice . . . / To appease their groaning shadows that are gone" (1.1.124–9), but goes on to kill his own son Mutius for challenging his authority over his daughter's marriage. By sacrificing both Tamora's son and his own, Titus not only eschews the sympathetic identifications linked with tragic power, but positions himself directly as their opponent.

In the wake of Titus's sacrifices, Tamora takes on the authority of Greek tragic maternity. Paralleling Titus's comparison of himself to Priam, Demetrius turns directly to Hecuba as a symbol for his mother's hopes of revenging her son's murder. "Then, madam, stand resolved," he tells her,

> but hope withal,
> The self-same gods that armed the Queen of Troy
> With opportunity of sharp revenge
> Upon the Thracian tyrant in his tent,
> May favor Tamora, the Queen of Goths.   (1.1.135–9)

Demetrius, whose name is self-consciously Greek, turns to Greek tragic tradition to authorize his mother's violence. Aligning Tamora's regal status as Queen of Goths with Hecuba's role as Queen of Troy, he similarly links Titus with the Thracian tyrant, Polymestor, who incurs Hecuba's violent wrath by killing her son. Serving as a curse, his words are performative, both prophesying and bringing about the violent revenge that lies in wait for his mother's enemy. They are also curiously detailed; not only does Demetrius explicitly invoke the period's most prestigious icon of Greek tragedy, but he specifically refers to Euripides' play, in which Hecuba takes her revenge on Polymestor in a tent. Claiming that she has jewels to give him, she asks him to accompany her to their hiding place, where the treasure "is safe in a heap of spoils inside these tents."[38] Ovid, by contrast, does not situate Hecuba's revenge in a tent, and Seneca does not depict her revenge at all.[39] Out of a range of literary options and associations, Demetrius insists on channeling the particular conversion from grief to revenge rooted in Euripides' tragic Hecuba.

I suggest that this uncharacteristically detailed Greek allusion raises the specter of Peele, whom growing scholarly consensus has identified as the author of this scene.[40] As discussed in this book's introduction, Peele had translated one of Euripides' Iphigenia plays, probably *Iphigenia in Aulis*, which, like *Hecuba*, featured a mother's grief and rage over a child's sacrifice to the Trojan War. *Iphigenia* only appeared in print in conjunction with *Hecuba*, so Peele would certainly have known the latter play.

As previously observed, his *Iphigenia* translation earned Peele a reputation as a privileged ventriloquist for Euripides—William Gager claimed that, "If Euripides lived, he would consider himself indebted to [Peele]"—and Hecuba lingered in his imagination as he moved out of the university realm and into London's commercial literary world.[41] In his epyllion *The Tale of Troy*, printed 1589 but written earlier, Peele described Priam as "Blest in his queen," whom he praised with an emphasis on her prolific maternity:[42]

> Y-clypped Stately Hecuba was she,
> A goodly creature of such majesty
> As well became her princely personage;
> And long before she tasted fortunes rage,
> With many sonnes and daughters, wondrous thing,
> This lustie Ladie did enrich her King,
> Fruite not unlike the Tree from whence they sprong,
> The daughters lovely, modest, fair, and yong.   (183–4, ll.10–18)

Peele introduces Hecuba by emphasizing not only her beauty and regal bearing, but primarily her famed fertility, through which she reproduced her own traits in others. Her children, especially her daughters, are "Fruite not unlike the Tree from whence they sprong." This botanical metaphor resonates with both Isabella's fertile tree in *The Spanish Tragedy* and the merging of bodies with trees in *Titus*, where, as critics including Tzachi Zamir and Roya Biggie have noted, limbs are lopped, hewed, and trimmed, and Lavinia becomes a hybrid sylvan-human figure.[43] Linking Hecuba's famous fertility with the natural reproduction of plants, the metaphor also suggestively recalls Euripides' own juxtaposition of trees with maternal investments. Demanding the right to die alongside her daughter, Hecuba tells Odysseus, "I will cling to her like ivy to an oak."[44]

Shortly after introducing Hecuba in *The Tale of Troy*, Peele returns to her fertility in describing her legendary dream while pregnant with Paris:

> A dreadful Dreame, and as it did befall,
> To Priams Troy, a dreame deadly and fatall.
> For when the time of Mothers payne drewe nie,
> And now the loade that in her wombe did lie
> To move beganne to stir with proper strength,
> Readie to leave his place, behold at length
> She dreames, and gives her pheere to understand,
> That she should soone bring foorth a firy brand,
> Whose flame and fatal smoke would grow so great
> That Ilium's towers it should consume with heat.   (184–5, ll.37–46)

Hecuba's firebrand dream was one of her most conspicuous literary motifs, transmitted to early moderns in texts including Euripides' *Trojan Women*, Virgil's *Aeneid*, Apollodorus' *Library*, Ovid's *Heroides*, and Conti's *Mythologia*.[45] Shakespeare, notably, refers to it in *Troilus and Cressida* (*c.*1602), when Cassandra laments, "Our firebrand brother, Paris, burns us all," as well as indirectly in *Henry IV, Part Two* (*c.*1597), when a page conflates the story with another classical firebrand.[46] Explaining his reference to Bardolph as "you rascally Althea's dream," the page tells Hal, "Marry, my lord, Althea dreamt she was delivered of a firebrand, and therefore I call him her dream," overlaying Hecuba's doomed pregnancy with Althea's angry destruction of the firebrand that represented her son Meleager's life.[47] Peele's early and explicit interest in this emblem of Hecuba's dangerous gestation offers a suggestive backdrop both for Shakespeare's later fascination with firebrand dreams, and for Tamora, whose pregnancy with an illegitimate son similarly threatens her own security.

Paris eventually burns all of Troy, but Peele depicts Hecuba as the most profoundly affected by the firebrand she bore. Towards the end of *The Tale of Troy*, Hector's death unleashes a destructive fury in her. "The Mother Queene withouten more adoe," Peele writes, "Gins whet her wits to wreak this malice donne,/ And tragic murther of her valiant sonne" (196, ll.323–5). Emphasizing both her maternity and her regal status, he shows how Hecuba's anger leads to Achilles' death, bringing on greater losses and ultimately the end of Troy. Peele describes her as "she that erst brought forth the fatall brand/ That firde the town, the most unhappy Queene,/ Whose like for wretchedness was never seene" (200, ll.433–5). His final portrait of Hecuba features grief, rage, and insanity:

> My penne forbeare to write of Hecuba,
> That made the Sunne his glistering Chariot stay,
> And rayning teares his golden face to hide,
> For ruth of that did after her betide,
> Sith this thrice-wretched lady lived the last,
> Till Fortune's spight and mallice all was past.
> And worn with sorrows, wexen fell and mad.   (201, ll.458–64)

In *The Tale of Troy*, Peele depicts Hecuba's transformation from happiness to ruin as hinging especially on her experience of maternity. And despite her violence she earns pity and sympathy, even from the gods; the intensity of her suffering causes the flaming sun to melt his fire into tears, perhaps inspiring the player's account in *Hamlet* of Hecuba as "threat'ning the flames/ With bisson rheum" and making "milch the burning eyes of heaven."[48] Like Kyd's Isabella and his own Tamora,

Peele's Hecuba inhabits a liquid realm of tears, which she recreates in those who witness her grief.

Peele's meditations on the consequences of Hecuba's maternal suffering offer a telling prehistory for her invocation in *Titus Andronicus*. Like Hecuba, Tamora witnesses a child's sacrifice to the violence of war, after pleading unsuccessfully for that life to be spared. She also emphasizes her maternal status as a source of authority, not only rooting her pleas in a "mother's tears in passion for her son," but also describing her marriage to Saturninus in curiously parental terms, offering to be "A loving nurse, a mother to his youth" (1.1.336–7). Depicting child-sacrifice and maternal grief, and bolstered by explicit allusions to Hecuba, the play's opening scene draws on Greek tragic models that direct sympathies away from Titus.[49] Despite important insights, then, Jones's account of Titus as "a male Hecuba," moved to revenge by his grief for violated children, misses a crucial function of the play's allusions.[50] Titus eventually becomes a bereaved revenger, but he only attains this role's affective authority after learning from the female grief he witnesses. Before then, Tamora's mimetic revenge—sacrificing Titus' children as he sacrificed hers—mobilizes new sympathies, realigning the gods of tragedy whom Demetrius had enlisted in her support.

Just as Tamora's maternal suffering links her with an icon of the Greek tragic tradition, the suffering of Titus' virginal daughter Lavinia implicitly evokes the same tradition's sacrificial daughters. As a crucial vessel for the Andronici's bloodline, Lavinia begins the play as the object of argument and abduction. After agreeing to marry Saturninus in response to her father's promise, she is seized by Bassianus, to whom she was previously betrothed, sparking accusations of rape that prefigure her literal rape later in the play. Throughout the play, as Coppelia Kahn has observed, she is defined by references to her virginal womb, described as her "treasury" and implicitly paralleled with the tomb that is "sacred receptacle" of Titus' bloodline (1.1.631, 95).[51] Even after marriage, her rape is described as a deflowering (2.2.191, 2.3.26). Twinned as objects of Saturninus' courtship and representatives of the fertility needed to continue Rome's bloodlines, Lavinia and Tamora offer mirror images of each other.[52] Yet although their similarities suggest a potential alliance, supported by Tamora's initial intercession to Saturninus on Lavinia's behalf, the play quickly flouts this possibility by pitting them against each other.

Although Tamora's unsuccessful supplication opens the play, Lavinia's rape and mutilation make her the play's most spectacular symbol of suffering. Like Tamora, she is a failed supplicant. "O Tamora, thou bearest a woman's face," she pleads; "Be not obdurate, open thy deaf ears." "O Tamora," she attempts again, "be called a gentle queen"

(2.2.136, 160, 168). Emphasizing Tamora's regal status, Lavinia suggests that both her sex and high birth should signal compassion. Yet she, like her father, has treated Tamora cruelly, and Tamora points out that her failed supplication mirrors Tamora's own. "Remember, boys, I poured forth tears in vain," Tamora tells her sons, "To save your brother from the sacrifice,/ But fierce Andronicus would not relent" (2.2.163–5). The play identifies Tamora, like Hecuba, with the liquid force of tears, but when her tears fail to melt her audience into identification and support, she turns to other strategies. Like Hieronimo, she will reproduce her pain in her audience through violence. The play dramatizes both the repeated failure of deliberate sympathy and the inescapably sympathetic transmission of suffering.

While Lavinia's pleas to Tamora fail, her suffering catalyzes a more self-conscious interrogation of tragic sympathy. Witnessing Lavinia's pain prompts Titus to explore the nature of the bond that drives his response. Listing his other terrible losses, he reflects,

> But that which gives my soul the greatest spurn,
> Is dear Lavinia, dearer than my soul.
> Had I but seen thy picture in this plight,
> It would have madded me; what shall I do
> Now I behold thy lively body so? (3.1.102–6)

Confronted with Lavinia's terrible impact, Titus reflects on both the impact of viewing her "picture in this plight" and the more potent consequences of her "lively body." The picture itself would be damaging enough, but the presence of her actual body exerts a more profound gravitational pull, suggesting a model of sympathy that is physical as well as emotional, translating between the realms of body and soul.

Titus draws on this physical gravitational force in identifying his ideal audience with stones, whose paradoxical receptivity allows him, too, to melt. Tribunes will neither hear nor pity him, he explains,

> Therefore I tell my sorrows to the stones,
> Who, though they cannot answer my distress,
> Yet in some sort they are better than the tribunes,
> For that they will not intercept my tale:
> When I do weep, they humbly at my feet
> Receive my tears and seem to weep with me (3.1.36–41)

Titus, like Tamora, wants his listeners to weep with him. The tribunes repel his sorrows, but stones, incapable of resistance, paradoxically prove "soft as wax" (3.1.45). As Biggie has argued, the play imagines kinship between pointedly dissimilar elements in order to emphasize the imaginative leaps necessary to interpersonal identification and empathy.[53]

Similarly, I suggest, Titus' experience of witnessing and responding to female tears leads him to reflect on the possibility of transferring emotions between bodies. In his fantasy of softening stones to receive and share his tears, he begins to model himself after Greek tragic icons such as Hecuba, whose power lay especially in communicating her pain to audiences.

As Titus' account of weeping with wax-soft stones suggests, his inter-elemental model emphasizes the melting effect that Peele, among others, links with Hecuba. Like Isabella, he adopts an environmental vocabulary to identify with the liquidity of the sea. "When heaven doth weep," he asks Marcus,

> doth not the earth oerflow?
> If the winds rage, doth not the sea wax mad,
> Threatening the welkin with his big-swollen face?
> And wilt thou have a reason for this coil?
> I am the sea. Hark how her sighs doth blow.
> She is the weeping welkin, I the earth.
> Then must my sea be moved with her sighs,
> Then must my earth with her continual tears
> Become a deluge, overflow'd and drown'd ...   (3.1.222–30)

Titus imagines Lavinia as the moving force—cloud, sky, heavens—that melts and stirs his emotions through her sighs and tears, creating "a sympathy of woe" (3.1.149). In a recent study of the play's depiction of sympathy, Richard Meek suggests that it problematizes critical accounts of the passions as humoral forces, emphasizing instead "the extent to which pity and compassion are bound up with language, narrative and the imagination."[54] Yet Titus' strikingly material terms for experiencing sympathy—stones, sea, sky, tears—also point explicitly to the physical force emphasized in the word's early modern usage, rooted in a Greek medical model fusing physical and emotional forces. In 1574, the physician John Jones cited Galen to define "*Simpathia*" as "unity, agreements of the spirites, humors and members," and observed that "Plato also testifieth suche a *sympathia* to be betweene the body and the soule."[55] Titus' own account of Lavinia's "lively body" as "dearer than my soul" and "that which gives my soul the greatest spurn" suggests precisely this crossing between the realms of body and soul.

As the figure who sparks and symbolizes Titus' own exploration of sympathy, Lavinia becomes a tragic icon herself. "I have heard my grand-sire say full oft," young Lucius announces in response to Lavinia's frenzied behavior, "Extremity of griefs would make men mad;/ And I have read that Hecuba of Troy/ Ran mad through sorrow" (4.1.18–21). Although the youthful childless Lavinia more conspicuously evokes sacrificial Greek daughters such as Iphigenia, the immediacy and intensity of her suffering identify her also with Hecuba as icon of authoritative tragic grief. Alongside this allusion, this scene also features the play's most self-consciously intertextual moment, in which Lavinia uses the pages of Ovid's *Metamorphoses* to communicate her sufferings to her father and uncle. In his response to this revelation, Marcus wonders "O, why should nature build so foul a den,/ Unless the gods delight in tragedies?" (4.1.59–60). As Bate suggests in a note on this line, the more general association of tragedy with terrible events shades into the specific theatrical term, echoing Tamora's earlier reference to "the complot of this timeless tragedy" (2.2.265).[56] In the light of Peele's authorship of this scene, as well as the scene that previously invoked Hecuba, I argue that his experience of Euripides contributed crucially to the play's focus on female suffering, and in particular the iconic specter of Hecuba, as a symbol for the theater's ability to transmit emotions. When the play confronts question about tragedy and its effects on audiences, characters turn to the figure of Hecuba to reflect on the potent grief, madness, and violence that the genre depicts and unleashes.

While Lavinia channels Hecuba's grief especially through a parent–child bond, Tamora imitates the tragic icon by giving birth to a son who threatens to destroy the heart of the court. Describing the baby as "A joyless, dismal, black, and sorrowful issue . . . as loathsome as a toad," the Nurse explains to Aaron that "The empress sends it thee, thy stamp, thy seal,/ And bids thee christen it with thy dagger's point" (4.2.68–72). Like Paris, Tamora's son is a firebrand of sorts, destined to destroy his mother and his country. Yet whereas Hecuba refused to let Paris die, smuggling him away for dangerous preservation, Tamora is eager to destroy the evidence of her infidelity. In an unexpected contrast, it is Aaron who insists on protecting the baby. Extending the nurse's account of the baby as his stamp and seal, he describes his son in the language not of resemblance, but of shared identity. "My mistress is my mistress," he explains when accused by Demetrius of betraying Tamora, "this myself,/ The vigour and the picture of my youth./ This before all the world do I prefer" (4.2.109–11). Aaron, like Hecuba, reproduces himself in another, a child who not only represents him, but *is* him. Like Titus, he is mobilized by a threat to his child, again emphasizing the privileged transmission of sympathies between parent and child.

Protected by Aaron, Tamora's firebrand baby will live, but like Paris he will be removed from the court. Aaron formulates an exchange, a bed-trick of sorts. "Not far," he tells Demetrius and Chiron, "one Muly lives, my countryman:/ His wife but yesternight was brought to bed;/ His child is like to her, fair as you are" (4.2.154–6). Instructing them to offer the family gold, and the promise that their child will "be received for the emperor's heir" (4.2.160), he arranges to have the baby "substituted in the place of mine,/ To calm this tempest whirling in the court" (4.2.161–2). As Francesca Royster has observed, although the substitution avoids exposing Tamora, it nonetheless replicates the invasion of Rome's blood-line with an outsider—one that is not only non-Roman, but like Aaron's baby, mixed-race.[57] Being fair like his mother, the baby can pass, but his father is Aaron's "countryman"; like Aaron's son, he represents the mingling of blood across national lines. Although Aaron will not directly invade Rome's imperial genealogy with his own blood, then, he succeeds in invading it with mixed Moorish blood that resembles and represents his own genetic investments. Both Aaron's and Muly's children serve as firebrands, invading foreign households and threatening destruction.

These firebrand sons prefigure another threat from the Andronici: a military invasion led by Titus' son Lucius. In response, Tamora plots a figurative counter-invasion, through a self-conscious tragic performance. "I will enchant the old Andronicus," she assures Saturninus, "With words more sweet and yet more dangerous/ Than baits to fish or honey-stalks to sheep" (4.4.88–90). Channeling the language of poetic seduction, she vows to "smooth and fill his aged ears/ With golden promises" (4.4.95–6). Rather than woo in her own person, Tamora presents herself as a staged allegory. "Thus, in this strange and sad habiliment," she tells her sons,

> I will encounter with Andronicus
> And say I am Revenge, sent from below
> To join with him and right his heinous wrongs.
> Knock at his study, where they say he keeps
> To ruminate strange plots of dire revenge;
> Tell him Revenge is come to join with him
> And work confusion on his enemies.   (5.2.1–8)

By staging herself as the figure of Revenge, Tamora imitates the metathea-trical frame of *The Spanish Tragedy*, in which Revenge leads Andrea to watch his murderer's punishment. Yet unlike Kyd's Revenge, Tamora miscalculates. Overconfident in her performance, she assumes that Titus will accept her story. After her performance, she believes that in his "lunacy" and "brainsick humours," Titus "firmly takes [her] for Revenge" (5.2.70, 71, 73). Yet Tamora has already succeeded at remaking Titus in her own image; he has acquired not only her grief and ferocity, but also her resourceful wiliness. Ultimately, she proves audience rather than performer, victim rather than victor.

Trained by Tamora, Titus carries out his own revenge in a theatrical plot. His grotesque plan—chopping Tamora's remaining sons and serving them to her in a pie–suggests Greek tragic scenes of dismemberment such as that of Euripides' *Bacchae*, transmitted especially through Ovid's Procne and Seneca's *Thyestes*. In announcing "I'll play the cook" (5.2.204), moreover, he emphasizes the scene's theatrical overtones.[58] Although the scene is attributed to Shakespeare, it also recalls the "bloudie banket" of "*Dead mens heads in dishes*" in Peele's *Battle of Alcazar* (c.1588–91), when a Moor named Muly attempts to usurp the throne of another Moor by the same name.[59] The echoes of dismemberment, invasion, Moors, Muly, and revenge suggest lines of influence between the plays, supporting arguments that *Titus* represents a genuine collaboration between Shakespeare and Peele, rather than a fitting together of scenes written separately.[60] Closing his performance by stabbing Lavinia, and then killing Tamora, Titus dies by Saturninus' sword, but, like Hieronimo, he dies satisfied that he has achieved his revenge.

The play's self-consciously theatrical ending echoes *The Spanish Tragedy* in reflecting not only on grief, violence, and revenge, but also on the genre of tragedy. Both plays offer startlingly literal enactments of tragic motifs, rooted in the dead bodies of bold young women who spur the revenge plots. Tracing the play's metatheatrical reflections on the genre, Tzachi Zamir describes *Titus* as "a tragedy about tragedy."[61] After Bassianus' death, Tamora presents her forged letter as a "fatal writ,/ The complot of this timeless tragedy" (2.2.264–5), underscoring the painful subject and the dark plotting it represents, as well as implicitly suggesting the genre's time-traveling nature.[62] Titus similarly turns to the vocabulary of tragedy on observing Lavinia's reading "the tragic tale of Philomel" (4.1.47), implicitly linking Ovid's prose with the theatrical frame it evokes, and Marcus wonders, at the site of Lavinia's violent rape, "O, why should nature build so foul a den,/ Unless the gods delight in tragedies?" (4.1.59–60). I argue that the play's invocations of Hecuba, and its pairing of a bereaved mother with a sacrificial daughter, serve a crucial function in its metadramatic vocabulary. Like *The Spanish Tragedy*, *Titus* identifies tragedy with the transmission of sympathies between bodies, and channels Greek tragic icons to identify these circuits of transmission with suffering women, whose distinctive access to grief gives them a privileged ability to instill their emotions in others.

Both *Titus Andronicus* and *The Spanish Tragedy* reflect on the new tragic genre by featuring performances through which characters transmit their grief to listeners, remaking audiences into versions of themselves. Both plays, similarly, link bereaved mothers and sacrificial daughters with Greek tragic female icons, giving them a privileged authority for transferring sympathies. Beginning with Proserpine, whose pity for Andrea moves her to stage a play, *The Spanish Tragedy* depicts a chain of passionate performances, through which Bel-Imperia and Isabella shape Hieronimo into a theatrically sophisticated Greek-speaking revenger. Identifying both a supplicating queen and a ravaged daughter with Hecuba's vindictive grief, *Titus Andronicus* similarly shows these figures shaping their audiences, especially Titus, into versions of their destructive power. Both plays, that is, reflect on tragedy's nature and consequences by turning to Greek tragic women and exploring their powerful solicitation of audience sympathies. Layering Roman literary models on Greek ghosts to form new English originals, the plays' palimpsests reveal crucial debts to unfamiliar origins.

NOTES

1. Shakespeare's tragedies include only two exceptions to this pattern, both in plays that share extensive overlap with romantic comedy: *Romeo and Juliet* and *Antony and Cleopatra*. The lower modern visibility of important female-centered tragedies, such as Webster's *The White Devil* (1612) and *The Duchess of Malfi* (1614), and Marston's *The Insatiate Countess* (c.1610), responds to Shakespeare's centrality in processes of canonization, but it is also the case that titles of early modern tragedies feature male names considerably more frequently than female names.
2. Ben Jonson, *Bartholomew Fair*, ed. John Creaser, in *The Cambridge Edition of the Works of Ben Jonson*, ed. David Bevington, Martin Butler, and Ian Donaldson, vol. 4: *1611–1616* (Cambridge: Cambridge University Press, 2012), 271–428, Induction, 95–8.
3. On Senecan backdrops, see Jessica Winston, "Early 'English Seneca': From 'Coterie' Translations to the Popular Stage," in *Brill's Companion to the Reception of Senecan Tragedy*, ed. Eric Dodson-Robinson (Leiden: Brill, 2016), 174–202; Scott McMillin, "The Book of Seneca in *The Spanish Tragedy*," *Studies in English Literature, 1500–1900* 14:2 (1974), 201–8; Gordon Braden, *Renaissance Tragedy and the Senecan Tradition* (New Haven, CT: Yale University Press, 1985); Robert Miola, *Shakespeare and Classical Tragedy: The Influence of Seneca* (Oxford: Clarendon Press, 1992), 18–31; and E.D. Hill, "Senecan and Vergilian perspectives in *The Spanish Tragedy*," *English Literary Renaissance* 15 (1985), 143–65. On Ovid, see Heather James, *Shakespeare's Troy* (Cambridge: Cambridge University Press, 1997), 42–84; Jonathan Bate, *Shakespeare and Ovid* (Oxford: Clarendon Press, 1994); Cora Fox, "Grief and Ovidian Politics of Revenge in *Titus Andronicus*," in *Ovid and the Politics of Emotion in Elizabethan England* (Basingstoke: Palgrave Macmillan, 2009), 105–24.
4. On the play's impact, see Lukas Erne, *Beyond The Spanish Tragedy: A Study of the Works of Thomas Kyd* (Manchester: Manchester University Press, 2001); Clara Calvo, "Thomas Kyd and the Elizabethan Blockbuster: *The Spanish Tragedy*," in *The Cambridge Companion to Shakespeare and Contemporary*

Dramatists, ed. Ton Hoenselaars (Cambridge: Cambridge University Press, 2014), 19–33; *The Works of Thomas Kyd*, ed. Frederick S. Boas (Oxford: Clarendon Press, 1901, repr. 1962); Rebekah Owens, "Parody and *The Spanish Tragedy*," *Cahiers Élisabéthains* 71 (2007), 27–36; and Emma Smith, "Hieronimo's Afterlives," in *The Spanish Tragedie with the First Part of Jeronimo*, ed. Emma Smith (London: Penguin, 1998), 133–59. On plays exploring revenge before Kyd, see Bradley J. Irish, "Vengeance, variously: revenge before Kyd in early Elizabethan Drama," *Early Theatre* 12:2 (2009), 117–34.

5. See Clara Calvo and Jesús Tronch, "Introduction," *The Spanish Tragedy*, ed. Calvo and Tronch, Arden Early Modern Drama (London: Bloomsbury, 2013), 1–112, 20. All citations to the play are to this edition.

6. In *Cynthia's Revels*, Child #2 mocks a hypothetical audience member who "swears down all that sit about him, 'that the old *Hieronimo*', as it was first acted, 'was the only, best, and judiciously penned play of Europe.'" See Ben Jonson, *Cynthia's Revels*, ed. Eric Rasmussen and Matthew Steggle, in *The Cambridge Edition of the Works of Ben Jonson*, ed. David Bevington, Martin Butler, and Ian Donaldson (Cambridge: Cambridge University Press, 2012), vol. 1, 429–548, Praeludium, 165–7. Philip Henslowe refers in his diary several times to payments made for "additions to Hieronimo"; see *Henslowe's Diary*, ed. R. A. Foakes and R. T. Rickert (Cambridge: Cambridge University Press, 1961), 182, 203. For more on focus of parodies and imitations, see Owens, "Parody," 29–31, and Smith, "Hieronimo's Afterlives."

7. See Pamela Allen Brown, "Anatomy of an Actress: Bel-imperia as Tragic Diva," *Shakespeare Bulletin* 33:1 (2015), 49–65. Because Renaissance reception of Greek began in Italy, I suggest that Italian interest in female roles also responds to early interest in Greek plays.

8. References to Persephone appear frequently in the particular Greek plays popular in this period; see Euripides' *Hecuba*, 137; *Alcestis*, 746; *Orestes*, 963; Sophocles' *Antigone*, 894; and *Electra*, 110. On the myth of Persephone, and her Latin translation Proserpine, behind Euripides' redeemed tragic women, see Helene P. Foley, "*Anodos* Dramas: Euripides' *Alcestis* and *Helen*," in *Innovations of Antiquity*, ed. Ralph Hexter and Daniel Selden (London: Routledge, 1992), 133–60 (also Foley, *Female Acts in Greek Tragedy* [Princeton: Princeton University Press, 2001], 301–32), and J. P. Guépin, *The Tragic Paradox: Myth and Ritual in Greek Tragedy* (Amsterdam: Adolf M. Hakkert, 1968).

9. On the significance of the play's metatheatrical frame, see Gregory M. Colón Semenza, "*The Spanish Tragedy* and Metatheatre," in *The Cambridge Companion to English Renaissance Tragedy*, eds. Emma Smith and Garrett Sullivan (Cambridge: Cambridge University Press, 2010), 153–62, and Barry Adams, "The Audiences of *The Spanish Tragedy*," *Journal of English and Germanic Philology* 68 (1969), 221–36.

10. Ben Jonson, *Poetaster*, ed. Gabriele Bernhard Jackson, in *The Cambridge Edition of the Works of Ben Jonson*, ed. David Bevington, Martin Butler,

and Ian Donaldson, vol. 2: *1601–1606* (Cambridge: Cambridge University Press, 2012), 1–181, 3.4.195–9.

11. See Owens, "Parody," and Smith, "Hieronimo's Afterlives."

12. I count Isabella's scenes from the original version of the play, not the later additions.

13. In some editions, these lines are numbered 104–109 because of interceding lines added to the play at a later date. See Calvo and Tronch, 178, n.45.

14. On printing in red ink as signaling urgency, authenticity, and bodily interiority, see Bianca Calabresi, "'Red Incke': Reading the Bleeding on the Early Modern Page," in *Printing and Parenting in Early Modern England*, ed. Douglas A. Brooks (Aldershot: Ashgate, 2005), 237–64.

15. On handkerchiefs' paradoxical associations with both cleanliness and intimate bodily fluids, see especially Bella Mirabella, "'Embellishing Herself with a Cloth': The Contradictory Life of the Handkerchief" in *Ornamentalism: The Art of Renaissance Accessories*, ed. Bella Mirabella (Ann Arbor: University of Michigan Press, 2011), 59–82.

16. See Tanya Pollard, "A Kind of Wild Medicine: Revenge as Remedy in Early Modern England," *Revista Canaria de Estudios Ingleses* 50 (2005), 57–69.

17. On the significance of the play's pervasively ecological language for grief, see Roya Biggie, "Ecologies of the Passions in Early Modern English Tragedies," Ph.D. thesis, CUNY Graduate Center, 2016.

18. Tzachi Zamir, "Wooden Subjects," *New Literary History* 39:2 (2008), 277–300, 282–4.

19. On the play's additions, see Calvo and Tronch, 319–28, and Vin Nardizzi, "'No Wood, No Kingdom': Planting Genealogy, Felling Trees, and the Additions to *The Spanish Tragedy*," *Modern Philology* 110:2 (2012), 202–25.

20. Nardizzi describes Isabella's attack as "misguided in its aims and superfluous to the play's plot; at best, it is a 'symbolic prologue' to Hieronimo's more elaborate and direct method for retribution"; Nardizzi, "No Wood, No Kingdom," 219.

21. Giovan Battista Giraldi Cinthio, *Discourse or Letter on the Composition of Comedies and Tragedies*," trans. Daniel Javitch, *Renaissance Drama* 39 (2011), 207–55, 242. Giraldi's Italian reads, "Polissena . . . andasse animosamente alla morte . . . E fu cosa degna del real animo di Polissena giudicar men male il morire, che star sempre uituperosamente col collo sopposto al seruil giogo"; see *Discorsi di M. Giovambattista Giraldi Cinthio* (Ferrarra, 1554), 262.

22. See Sarah Knight, "'Goodlie anticke apparrell?': Sophocles' *Ajax* at Early Modern Oxford and Cambridge," *Shakespeare Studies* 38 (2009), 25–42.

23. See B. M. W. Knox, "The *Medea* of Euripides," *Yale Classical Studies* 25 (1977), 197–202, and Mary Whitlock Blundell, *Helping Friends and Harming Enemies* (Cambridge: Cambridge University Press, 1991).

24. Henry Medwall's *Fulgens and Lucres* (1497) is earlier, but its inset play is not part of an external play—rather, it *is* the play, and the external play is merely a frame. On Kyd's metatheatrical innovation, see Anne Barton, *Shakespeare and the Idea of the Play* (London: Chatto and Windus, 1962), 77–81.

25. Jonathan Bate has argued, "theatrical self-referentiality is the very essence, not some contingent feature, of the genre of English Renaissance revenge drama"; see Jonathan Bate, "The Performance of Revenge: *Titus Andronicus* and *The Spanish Tragedy*," in *The Show Within: Dramatic and Other Insets: English Renaissance Drama (1550–1642)*, ed. Francois Laroque (Montpellier: Paul-Valery University Press, 1990), 267–83, 268.

26. On the importance attributed to audiences in early modern plays, see Allison Hobgood, *Passionate Playgoing in Early Modern England* (Cambridge: Cambridge University Press, 2014).

27. See Jean-Pierre Vernant and Pierre Vidal-Naquet, *Myth and Tragedy in Ancient Greece*, trans. Janet Lloyd (New York: Zone Books, 1990), esp. 23–4; also Odonne Longo, "The Theater of *Polis*," in *Nothing to Do with Dionysos?: Athenian Drama in Its Social Context*, eds. John Winkler and Froma Zeitlin (Princeton: Princeton University Press, 1990), 12–19, 17.

28. Bate links Revenge and Andrea's Ghost with Seneca's uses of chorus and ghosts, but I note that both devices originate in Greek tragedies; see Bate, "The Performance of Revenge," 269.

29. Although *Cornelia* was published later than *The Spanish Tragedy*'s probable date, Erne argues that Andrea's account of the underworld is indebted to a related passage in Garnier's *Cornélie*, and accordingly that Kyd knew the play earlier; see *Beyond The Spanish Tragedy*, 53–5.

30. James Whitelocke, who began studies at Merchant Taylors' at some point in the mid-1570s and stayed until 1588, wrote that "I was brought up at School under mr. Mulcaster, in the famous school of the Merchantaylors in London, whear I continued untill I was well instructed in the Hebrew, Greek, and Latin tongs"; see John Bruce, *Liber Famelicus of Sir James Whitelocke* (Camden Society, vol. 70), 12.

31. See Arthur Freeman, *Thomas Kyd: Facts and Problems* (Oxford: Clarendon Press, 1967), 5. Kyd found the story of Soliman and Perseda in Henry Wotton's *Courtlie Controuersie of Cupids Cautels*, published by Coldock.

32. Although Shakespeare's earlier history plays overlap with tragedy in titles and style, the genres have been distinguished beginning in Shakespeare's First Folio. On *Titus*'s date, and status as "Shakespeare's earliest and bloodiest tragedy," see Jonathan Bate, "Introduction," *Titus Andronicus*, Arden Shakespeare (London: Routledge, 1995, rprt. 2005), 1–121, 1.

33. See Bate, "The Performance of Revenge"; Roslyn Lander Donald, "Formulas and Their Imitations: *The Spanish Tragedy* and *Titus Andronicus*," *Publications of the Arkansas Philological Association* 4.2 (1978), 13–18; and Zamir, "Wooden Subjects."

34. Important readings of the play's debts to Latin literature include James, *Shakespeare's Troy*, 42–84; Bate, *Shakespeare and Ovid*; Fox, "Grief and Ovidian Politics of Revenge in *Titus Andronicus*"; Miola, "*Titus Andronicus* and the Mythos of Shakespeare's Rome," *Shakespeare Studies* 14 (1981), 85–98; Pramit Chaudhuri, "Classical Quotation In *Titus Andronicus*," *ELH* 81:3 (2014), 787–810; and Naomi Conn Liebler, "Getting it all Right: *Titus*

Andronicus and Roman History," *Shakespeare Quarterly* 45:3 (1994), 263–78. On the influence of Herodotus, see Jane Grogan, "'Headless Rome' and Hungry Goths: Herodotus and *Titus Andronicus*," *English Literary Renaissance* (2013), 30–61.

35. See Emrys Jones, *The Origins of Shakespeare* (Oxford: Clarendon Press, 1977), 85–107; Penelope Meyers Usher, "Greek Sacrifice in Shakespeare's Rome: *Titus Andronicus* and *Iphigenia in Aulis*," in *Rethinking Shakespeare Source Study: Audiences, Authors, and Digital Technologies*, ed. Dennis Britton and Melissa Walter (Abingdon: Routledge, forthcoming); I am grateful to Meyers Usher for sharing this essay with me prior to publication.

36. On the play's collaborative authorship, see Brian Vickers, *Shakespeare, Co-Author: A Historical Study of Five Collaborative Plays* (Oxford: Oxford University Press, 2002) and Macdonald P. Jackson, "Stage Directions and Speech Headings in Act 1 of *Titus Andronicus* Q (1594): Shakespeare or Peele?" *Studies in Bibliography* 49 (1996), 134–48. For a reading based on this scholarship, see Brian Boyd, "Mutius: An Obstacle Removed in Titus Andronicus," *The Review of English Studies* 55:219 (2004), 196–209. Robert Miola suggests that *Titus* is indebted to Seneca's *Troades*, which both imitates Euripides and features Hecuba as protagonist; his account of child-killing children in Renaissance neoclassical drama as a Senecan legacy implicitly offers another model for the transmission of Euripides' plays to early modern readers. See Miola, *Shakespeare and Classical Tragedy*, 18–31.

37. All citations from *Titus Andronicus* are to Jonathan Bate's Arden edition, cited in note 32.

38. "σκύλων ἐν ὄχλῳ ταῖσδε σῴζεται στέγαις"; Euripides, *Hecuba*, 1014. Erasmus translates closely, "Spoliorum acervo his delitent tentoriis"; Erasmus, *HECUBA, & Iphigenia in Aulide Euripidis tragoediae in Latinum tralatae Erasmo* (Venice: Aldus, 1507), Eiir.

39. See J. A. K. Thomson, *Shakespeare and the Classics* (London: George Allen & Unwin, 1952), 57–8.

40. Most scholars now attribute Act 1, 2.1, 2.2, and 4.1 to Peele. On the linguistic patterns behind this attribution—such as Peele's propensity for the word "brethren," in contrast to Shakespeare's characteristic use of the plural "brothers"—see Jackson, "Stage Directions and Speech Headings," and Vickers, *Shakespeare, Co-Author*.

41. See William Gager, "In Iphigenia[m] Georgij Peeli Anglicanis Versibus Reddita[m]," in *The Life and Minor Works of George Peele*, ed. David H. Horne (New Haven, CT: Yale University Press, 1952), vol. 1, 43.

42. All citations to *The Tale of Troy* are from *Life and Minor Works*, 183–202. In his 1589 edition, Peele referred to it as "an olde Poeme of myne owne" (A2); Horne suggests that Peele probably wrote it around 1581, when he left Oxford (*Life and Minor Works*, 149).

43. See Zamir, "Wooden Subjects," and Biggie, "Ecologies of the Passions in Early Modern English Tragedies."

44. "ὁποῖα κισσὸς δρυός, ὅπως τῇσδ᾽ ἕξομαι"; Euripides, *Hecuba*, 398. Erasmus translates, "Ut hedera quercu: sic ego huic inhesero"; *Hecuba*, Ciiir.

45. See Pollard, "Hecuba," in *A Dictionary of Shakespeare's Classical Mythology*, ed. Yves Peyré (2009–), http://www.shakmyth.org/myth/107/hecuba/analysis.

46. Shakespeare, *Troilus and Cressida*, ed. David Bevington, Arden Shakespeare (London: Bloomsbury, 1998), 2.2.110.

47. Shakespeare, *Henry IV, Part 2*, ed. James Bulman, Arden Shakespeare (London: Bloomsbury, 2016), 2.2.85–9; see note, pp. 236–7. On Althea, see Hyginus, *Fabulae*, 171.

48. Shakespeare, *Hamlet*, ed. Ann Thompson and Neil Taylor, Arden Shakespeare (London: Thompson Learning, 2006), 2.2.443–4, 455.

49. Sarah Carter argues that by making Tamora an anti-hero, Shakespeare critiques women's place in tragedy; see Carter, "*Titus Andronicus* and Myths of Maternal Revenge," *Cahiers Élisabéthains* 77 (2010), 37–49. Douglas E. Green, on the other hand, argues for the central significance of both Tamora and Lavinia, claiming, "It is largely through and on the female characters that Titus is constructed and his tragedy inscribed." See Green, "Interpreting 'Her Martyr'd Signs': Gender and Tragedy in *Titus Andronicus*," *Shakespeare Quarterly* 40:3 (1989), 317–26, 319.

50. Jones, *Origins of Shakespeare*, 101.

51. See Coppelia Kahn, *Roman Shakespeare: Warriors, Wounds, and Women* (London: Routledge, 1997), 46–76.

52. In the context of different classical literary models, Heather James has observed, "the bodies of Tamora and Lavinia are twinned and understood as sites of physical mayhem and literary contamination." See James, *Shakespeare's Troy*, 48.

53. See Biggie, "Ecologies of the Passions"; on the period's interpersonal and material models of selfhood, see Nancy Selleck, *The Interpersonal Idiom in Shakespeare, Donne and Early Modern Culture* (New York: Palgrave Macmillan, 2008).

54. Meek, "'O, what a sympathy of woe is this': Passionate Sympathy in *Titus Andronicus*," *Shakespeare Survey* 66 (2013), 287–97, 291. On emerging notions of sympathy in this period, in conjunction with classical female models, see Heather James, "Dido's Ear," *Shakespeare Quarterly* 52:3 (2001), 360–82; on early modern notions of sympathy as a material attraction between both animate and inanimate bodies, see Mary Floyd-Wilson, *Occult Knowledge, Science, and Gender on the Shakespearean Stage* (Cambridge: Cambridge University Press, 2013).

55. John Jones, *A briefe, excellent, and profitable discourse, of the naturall beginning of all growing and liuing things* (London: William Iones, 1574), 29; Jones, *The arte and science of preseruing bodie and soule* (London: Henrie Bynneman, 1579), aivv.

56. Bate, ed. *Titus*, 214.

57. See Francesca Royster, "White-limed walls: Whiteness and Gothic Extremism in Shakespeare's *Titus Andronicus*," *Shakespeare Quarterly* 51:4 (2000),

432–55. Royster writes, "the danger of invasion is displaced onto the danger of infiltration by foreign peoples. The barbarians are not at the gate but inside the gate...The mixed race of the child they produce compromises Roman racial purity, and he is not the only mixed-race baby in town" (450).

58. Bate suggests that his banquet is sufficiently stylized and theatrical to become a play in itself; see "The Performance of Revenge," 272.

59. Peele, *Battle of Alcazar,* ed. John Yoklavich, in *The Dramatic Works of George Peele* (New Haven, CT: Yale University Press, 1961), 4, 983 and S.D. 984.

60. Vickers examines links between scenes by Shakespeare and Peele to support the claim that "both dramatists had shared the planning of the whole play" (*Shakespeare as Co-Author*, 161).

61. Zamir, "Wooden Subjects," 281.

62. Zamir suggests that this metatheatrical comment "draws the audience's attention not merely to the very genre it is witnessing, but also foregrounds the unsavory modes of pleasure that are mobilized at that very moment; Zamir, "Wooden Subjects," 278–9.

3

What's Hecuba to Him?

In Shakespeare's first tragedy, grief and rage prompt thoughts of Hecuba, the period's most prominent representative of the Greek tragic tradition. As we have seen in Chapter 2, allusions to Hecuba in *Titus Andronicus* cite details that only appear in Euripides' play, and occur in scenes widely attributed to Euripidean translator George Peele, suggesting direct Greek tragic influence.[1] These same allusions and associations haunt Shakespeare's return to the genre with *Hamlet* (*c.*1600), a play that has come to epitomize tragedy for modern readers and audiences. When Hamlet reflects on the charged power of the tragic theater, he too turns to Hecuba: "What's Hecuba to him, or he to Hecuba,/ That he should weep for her?" (2.2.494–5).[2] Hecuba offers a privileged symbol for a genre defined especially by its power to move audiences' emotions.

Of all Shakespeare's characters, Hamlet is the most self-consciously preoccupied with the theater: he makes pronouncements on the purpose of playing, interrogates the effects of a player's performance, and stages a version of his own story in order to reveal his uncle's guilt. Yet despite the play's extended reflections on the nature of tragedy, critics have paid little attention to Hamlet's fascination with the protagonist of the period's most popular Greek tragedy. A number of scholars have situated Hamlet's metatheatrical reflections in the context of Shakespeare's competition with contemporary playwrights, as a response to the Ur-*Hamlet* typically attributed to Kyd (*c.*1588–9), *The Spanish Tragedy*, and the "little eyases" of the boys' companies, which offered new catalysts for reconceiving tragedy's shape and function.[3] Scholars attentive to the play's classical echoes have proposed that *Hamlet* invokes the shadow of Orestes, another melancholy avenger haunted by loyalty to a murdered father and ambivalence towards an unfaithful mother.[4] Yet it is significant that Shakespeare turns Hamlet's attention to a female tragic protagonist. Examining the play in the context of contemporary responses to Greek tragic women illuminates the implications of his confrontation with a specific kind of dramatic authority. In staging Hamlet's imagined encounter with Hecuba, Shakespeare reflects on his own negotiations with a genre identified especially with the affective impact of female lament.

WHAT'S HECUBA TO HAMLET?

Unlike *The Spanish Tragedy* and *Titus Andronicus*, which both depict powerful female revengers alongside their male counterparts, *Hamlet* is monopolized by its male protagonist. In his sheer quantity of speech, Hamlet dominates his play more thoroughly than any other Shakespeare character.[5] The play further challenges the popular Greek tragic conventions imitated by previous English plays in shifting its emotional center from a bereaved parent to a mourning son. Yet the play underlines the strangeness of these choices by highlighting the earlier tradition with which they break. When Hamlet meets the players, he asks them for "a passionate speech," and quickly identifies the quintessential classical tragic material of the Trojan War: "Aeneas' talk to Dido, and thereabout of it especially where he speaks of Priam's slaughter" (2.2.369–70, 384–5).[6] Although Hamlet refers to Priam, and implicitly evokes Virgil, he soon hurries the player towards the speech's true center: "Say on; come to Hecuba." As his eagerness suggests, the scene finds its climactic force in Hecuba's passions:

> But who—ah, woe—had seen the mobled queen—...
> —Run barefoot up and down, threatening the flames
> With bisson rheum, a clout upon that head
> Where late the diadem stood and, for a robe,
> About her lank and all-o'erteemed loins,
> A blanket, in the alarm of fear caught up.
> Who this had seen, with tongue in venom steeped,
> 'Gainst Fortune's state would treason have pronounced.
> But if the gods themselves did see her then...
> The instant burst of clamour that she made
> (Unless things mortal move them not at all)
> Would have made milch the burning eyes of heaven
> And passion in the gods.   (2.2.439–56)

Hecuba's wretched state—bereaved, barefoot, and clothed only in rags—suggests powerlessness, but paradoxically intensifies her affective power. Threatening Troy's flames with her "bisson rheum," she both embodies tears and incites them in others, making "milch the burning eyes of heaven." As these examples suggest, the passage's insistently Anglo-Saxon vocabulary implicitly translates Hecuba's foreign and classical origins to an intimate, local setting, just as "milch" and "o'erteemed loins" emphasize her maternity. In evoking her, the player brings classical tragedy to Elsinore, England, and the domestic sphere, with a promise of powerful consequences for audiences. Other moments in the play, such as the ghost's account of how his terrible story would affect "ears of flesh and blood" (1.5.22), also dramatize the affective and physiological consequences of tragic performances on their audiences, evoking the period's discussions about the effects of tragic pathos on audiences.[7] Yet while the ghost warns that his tragedy will freeze and stiffen its audiences, Hecuba's tragedy promises the opposite effect: it will melt, liquefy, even douse flames. The performance of female grief, the player suggests, offers a distinctive model of tragic impact, one that shadows, complements, and competes with that produced by men.

Beyond Hecuba's reported effects on her mortal and immortal audiences, her most obvious immediate impact is on the player, whose passionate performance Polonius breaks off in concern: "Look where he has not turned his colour and has tears in's eyes.—Prithee no more!" (2.2.457–8). Yet her deeper impact is on Hamlet himself. Disconcerted by the player's tears and broken voice, Hamlet famously condemns his display of grief as "monstrous":

> and all for nothing–
> For Hecuba?
> What's Hecuba to him, or he to Hecuba,
> That he should weep for her?   (2.2.486, 492–5)

Although it is the player whose reaction Hamlet attacks, it is Hecuba who occupies his thoughts. He tries to reduce her to "nothing," but she proves a substantial presence. He harps insistently on her name, three times in two lines, echoing it with surrounding alliteration of sighing "h" sounds as he puzzles over her apparently inexplicable effect on a man lacking any direct ties to her. Hecuba is a distant figure, who has neither appeared nor even been given a direct voice. Nonetheless, the mere evocation of her suffering is enough to produce tears in audiences both within and beyond the player's speech.

The moving power of Hecuba's laments directly highlights Hamlet's sense of his own failings. "Yet I," he complains, "A dull and muddy-mettled rascal, peak/ Like John-a-dreams, unpregnant of my cause,/ And can say nothing" (2.2.501–4). Technically he compares himself with the player, but Hamlet's curious indictment of himself as "unpregnant" suggests that it is Hecuba herself against whom he fails to measure up. Although editors and critics have taken pains to distance the word from its maternal connotations, its literal sense was known and used in Shakespeare's time.[8] More compellingly, its appearance here resonates with later passages linking Hamlet with pregnancy: Claudius meditates on "the hatch and the disclose" of "something in his soul/ O'er which his melancholy sits on brood" (3.1.163–5), and he is later imagined (by Claudius in F, and

Gertrude in Q2) as "the female dove/ When that her golden couplets are disclosed" (5.1.275–6). The play's insistent interest in Hamlet's potential maternity highlights the player's identification of Hecuba with milk and teeming loins: described by Euripides as a mother fifty times over, she was also a strikingly fertile literary figure, widely cited and imitated.[9] Although her grief most conspicuously indicts Gertrude, the play's other widowed mother, for her failure to mourn, at a deeper level it calls attention to Hamlet's unlikely status as tragic protagonist. Hamlet, in contrast with Hecuba, is incapable of fertility: male rather than female, child rather than parent, belated literary imitator rather than origin.[10] These recurring allusions to female fertility, combined with Hamlet's powerful response to the player's depiction of Hecuba, suggest that there is more than one ghostly parent haunting this play.

WHAT'S HECUBA TO SHAKESPEARE?

As we have seen, the exceptional popularity of Euripides' *Hecuba*, and the wealth of allusions to Hecuba in early modern writings, made her an icon for the re-emerging tragic genre. Shakespeare's insistent interest in Hecuba shows his awareness both of her prominence and of her particular associations. He invokes her considerably more frequently than comparable figures from myth: fifteen times by name as well as once by status, as "the queen of Troy."[11] Tracing these references suggests that Shakespeare forcefully revised Hecuba's prevailing literary legacy, remaking her specifically in Euripides' powerful and darkly triumphant image. In antiquity and beyond, most writers identified Hecuba especially with her Homeric legacy of sorrow.[12] The magnitude of her losses—her husband, her many children, and Troy itself—made her a symbol of grief, and of Fortune's precariousness. For the most part, accordingly, literary depictions of Hecuba emphasized her suffering, grief, and futile supplication of both gods and Greeks. They also showcased the vulnerability intrinsic in her maternity, especially through references to pregnancy: as observed in Chapter 2, her famous dream of delivering a firebrand, while pregnant with Paris, features in multiple texts, including Euripides' *Trojan Women*, Virgil's *Aeneid*, Apollodorus' *Library*, Ovid's *Heroides*, and Conti's *Mythologia*, all of which circulated in the early modern period.[13]

In the context of Hecuba's widespread association with mourning, it is striking that when she appears in *Titus Andronicus* (*c.*1592), she serves as a symbol not only of grief, but also of armed vengeance, identified with both justice and satisfaction. As discussed in Chapter 2, Demetrius invokes her when his mother Tamora agonizes over the murder of her son, calling upon

"The self-same gods that armed the Queen of Troy/ With opportunity of sharp revenge/ Upon the Thracian tyrant in his tent" (1.1.136–8).[14] Tamora's terrible loss prompts the revenge that sets the play's plot into motion, but the resulting violence ultimately turns audiences against her by inviting sympathetic identification with a new Hecuba figure, Titus' daughter Lavinia, whose brutal punishment Tamora directs. Young Lucius' comparison of Lavinia with "Hecuba of Troy," who "Ran mad through sorrow" (4.1.20–1), implicitly predicts Lavinia's imminent imitation of Hecuba by exacting revenge. These passages, written by George Peele, reflect not only his study of Greek and his 1570s translation of Euripides' *Iphigenia*, but also his depiction of Hecuba's revenge in his epyllion *The Tale of Troy* (*c*.1581).[15] Shakespeare's subsequent depictions of Hecuba share these figures' conversion of passive sorrow into active rage and violence, suggesting that his early collaboration with Peele left a Euripidean imprint on his tragic imagination.

Shakespeare returns to Hecuba independently in *The Rape of Lucrece* (1594), where Lucrece's ekphrastic meditation on "despairing Hecuba" enables her to see herself as a classical tragic heroine, one who "shapes her sorrow to the beldame's woes" and transforms it into a plan for taking action against her wrongdoer (1447, 1458). Reflecting on Hecuba's woes rouses her to imagine responding violently: she promises her imaginary interlocutor that she will "with my knife scratch out the angry eyes/ Of all the Greeks that are thine enemies" (1469–70). As in *Titus*, the figure serves as a pivot between generic directions, converting Lucrece from the passive genre of complaint towards an actively heroic role. As discussed in Chapter 2, Hecuba makes a more oblique appearance in *Henry the Fourth Part Two* (1597–8), when Falstaff's page claims "Althea dreamt she was delivered of a firebrand, and therefore I call him her dream," implicitly invoking Hecuba's dream through a misidentified allusion to another tragic Greek mother.[16] Her place in the play's pantheon of mythic allusions again highlights generic multiplicity, juxtaposing the history play's dreams of epic grandeur and tragic decline with undertones of domestic comedy.

Shortly after her invocation in *Hamlet*, Hecuba emerges as an actual dramatic character in *Troilus and Cressida* (*c*.1602). Although she does not appear directly on the stage, other characters discuss her, in contexts that identify her with emotional intensity. Describing Helen finding a white hair on Troilus' chin, Pandarus tells Cressida, "But there was such laughing! Queen Hecuba laughed that her eyes ran o'er" (1.2.137–8). Imagining responses to his own death, however, Troilus later prophetically pictures, "Priamus and Hecuba on knees,/ Their eyes o'ergalled with recourse of tears" (5.3.54–5), and Cassandra predicts Hector's terrible death with descriptions of "how Hecuba cries out" (5.3.86). These lines emphasize Hecuba's association with tears as signs of emotional excess, whether of laughter or distress; her insides cannot contain her passions, which spill out from her body in liquid form.[17] Marked by the generic instability of its vacillations between epic, farce, and tragedy, the play turns to Hecuba as a symbol of each genre's possible affective extremes. In the context of her significance and many references, it is curious that Hecuba herself never appears on the stage. As in the earlier *Titus*, *Lucrece*, and *Hamlet*, she is invoked, described, and depicted, but she challenges or even defies direct representation, suggesting that her actual theatrical presence might prompt uncontainable consequences.

Hamlet's encounter with the Trojan queen, then, joins a substantial body of Shakespeare's reflections on Hecuba as symbol for tragedy's affective and generic capaciousness. The combination of grief and triumphant action that she signals in these settings carries over into later plays. In *Coriolanus* (1608–9), Volumnia uses Hecuba's associations with maternal tenderness to chide her daughter-in-law for her concern for Coriolanus' safety over his honor by juxtaposing nurture with violence: "The breasts of Hecuba,/ When she did suckle Hector looked not lovelier/ Than Hector's forehead when it spit forth blood/ At Grecian sword" (1.3.42–5). And in *Cymbeline* (1610–11), upon mistaking Cloten's corpse for that of Posthumus, Imogen invokes her as a kindred spirit of bereaved vindictive fury: "Pisanio,/ All curses madded Hecuba gave the Greeks,/ And mine to boot, be darted on thee!" (4.2.314–16). Throughout these allusions, Shakespeare's Hecuba continues to represent not simply the passive suffering we see in Seneca, but active responses to wrongdoers. Transforming grief into the satisfaction of achieving justice, this Hecuba offers a symbol of tragedy both emotionally affecting and potentially triumphant. She has, in short, Euripides' fingerprints all over her.

Hecuba and the model of tragedy she embodies form as haunting a presence to Shakespeare as the ghost to Hamlet, challenging the prevailing belief that Shakespeare was untouched by Greek plays. As critics have noted, Shakespeare would not have needed to know Euripides in order to be familiar with Hecuba from other classical sources such as Ovid, Virgil, and Homer.[18] Yet with even a minimal grammar school education he could easily have read the bilingual Greek–Latin editions of Euripides' play and/or any of the vernacular translations.[19] In the light of the explicit invocations of Euripides' *Hecuba* in *Titus*, and Shakespeare's repeated returns to the figure of Hecuba, it seems extremely unlikely that he did not. Martin Mueller has suggested that the player's account of Pyrrhus' pause before slaying Priam in *Hamlet*—"neutral to his will and matter" (2.2.484)—closely resembles Pyrrhus' similarly charged pause before slaying Polyxena in *Hecuba*, where he is "not willing and willing" ("οὐ θέλων τε καὶ θέλων"; Erasmus, "volensque & non volens"), invoking the play's particular interest in the tension between revenge and conscience.[20] Volumnia's invocation of "The breasts of Hecuba,/ When she did suckle Hector" in *Coriolanus* also suggests Polyxena's famous lament to Hecuba, "Oh chest and breasts, that suckled me sweetly" ("ὦ στέρνα μαστοί θ', οἵ μ' ἐθρέψαθ' ἡδέως"; Erasmus, "O pectus e quis alita blande sum ubera").[21] And as observed Chapter 2, Demetrius' reference in *Titus* to "the Thracian tyrant in his tent" (1.1.138) indicates specific knowledge of Euripides' play: no other literary version depicts Hecuba's violence as taking place in a tent.[22] Whether or not these moments indicate that Shakespeare had direct access to the play in Greek, the nature of his extended reflections and the growing consensus that he collaborated with Peele on his first tragedy combine to suggest that at the very least he knew salient details of Euripides' *Hecuba*, and that *Hecuba*'s authority as representative of tragedy's origins loomed behind his ongoing engagement with its protagonist.

In arguing that Hecuba's association with Euripidean tragedy is crucial to understanding her meanings for Shakespeare, I do not exclude other depictions of Hecuba from his web of literary engagement. Shakespeare's compounding and confounding of literary models have been widely acknowledged, and critics have persuasively demonstrated his engagement with Virgil and Ovid, among other classical sources. Yet as Emrys Jones rightly notes, "we are not faced with a choice between Euripides and Ovid, since no one denies Ovidian influence. The choice is between Ovid alone and Ovid together with Euripides."[23] Identifying Euripides' role in this intertextual web points to Shakespeare's particular interest in the effects of tragic performance on audiences. As Jones has also pointed out, *Hecuba* offered Shakespeare a classical model for a highly successful, publicly performed tragedy, something he could not find elsewhere.[24] Euripides' play offered Shakespeare not only the generic conventions he exploits in *Hamlet*—a pre-existing crime, ghost, delay, deceit, and violence—but also a dramatic model for engaging audiences with tragic affect. In particular, it offered him a tradition of emotionally affecting and generically hybrid tragedy that was female-centered, rooted in lament, and culminating in triumphant action: a tradition that served as a crucial foundation for his own experiments with transmitting powerful emotions onstage.

In the context of Hecuba's strong association with maternal lament, it is unsurprising that Shakespeare most frequently evokes Hecuba in the context of suffering women. Tamora, Lavinia, Lucrece, Virgilia, and Imogen are all linked with Hecuba in ways that suggest active responses to tragic grief. Oddly, however, it is Hamlet—male, unmarried, childless—through whom Shakespeare most fully explores Hecuba's dramatic possibilities. At least at first glance, the play's central drama moves its mothers and daughters to the sidelines in order to focus on a son's commemoration of his father, apparently bearing out the critical truism that Shakespeare's tragedies primarily attend to male experience.[25] Yet Hecuba's name occurs four times in *Hamlet*, more often than in any Shakespeare text beyond *Troilus and Cressida*, in which she has an actual role in the plot. Why should *Hamlet* provide such a focal point for Shakespeare's fascination with Hecuba, and how does the play respond to the tragic tradition she represents?

HAMLET'S ALTERED HECUBAS

Hamlet appeared among a spate of English playwrights' depictions of tragic Trojan figures. In 1598 George Chapman published the first seven books of his English translation of Homer's *Iliad*, providing newly widespread access to Hecuba and her Trojan peers in their first literary incarnations.[26] In 1599, the Admiral's Men staged plays at the Rose Theater titled *Orestes Furies* and/or *Agamemnon*, and *Troilus and Cressida*, by Henry Chettle and Thomas Dekker, as well as *Troy's Revenge*, by Chettle.[27] *Hamlet* arrived on the heels of these plays by Shakespeare's competitors, probably in 1600; Shakespeare went on to write *Troilus and Cressida*, his most direct exploration of the Trojan story, soon after.[28] Colin Burrow has recently argued that Shakespeare's engagement with classical texts changes significantly around 1600, developing more subtlety and complexity.[29] I suggest that this shift owes crucial debts to the explosion of interest in newly visible Greek tragic texts at around this moment. Greek tragic sagas would continue to increase their hold on playwrights' attention through the following decade. The 1609 publication of Chapman's complete *Iliad* translation corresponded with Thomas Heywood's *Troia Britannica* (also 1609), followed by Heywood's popular dramatizations of Greek gods and heroes in his Ages plays (1609–13), and more esoteric plays such as Thomas Goffe's *Tragedy of Orestes* (c.1609–16).[30] Poised at the start of an expanding series of dramatic conversations about the uses of Greek tragic material, *Hamlet* showcases Shakespeare's most self-conscious exploration of tragedy and its effects.[31] The play accordingly offers an important site for reflecting on Hecuba's dramatic legacy, and recovering this legacy allows us to recognize Shakespeare's responses to it.

Perhaps most conspicuously, evoking Hecuba's model of tragedy directs audiences to expect that Gertrude, a widow and mother, will be the play's primary grieving figure.[32] Despite the prominence of their father–son relationships, *The Spanish Tragedy* and *Titus Andronicus* both continued a tradition of dramatizing maternal grief as a catalyst to revenge. Shakespeare's decision to withhold this convention in *Hamlet* is striking. As Katharine Goodland has observed, acts of female mourning in the play are consistently dismissed, interrupted, or otherwise contained.[33] Whatever mourning Gertrude may have done is blocked from the audience's view, as are her thoughts more broadly: she says surprisingly little in the play, especially in contrast with Hamlet's outsized role. Situating the play in the context of Hecuba's tragic genealogy sheds a new light on one of Hamlet's most vehement fixations: Gertrude's insufficient mourning. "Heaven and earth," he exclaims,

> Must I remember? Why, she would hang on him
> As if increase of appetite had grown
> By what it fed on. And yet, within a month
> (Let me not think on't—Frailty, thy name is Woman),
> A little month, or e'er those shoes were old
> With which she followed my poor father's body,
> Like Niobe, all tears. Why she—
> O God, a beast that wants discourse of reason
> Would have mourned longer—married with mine uncle ...   (1.2.142–51)

As this passage suggests, Hamlet speaks more easily and extensively about his mother's failure to grieve than about his own grief. His preoccupation with Gertrude has been widely read as a sign of his misogyny, and his Oedipal fixation on her sexuality.[34] But in the context of Shakespeare's interest in Hecuba, we might more fruitfully understand it as representing a confrontation with the genre's conventions. Although Hamlet depicts Gertrude as passionately attached to his father, and as having mourned him "like Niobe, all tears," he insists that her grief is not substantial enough to merit its traditional place at the tragedy's emotional center. Like Hecuba, with whom Achilles indirectly links her in the *Iliad*, Niobe was primarily known for mourning her numerous children, of whom she was so excessively proud that the gods punished her with their deaths.[35] Yet although Gertrude evokes Niobe's emotional excess, she falls short of this iconic grief. By contrasting Niobe's tears with the speed of Gertrude's remarriage, Hamlet insists that Gertrude represents a fallen version of mythic female mourning.[36]

Gertrude, of course, is not the play's only female mourner. Recognizing early modern English fascination with Greek mother–daughter dyads illuminates the play's identification of Ophelia with another iconic tragic figure. Not only did Shakespeare give Ophelia an explicitly Greek name, but allusions in the play link her with the famous self-sacrificing virgins central to the Greek dramatic tradition.[37] Between Polonius' announce-ment of the players and their entrance, Hamlet announces, "O Jephthah, judge of Israel, what a treasure hadst thou?," to which Polonius concedes, "If you call me Jephthah, my lord, I have a daughter that I love passing well" (2.2.340–8). As editors and critics have observed, Jephthah vowed to sacrifice the first living thing he met if he returned successfully from war, which led to sacrificing his daughter.[38] Although most conspicuously a biblical allusion, Jephthah implicitly invokes Euripides' *Iphigenia in Aulis*, which served as model for the *Jephthes, Sive Votum* (1540–7, published 1554) of George Buchanan, a humanist scholar who translated Euripides, and John Christopherson's *Jephthah* (c.1544), the first English play com-posed in Greek.[39] Both plays self-consciously imitated Euripides' story of a father sacrificing a daughter for the sake of a war, which was (after *Hecuba*) the period's second-most popular Greek play.

As discussed in Chapter 1, *Iphigenia in Aulis* was especially popular in England: translated by Erasmus, then Lumley, then Peele, it was staged by St. Paul's boys, and implicitly invoked in *Titus*. Its mediation through Buchanan's exceptionally well-received Jephthah play, which was widely reprinted, translated, and praised by writers including Roger Ascham and Philip Sidney, forged a link between classical drama and the English stage. A Jephthah play was performed at Trinity College, Cambridge, in 1566–7, and a commercial play about Jephthah, written by Dekker and Munday, was performed by the Admiral's Men in 1601–2.[40] With their focus on a sacrificial daughter, these plays implicitly evoke not only *Iphigenia* but also *Hecuba*, which similarly dramatizes a daughter's sacrifice as preamble to a mother's revenge.[41] Between hearing of the players and watching them represent Hecuba, then, Hamlet is already thinking about female sacrifice linked to classical tragedy: his medita-tion on Jephthah's daughter implicitly frames the speech he requests a few dozen lines later. The allusion suggests that Ophelia—who, like Iphigenia, is sacrificed by her father for matters of state negotiated between men—will both mirror Hamlet and compete with him for the play's tragic center.

Like Hamlet, Ophelia responds to a father's death by staging spectacles for audiences. And, like Hecuba, she seems to outdo Hamlet in her ability to produce an emotional impact with her performances. Just as the player reports that Hecuba's grief would melt her audiences, Claudius says of Ophelia's singing that "this,/ Like to a murdering-piece in many places/ Gives me superfluous death" (4.5.94–6). Laertes identifies her painful performance as a catalyst to revenge: "Hadst thou thy wits and didst persuade revenge/ It could not move thus" (4.5.163–4). Although Ophelia does not perform either Hecuba's direct revenge or Iphigenia's boldly altruistic self-sacrifice, the affective power of her grief, madness, and suicide serves to melt and mobilize her audiences as did her Greek forerunners. With her songs of grief, Ophelia offers the play's closest approximation to the lyrically lamenting female figures of classical tragedy.[42] Her combination of female grief, madness, and sexuality melds Hecuba and Iphigenia with the passionate performances of Renaissance Italian actresses, through what Eric Nicholson has described as "the process of transnational *contaminatio.*"[43]

Despite surprisingly little direct speech in the play, Ophelia acquires an acutely moving power in her performances, especially in her striking death, which has developed a substantial afterlife through later responses to the play.[44] As reported by Gertrude, Ophelia's death literalizes the liquidity frequently linked with tragic female lament: like the tears she elicits, she melts into the kindred medium of a "weeping brook" (4.7.173). "[L]ong it could not be," Gertrude explains, "Till that her garments, heavy with their drink,/ Pulled the poor wretch from her melodious lay/ To muddy death" (4.7.178–81). In reply to Laertes' question, "Alas, then, she is drowned?," she echoes his words in a sort of chorus, "Drowned, drowned." In his response, Laertes conflates the weeping brook with his own weeping eyes, and links both liquid forms with Ophelia herself. "Too much of water hast thou, poor Ophelia," he reflects,

> And therefore I forbid my tears: but yet
> It is our trick; nature her custom holds,
> Let shame say what it will: when these are gone,
> The woman will be out. Adieu, my lord:
> I have a speech of fire, that fain would blaze,
> But that this folly drowns it.   (4.7.181–9)

Like Ophelia herself, the blazing fire of Laertes' rage is drowned by the grief she elicits, just as Hecuba's passionate lament "made milch the burning eyes of heaven" (2.2.455). These melting effects have an ambivalent status for Hamlet, who famously opens the play wishing "that this too too solid flesh would melt/ Thaw and resolve itself into a dew" (1.2.129–30), but later identifies liquefaction with unsettling fragility. If lust can overtake his mother, he proclaims, "To flaming youth let virtue be as wax,/ And melt in her own fire" (3.4.86–7). The play similarly shows the melting consequences of female lament to be both desirable and dangerous. Like the liquid poison that courses through King Hamlet's ears, or the wine that dissolves a pearl and multiple lives at the play's end, Ophelia's performances invade and disintegrate their consumers.

As versions of the Euripidean mother–daughter dyads linked with tragic origins, Gertrude and Ophelia highlight Hamlet's struggle to achieve Hecuba's power, and his preoccupation with the possibility of communicating emotion through tragic performance. If the implicit corollary to Hamlet's attacks on Gertrude and Ophelia is that his own grief, by contrast, constitutes the rightful heart of the tragedy, he seems to protest too much. For Hamlet's quickness to attack Gertrude masks his own discomfort with confronting his father's death. Whenever he begins to remember his father, he immediately reverts to outrage about his mother and her remarriage. "Remember thee?," he addresses the ghost, "Yes, by heaven,/ O most pernicious woman" (1.5.95, 104–5). As his frequent slippage from his father's memory to his mother's marriage shows, it is not only acts of female mourning that are interrupted, pre-empted, or otherwise prevented in the play. Hamlet's relationship to his grief is vexed: unlike Hecuba's passionate laments, his are fraught with ambivalence, uncertainty, and anxiety.

It is not simply that, as has been widely observed, Hamlet cannot bring himself to act—or, at least, act in accordance with the ghost's mandate. More surprisingly, and in contrast to the critical consensus on the play, he cannot actually *speak*: at least not "to th' purpose" of his grief (2.2.244). Hamlet's preoccupation with Gertrude masks his anxiety that he, like she, is no Hecuba. If Hecuba, to early modern readers in general and to Shakespeare in particular, represents the power of passionate lament both as a speech act in itself and as a catalyst to righteous action, Hamlet is striking precisely for his struggle to fulfill these ends. On a broader level, whereas *Hecuba* embodies both the tragedy of pathos and the tragedy of triumph, *Hamlet* is caught uneasily between the two: it cannot fully provide the cathartic pleasures of unfettered grief, nor the satisfaction of seeing a victim heroically bring down a wrongdoer. Instead, Shakespeare reconfigures structural features popular from *Hecuba* to demonstrate an alternative approach to conjuring emotional intensity. Hamlet's reflections on his failure to match Hecuba paradoxically lead him to develop his own form of tragic power.

Hamlet confronts this failure most fully in his meditation on the player's reaction to Hecuba. "O, what a rogue and peasant slave am I!" he castigates himself (2.2.485). Comparing himself with the tragic passion that she has inspired in the player, he asks:

> What would he do
> Had he the motive and that for passion
> That I have? He would drown the stage with tears
> And cleave the general ear with horrid speech,

> Make mad the guilty and appal the free,
> Confound the ignorant and amaze indeed
> The very faculties of eyes and ears. Yet I,
> The dull and muddy-mettled rascal, peak
> Like John-a-dreams, unpregnant of my cause,
> And can say nothing.   (2.2.495–504)

Technically Hamlet compares himself here with the player, and proclaims the superiority of his own motive for passion. Yet although he criticizes the player's response, he also compares Hecuba's pain to his own, suggesting that the player would conjure even more tragic power if inspired by Hamlet's woes. At the same time, he implicitly competes with Hecuba's invoked performance, which includes drowning the stage with tears, maddening the guilty murderer of her son, and amazing her audiences, both onstage and off. Despite his claim to possess a stronger motive for passion, he sees himself as unable to match either the moving power of a theatrical fiction or Hecuba's ability to speak and act on her passion.

Yet Hamlet revises his indictment of his inability to speak when he considers the even greater problem of his inability to demonstrate filial loyalty through revenge. "Why, what an ass am I," he reflects:

> this is most brave,
> That I, the son of a dear murdered,
> Prompted to my revenge by heaven and hell,
> Must like a whore unpack my heart with words
> And fall a-cursing like a very drab,
> A stallion!   (2.2.517–22)

Although Hamlet earlier described himself as insufficiently female to match Hecuba's pregnant capacity for emotion-laden speech, here he worries that his predilection for words over action makes him overly feminine. He is not alone in this interpretation: critics, directors, and the many actresses who have played his role have emphasized what Tony Howard has called "the issue of Hamlet's 'femininity.'"[45] Nor does he see his feminine verbal facility as an asset. His comparisons of himself to a "whore," a "very drab," and either a "stallion" (Q2), male prostitute, or a "scullion" (F), suggest that his failure to act makes him both subservient and unfaithful to his father's memory, closer to Gertrude's "wicked speed . . . to incestuous sheets" (1.2.156, 157) than to Hecuba's passionate commemoration of her husband and children. If Gertrude and Ophelia offer altered Hecubas, constricted and compressed versions of original tragic icons, Hamlet worries that he cannot even emulate the model they evoke.

AS GOOD AS A CHORUS?

By moving tragic female characters to the margins of the play, and centering our attention on a protagonist who observes and comments on them, Shakespeare self-consciously reflects on a male character's experience of watching traditional—that is, female—tragic protagonists. *Hamlet* constructs, scrutinizes, and critiques an emerging English model of tragedy through conversation with its earlier counterpart. His reflections on Hecuba lead him to unearth and adapt alternative Greek tragic roles, predicated more on watching and reflecting than on action. If the player's evocation of Hecuba's tragic power makes Hamlet question his status as a tragic protagonist, it simultaneously inspires him to stage a performance of a tragedy. Shakespeare explicitly returns to the innovation of the play-within-the-play, and makes it a centerpiece of his tragedy, reinforcing its prominence in the revenge tragedy tradition. In confronting an unjust ruler with a theatrical version of Hecuba's story—a newly widowed queen who "makes passionate action" (s.d. 3.2.128.7) upon discovering her dead husband—he gestures to the tyrant-melting powers attributed by both Plutarch and Sidney to Euripides' play.[46] If he cannot play Hecuba's role himself, he will find another way to exploit her tragic formula for his purposes.

In *Hamlet*, the performance that introduces Hecuba prompts not only a revival of Kyd's play-within-the-play, but a preceding dumb-show, often seen by critics as unnecessarily repetitive. As discussed in Chapter 2, both dumb-show and play-within-the-play suggest versions of the classical theater's chorus, and, as the performance begins, Ophelia identifies Hamlet's commentary as the missing element of this classicizing trio: "You are as good as a chorus, my lord" (3.2.238). Although Ophelia does not technically refer to a Greek tragic chorus, her diction is telling. The word "chorus" not only originates in Greek, but was also a technical theatrical term; in 1600 it was a recent import into the English language, appearing almost exclusively in Latin and/or dramatic texts.[47] Ophelia's observation highlights the strangeness of Hamlet's relationship to the performance he has arranged. Unlike Hieronimo, who plays the vengeful lead character in his play-within-the-play, Hamlet has no part in the play's action, but neither is he a conventional spectator. Armed with a privileged knowledge of the plot, he hovers in a liminal position between the play and its audience, meting out information to the other audience members at intervals. "Marry, this is munching mallico!," he tells Ophelia of the dumb-show; "It means mischief." "We shall know all by this fellow," he announces of the Prologue (3.2.130–4). When Ophelia identifies him as a chorus, he tacitly agrees: "I could interpret between you and your love if I could see the puppets dallying" (3.2.239–40).

Hamlet's choric position toward the play he stages offers a model for his role within his own drama. It is not simply that he finds himself unable to embody the traditional figure of lament and revenge represented by Hecuba: he cannot find any way to undertake the action that the ghost has required of him. When Hamlet is served up a chance to play a conventional active role in his own drama, he balks. Just after the performance, he stumbles upon the opportunity to kill Claudius— "Now might I do it. But now 'a is a-praying./ And now I'll do it"—but stops short of action (3.3.73–4). In considering but refusing to play a part in revenge, he evokes Hecuba's own chorus of Trojan women, who wonder whether they should help Hecuba attack Polymestor, but hold back from taking action.[48] Rather than accepting the revenger's role, Hamlet instead reverts to observing and interpreting his mother. "You go not till I set you up a glass," he tells her upon subsequently finding her in her closet, "Where you may see the inmost part of you" (3.4.18–19).[49] As in his famous claim that "the purpose of playing . . . is to hold as 'twere the mirror up to Nature" (3.2.20–22), Hamlet uses the vocabulary of mirroring to describe his metatheatrical reflections on the tragic characters and events that he observes and discusses.

Hamlet's choric role not only offers him a position from which to reflect on the play he inhabits, but also establishes parameters for the melancholy malcontent revengers who follow him on the early modern stage, who also frequently step outside of their tragic events in order to contemplate them. Robert Miola has observed that Hamlet's "To be or not to be" speech echoes a choral ode from Seneca's *Troas*, and suggested that Hamlet follows the Senecan chorus in voicing "an ancient and profound world-weariness, infusing the choral perspective with anguished awareness of his own situation."[50] Stepping outside of the tragedy's conventional center also allows Hamlet to reflect on the female characters who represent the more paradigmatic tragic protagonists. His choric status on one hand puts him in a position more typically feminine than theirs—marginal, passive, and observing, rather than central, active, and defining—and yet paradoxically strengthens him by giving him the leverage of an external vantage point on their drama.[51] As a male figure reflecting on female characters, he also finds himself in the relatively unusual position of a cross-sex chorus: a situation usually unfavorable to the protagonist.[52] Perhaps most strikingly, reducing the typically collective choral voice to a singular one emphasizes the painful isolation of Hamlet's reflections while intensifying his own particular importance, and converting the typically sung choral odes to speech removes him further from the distinctive affective impact of lyric performance.[53] As a quasi-choral figure, Hamlet mediates between the audience and the play's female figures, framing and shaping our perspectives on them.

In carving out this curiously decentered position for his tragic protagonist, Shakespeare may well have drawn inspiration from the figure of Orestes, as several critics have proposed.[54] Although Orestes' name never appears in the play, he haunted English stages in this period. At least three Orestes plays appeared in England before 1600—John Pickering's interlude *Horestes* (between 1550–67), a 1567 production of Euripides' *Orestes* staged by Westminster schoolboys, and the 1599 *Orestes Furies* at the Rose Theatre—followed slightly later by Thomas Heywood's *Second Part of the Iron Age* (*c.*1613); Thomas Goffe's *Tragedy of Orestes*, performed in Christ Church College, Oxford (*c.*1609–1616); and a manuscript play titled *Pylades and Orestes*, probably from around the turn of the century.[55] Although these plays represent considerable mediation, performance records suggest that no other Greek or Roman tragedy attracted this much theatrical interest in England in the late sixteenth and early seventeenth centuries, in surprising contrast to the predominance of female tragic figures both in earlier decades and in continental Europe.[56] Shakespeare could not have missed rising interest in Orestes, whose name features in plays by Kyd, Greene, Marlowe, Marston, and Jonson.[57] Beyond its proliferation of malcontented young men intent on revenging their father's deaths, *Hamlet* suggests possible echoes of Euripides' play. When Menelaus asks, "Does your father's vengeance help (*ōphelei*) you at all?," Orestes replies, "Not yet; I call delay the same as inaction," responding to the word that forms Ophelia's name.[58] Just after this, Menelaus asks Orestes what fate the townspeople will decide for him: "to die or not to die?" ("*ē thanein ē mē thanein?*").[59] Hamlet famously asks himself a similar version of this question. Whether or not these and other resonant lines indicate Shakespeare's direct familiarity with Euripides' play, his contemporaries saw the figures as linked; both Heywood and Goffe echoed lines from *Hamlet* in their Orestes plays.[60]

If Shakespeare channeled Orestes in *Hamlet*, what ends might this ghostly figure serve? Louise Schleiner has argued that *Hamlet* recreates "full-fledged tragedy in the Greek spirit" by responding to the influence of Saint Ravy's 1555 Latin translation of Aeschylus, which circulated in various editions during this period, and Euripides' *Orestes*.[61] Yet Shakespeare's conspicuous interest in Hecuba suggests that Euripides' *Orestes*, considerably more visible than Aeschylus' plays in this period, could have appealed to Shakespeare especially for its deliberate identification of Orestes with female tragic figures.[62] Orestes is framed by women throughout the play—during the first 210 lines, he sleeps onstage while his sister Electra and then his aunt Helen speak, and during the last 140 lines, he stands, like Medea, defiantly on top of the house, in a position typically reserved for the gods. His mimetic relation to these figures reflects the play's broader interest in revisiting earlier models of tragedy. Euripides wrote *Orestes* in 408 BCE, near the end of his life, and the play reflects self-consciously on his own earlier *Medea* (431) and *Hecuba* (424), as well as Aeschylus' *Oresteia* (458). Orestes himself similarly reacts belatedly to the previous generation's tragedy: as the youngest member of the House of Atreus, he confronts not only his own mother's violence, but also the larger traumatic aftermath of the Trojan War. I suggest that Orestes' status as belated outsider made him a particularly compelling literary model for the even more belated English. As Chapter 1 has shown, English translators, writers, readers, and audiences took a particular interest in younger tragic protagonists, especially Orestes' sister Iphigenia, forced to respond to their parents' legacies.[63] And importantly, Orestes modeled not only a later respondent to an older tradition, but also a male version of iconic female tragic roles. I suggest that in this capacity he offered an especially useful resource to a playwright whose playing company featured increasingly established adult male actors, especially Richard Burbage, with personal reputations in the prestigious vehicle of tragedy.[64] As a popular male representative of the Greek tragic tradition, Orestes offered a model for transferring Hecuba's tragic legacy to a later generation's male protagonists.

Like Orestes, Hamlet occupies an uneasy relationship toward both the bereaved mother and sacrificial daughter figures who are more representative of iconic tragic protagonists. Yet his active reflections on these female figures identify him with the same Greek tradition they represent, both as a kind of chorus and as an heir to the returned exile Orestes. Presented as audience and mirror to the play's female figures, Hamlet simultaneously usurps and highlights their centrality in the genre. In his decision to pursue vengeance by staging a play, Hamlet seems to follow Hieronimo in turning to tragic performance as a source of affective power, yet in contrast to *The Spanish Tragedy*, *Hamlet*'s play-within-the-play does not directly bring about the results it seeks. Instead, Ophelia's performances, both of songs and of suicide, offer more urgent catalysts, prompting both Laertes and Hamlet to the play's culminating action; Gertrude's insistence on drinking from Hamlet's poisoned cup, in defiance of Claudius' warning, similarly spurs Hamlet's final burst of retributive violence. If Hamlet serves crucially as observer of tragedy, his responses to female tragic performance show Shakespeare reflecting on the genre's consequences on audiences.

TRANSFORMING GREEK TRAGEDY

Hamlet has long been recognized as a self-conscious exploration of tragedy and its effects, written in the long aftermath of *The Spanish Tragedy*. Observing its proximity to a new surge of tragic Trojan material on commercial stages shows the play also responding to the ghosts of tragedy's Greek past, and Hamlet's fixation on Hecuba illuminates a larger fascination with a model of tragedy rooted in female affect. Just as Hecuba represents the power of passionate lament to move listeners to both sympathetic feeling and action, Hamlet reflects on the experience of receiving and responding to this tragic mode.

Male, childless, reticent of passionate speech and action, Hamlet is no Hecuba. Our icon of grief and revenge tragedy struggles both to grieve and to revenge. Yet Shakespeare constructs Hamlet's distinctive innovation to the genre—a new focus on audiences' relationship with the moving spectacles they watch, at a moment when theaters were rapidly rising in prominence—in intimate conversation with paradigmatic elements of Greek tragedy. Although Hamlet's question—"What's Hecuba to him, or he to Hecuba,/ That he should weep for her?"—has often been understood as skeptical, even hostile, I suggest that it contains admiration, as well as competitive envy. Shakespeare's long-running preoccupation with Hecuba emphasizes not only her iconic power to stir sympathetic emotion in audiences, but also his investments in achieving this power in his own plays. By reversing traditional tragic models to center his play on a young male figure responding to the loss of a parent, Shakespeare suggests that it is possible for latecomers to the tragic tradition to inherit her mantle. Through recognizing, studying, and identifying themselves with her authority, not only daughters, but also sons can reproduce the transmissions of sympathy she represents. In reflecting on weeping for Hecuba, Shakespeare learns how to make audiences weep with and for Hamlet as well.

NOTES

1. On Peele's collaborative role in *Titus Andronicus*, see Brian Vickers, *Shakespeare, Co-Author: A Historical Study of Five Collaborative Plays* (Oxford: Oxford University Press, 2002) and Macdonald P. Jackson, "Stage Directions and Speech Headings in Act 1 of *Titus Andronicus* Q (1594): Shakespeare or Peele?," *Studies in Bibliography* 49 (1996), 134–48. On Peele's Euripides translation, see William Gager, "In Iphigenia[m] Georgij Peeli Anglicanis

Versibus Reddita[m]," printed in *The Life and Minor Works of George Peele*, ed. David H. Horne (New Haven, CT: Yale University Press, 1952), vol. 1, 43.

2. Citations are to William Shakespeare, *Hamlet*, ed. Ann Thompson and Neil Taylor, Arden Shakespeare (London: Thompson Learning, 2006). See Pollard, "What's Hecuba to Shakespeare?," *Renaissance Quarterly* 65:4 (2012), 1060–93.

3. Recent discussions of Shakespeare's responsiveness to Kyd include Emma Smith, "Shakespeare and Early Modern Tragedy," in *The Cambridge Companion to English Renaissance Tragedy*, ed. Emma Smith and Garrett Sullivan (Cambridge: Cambridge University Press, 2010), 132–50, and Clara Calvo, "Thomas Kyd and the Elizabethan Blockbuster," in *The Cambridge Companion to Shakespeare and Contemporary Dramatists*, ed. Ton Hoenselaars (Cambridge: Cambridge University Press, 2012), 19–33. On the Ur-Hamlet, see Lukas Erne, *Beyond The Spanish Tragedy: A Study of the Works of Thomas Kyd* (Manchester: Manchester University Press, 2001), 146–56, and Emma Smith, "Ghost Writing: *Hamlet* and the *Ur-Hamlet*," in *The Renaissance Text*, ed. Andrew Murphy (Manchester: Manchester University Press, 2000), 177–90. On *Hamlet* as responding to children's companies, see, for instance, David Farley-Hills, *Shakespeare and the Rival Playwrights 1600–1606* (London and New York: Routledge, 1990), esp. 7–40, and R. A. Foakes, "Tragedy at the Children's Theatres after 1600: A Challenge to the Adult Stage," in *The Elizabethan Theatre II*, ed. David Galloway (Toronto: Macmillan, 1970), 37–59.

4. See especially Louise Schleiner, "Latinized Greek Drama in Shakespeare's Writing of *Hamlet*," *Shakespeare Quarterly* 41:1 (1990), 29–48; John Kerrigan, *Revenge Tragedy: Aeschylus to Armageddon* (Oxford: Clarendon Press, 1996); Martin Mueller, "*Hamlet* and the World of Ancient Tragedy," *Arion* 5:1 (1997), 22–45; Gilbert Murray, *Hamlet and Orestes, a Study in Traditional Types* (Oxford: Oxford University Press, 1914); and Jan Kott, "Hamlet and Orestes," trans. Boleslaw Taborski, *PMLA* 82:5 (1967), 303–13. Earl Showerman proposes the influence of Orestes to argue that that *Hamlet* was written by the Earl of Oxford; see Showerman, "Orestes and Hamlet: From Myth to Masterpiece, Part I," *The Oxfordian* 7 (2004), 89–114.

5. Jonathan Bate and Eric Rasmussen calculate that Hamlet speaks 37 percent of the play's lines; see Shakespeare, *Hamlet*, ed. Bate and Rasmussen, The RSC Shakespeare (New York: Modern Library, 2008), xxx.

6. On the significance of Shakespeare's engagement with Marlowe's *Dido*, see Laurie Maguire and Emma Smith, "What is a Source? Or, How Shakespeare read his Marlowe," *Shakespeare Survey* 68 (2015), 15–31.

7. On the ghost's account of his story's effects, see Kenneth Gross, *Shakespeare's Noise* (Chicago: University of Chicago Press, 2001), 10–32; David Hillman, *Shakespeare's Entrails* (Basingstoke: Palgrave, 2007), 81–116; and Tanya Pollard, *Drugs and Theater in Early Modern England* (Oxford: Oxford University Press, 2005), 123–41.

8. From 1425, the word meant "Of a woman or other female mammal: having offspring developing in the uterus. †Also of the womb (*obs.*). Freq. with *with*

(the offspring), *by* (the male parent)." *OED*, "pregnant," II.3.a; www.oed. com, accessed August 26, 2015. Shakespeare's usage here has been glossed as "unapt" (Shakespeare, *The Complete Works*, ed. Stanley Wells and Gary Taylor [Oxford: Clarendon Press, 1986], 1429), "barren of realization" (Shakespeare, *The Tragical History of Hamlet Prince of Denmark*, ed. A. R. Braunmuller, The Pelican Shakespeare [New York: Penguin Classics, 2001], 61), and "insensible, unmindful, unready" (Swynfen Jervis, *A Dictionary of the Language of Shakspeare* [London: John Russell Smith, 1868], 349); Philip Edwards claims that "'pregnant' is not used by Shakespeare to mean 'with child'" (*Hamlet, Prince of Denmark*, ed. Philip Edwards [Cambridge: Cambridge University Press, 2003], 153). Mary Thomas Crane similarly argues that Shakespeare did not use the term to refer to child-bearing, though she notes that Shakespeare would have been aware of that definition; see "Male Pregnancy and Cognitive Permeability in *Measure for Measure*," *Shakespeare Quarterly* 49:3 (1998), 269–92, esp. 275–85, and Pollard, "Conceiving Tragedy," in *Shakespearean Sensations: Experiencing Literature in Early Modern England*, ed. Katharine Craik and Tanya Pollard (Cambridge: Cambridge University Press, 2013), 85–100.

9. As discussed in the Introduction, in having Hecuba lament her "fifty children" [πεντήκοντά . . . τέκνων], Euripides expands strikingly on the nineteen children attributed to Hecuba by Homer, suggesting his especially acute interest in Hecuba's prolific maternity (Euripides, *Hecuba*, 421).

10. Most immediately, though not exclusively, he imitates an earlier *Hamlet*, which itself imitates two European sources. On pregnancy imagery as representing literary fecundity in the period, see Katharine Eisaman Maus, "A Womb of His Own: Male Renaissance Poets in the Female Body," in *Sexuality and Gender in Early Modern Europe*, ed. James Grantham Turner (Cambridge: Cambridge University Press, 1993), 266–88.

11. Shakespeare mentions Dido, to whom he has been described as "mysteriously attracted," thirteen times (see Heather James, "Dido's Ear: Tragedy and the Politics of Response," *Shakespeare Quarterly* 52:3 [2001], 360–82, 364); Hippolyta six times (plus four in stage directions, all in *A Midsummer Night's Dream*); and Medea once; Iphigenia, Clytemnestra, and Antigone do not feature at all, nor do Oedipus, Orestes, Hippolytus, Thyestes, or Atreus. The only classical literary characters who appear more frequently are those with active roles in *Troilus and Cressida*, such as Achilles, Hector, Priam, Agamemnon, and Aeneas, and demigods such as Hercules.

12. On Hecuba's literary afterlife in this period, see Lizette Westney, "Hecuba in Sixteenth-Century English Literature," *College Language Association Journal* 27:4 (1984), 436–9. On the reception of Euripides' *Hecuba*, see Judith Mossman, *Wild Justice: A Study of Euripides'* Hecuba (Oxford: Clarendon Press, 1995); Malcolm Heath, "'Jure principem locum tenet': Euripides' *Hecuba*," in *Bulletin of the Institute of Classical Studies* 34 (1987), 40–68; and Helene Foley, *Euripides: Hecuba* (London: Bloomsbury, 2014). On Shakespeare's response to Hecuba, especially in *Titus*, see Emrys Jones,

The Origins of Shakespeare (Oxford: Clarendon Press, 1977); Amy Cook, "For Hecuba or for Hamlet: Rethinking Emotion and Empathy in the Theatre," *Journal of Dramatic Theory and Criticism* 25:2 (2011), 71–87; Marina Warner, "'Come to Hecuba': Theatrical Empathy and Memories of Troy," *The Shakespearean International Yearbook* 11 (2011), 61–87; Mary Jo Kietzman, "'What Is Hecuba to Him or [S]he to Hecuba?' Lucrece's Complaint and Shakespearean Poetic Agency," *Modern Philology* 97:1 (1999), 21–45; and Katharine Goodland, *Female Mourning in Medieval and Renaissance English Drama: From the Raising of Lazarus to King Lear* (Aldershot: Ashgate, 2006).

13. See Pollard, "Hecuba" (2015), in *A Dictionary of Shakespeare's Classical Mythology* (2009–), ed. Yves Peyré, http://www.shakmyth.org/myth/107/hecuba (viewed August 5, 2015).

14. William Shakespeare, *Titus Andronicus*, ed. Jonathan Bate, Arden Shakespeare (London: Routledge, 1995, rprt 2005).

15. *The Tale of Troy* was published in 1589, but dates from earlier; see Horne, ed., *The Life and Works of George Peele*, 149.

16. Shakespeare, *Henry IV, Part 2*, ed. James Bulman, Arden Shakespeare (London: Bloomsbury, 2016), 2.2.88–9; see note, pp. 236–7.

17. On early modern concerns about the excess that characterizes both weeping and laughing, and on Shakespeare's particular interest in the juxtaposition of the two, see Matthew Steggle, *Laughing and Weeping in Early Modern Theatres* (Aldershot: Ashgate, 2007).

18. Latin poets' considerable debts to Euripides point to overlapping forms of influence; see Robert Garland, *Surviving Tragedy* (London: Duckworth, 2004), 60, and Bate's suggestion that Shakespeare "derived a Euripidean spirit from Ovid" (Jonathan Bate, *Shakespeare and Ovid* [Oxford: Clarendon Press, 1994], 239).

19. As discussed in Chapter 1, scholars generally agree that Shakespeare had a standard grammar school education, and by the 1570s this would typically have included at least some Greek; see T. W. Baldwin, *William Shakspere's Small Latine and Lesse Greeke*, 2 vols. (Urbana: University of Illinois Press, 1944).

20. See Mueller, "*Hamlet* and the World of Ancient Tragedy." Euripides, *Hecuba*, 566; Erasmus, *Hecuba et Iphigenia in Aulide* (1507) cviiv.

21. Shakespeare, *Coriolanus*, ed. Peter Holland, Arden Shakespeare (London: Bloomsbury, 2013), 1.3.37–38; Euripides, *Hecuba*, 424; Erasmus, *Hecuba*, ciiiir.

22. See J. A. K. Thomson, *Shakespeare and the Classics* (London: George Allen & Unwin, 1952), 57–8. I would add that Erasmus's translation underscores the play's emphasis on the tent; his Hecuba tells Polymestor that she has hidden additional treasures for him in "tentoriis," or tents, and he replies that he will enter her "tabernacula," tabernacles, or tents; see Erasmus, *Hecuba*, eiir.

23. Jones, *The Origins of Shakespeare*, 102.

24. Jones, *The Origins of Shakespeare*, 102–3.

25. See Linda Bamber, *Comic Women, Tragic Men: A Study of Gender and Genre in Shakespeare* (Palo Alto: Stanford University Press, 1982), On the apparent erasure of mothers, in particular, in Shakespeare's plays, see Mary Beth Rose, "Where are the Mothers in Shakespeare?: Options for Gender Representation in the English Renaissance," *Shakespeare Quarterly* 42:3 (1991), 291–314, and Janet Adelman, *Suffocating Mothers* (New York and London: Routledge, 1992).

26. On Chapman's influence on early modern dramatic depictions of Troy, see Tania Demetriou, "'Strange appearance': The Reception of Homer in Renaissance England" (Cambridge, D.Phil, 2008), and Demetriou, "Chapman's Odysses (1614–1615): Translation and Allegory," in *Homère à la Renaissance: Le Mythe et Ses Transfigurations*, ed. Luisa Capodieci and Philip Ford (Rome: Somogy/Académie de France à Rome, 2011), 245–60.

27. *Agamemnon* and *Orestes' Furies* may be the same play; records are indeterminate. For details on these plays, see Martin Wiggins, with Catherine Richardson, *British Drama 1533–1642* (Oxford: Oxford University Press, 2014), 4 vols, vol. 4, 1598–1602, entries 1182 (pp. 96–8), 1186 (pp. 111–12), and 1202 (pp. 142–3); see APGRD for details of these and other performances. On these and other lost Trojan plays, see Misha Teramura, "Brute Parts: From Troy to Britain at the Rose, 1595–1600," in *Lost Plays in Shakespeare's England*, ed. David McInnis and Matthew Steggle, (New York: Palgrave Macmillan, 2014), 127–47; see also Lost Plays Database, ed. Roslyn L. Knutson, David McInnis, and Matthew Steggle http://www.lostplays.org, accessed August 20, 2015. On early modern dramatic responses to Trojan material more broadly, see Inga-Stina Ewbank, "'Striking too short at Greeks': The Transmission of *Agamemnon* on the English Renaissance Stage," in Agamemnon *in Performance: 458 BC to AD 2004*, ed. Fiona Macintosh, Pantelis Michelakis, Edith Hall, and Oliver Taplin (Oxford: Oxford University Press, 2005), 37–52; Schleiner, "Latinized Greek Drama in Shakespeare's Writing of *Hamlet*"; and John S. P. Tatlock, "The Siege of Troy in Elizabethan Literature, Especially in Shakespeare and Heywood," *PMLA* 30:4 (1915), 673–770.

28. For a recent discussion of the probable dating of *Hamlet* and *Troilus and Cressida*, see Wiggins, *British Drama 1533–1642*, vol. 4, entries 1259 (pp. 241–51) and 1325 (pp. 372–7).

29. See Colin Burrow, *Shakespeare and Classical Antiquity* (Oxford: Oxford University Press, 2013), 70–1.

30. On Heywood's role in introducing Greek mythology to the large popular audiences of the Red Bull playhouse, see Charlotte Coffin, "The Gods' Lasciviousness, Or How To Deal With It? The Plight Of Early Modern Mythographers," *Cahiers Élisabéthains* 81 (2012), 1–14; Coffin, "Théorie et pratique des mythes: les paradoxes de Thomas Heywood," *Revue de la Société d'Études Anglo-Américaines des XVIIe et XVIIIe Siècles* 60 (2005), 63–76; and Angus Vine, "Myth and Legend," in *The Ashgate Research Companion to Popular Culture in Early Modern England*, ed. Abigail Shinn, Matthew Dimmock, and Andrew Hadfield (Aldershot: Ashgate, 2014), 103–18.

31. Bruce Louden describes parallels between *Hamlet* and Homer's *Odyssey*, although he does not explore Shakespeare's access to Homer's text. See Louden, "Telemachos, The *Odyssey* and *Hamlet*," *Text & Presentation* 11 (2014), 33–50.

32. On Hecuba as an affront to Gertrude's own failure to mourn properly, see Robert S. Miola, "Aeneas and Hamlet," *Classical and Modern Literature* 8:4 (1988), 275–90, 284, and Heather James, *Shakespeare's Troy* (Cambridge: Cambridge University Press, 1997), 40.

33. Goodland, *Female Mourning*, esp. 171–2.

34. On critical responses to this preoccupation, and on Gertrude as evoking ambivalence toward the aging Elizabeth, see Steven Mullaney, "Mourning and Misogyny: *Hamlet, The Revenger's Tragedy*, and the Final Progress of Elizabeth I, 1600-1607," *Shakespeare Quarterly* 45:2 (1994), 139–62, esp. 150–4.

35. Achilles cites Niobe as an analogy for Priam's grief over his (and Hecuba's) son Hector's death: Homer, *Iliad*, Loeb edition (Cambridge, MA: Harvard University Press, 1924), 24:602–14. Curiously, Sophocles' Antigone—who dies a virgin—likens her tearful death to Niobe's, though the chorus reminds her that, as a mortal, she is not comparable to the goddess-born Niobe. Thomas Watson rendered the exchange faithfully in his 1581 Latin translation of the play, which would have been easily available to Shakespeare.

36. On the text's relative silence on Gertrude's moral status, and critical tendencies to follow Hamlet's disapproval despite this lack of evidence, see Rebecca Smith, "A Heart Cleft in Twain: The Dilemma of Shakespeare's Gertrude," in *The Woman's Part: Feminist Criticism of Shakespeare*, ed. Carolyn Ruth Swift Lenz, Gayle Greene, and Carol Thomas Neely (Urbana: University of Illinois Press, 1980), 194–210, and Richard Levin, "Gertrude's Elusive Libido and Shakespeare's Unreliable Narrators," *SEL* 48:2 2008 (305–26).

37. The name Ophelia comes from the Greek ὀφέλλεια (*opheleia*), help, aid, from ὄφελος (*ophelos*), advantage, help, and ὀφέλλειν (*ophelein*), to increase, enlarge, and strengthen.

38. See Nona Fienberg, "Jephthah's Daughter: The Part Ophelia Plays," in *Old Testament Women in Western Literature*, eds Raymond-Jean Frontain and Jon Wojcik (Conway, AR: UCA Press, 1991), 128–43; James G. McManaway, "Ophelia and Jephtha's Daughter," *Shakespeare Quarterly* 21.2 (1970), 198–200; Cameron Hunt, "Jephthah's Daughter's Daughter: Ophelia," *ANQ: A Quarterly Journal of Short Articles, Notes, and Reviews* 22:4 (2009), 13–16; and Goodland, *Female Mourning*, 188–9.

39. Just prior to writing his play, Buchanan had translated Euripides' *Alcestis* and *Medea* from Greek into Latin. See Wilbur Sypherd, *Jephthah and his Daughter* (Newark: University of Delaware Press, 1948); Debora Shuger, *The Renaissance Bible: Scholarship, Sacrifice, and Subjectivity* (Berkeley: University of California Press, 1994); and Paul D. Streufert, "Christopherson at Cambridge: Greco-Catholic Ethics in the Protestant University," in *Early Modern*

Academic Drama, ed. Jonathan Walker and Paul Streufert (Burlington: Ashgate, 2008), 45–64.

40. Ascham described the play as one of only two modern tragedies "able to abide the true touch of Aristotle's precepts and Euripides' examples" (*The Scholemaster* [London, 1571], 174), and Sidney claimed that "the tragedies of Buchanan do justly bring forth a divine admiration" (*Defence*, K3v). The Cambridge performance could have been either Buchanan's or Christopherson's play; see Sypherd, *Jephthah*, 15; on Dekker and Munday's play, see R. A. Foakes, ed., *Henslowe's Diary*, 2nd edition (Cambridge: Cambridge University Press, 2002), 200–3, 296. See also "Jephthah," *Lost Plays Database*, https://www.lostplays.org/index.php?title=Jephthah, accessed August 19, 2016.

41. Although it is the murder of her son Polydorus that ultimately catalyzes Hecuba's revenge on his killer, Polymestor, the sacrifice of her daughter Polyxena lays a foundation for the grief that eventually turns into murderous rage. On the centrality of female sacrifice in Renaissance translations of Greek tragedy, see Shuger, *Renaissance Bible*, 129.

42. On the significance of song in shaping her meaning in the play, see Leslie C. Dunn, "Ophelia's Songs in Hamlet: Music, Madness, and the Feminine," in *Embodied Voices: Representing Female Vocality in Western Culture*, ed. Leslie C. Dunn and Nancy A. Jones (Cambridge: Cambridge University Press, 1994), 50–64, and Jacquelyn Fox-Good, "Ophelia's Mad Songs: Music, Gender, Power," in *Subjects on the World's Stage: Essays on British Literature of the Middle Ages and the Renaissance*, ed. David C. Allen and Robert A. White (Newark: University of Delaware Press, 1995), 217–38.

43. Eric Nicholson, "Ophelia Sings Like a *Prima Donna Innamorata*: Ophelia's Mad Scene and the Italian Female Performer," in *Transnational Exchange in Early Modern Theater*, ed. Robert Henke and Eric Nicholson (Aldershot: Ashgate, 2008), 81–98, 93; see also Pamela Allen Brown, "The Counterfeit *Innamorata*, or, The Diva Vanishes," *Shakespeare Yearbook* 10 (1999), 402–26.

44. On Ophelia's remarkable tenacity in other centuries and media, see *The Afterlife of Ophelia*, ed. Kaara L. Peterson and Deanne Williams (Basingstoke: Palgrave Macmillan, 2012), and Elaine Showalter, "Representing Ophelia: Women, Madness, and the Responsibility of Female Criticism," in *Shakespeare and the Question of Theory*, ed. Patricia Parker and Geoffrey Hartman (London: Methuen & Co., 1985), 77–94.

45. See Tony Howard, *Women as Hamlet: Performance and Interpretation in Theatre, Film and Fiction* (Cambridge: Cambridge University Press, 2007), 1.

46. On Sidney's depiction of the play's effects on tyrants, drawing on Plutarch, see Pollard, "What's Hecuba to Shakespeare?,"; D. M. Gaunt, "Hamlet and Hecuba," *Notes and Queries* 16 (1969), 136–7; Patricia Gourlay, "Guilty Creatures Sitting at a Play: A Note on *Hamlet*, Act II, Scene 2," *Renaissance Quarterly* 24:2 (1971), 221–5; James Freeman, "Hamlet, Hecuba, and

Plutarch," *Shakespeare Studies* 7 (1974), 197–202; and Goodland, *Female Mourning*, 173–4.

47. "Chorus" comes from the Greek χορός, by way of the Latin *chorus*; its first English definitions are "1a) An organized band of singers and dancers in the religious festivals and dramatic performances of ancient Greece; 1b) The song sung by the chorus; and 1c) In English drama, imitated or adapted from the chorus of Attic tragedy, as in *Gorboduc*, and Milton's *Samson Agonistes*; by Shakespeare and other Elizabethan dramatists reduced to a single personage, who speaks the prologue, and explains or comments upon the course of events." Other definitions do not enter English usage until later centuries. See "chorus," *Oxford English Dictionary*, www.oed.com, accessed August 21, 2015. An EEBO search for "chorus" before 1600 turns up 548 instances in 111 records, in texts that are either in Latin, translated from or commenting on classical sources, and/or dramatic.

48. The chorus wonders, "Should we burst in on them? The moment requires us to stand with Hecuba and the Trojan women as allies" ("βούλεσθ' ἐπεσπέσωμεν; ὡς ἀκμὴ καλεῖ / Ἑκάβῃ παρεῖναι Τρῳάσιν τε συμμάχους"); Euripides, *Hecuba*, 1042–3. This pattern of considering but refusing action is common in Euripides' choruses. In response to Medea's children's offstage cries for help while their mother attempts to murder them, the chorus of Corinthian women wonders, "Shall I go into the house? I must prevent the children's death" ("παρέλθω δόμους; ἀρῆξαι φόνον/ δοκεῖ μοι τέκνοις"). Although the children, breaking tragic convention, hear this from offstage and reply, "Yes, by the gods, help, for it must be done now!" ("ναί, πρὸς θεῶν, ἀρήξατ᾽· ἐν δέοντι γάρ"), the chorus does nothing but lament; Euripides, *Medea*, 1275–7. On varieties of the Euripidean chorus, see Rush Rehm, "Performing the Chorus: Choral Action, Interaction and Absence in Euripides," *Arion* 3rd series 4:1 (1996), 45–60; and Donald J. Mastronarde, *The Art of Euripides: Dramatic Technique and Social Context* (Cambridge: Cambridge University Press, 2010), 88–152.

49. Like Hecuba, Hamlet is frequently depicted as a mirror in which others see themselves. Ophelia describes him as "The glass of fashion and the mould of form,/ Th'observed of all observers" (3.1.152–53).

50. Robert Miola, *Shakespeare and Classical Tragedy: The Influence of Seneca* (Oxford: Clarendon Press, 1992), 38–9.

51. Noting that most tragic choruses are female, Oliver Taplin suggests that "Women and weak old men seem to be favoured for choruses partly because of their ineffectuality in action"; see Taplin, "Comedy and the Tragic," in *Tragedy and the Tragic: Greek Theatre and Beyond*, ed. M. S. Silk (Oxford: Clarendon Press, 1996), 188–202, 183.

52. Female tragic figures who succeed in their undertakings, such as Medea and Hecuba, benefit from the sympathetic support of their female choral figures; those without such support, such as Clytemnestra and Antigone, are more likely to be destroyed.

53. On the importance of the chorus's collective nature, see John Gould, "Tragedy and Collective Experience," in *Tragedy and the Tragic: Greek Theatre and Beyond*, 217–43.

54. See note 4, this chapter.

55. See Appendices; Lost Plays Database; and Wiggins, *British Drama*, vol. 4, for details. *Pylades and Orestes* has been dated to about 1620 by some scholars, but more recently has been estimated to be around the end of the sixteenth century; see Lost Plays Database, and Wiggins, *British Drama*, vol. 4, Entry 1261, pp. 252–3.

56. If we conflate Greek and Roman versions of similar material, *Hippolytus* and *Troades/Hecuba* come close; see Appendices and APGRD database. Among comedies, only Plautus' *Menaechmi* overtakes it, with five performances.

57. Jonson owned an edition of Euripides' *Orestes*; John Selden wrote of finding a copy "of *Euripides* his *Orestes* . . . in the well-furnisht Librarie of my beloved friend that singular Poet M. *Ben: Ionson.*" See John Selden, *Titles of Honour* (London: William Stansby, 1614), Preface, d1r.

58. "πατρὸς δὲ δή τι σ' ὠφελεῖ τιμωρία; οὔπω· τὸ μέλλον δ' ἴσον ἀπραξίᾳ λέγω," Euripides, *Orestes*, 425–6.

59. "ἢ θανεῖν ἢ μὴ θανεῖν," *Orestes*, 441.

60. See Mueller, "*Hamlet* and the World of Ancient Tragedy," esp. 27.

61. See Schleiner, "Latinized Greek Drama in Shakespeare's *Hamlet.*"

62. On the play's lateness, self-reflexivity, and allusions to previous Euripidean female revengers, see Froma Zeitlin, "The Closet of Masks: Role-playing and Myth-making in the *Orestes* of Euripides," *Ramus: Critical Studies in Greek and Roman Literature* 9 (1980), 51–77, esp. 62–3; also Matthew Wright, "Orestes, a Euripidean Sequel," *Classical Quarterly* 56:1 (2006), 33–47; and Wright, *Euripides' Orestes* (London: Bloomsbury, 2008).

63. Written even later than *Orestes*, Euripides' popular *Iphigenia in Aulis* was staged in 405 BCE after the playwright's death the previous year.

64. On Richard Burbage and his particular affinity with tragedy, see especially Bart Van Es, "Richard Burbage," in *Shakespeare in Company* (Oxford: Oxford University Press, 2013), 232–48, and Tiffany Stern and Simon Palfrey, *Shakespeare in Parts* (Oxford: Oxford University Press, 2007).

4

Iphigenia in Illyria

Greek Tragic Women on Comic Stages

Just as the specter of Hecuba summons the theatrical legacy of Greek tragic women into English tragedies, versions of these figures also invade and reshape the genre of comedy. Shakespeare's comedies self-consciously advertise their debts to Latin and Italian literary models: in particular, *The Comedy of Errors* closely imitates Plautus' popular comedy *Menaechmi*, and *Twelfth Night* revisits the earlier play's shipwrecked twins by way of Italian variations.[1] Yet although these plays flirt with farce and end with festivity, they depart from their Latin and Italian models in the haunting melancholy that underpins their central plots of loss and restoration. Both plays begin with mourning, and both develop heightened affective power through unexpected performances of female lament. This chapter argues that Greek tragic women played a crucial role in shaping Shakespeare's sense of comedy's affective possibilities. I suggest that in the wake of Greek-inspired experiments with tragedy, Shakespeare turned to versions of these tragic icons from mediating Greek texts to explore the resources of female lament—a trans-generic literary feature intimately linked with tragic performance—in order to solicit sympathies in comedy.

To trace the shadowy outlines of these figures in new comic settings, this chapter explores different forms of literary transmission than those pursued in the preceding chapters. Whereas translators such as Lumley, Gascoigne, Kinwelmersh, and Watson worked directly with Greek plays and their Latin and vernacular translations, and playwrights such as Peele drew on their experience of translating Greek, the eloquent female figures in Shakespeare's comedies signal their affinities with Greek tragic origins through layered literary genealogies. Shakespeare's proliferating allusions to Hecuba after collaborating with Peele in *Titus Andronicus* (*c.*1592) show that her privileged status as tragic icon lingered in his mind. In the context of this continuing interest, I suggest that allusions to similar Greek female figures from intermediary sources offer variations on Hecuba's legendary transmission of sympathies. As discussed in the Introduction,

Greek prose fiction played an especially prominent role in transmitting Euripides' tragic figures and structures to early modern readers, with some important alterations. Sacrificial virgins overshadow bereaved mothers, with an increasing emphasis on their status as potential brides—both Iphigenia and Polyxena are presented for sacrifice under the auspices of marriage to Achilles—giving the precarious pleasures of romantic love a central role in their stories.[2] Euripides' own interest in erotic passions, startling recognitions, and unexpected reunions attracted imitation from writers of prose fictions and New Comedy, both of which shaped Shakespeare's comedies through popular vernacular translations, as well as indirectly through their influence over sixteenth-century Italian and English romances.[3] In *The Comedy of Errors* and *Twelfth Night*, his responses to Plautus' *Menaechmi*, *Apollonius of Tyre*, and Heliodorus' *Aethiopica* show an emerging sense of new theatrical possibilities for eloquent suffering women.

Taking as a starting point Greek allusions in *The Comedy of Errors* and *Twelfth Night*, I suggest that these apparently superficial details signal deeper underlying borrowings, diffusely in the earlier *Comedy of Errors*, and more directly in *Twelfth Night*. In particular, I argue that Shakespeare revises the intrinsically hybrid female characters associated with Greek tragedy to develop new comic outcomes. Although these iconic figures carry tragic meanings, comic settings showcase the resourcefulness linked with their affective power, and highlight their crucial role in bringing about the recognitions, revelations, and reunions of Euripidean tragicomic endings. I suggest, in fact, that comedy offered Shakespeare an especially receptive setting for developing these figures' theatrical power. Because the genre's popularity with commercial audiences jarred with its ambivalent literary and ethical status in early modern England, playwrights and theorists alike frequently drew on the authority of both tragedy and antiquity in developing new comic models.[4] In contrast with satiric playwrights such as Ben Jonson, Thomas Middleton, and John Marston, whose comedies typically featured male protagonists seeking revenge and usurpation, Shakespeare developed his distinctive hybrid version of comedy in conversation with a Greek dramatic model that emphasized moving audiences through the performance of female passions.

LOSS AND RESTORATION IN EPHESUS

One of Shakespeare's earliest comedies, *The Comedy of Errors* (*c.*1594) follows *Titus Andronicus* in turning not only to Rome but also to Greece as gateway to its genre's possibilities. With its shipwreck-separated twins, indistinguishable slaves, and locked-out husband, the play adapts Plautus'

Menaechmi and *Amphitryo*, both of which had crucial roles in introducing classical comedy to Renaissance audiences: *Menaechmi* was easily the most popular classical play of any genre in the period, and *Amphitryo* stood at the center of early modern debates about tragicomedy.[5] Yet while under-scoring the pleasurable disorientation rooted in these dramas of mistaken identity, Shakespeare's revisions create a distinctively Greek geography, and draw on Greek-rooted literary models—especially the popular romance *Apollonius of Tyre*—to expand tragic frames and female roles.[6] Critics have nuanced our understanding of the play's generic mixture by exploring its interweaving of comic farce with romance; I argue that tracing Greek elements and allusions shows tragedy also contributing to this mixture.[7] Although the play's engagement with Greek models is diffuse and mediated, recognizing its debts to a tragic tradition linked with female suffering and sympathies illuminates the affective power of its bewilderment, separations, and laments, and shows it establishing a foundation for Shakespeare's later tragicomic depictions of sea-separated families in Greek settings, in *Twelfth Night*, *Pericles*, and *The Winter's Tale*. Far from simple farce, *Comedy of Errors* develops a template for the tragic underpinnings and female eloquence that come to mark Shakespeare's distinctive approach to the making of comedy.

Shakespeare's departures from Plautus begin with the play's self-consciously Greek setting.[8] Shifting the story to Ephesus—famously identified with its temple to the goddess Artemis, or Diana—situates the play in an implicitly pagan realm ruled by the goddess of both chastity and childbirth.[9] Shakespeare would have known of Diana's prominence in Ephesus from Plutarch; he would similarly have known of its link with Scythian Amazons.[10] In keeping with the city's invocation of mythic female power, the Syracusan Antipholus casts himself as a spellbound Odysseus when he tells Luciana, "Sing, siren, for thyself and I will dote" (3.2.47), and Duke Solinus later complains, "I think you all have drunk of Circe's cup" (5.1.271).[11] The threatening enchantments of *The Odyssey*'s seductresses link the mysterious delirium of Ephesus with Greek literary shadows, underscoring Homer's association in the period with tragicom-edy and the roots of dramatic performance.[12]

In keeping with this backdrop of enchanted Greek literary travels, Shakespeare departs more substantively from his Plautine model in the haunting melancholy of Egeon's frame narrative, which establishes a recurring Shakespearean pattern of beginning a comedy with the threat of imminent death.[13] "Proceed, Solinus, to procure my fall," Egeon pronounces, "And by the doom of death end woes and all" (1.1.1–2). The tale that follows is not the simple backstory of separated twins that we see in Plautus, but a lengthy lament relating the "griefs unspeakable"

(1.1.32) of losing a wife and son at sea. Shakespeare borrowed this story of dangerous Mediterranean travels from the story of *Apollonius of Tyre*, which he would revisit obliquely in *Twelfth Night* and more extensively in *Pericles*. The romance—in which a young king loses his wife and newborn daughter to disasters at sea before miraculously reuniting with them many years later—was well known in sixteenth-century England. It circulated most visibly in the eighth book of John Gower's *Confessio Amantis* (*c*.1390), which Shakespeare cited in *Pericles*, but also through the late medieval *Gesta Romanorum*, Robert Copland's *King Apollyn of Thyre* (1510), Belleforest's *Histoires Tragiques* (1582), and Lawrence Twine's *The Pattern of Painful Adventures* (1576, reprinted 1594 and 1607).[14] Although Gower did not directly advertise the story's Greek roots, he maintained its Greek names and settings, and followed it with discussions of Greek tragic women including Helen of Troy, Medea, Polyxena, Penelope, and Alcestis.[15] Shakespeare's expansions of the story's Greek references suggest that these associations made an impression on him; Linda McJannet has shown that Egeon's itinerary is more Greek than that of his source, as Peter Holland has similarly observed about the geography of *Pericles*.[16] Recognizing Shakespeare's attention to the ancient story's Greek elements suggests links with the kinds of Greek allusions *Titus Andronicus* had recently explored. Discussions of Shakespeare's *Apollonius* have observed the romance's debts to Homeric seafaring, but not to Euripides' female-centered dramas of passion, separation, and recognition.[17] Identifying the romance's transmission of Greek tragic women highlights important elements of *Comedy of Errors* that cannot otherwise be fully accounted for: the grief, never fully explained, that echoes in Adriana's passionate laments, and the pervasive identification of this grief with the language of maternity, which frames and animates the play's tragic underpinnings.

Taking its cue from *Apollonius*, Egeon's story channels tragedies of suffering women by identifying grief with the painful consequences of pregnancy and childbirth. He reports a happy life of prosperous sea voyages and marriage until his wife, "almost at fainting under/ The pleasing punishment that women bear,/ ... became/ A joyful mother of two goodly sons" (1.1.46–50), while "That very hour, and in the self-same inn,/ A mean woman was delivered/ Of such a burden male, twins both alike" (1.1.53–5). Egeon's use of the word "burden" to describe the birth of his sons' slaves opens a surprisingly resonant set of echoes throughout the play.[18] Frequently spelled in the period as "burthen," and sharing etymological roots with "birth," "bear," and "born," the word includes among its definitions "That which is borne in the womb; a child."[19] The word "burden" appears seven times in *Comedy of Errors*, far more frequently than in any other Shakespeare play, suggesting a particular preoccupation with the labors and sorrows of child-bearing; versions of the related word "bear" occur twenty-five times, also unusually frequently.[20] Egeon turns to the word "burden" again in describing the "tragic instance of our harm" (1.1.64), his terrible separation from his wife and son. "We were encountered by a mighty rock," he tells Duke Solinus,

> Which being violently borne upon,
> Our helpful ship was splitted in the midst;
> So that, in this unjust divorce of us,
> Fortune had left to both of us alike
> What to delight in, what to sorrow for.
> Her part, poor soul!, seeming as burdened
> With lesser weight but not with lesser woe,
> Was carried with more speed before the wind.   (1.1.101–9)

Egeon's ship is borne as uncontrollably as were his children and their attendants, and the resulting "unjust divorce" leaves both him and his wife each bearing a burden that is paradoxically both lighter by the weight of one child, and heavier with additional woe. Bereft of wife and son, Egeon acquires the suffering and sympathy of a tragic protagonist. "Hapless Egeon," Solinus proclaims, "whom the fates have marked/ To bear the extremity of dire mishap!" (1.1.14–41). As the duke emphasizes in his self-consciously tragic vocabulary, Egeon must bear the extremity of a genre at odds with the play's title.

Comedy, however, brings unexpected transformations to Egeon's burdens. His lost son and tragic language meet in Adriana, whose passionate laments mark Shakespeare's most striking departure from Plautus. While the wife in *Menaechmi*, cartoonishly named Matrona, speaks little and lacks persuasive power, Adriana has the second largest role in the play, with almost as many lines as the play's primary speaker (Antipholus of Syracuse). Her plaints offer a revised version of the loss that haunts the frame narrative. Chiding Luciana for failing to understand the impact of a husband's negligence, she accuses her sister of lacking empathy, insisting "were we burdened with like weight of pain/ As much or more would we ourselves complain" (2.1.36–7). Adriana's verbal echoes of Egeon's burdens and weights forge a link between her husband's past and current worlds, while invoking identification in order to arouse sympathy. Also like Egeon, she tells a backstory of loss, in her husband's regular disappearances. "[T]oo unruly deer," she laments, "he breaks the pale/ And feeds from home; poor I am but his stale" (2.1.100–1). Although their generic frames differ, her words suggest a prehistory to Portia's poignant queries to her husband in *Julius Caesar* (1599): "Dwell I but in the suburbs/ Of your good pleasure? If it be no more,/ Portia is Brutus' harlot, not his wife."[21] Reflecting on the play's dominant and vexed symbol of their marital bond, she recalls,

> Sister, you know he promised me a chain;
> Would that alone a toy he would detain,
> So he would keep fair quarter with his bed...
> Since that my beauty cannot please his eye,
> I'll weep what's left away, and weeping die. (2.1.106–8, 114–15)

To Adriana, the absence of the promised chain represents the absence of her husband's person and affections, resulting in the melting effects of tears discussed in Chapters 2 and 3. Although her hyperbolic emotion can translate into comic melodrama in performance, even apparently anti-tragic stagings underscore the complex theatrical resources of lament, highlighting the tenuous line between extreme tears and laughter.[22]

When we next see Adriana, confronted with a disoriented Antipholus who is not her husband, her passionate liquid imagery becomes even more lyrically haunting. In his first scene, Antipholus of Syracuse voiced his melancholy isolation with the striking image of a lone drop of water lost in a larger body: "I to this world am like a drop of water/ That in the ocean seeks another drop" (1.2.35–6). As if in reply, Adriana denies the possibility of this individuated drop, transforming the metaphor into a metaphysical reflection on marriage. "O, how comes it," she asks the wrong Antipholus,

> That thou art then estranged from thyself?—
> Thyself I call it, being strange to me,
> That, undividable, incorporate,
> Am better than thy dear self's better part.
> Ah, do not tear away thyself from me;
> For know, my love, as easy mayst thou fall
> A drop of water in the breaking gulf,
> And take unmingled thence that drop again
> Without addition or diminishing,
> As take from me thyself, and not me too (2.2.119–129)

In her oceanic simile, Adriana—whose name itself allies her with the Adriatic Sea—echoes not only her brother-in-law, but also Plautus, who included variations on this image in both *Menaechmi* and *Amphitryo*.[23] Yet she redirects the image into a paradox, juxtaposing grief at abandonment with insistence that separation is not possible. Whereas the Syracusan Antipholus imagines the prospect of reuniting with his lost twin as a near-impossible fantasy, Adriana sees the bonds of flesh as irrevocable, even when disclaimed. In contrast with most of the play's characters, she understands identity as both interpersonal and corporeal.[24] As a result, she offers an unsettling portrait of the vulnerability underpinning the play's haphazard accidents. Colin Burrow has described Adriana's complexity as Shakespeare's most distinctive break from classical precedent in the play, but I suggest that she signals a different kind of classical precedent, continuing the exploration of eloquently affecting Greek tragic heroines recently invoked in *Titus Andronicus*.[25]

After Adriana's ongoing intersections with the confusions sparked by the twins' misadventures in Ephesus, she plays a central role in the play's closing scene, alongside another female figure. Refuting her husband's account of the day's dramas, Adriana returns to the language of burdens: "As this is false he burdens me withal!" (5.1.209). Her husband echoes the same language in refuting her: "And this is false you burden me withal" (5.1.269). Yet the nature of the play's burdens remains mysterious until the abbess steps forth as a *dea ex machina* with the revelation—all the more astonishing because never revealed to or anticipated by the audience—that she is their bearer. "Whoever bound him," she says of Egeon,

> I will loose his bonds
> And gain a husband by his liberty.
> Speak, old Egeon, if thou be'st the man
> That hadst a wife once call'd Emilia
> That bore thee at a burden two fair sons:
> O, if thou be'st the same Egeon, speak,
> And speak unto the same Emilia! (5.1.340–6)

Bonds, like burdens, offer a persistent linguistic thread that unites the play's array of obligations, including the financial bond looming over Egeon's head, the indentured servitude of the Dromio bondsmen, the ambivalent bonds of marriage, and the invisible bonds linking twin to twin and sons to parents.[26] In revealing herself as the central figure reuniting a lost and dispersed family, Emilia simultaneously loosens and strengthens the mysterious bonds that have shaped the play. She also illuminates the nature of the burdens that have shaped the play's unsettling errors.

Curiously, in a play apparently centered on male twins and their male servants, the play's denouement hinges on a woman—a variation on a virgin priestess—who presents the final scene's consummation as a delivery crowning arduous labor. "Thirty-three years have I but gone in travail/ Of you, my sons," Emilia observes; "and till this present hour/ My heavy burden ne'er delivered" (5.1.401–2). The language of labor and delivery culminates in her subsequent insistence that "After long grief," they will celebrate "their nativity" (5.1.406, 404). Just as the play's griefs evoke the labor pangs that spur and valorize a tradition of female tragic lament, the closing resurrection of an apparently dead wife draws on *Apollonius of Tyre* to channel the astonishing tragicomic reversals of Euripides' revived women, establishing a motif that Shakespeare will go on to explore more fully in later plays. This departure from Plautine comedy toward Greek tragic motifs suggests that Greek echoes and elements in the *Apollonius* story directed Shakespeare toward new theatrical uses for Greek tragic models. After exploring Greek tragic women as a resource for soliciting sympathies in tragedy, in *Comedy of Errors* Shakespeare develops alternate versions of these figures to shape his experimentation with comedy.

IPHIGENIA IN ILLYRIA

Shakespeare turns more directly to Greek intertexts in *Twelfth Night* (1600–1), shortly after reflecting on Hecuba's tragic power in *Hamlet* (1599–1600). Shifting Hamlet's preoccupations with mourning and dis-simulation into a comic setting, the play mingles tragic threats and eloquent female suffering with the Plautine shipwrecked twins already explored in *Comedy of Errors*. Shakespeare borrowed *Twelfth Night*'s plot most directly from Italian reworkings of Plautus, especially the play *Gl'Ingannati*, and their English prose adaptations, such as Barnabe Rich's *Apollonius and Silla* (which borrowed its protagonist's name, as well as plot elements, from *Apollonius of Tyre*).[27] Yet as in *Comedy of Errors*, the play's preoccupations with grief, eloquent female lament, and unexpected recognitions also show the lingering influence of Greek tra-gedy. When Orsino, towards the end of the play, explicitly alludes to the threatened sacrifice of a virgin from Heliodorus' popular tragicomic romance *Aethiopica*, he highlights subtler Greek borrowings throughout the play. I suggest that Viola's enigmatic interiority and moving power draw on a tradition of tragic female lament that forges bonds by melting audiences' sympathies.

As in *Comedy of Errors*, the play's implicit Greek allusions begin with its setting. Worlds apart from Shakespeare's more familiar Italian and French comic backdrops, Illyria has been linked with its name's poetic merger of illusion, delirium, and lyricism,[28] and recent scholarship has explored the region's early modern associations with piracy, violence, Turks, and romance.[29] Yet critics have not observed that the Greek name Illyria refers to a kingdom rooted in classical antiquity and iden-tified with the literary legacy of tragedy.[30] Illyria was notable as the final resting place for Cadmus, the father of Thebes, central to tragic legend; both Apollodorus and Ovid described how Cadmus and Harmonia settled in Illyria before being sent to Elysium, the Greek afterworld with which Viola also juxtaposes the country. "And what should I do in Illyria?," she asks as the play opens; "My brother he is in Elysium" (1.2.3–4).[31] In his last moments before this presumed passage to Elysium, moreover, Sebastian is seen riding the waves "like Arion on the dolphin's back" (1.2.14), evoking a mythic Greek poet and musician widely associated with the origins of tragedy through his reputed invention of dithyrambic verse.[32]

Viola's opening grief, disguise, and emphasis on musical skill recall these Greek tragic backdrops. "Conceal me what I am," she tells the captain,

> and be my aid
> For such disguise as haply shall become
> The form of my intent. I'll serve this duke.
> Thou shall present me as an eunuch to him.
> It may be worth thy pains, for I can sing
> And speak to him in many sorts of music (1.2.50–5)

Just as the play's shipwreck-torn opening nods to Plautus, Viola's plan to disguise herself as a eunuch to gain access to a home, and ultimately to a secret love-object, deepens the play's New Comedy borrowings by echoing Terence's *Eunuch*.[33] Yet her sex complicates both these debts. Her transvestite identity has roots in the play's most conspicuous sources—the Italian Renaissance comedies and *novelle* mentioned earlier—which reflected both the popularity of emerging Italian actresses, as Pamela Allen Brown has shown, and early Italian interest in Greek theater.[34] Although Shakespeare's female-centered rewriting of New Comedy may most immediately evoke Italy, then, it also suggests Greek tragic female interiority and lament, which become more central as the play progresses.

The play never revisits the idea of Viola as a musically talented eunuch, but her performances of lament inspire painfully unachievable yearnings in both herself and others, developing a poignant intensity that complicates the play's comedy of misunderstandings.[35] Sent as a proxy to represent Orsino's love, Viola captivates Olivia by conveying instead her own sense of frustrated desire. "If I did love you in my master's flame," she insists, "With such a suffering, such a deadly life,/ In your denial I would find no sense;/ I would not understand it" (1.5.256–9). When Olivia asks, "Why, what would you?," Viola describes an urgency unmoored from Orsino's conventional tropes. "Write loyal cantons of contemned love," she explains,

> And sing them loud even in the dead of night;
> Hallow your name to the reverberate hills
> And make the babbling gossip of the air
> Cry out "Olivia!"   (1.5.262–6)

Implicitly recalling her original plan to seek work as a musician, Viola insists that her songs of love will move both hills and winds to join her in sympathy, creating an integrated aural assault that will overpower her audience. "O, you should not rest," she assures Olivia, "but you should pity me" (1.5.266–8). Her confidence proves justified. Rooted in her own experience of desire, her performance of passions succeeds in melting her audience: Olivia tells her, "You might do much" (1.5.268).

After Viola's departure, Olivia reflects on the encounter's overwhelming force in physical terms. "How now?," she wonders,

> Even so quickly may one catch the plague?
> Methinks I feel this youth's perfections
> With an invisible and subtle stealth
> To creep in at mine eyes.   (1.5.286–90)

Complementing Viola's emphasis on her words' aural impact, Olivia emphasizes the visual force of the performance, which "creep[s] in at [her] eyes." Together, these aural and visual elements confirm Olivia's initial jesting query into her visitor's theatrical talent: "Are you a comedian?" (1.5.177). Darryl Chalk has persuasively described this exchange as responding to antitheatrical accounts of the physically invasive power of performance.[36] The play's characters reflect self-consciously on the impact of performances; observing Malvolio's transformations, Fabian notes, "If this were played upon a stage, now, I could condemn it as an improbable fiction" (3.4.114–15). Yet as feminist and queer readings have demonstrated, Olivia's response to Viola/Cesario also draws on a passionate sympathy between two female characters.[37] I suggest that the attraction underscores the resemblance between the two women, who are both virgins mourning dead brothers. In conjuring the transfer of emotion between a passionate performer and a receptive listener, the scene offers an alternative version of the female dyads central to the period's preferred models of Greek tragedy.

Although this scene leaves its most potent imprint on Olivia, Viola also responds uneasily to the sympathies she sparks, especially after Malvolio's presentation of Olivia's ring stirs her to recognition, pity, and introspection. "What means this lady?," she muses; "Fortune forbid my outside have not charmed her" (2.2.17–18). She quickly arrives at her bemused realization:

> Poor lady, she were better love a dream.
> Disguise, I see, thou art a wickedness,
> Wherein the pregnant enemy does much.
> How easy is it for the proper false
> In women's waxen hearts to set their forms.
>   . . . My master loves her dearly,
> And I, poor monster, fond as much on him,
> And she, mistaken, seems to dote on me.
> What will become of this?   (2.2.26–36)

Rather than stopping at mockery, Viola's reflections on Olivia's hapless desire extend to empathy and identification. In recounting a chain of unrequited longings, she recognizes that Olivia suffers the same hopeless affection that she herself feels towards Orsino. Her sympathetic response leads her to reflect on the susceptibility of "women's waxen hearts," implicitly evoking the vocabulary of melting associated with female tragic performance in *Titus Andronicus* and *Hamlet*.

Viola's curious reference to "the pregnant enemy" implicitly underscores the relation between erotic susceptibility and the impressionable, receptive nature she attributes to the waxen female body. Keir Elam glosses "the pregnant enemy" as the devil, a suggestion that Maurice Hunt has developed into a claim that the play presents the devil "as capable of conceiving and delivering issue, usually of a monstrous kind."[38] Yet despite editors' routine claims that Shakespeare only uses "pregnant" in a figurative sense, Viola's usage here, like Hamlet's concern about being "unpregnant," links the term with the receptive and generative nature of female passions.[39] The word also resonates in her later insistence to Olivia, that "My matter hath no voice, lady, but to your own most pregnant and vouchsafed ear" (3.1.86–7). This striking phrase impresses Andrew so much that he takes careful note to reuse it: " 'Odours,' 'pregnant' and 'vouchsafed'—I'll get 'em all three all ready" (3.1.88–9). Yet if his naïve awe suggests an ironic critique of Viola's grandiloquence, it also underlines the intimately female and physiological language with which Viola succeeds where others have failed, in awakening Olivia's desire.

Viola's empathetic observation of Olivia's passions in this passage leads her to acknowledge her own love for Orsino: "And I, poor monster, fond as much on him." Her identification with monstrosity echoes her concern with pregnancy and impressionable organs, implicitly recalling the period's notions of monsters as shaped by the vivid fantasies of the maternal imagination.[40] The soliloquy prefigures her fuller anatomy of tragic female passions in her near-confession of love to Orsino. Claiming that she knows "Too well what love women to men may owe," she offers a cryptic defense of women's capacity for powerful emotion: "In faith, they are as true of heart as we" (2.4.105–6). "My father had a daughter loved a man," she goes on to tell him, "As it might be, perhaps, were I a woman,/ I should your lordship" (2.4.107–9). At his inquiry, she recounts more of this sad history:

> She never told her love,
> But let concealment, like a worm i' the bud,
> Feed on her damask cheek: she pined in thought,
> And with a green and yellow melancholy
> She sat like patience on a monument,
> Smiling at grief. Was not this love indeed?
> We men may say more, swear more, but indeed
> Our shows are more than will, for still we prove
> Much in our vows, but little in our love.   (2.4.110–18)

Viola presents female desire as deep and hidden, countering the showy proclamations of Petrarchan suffering with which Orsino opened the play, and challenging comedy's purported emphasis on love's pleasures by linking it to the mourning with which both she and Olivia began the play. She even hints that the suffering of hidden, unrequited love could be fatal: when her story, framed in the past tense, prompts Orsino to wonder, "But died thy sister of her love, my boy?," Viola replies enigmatically, "I am all the daughters of my father's house,/ And all the brothers too: and yet I know not" (2.4.119–21). In her evocation of grief, and refusal to refute the unhappy ending he imagines, Viola suggests that love threatens tragic consequences.

This threat sharpens towards the play's end, when Orsino responds with fury to Olivia's claim to have married Cesario. "Why should I not, had I the heart to do it," he asks, "Like to th' Egyptian thief, at point of death/ Kill what I love...?" (5.1.113–15). Orsino alludes here to a scene in Heliodorus' *Aethiopica* in which the Egyptian thief Thyamis threatens to kill the beautiful heroine Chariclea, whom he loves and hopes to marry.[41] Editors and critics typically identify Orsino as directing this threat towards Olivia, yet he goes on to specify "this your minion, whom I know you love" (5.1.121), and tells Viola/Cesario directly, "Come, boy.../ I'll sacrifice the lamb that I do love" (5.1.126).[42] While earlier moments in the play indirectly evoke popular Greek suffering heroines, this moment offers explicit intertextual contact. Critics have discussed the implications of Orsino's likeness to Thyamis, but the alignment of Viola with Chariclea invokes a Greek tragic motif of female sacrifice, which Viola self-consciously embraces. She responds to Orsino's threat not by confessing her sex and disproving her marriage, but by volunteering to be sacrificed: "And I, most jocund, apt and willingly/ To do you rest, a thousand deaths would die" (5.1.128–9). As a sacrificial victim willing to die for love, Viola merges Chariclea's passionate monogamy with the heroism of Iphigenia and Polyxena, the sacrificial tragic virgins that the *Aethiopica* invokes and imitates.[43] Signaling a shift from the play's Latin dramatic model centered on comic men to a Greek model centered on tragic women, Orsino's allusion points to a distinctly Greek literary legacy highlighting the affective power of female suffering.

Among its many features, the *Aethiopica* offered early moderns a prose version of Euripides' sacrificial virgins and tragicomic plotting, which Heliodorus imitates both directly and indirectly. The romance tells the story of Chariclea, who is separated at birth from her parents (the King and Queen of Ethiopia), becomes a priestess to Artemis at Delphi, falls in love with the handsome Theagenes, encounters many threats over the course of perilous travels, and is nearly killed by her father in a religious sacrifice just before her identity is miraculously revealed. In the episode to which Orsino alludes, the Egyptian thief Thyamis demands Chariclea's hand in marriage. In Thomas Underdowne's popular 1569 English translation, Thyamis assumes that Chariclea is "Priest of somme *Goddesse*" and "consecrated to somme God."[44] Chariclea, who is as clever as she is beautiful, confirms that she is "consecrated to the Goddes," and requests a postponement until she can visit an "an Altare, or Church sacred to *Appollo*, to surrendre mine office, and the tokens thereof."[45] Her language of religious consecration hints at her kinship with tragic sacrificial heroines such as Iphigenia and Polyxena, and she pursues this identification even more explicitly when she later directly quotes Polyxena from just before her sacrifice in *Hecuba*—"why should I live?"—prefaced by the self-consciously dramatic verb "she tragedized" (*epetragoidei*).[46] Early modern responses suggest particular interest in both Chariclea's heroic suffering and Heliodorus' metatheatrical language. Underdowne does not attempt to capture the theatrical verb *epetragoidei*, which he translates as "lamented," but elsewhere he echoes and intensifies Heliodorus' pervasive use of theatrical terms, especially through his repeated and almost invariably capitalized references to "Tragedy."[47] His translation's title, moreover—*An AEthiopian Historie Written in Greeke*—underscores his identification of the romance with the distinctively Greek literary tradition newly emerging into visibility.

Shakespeare's turn to the *Aethiopica* reflects a broader cultural fascination with Heliodorus, whose early modern popularity has been well established.[48] James Sanford translated parts of the romance into English in 1567, and Thomas Underdowne's 1569 full translation was so popular that it was reprinted in 1577, 1587, 1605, 1606, 1622, and 1627; by 1620, the satirist

Joseph Hall wondered, "What Schole-boy, what apprentice knows not Heliodorus?"[49] Chariclea had a particular attraction for playwrights: France saw a surge of tragicomic plays named for her, and in England a *Chariclea* was staged at court in 1572, and a *Queen of Ethiopia* in Bristol in 1578.[50] There were probably others; in 1582 the antitheatrical critic and former playwright Stephen Gosson claimed that romances including "*the Palace of pleasure, the Golden Asse, the Aethiopian historie . . .* haue beene throughly ransackt, to furnish the playe houses in London."[51] Yet we have not identified Heliodorus' popularity with a larger interest in the suffering women, startling recognitions, and unexpected reversals that the *Aethiopica* imitated from Greek tragedies. I suggest that the romance participated in the phenomenon of the period's newly visible Greek texts, and that its audience-pleasing happy ending represented the same generic hybridity that captured attention in Euripides' plays. Just as Chariclea's eventual reunion with Theagenes "had of a Tragical beginninge a Comical endinge," her final reunion, with her parents, leaves onlookers marvelling at "the Gods, whose will it was that this shoulde fall out woonderfully, as in a Comedy."[52] As a suffering daughter, separated from parents and beloved, threatened with violent sacrifice but ultimately redeemed, reunited, and married, Chariclea offered early modern readers and audiences a romantically alluring version of Greek tragedy's sacrificial virgins. By identifying Viola with the new literary prototype of the suffering, nearly sacrificed Greek tragic virgin, Orsino's allusion both underscores the play's darker possibilities and hints at the swerve that will transform an apparently tragic trajectory towards a comic outcome.

Like the *Aethiopica*, *Twelfth Night* ends with a climactic revelation and reunion prompted by a recognition scene. Yet although the *Aethiopica*'s culminating recognitions take place between lovers, and between parents and child—motifs that Shakespeare would rework elsewhere—the primary reunion and recognition in *Twelfth Night* is fraternal, and brought about by an irrefutable family resemblance. "One face, one voice, one habit, and two persons," Orsino exclaims; "A natural perspective, that is and is not!" (5.1.212–13). Antonio similarly insists that the twins must be the same person: "How have you made division of yourself?," he wonders; "An apple cleft in two is not more twin/ Than these two creatures." (5.1.216–20). Like the equivalent moment in *Comedy of Errors*, the scene is indebted to Plautus. When the Epidamnian Menaechmus joins his twin onstage, Messenio asks "By the immortal gods, what do I see?" ("*Pro di immortales, quid ego video?*"); when his master repeats the question, he replies, "your mirror" ("*Speculum tuum*").[53] Yet Sebastian's disconcerted rejoinder—"I never had a brother" (5.1.222)—reminds the audience of the moment's crucial break from Plautus. Combined with the Heliodorus allusion, it also points to a series of iconic Greek recognition scenes, which loom behind *Menaechmi, The Aethiopica,* and *Twelfth Night* itself.

In the context of Viola's identification of Chariclea, this fraternal reunion recalls Chariclea's regular introduction of her betrothed, Theagenes, as her brother—beginning with the Thyamis episode—in order to justify the propriety of their intimacy as unmarried fellow travelers. Yet in the additional light of Chariclea's identification with Iphigenia, their mock-fraternal separation and reunion recalls Iphigenia's extended, irony-laden encounter with Orestes, the brother she has just mourned as dead, in Euripides' *Iphigenia in Tauris* (414-412 BCE). Upon discovering through identifying signs that the visitor is her brother, Iphigenia expresses amazement: "I have come upon things that are beyond wonder, far from speech."[54] In his 1562 preface, Gasparus Stiblinus seizes on this moment as a generic pivot: "As Iphigenia explains...she is suddenly revealed and recognized. As a result, mutual celebration and tears arise between brother and sister, for whom nothing could have been more welcome or more unexpected than this accident."[55] As discussed previously, Stiblinus's bilingual edition was easy to read, and accessible in England; early modern playwrights could easily have known this passage, as well as other Greek accounts of this moment. Orestes, whom Heliodorus mentions in the Thyamis episode of the *Aethiopica,* has a long literary legacy of drawn-out recognitions by startled sisters.[56] The reunion in *Iphigenia in Tauris* imitates his storied encounter with Electra, first dramatized by Aeschylus in his *Libation Bearers* (458), and later revisited by both Euripides and Sophocles in their *Electra* plays (413 and 409).[57] In each of these plays, an unexpected reunion with a brother believed dead hinges on secret bodily signs: matching footprints, matching locks of hair, and a scar, which self-consciously links these scenes to the famously cautious recognition of Odysseus.

These plays present the discovery of a presumed-dead brother as rooted in physical likeness to his sister. In *Libation Bearers,* Electra sees a freshly cut hair on her father's tomb resembling her own, followed by the sign (*tekmērion*) of footprints matching her own.[58] Although the chorus suggests the presence of Orestes, Electra greets her brother warily until presented directly with a lock of his hair that matches hers. Euripides' *Electra* features the same caution; the title character talks with Orestes for much of the play without knowing his identity, amid growing evidence not only of a lock of hair and footprint matching hers, but also some of her own weaving. Despite many proffered forms of proof, she demands an independent identifying sign—a mark (*charactēr*)—that appears in the form of a scar on his brow.[59] This physiological proof (*tekmērion*)—self-consciously alluding to Odysseus' famous recognition by his nurse, and implicitly to his testing by a highly wary Penelope—finally persuades Electra, who professes herself persuaded by the cumulative tokens (*symboloisi*).[60] Perhaps most strangely, in Sophocles' *Electra*, a disguised Orestes watches Electra mourn his death, holding an urn that she believes contains his ashes—presented as clear proof (*emphanē tekmēria*) of his death—before she learns of sure signs (*saphē sēmei*) that he is alive, in the form of a freshly cut lock of his hair, matching her own, on their father's tomb.[61]

If the return of a presumed-dead brother brings astonishment and wonder, it also urgently raises the question of evidence, and specifically the need for clear bodily signs—especially for women, whose dependence on men intensifies their vulnerability, and their vigilance. As Euripides' Medea laments, "Oh Zeus, why have you provided for mortals clear signs (*tekmēria . . . saphē*) to tell the counterfeit from the gold, but put no mark (*charactēr*) on the body of men (*andrōn*) by which to distinguish the false?"[62] Significantly, Medea refers specifically to the bodies of *andrōn* (members of the male sex) rather than *anthropōn* (humans). Euripides suggests that women especially need clear signs, because so much hinges on their embraces. Early moderns might well have known this plaint, as *Medea* was the third most popular Greek play in the period, and at least some saw Jason as its villain: in his commentary, Stiblinus asked rhetorically, "For what is more intolerable for wives to bear than the adultery and perfidy of their husbands?"[63] As discussed in Chapter 3, however, Orestes, like his sister Iphigenia, attracted particular attention in England, where he featured in the Westminster School's production of Euripides' *Orestes* (1567), John Pikering's *Horestes* (*c.*1567), Thomas Goffe's later *Tragedy of Orestes* (1609–16), and Henry Chettle and Thomas Dekker's *Orestes Furies* and *Agamemnon and Orestes*.[64] Marston's *Malcontent* (*c.*1603) makes him a symbol for returning revengers: "Orestes, beware Orestes!"[65] As the last generation of the House of Atreus, navigating the traumatic aftermath of the Trojan War, Iphigenia and Orestes offered especially compelling models for the even more belated English.[66]

Shakespeare clearly registered their dramatic possibilities. As also discussed in Chapter 3, *Hamlet*, written soon after Dekker and Chettle's plays, is haunted by Orestes: the son avenging his murdered father, furious at his adulterous mother and incestuous uncle, supported by a close male friend. In its fixation on Hecuba as symbol of tragic affect, moreover, the play echoes *Titus Andronicus*, co-written with Euripidean translator Peele. Written shortly after *Hamlet*, *Twelfth Night* replays its interest in mourning, deception, and revenge with a female protagonist.

In the context of increasingly visible Greek tragic material, Shakespeare's reference to Heliodorus highlights his interest in the affective possibilities of Greek sacrificial virgins. Shakespeare would not need to have known any of these plays in detail to have absorbed the legacy of a sister demanding proof of a brother's identity before embracing him, and his other responses to Greek tragic women suggest that this recurring motif would have attracted his attention. Yet even without any awareness of these staged sibling recognition scenes, their echoes in Heliodorus would have brought their preoccupations with proof, signs, and marks onto his literary horizon, and coded them as both Greek and theatrical. I argue, then, that the ending of *Twelfth Night* reflects not only the *Aethiopica*, but also the increasingly visible Greek tragic material that it imitated.

Recognizing Orsino's alignment of Viola with Chariclea, and the echoes of the fraternal recognitions embedded in Chariclea's Iphigenian legacy, suggests new meanings in *Twelfth Night*'s culminating reunion. Sebastian, whose appearance has not changed, should be easier to accept and recognize than Viola, who now appears as a boy, yet Sebastian, like Orestes, quickly suggests his willingness to embrace his sister. "Were you a woman," he offers, "as the rest goes even,/ I should my tears let fall upon your cheek,/ And say 'Thrice welcome, drowned Viola'" (5.1.235–7). Confronted with the ghost of an apparently dead brother, however, Viola toys with the cautious legacy represented by figures such as Iphigenia, Electra, and Penelope. Rather than directly revealing her sex, she turns to secret signs:

VIOLA My father had a mole upon his brow.
SEBASTIAN And so had mine.
VIOLA And died that day when Viola from her birth
    Had numbered thirteen years.
SEBASTIAN O, that record is lively in my soul!
    He finished indeed his mortal act
    That day that made my sister thirteen years. (5.1.238–44)

Viola's attention to bodily signs, which establishes a template for Shakespeare's later tragicomic recognitions, gestures to a Greek device for redirecting a potential threat into a happy outcome: originating in the *Odyssey*, acted on the Attic stage, and filtered through romances such as *Aethiopica*.[67] Viola, however, adds her own twist to this tradition of female wariness. Extending her adopted male role, she offers her own signs, rather than demanding her brother's. In doing so, she also emphasizes the uncertainty of her own identity, and insists that Sebastian and Orsino should wait for proof rather than trusting her word: they should be more cautious, more like Greek tragic women. Unlike their Greek models, though, they must continue waiting, beyond the play's end. "If nothing lets to make us happy both/ But this my masculine usurped attire," Viola tells her brother,

> Do not embrace me till each circumstance
> Of place, time, fortune, do cohere and jump
> That I am Viola—which to confirm,
> I'll bring you to a captain in this town,
> Where lie my maiden weeds   (5.1.245–51)

Just as Viola refuses to embrace Sebastian without firm evidence of his identity, she similarly won't let him embrace her without more evidence of hers: the "maiden weeds" that will establish who she is. Rather than announce herself, she will wait for proof.

In her caution, Viola pre-empts the fate of Chariclea, whose plea to avoid sacrifice on grounds that she is the king's daughter initially meets with disbelief. "Is not the mayde starke mad?," her father asks, "who of singulare boldenesse with lies seeketh t' auoide deathe, and saith shee is my Daughter, as if it were in a Comedy" (in Greek, "as if on a stage," "ὥσπερ ἐπὶ σκηνῆς").[68] Viola will not be mad or bold. Instead, she will look beyond Chariclea to her Euripidean models, to channel their insistence on proof. Her skepticism is contagious: Orsino frames his subsequent proposal in a conditional clause. "If this be so," he tells her, "as yet the glass seems true,/ I shall have share in this most happy wreck" (5.1.261–2). Until that time, he continues to call her "Boy" (5.1.264). "Cesario, come," he tells her at the play's close; "For so you shall be, while you are a man;/ But when in other habits you are seen,/ Orsino's mistress and his fancy's queen" (5.1.378–81). Viola will embrace and be embraced only when her identifying signs are sufficient.

Viola's caution actively surpasses the Greek models that she evokes. Although staging choices can counter her insistence on delay, her comedy ends with less satisfaction than the tragedies she channels: she insists that her identification, fraternal embrace, and marriage all remain stalled at the play's end. Orsino's request to see her "in thy woman's weeds" (5.1.269) waits on Malvolio, who leaves the stage crying, "I'll be revenged on the whole pack of you" (5.1.371). Despite the delight at the twins' encounter, the play's recognitions and reunions remain incomplete, leaving open the curious slight possibility—parodied in Ionesco's *Bald Soprano*—that maybe everyone has got it wrong.[69] In that play, Donald and Elisabeth embrace too soon, a prospect that Viola is determined to avoid. By leaving *Twelfth Night*'s climactic embraces waiting indefinitely for irrefutable evidence, Shakespeare multiplies Euripides' generic switchbacks, borrowing tragic strategies to heighten comedy's affective possibilities.

The Comedy of Errors and Twelfth Night represent very different moments in Shakespeare's experimentation with comedy. Marking one of his earliest, if not the earliest, of his comedies, The Comedy of Errors announces its engagement with classical dramatic models self-consciously, by wearing its debts to Plautus on its sleeve. Yet the play's distinctive effects come especially from its striking departures from Plautus: its tragic backdrop, lyrical enchantment, and especially its passionate, lamenting female voices. I argue that these features, rooted especially in *Apollonius of Tyre*, mark Shakespeare's growing attention to the affective potential of newly visible Greek tragic heroines. By Twelfth Night, these models loomed more conspicuously, and playwrights had begun engaging classical models with increasingly complex layers of *contaminatio*. Shakespeare's direct allusion to Heliodorus brings these new Greek figures and structures even more forcefully into play, crucially for both Viola's enigmatic passions and the complex hybridity of the final recognition scene. Twelfth Night shows Greek tragic women opening up new theatrical possibilities for Shakespeare, with important consequences for the increasingly hybrid tragicomic plays to come.

NOTES

1. On the influence of Roman comedy, see Robert S. Miola, *Shakespeare and Classical Comedy: The Influence of Plautus and Terence* (Oxford: Clarendon Press, 1994); Wolfgang Riehle, *Shakespeare, Plautus, and the Humanist Tradition* (Cambridge: Boydell and Brewer, 1990); George E. Duckworth, "The Influence of Plautus and Terence Upon English Comedy," in *The Nature of Roman Comedy: A Study in Popular Entertainment* (Princeton: Princeton University Press, 1952), 396–441; Richard F. Hardin, "*Menaechmi* and the Renaissance of Comedy," *Comparative Drama* 37:3,4 (2003–04), 255–74; and Hardin, "Encountering Plautus in the Renaissance: A Humanist Debate on Comedy," *Renaissance Quarterly* 60:3 (2007), 789–818. On Italian influences, see especially Louise Clubb, "Italian Stories on the Stage," in *The Cambridge Companion to Shakespearean Comedy*, ed. Alexander Leggatt (Cambridge: Cambridge University Press, 2001), 32–46.
2. On Euripidean elements in Greek romances see Silvia Montiglio, "The Call Of Blood: Greek Origins Of A Motif, From Euripides To Heliodorus," *Syllecta Classica* 22 (2011), 113–29; Montiglio, *Love and Providence: Recognition in the Ancient Novel* (Oxford: Oxford University Press, 2013); James Pletcher, "Euripides in Heliodorus' *Aethiopiaka* 7–8," *GCN* 9 (1998), 17–27; Anna Lefteratou, "Myth and Narrative in the Greek novel" (Oxford D. Phil, 2010); and Lefteratou, "Iphigenia revisited: Heliodorus' *Aethiopica* and the 'Der Tod und das Mädchen' pattern," in *Intende, Lector—Echoes of Myth, Religion and Ritual in the Ancient*

Novel, ed. Marília P. Futre Pinheiro, Anton Bierl, and Roger Beck (Berlin: de Gruyter, 2013), 200–22.

3. On Euripides and Greek romances, see note 2, above; on Euripides and comedy, see Bernard Knox, "Euripidean Comedy," *Word and Action* (Baltimore: Johns Hopkins University Press, 1979), 250–74, and Erich Segal, "'The Comic Catastrophe': An Essay on Euripidean Comedy," *Bulletin of the Institute of Classical Studies* 40:S66 (1995), 46–55. On Greek romances and early modern English literature, see Carol Gesner, *Shakespeare and the Greek Romance* (Lexington: University of Kentucky Press, 1970); Samuel Wolff, *The Greek Romances in Elizabethan Prose Fiction* (New York: Columbia, 1902); Steven Mentz, *Romance for Sale in Early Modern England: The Rise of Prose Fiction* (Aldershot: Ashgate, 2006); and Tanya Pollard, "Romancing the Greeks: A Look at *Cymbeline*'s Generic Models," in *How To Do Things With Shakespeare*, ed. Laurie Maguire (Oxford: Blackwell, 2007), 34–53.

4. For criticisms of comedy's dubious ethical status, see George Puttenham, *The Arte of English Poesie* (London, 1589), 27 and 25; Sir Thomas Elyot, *The Boke Named the Governour* (London: Thomas Berteleti, 1531), 50r and 35v; Philip Sidney, *The Defence of Poesie* (London: William Ponsonby, 1595), sig. F3r; and Ben Jonson, *Discoveries*, ed. Lorna Hutson, in *The Cambridge Edition of the Works of Ben Jonson*, ed. David Bevington, Martin Butler, and Ian Donaldson (Cambridge: Cambridge University Press, 2012), vol. 7, 481–596. On early modern ambivalence towards laughter, see Matthew Steggle, *Laughing and Weeping in Early Modern Theatres* (Aldershot: Ashgate, 2007), and Indira Ghose, *Shakespeare and Laughter: A Cultural History* (Manchester: Manchester University Press, 2008).

5. *Menaechmi* claimed not only the first recorded performance of a classical play in vernacular translation (in Ferrarra, in 1486), but also eight of the first fifteen recorded Plautus productions in post-classical Europe; no other classical play received more than two recorded performances by the same date. See the APGRD Database, http://www.apgrd.ox.ac.uk/research-collections/performance-database/productions, accessed February 17, 2014; and Hardin, "*Menaechmi* and the Renaissance of Comedy." On Renaissance interest in *Amphitryo* and especially in Plautus' use of the term "tragicomedia," see Hardin, "England's *Amphitruo* before Dryden: The Varied Pleasures of Plautus's Template," *Studies in Philology*, 109:1 (2012), 45–62; on the genre's classical debts more broadly in this period, see Pollard, "Tragicomedy," in *The Oxford History of Classical Reception in English Literature*, vol. 2, *The Renaissance*, ed. Patrick Cheney and Philip Hardie (Oxford: Oxford University Press, 2015), 419–32.

6. On *Apollonius of Tyre* and its transmission, see especially Elizabeth Archibald, *Apollonius of Tyre: Medieval and Renaissance Themes and Variations* (Woodbridge: Boydell and Brewer, 1991). Although its earliest extant forms are in Latin, the romance draws on earlier Greek roots; see G. A. A Kortekaas, *The Story of Apollonius, King of Tyre: A Study of Its Greek Origin and an Edition of the Two*

Oldest Latin Recensions (Leiden: Brill, 2004), and Alexander Haggerty Krappe, "Euripides' *Alcmaeon* and the *Apollonius Romance*," *Classical Quarterly* 18:2 (1924), 57–8. Linda McJannet suggests that *Apollonius* "provides the clearest evidence of a 'direct connection' between later medieval romance and its roots in Greek prose narratives of the first century B. C. to the third century A. D."; see McJannet, "Genre and Geography," in *Playing the Globe: Genre and Geography in English Renaissance Drama*, ed. John Gillies and Virginia Mason Vaughan (Madison, NJ: Fairleigh Dickinson University Press, 1998), 86–106, 87–8. On Shakespeare's expansion of the play's female roles, see especially Laurie Maguire, "The Girls from Ephesus," in *The Comedy of Errors: Critical Essays*, ed. Robert S. Miola (New York: Routledge, 1997), 355–91.

7. On mixing farce and romance, see especially Martine van Elk, "'This sympathizèd one day's error': Genre, Representation, and Subjectivity in *The Comedy of Errors*," *Shakespeare Quarterly* 60:1 (2009), 47–72; also Charles Whitworth, "Rectifying Shakespeare's Errors: Romance and Farce in Bardeditry," in *The Theory and Practice of Text-editing: Essays in Honour of James T. Boulton*, ed. Ian Small and Marcus Welsh (Cambridge: Cambridge University Press, 1991, 107–41.

8. See Sara Hanna, "Shakespeare's Greek World: The Temptations of the Sea," in *Playing the Globe*, 107–28, 107, and McJannet, "Genre and Geography," 93.

9. Attention to Shakespeare's shift to Ephesus has typically focused on the city's biblical associations; see, for example, Arthur F. Kinney, "Shakespeare's *Comedy of Errors* and the Nature of Kinds," *Studies in Philology* 85:1 (1988), 29–52. On the temple to Diana, see Randall Martin, "Rediscovering Artemis in *The Comedy of Errors*," *Shakespeare and the Mediterranean*, ed. Tom Clayton, Susan Brock, and Vicente Fores (Newark: University of Delaware Press, 2004): 363–79; Caroline Bicks, "Backsliding at Ephesus: Shakespeare's Diana and the Churching of Women," *Pericles: Critical Essays*, ed. David Skeele (Hove: Psychology Press, 2000), 205–27; and Maguire, "The Girls from Ephesus," 360–5.

10. Plutarch linked "the temple of *Diana* in the city of EPHESVS" with "priests, magitians and soothsayers" in "The Life of Alexander the Great," *The Lives of the Noble Grecians and Romanes*, trans. Thomas North (London: Thomas Vautroullier and John Wight, 1579), 723. Solinus wrote, "The beauty of *Ephesus* is the Temple of Diana, buylded by the *Amozons* . . ." Julius Solinus, "Of the Lesser Asia: of the Temple of Diana at Ephesus," *The Excellent and Pleasant Worke of Iulius Solinus Polyhistor*, trans. Arthur Golding (London: J. Charlewoode for Thomas Hacket, 1587).

11. All citations from the play refer to Shakespeare, *The Comedy of Errors*, ed. R. A. Foakes, Arden Shakespeare (London: Methuen, 1962).

12. On early modern responses to Homer's Circe, see Tania Demetriou, "'Essentially Circe': Spenser, Homer, and the Homeric Tradition," *Translation and Literature* 15:2 (2006), 151–76. On Homer's influence over early modern conceptions of

drama, see Sarah Dewar-Watson, "Shakespeare's Dramatic Odysseys: Homer as a Tragicomic Model in *Pericles* and *The Tempest,*" *Classical and Modern Literature* 25:1 (2005), 23–40, and Pollard, "Encountering Homer through Greek plays in Sixteenth-century Europe," in *Epic Performances: From the Middle Ages into the Twenty-First Century,* ed. Fiona Macintosh, Justine McConnell, Stephen Harrison, and Claire Kenward (Oxford: Oxford University Press, forthcoming).

13. *Midsummer Night's Dream,* for instance, opens with Egeus threatening Hermia with death; *As You Like It* begins with a murderous feud between Orlando and his brother Oliver.

14. On the romance's early modern reception, see especially Archibald, *Apollonius of Tyre.*

15. Gower refers to Helen of Troy at 8.2529, Medea at 8.2563, Polyxena at 8.2593, Penelope at 8.2621, and Alcestis at 8.2640; Greek literary figures Aristotle and Plato appear at 8.2705 and 8.2718. See John Gower, *Confessio Amantis,* ed. Russell A Peck (New York: Holt, Rinehart and Winston, 1968).

16. See McJannet, "Genre and Geography," 93. Peter Holland notes that "Shakespeare is the first person to move Pentapolis [from North Africa, in *Apollonius*] to Greece"; see Holland, "Coasting in the Mediterranean: The Journeyings of *Pericles,*" in *Charting Shakespearean Waters: Text and Theatre,* ed. Niels Bugge Hansen and Søs Haugaard (Copenhagen: Museum Tusculanum Press, 2005), 11–30, 14.

17. See Steve Mentz, *At the Bottom of Shakespeare's Ocean* (London: Continuum, 2009), 36, and Colin Burrow, *Shakespeare and Classical Antiquity* (Oxford: Oxford University Press, 2013), 143–4. On the centrality of female characters in the prose fiction of late antiquity, see Elizabeth Archibald, "Ancient Romance," in *A Companion to Romance from Classical to Contemporary,* ed. Corinne Saunders (Oxford: Wiley-Blackwell, 2004), 10–25, 14; Katharine Haynes, *Fashioning the Feminine in the Greek Novel* (London: Routledge, 2003); and Stanley Wiersma, "The Ancient Greek Novel and its Heroines: A Female Paradox," *Mnemosyne* 43 (1990), 109–23.

18. On the play's pregnancy vocabulary, see Patricia Parker, *Shakespeare from the Margins: Language, Culture, Context* (Chicago: University of Chicago Press, 1996), 58.

19. See "Burden," 4.a. in *Oxford English Dictionary* online, www.oed.com, accessed February 18, 2014.

20. Versions of "burden" (including "burdens" and "burdened") appear thirty-three times throughout Shakespeare's writings; *As You Like It* and *The Winter's Tale* feature the word four times, and *Romeo and Juliet* three times but not in direct association with childbirth; no other play uses it more than twice. See "Concordance of Shakespeare's complete works," http://www.opensourceshakespeare.org/concordance/, accessed February 18, 2014.

21. Shakespeare, *Julius Caesar*, ed. David Daniell, Arden Shakespeare (London: Thomson Learning, 1998, rprt. 2003), 2.1.284–6.

22. On the proximity of laughter and tears in Shakespeare, see Steggle, *Laughing and Weeping in Early Modern Theatres*.

23. See Miola, *Shakespeare and Classical Comedy*, 27; on Adriana's name, see Maguire, "The Girls from Ephesus," 365, 369.

24. See Nancy Selleck, *The Interpersonal Idiom in Shakespeare, Donne and Early Modern Culture* (London: Palgrave MacMillan, 2008), 35.

25. See Burrow, *Shakespeare and Classical Antiquity*, 150–1.

26. The word "bond" appears 7 times, in the play, alongside 8 instances of "bind" and 17 of "bound," markedly more often than in any other Shakespeare play besides *The Merchant of Venice*.

27. See Louise Clubb, "Italian Stories on the Stage," 40–1; also Clubb, *Italian Drama in Shakespeare's Time*, 65–8; Clubb, "Intertextualities: Some questions," in *The Italian World of English Renaissance Drama: Cultural Exchange and Intertextuality*, ed. Michele Marrapodi and A. J. Hoenselaars (Newark: University of Delaware Press, 1998), 179–89; and Clubb, ed., *Pollastra and the Origins of Twelfth Night* (Aldershot: Ashgate, 2010). On Shakespeare's debts to *Gl'Ingannati*, see also Susanne Wofford, "Foreign Emotions on the Stage in *Twelfth Night*," in *Transnational Exchange in Early Modern Theater*, eds. Robert Henke and Eric Nicholson (Aldershot: Ashgate, 2008), 141–58. On Rich's debts to Apollonius of Tyre, see Archibald, *Apollonius of Tyre*.

28. In the most recent Arden edition, Keir Elam argues that "for Shakespeare's early audiences, 'Illyria' probably did not ring distinct geographical bells" ("Introduction," Shakespeare, *Twelfth Night*, ed. Elam, Arden Shakespeare [London: Bloomsbury, 2008], 70–1). Citations to the play will refer to this edition. For reflections on the name's verbal resonances, see Leah S. Marcus, *Puzzling Shakespeare* (Berkeley and Los Angeles: University of California Press, 1988), 161, and Geoffrey Hartman, "Shakespeare's Poetical Character," in *Twelfth Night: New Casebooks*, ed. R. S. White (New York: St. Martin's Press, 1996), 27.

29. See Goran Stanivukovic " 'What country, friends, is this?': The Geographies of Illyria in Early Modern England," *Litteraria Pragensia* 12:23 (2002), 5–21, and "Illyria Revisited: Shakespeare and the Eastern Adriatic," in *Shakespeare and the Mediterranean*, 401–15; and Patricia Parker, "Was Illyria as Mysterious and Foreign as We Think?," in *The Mysterious and the Foreign in Early Modern England*, ed. Helen Ostovich, Mary V. Silcox, and Graham Roebuck (Newark: University of Delaware Press, 2008), 209–34. On Illyria's political implications for Shakespeare, see Lea Puljcan Juric, "Illyrians in *Cymbeline*," *English Literary Renaissance* 42:3 (2012), 425–51.

30. On Illyria's status in antiquity, see Marjeta Šašel Kos, "Mythological stories concerning Illyria and its name," in *L'Illyrie méridionale et l'Épire dans l'Antiquité*

IV, ed. Pierre Cabanes and Jean-Luc Lamboley (Paris: De Baccard, 2004),
493–504, and Kos, "Cadmus and Harmonia in Illyria," *Arheološki vestnik* 44
(1993), 113–36. Elizabeth Pentland juxtaposes Illyria's modern and classical
associations in "Beyond the 'Lyric' in Illyricum: Some Early Modern Backgrounds
to *Twelfth Night*," in *Twelfth Night: New Critical Essays*, ed. James Schiffer
(London: Routledge, 2011), 149–66.

31. Apollodorus writes: "And Cadmus ruled over the Illyrians, and a son Illyrius was
born to him. But afterwards he was, with Harmonia, turned into a serpent and
sent away by Zeus to the Elysian Fields" ("καὶ βασιλεύει Κάδμος Ἰλλυριῶν, καὶ
παῖς Ἰλλυριὸς αὐτῷ γίνεται. αὖθις δὲ μετὰ Ἀρμονίας εἰς δράκοντα μεταβαλὼν εἰς
Ἠλύσιον πεδίον ὑπὸ Διὸς ἐξεπέμφθη," *The Library of Greek Mythology*, 3.5.4). See
Sara Hanna, "From Illyria to Elysium: Geographical Fantasy in *Twelfth Night*,"
Litteraria Pragensia 12: 23 (2002), 21–45. Ovid, similarly, writes, "And fleeting
long like pilgrims, at the last/ Upon the coast of Illirie his wife and he were cast"
(longisque erroribus actus/contigit Illyricos profuga cum coniuge fines," *Meta-
morphoses*, 4.567–8, trans. Golding, 1567). On Ovid's Book 4, the "Theban
book," as the tragic center of the *Metamorphoses*, hearkening specifically to
Euripides, see Alison Keith, "Dionysiac Theme and Dramatic Allusion in
Ovid's *Metamorphoses* 4," in *Beyond the Fifth Century: Interactions with Greek
Tragedy from the Fourth Century BCE to the Middle Ages*, ed. Ingo Gildenhard and
Martin Revermann (Berlin and New York: de Gruyter, 2010), 187–217.

32. Arion was identified with the origin of tragedy in antiquity, at least as early as
Solon; see Eric Csapo and Margaret Christina Miller, *The Origins of Theater in
Ancient Greece and Beyond* (Cambridge: Cambridge University Press, 2007), 10.
His reputation reached the early modern period especially through Herodotus,
who described Arion as "the most excellent and skylfull musition on the harpe of
those rymers, by whom also chieflye was inuented, named, and taught the kynde
and forme of verse called *Dithyrambus*." See *The Famous Hystory of Herodotus*
(London: Thomas Marshe, 1584), 6v. Early modern English discussions of Arion
linked him with musical performance, and Robert Greene depicted him as the
author of "tragicall and comicall histories"; see *Greenes Orpharion* (London:
Edward White, 1599), 1.

33. See Keir Elam, "The Fertile Eunuch: *Twelfth Night*, Early Modern Intercourse,
and the Fruits of Castration," *Shakespeare Quarterly* 47:1 (1996), 1–36; Robert S.
Miola, "New Comedic Errors: *Twelfth Night*," in *Shakespeare and Classical
Comedy* (Oxford: Oxford University Clarenden Press, 1994), 38–61; and Martine
van Elk, "'Thou Shalt Present Me as an Eunuch To Him': Terence in Early
Modern England," in *A Companion to Terence*, ed. Antony Augoustakis and
Ariana Trill (Oxford: Wiley-Blackwell, 2013), 410–28.

34. On actresses, see Pamela Allen Brown, "Anatomy of an Actress: Bel-imperia as
Tragic Diva," *Shakespeare Bulletin* 33:1 (2015), 49–65; "Dido, Boy Diva of
Carthage," in *Transnational Mobilities in Early Modern Theater*, ed. Robert

Henke and Eric Nicholson (Aldershot, Ashgate, 2014), 113–30; " 'Cattle of this Colour': Boying the Diva in *As You Like It*," *Early Theatre* 15.1 (2012): 145–66; and "The Counterfeit *Innamorata*, or, The Diva Vanishes," *Shakespeare Yearbook* 10 (1999): 402–26; see also Eric Nicholson, "Ophelia Sings Like a *Prima Donna Innamorata*: Ophelia's Mad Scene and the Italian Female Performer," in *Transnational Exchange in Early Modern Theater*, ed. Robert Henke and Eric Nicholson (Aldershot: Ashgate, 2008), 81–98. On Greek influences, Rich's *Apollonius and Silla* (1581) drew on a novella by Matteo Bandello, who, as previously discussed, had translated Euripides' *Hecuba* in 1539. On Italy as the crucible of European reception of Greek plays, see especially Salvatore Di Maria, "Italian Reception of Greek Tragedy," in *A Companion to Greek Tragedy*, ed. Justina Gregory (Oxford: Wiley-Blackwell, 2005), 428–43, and Agostino Pertusi, "Il Ritorno alle fonti del teatro Greco classico: Euripide nell'Umanesimo e nel Rinascimento," *Venezia e l'Oriente fra tardo Medioevo e Rinascimento* (Firenze: Sansoni, 1966), 205–24.

35. On the play's exploration of sympathies and antipathies, see Mary Floyd-Wilson, " 'As secret as maidenhead,' " in *Occult Knowledge, Science, and Gender on the Shakespearean Stage* (Cambridge: Cambridge University Press, 2013), 73–90.

36. See Darryl Chalk, "To Creep In At Mine Eyes": Theatre And Secret Contagion In *Twelfth Night*," in *Rapt in Secret Studies: Emerging Shakespeares*, ed. Darryl Chalk and Laurie Johnson (Newcastle: Cambridge Scholar Publishing, 2010), 171–94.

37. See Valerie Traub, *The Renaissance of Lesbianism in Early Modern England* (Cambridge: Cambridge University Press, 2002), 56–7; Laurie Shannon, "Nature's Bias: Renaissance Homonormativity and Elizabethan Comic Likeness," *Modern Philology* 98:2 (2000), 183–210.

38. See Elam, ed. *Twelfth Night*, 210, and Maurice Hunt, "Shakespeare's *Twelfth Night* and 'The Pregnant Enemy': The Devil in *What You Will*," *The Upstart Crow: A Shakespeare Journal* 30 (2011), 5–17.

39. See Tanya Pollard, "Conceiving Tragedy," in *Shakespearean Sensations*, ed. Katharine Craik and Tanya Pollard (Cambridge: Cambridge University Press, 2013), 85–100.

40. See Marie-Hélène Huet, *Monstrous Imagination* (Cambridge, MA: Harvard University Press, 1993), and Katharine Park and Lorraine J. Daston, "Unnatural Conceptions: The Study Of Monsters In Sixteenth-And Seventeenth-Century France And England," *Past and Present* 92:1 (1981), 20–54.

41. Elam notes the implications of barbarity (*Twelfth Night*, 330), which Wofford also explores in "Foreign Emotions on the Stage in *Twelfth Night*," 147–50; Steve Mentz identifies Orsino's misreading of the situation with a pattern of "generic misdirection" in Heliodorus (*Romance for Sale in Early Modern England*, 50). In the most sustained reading of this allusion, Mark Houlahan observes the contrast between passive Orsino and the forceful Thyamis, whom he links more closely with the "pirate" Antonio, but his primary focus is on the play's engagement with the tonal

complexity of Heliodorus' romance; see "'Like To Th'Egyptian Thief': Shakespeare Sampling Heliodorus in *Twelfth Night*," in *Rapt in Secret Studies*, 305–17.

42. Elam describes "a shift in the object of Orsino's affections, from *what I love* (presumably Olivia) at 115, to whom *I tender dearly* (Cesario) at 122" (*Twelfth Night*, 33); Wofford similarly writes, of the words "Kill what I love," "he presumably refers to Olivia, yet the next time he refers to killing someone he loves, he will shift focus to Cesario" ("Foreign Emotions," 149).

43. On Chariclea's identification with Iphigenia, see Lefteratou, "Myth and Narrative in the Greek novel" and "Iphigenia revisited"; on Chariclea's echoes of Polyxena, see Pletcher, "Euripides in Heliodorus' *Aethiopiaka* 7–8."

44. *An AEthiopian historie written in Greeke by Heliodorus*, trans. Thomas Underdowne (London: Frances Coldock, 1569), 13r; Heliodorus, *Aethiopica*, I.20.

45. *An AEthiopian historie*, 14v.

46. "Καὶ ὁ Θεαγένης ἐπεῖχεν ἐπιλαμβανόμενος σὺν ἱχεσίας τῶν χειρῶν, ἡ δὲ ἐπετραγῳδίδει, τί γάρ με δεῖ ζῆν;" Heliodorus, *Aethiopica*, VII.14.7. See Pletcher, "Euripides in Heliodorus' *Aethiopiaka* 7–8," and J. W. H. Walden, "Stage-Terms in Heliodorus's *Aethiopica*," *Harvard Studies in Classical Philology* 5 (1894), 1–43.

47. *An AEthiopian historie*, 96v.

48. See Gesner, *Shakespeare and the Greek Romance*; Wolff, *The Greek Romances in Elizabethan Prose Fiction*; Mentz, *Romance for Sale in Early Modern England*; Pollard, "Romancing the Greeks."

49. Joseph Hall, "The Honour of the Married Clergy Maintained," in *The Works of the Right Reverend Father in God, Joseph Hall*, ed. Josiah Pratt (London, 1808), 10 vols, 9:148. See Douglas Bush, *English Literature in the Earlier Seventeenth Century* (Oxford: Oxford University Press, 1945), 53.

50. See Wes Williams, *Monsters and Their Meanings in Early Modern Culture: Mighty Magic* (Oxford: Oxford University Press, 2011), and *Lost Plays Database*, http://www.lostplays.org/index.php/Chariclea_(Theagenes_and_Chariclea), accessed October 10, 2014.

51. Stephen Gosson, *Playes Confuted in Five Actions* (London: Thomas Gosson, 1582), D5v.

52. *An AEthiopian historie*, 91v and 148r.

53. Plautus, *Menaechmi*, 5.9.3–4.

54. "θαυμάτων/ πέρα καὶ λόγου πρόσω τάδ' ἐπέβα" (839–40). The Latin of Stiblinus's edition reads "Omne superant miraculum/ Omnemqu. sermonem ea quae acciderunt"; see Gasparus Stiblinus, *Evripides Poeta Tragicorum princeps* (1562), 368.

55. "Hinc mutua congratulatio et lacrimae inter fratrem et sororem oriuntur, quibus hoc casu nihil nec optatius nec insperatius accidere poterat." Stiblinus, "Argumentum Et Praefatio Gaspari Stiblini In Iphigeniam Tauricam," in *Evripides Poeta Tragicorum princeps*, 381.

56. In Book Two, shortly after the Thyamis episode, Calasiris tells Cnemon of how he came to meet Chariclea when visiting Delphi, at the time of an important

sacrifice: "This Sacrifice the *Aenians* sende to *Pirrhus Achilles* sonne euery fourthe yéere, at suche time as the feaste *Agon* is kepte to *Apollo* (whiche is now as you knowe) for here was he killed at the very Aultars of *Apollo*, by guile of *Orestes Agamemnons* Sonne" (*An AEthiopian historie*, 37r).

57. On this scene, see especially Friedrich Solmsen, *Electra And Orestes: Three Recognitions in Greek Tragedy* (Amsterdam: N.V. Noord Hollandsche Uitgevers Maa Tschappij, 1967), and Froma Zeitlin, "A Study in Form: Recognition Scenes in the Three Electra Plays," *Lexis* 30 (2012), 361–78.

58. "καὶ μὴν στίβοι γε, δεύτερον τεκμήριον,/ ποδῶν ὅμοιοι τοῖς τ᾽ ἐμοῖσιν ἐμφερεῖς." Aeschylus, *Choephoroi*, in *Septum Quae Supersunt Tragoedias*, ed. Denys Page (Oxford: Clarendon Press, 1972, 1975), 199–244; ll. 205–6.

59. "ποῖον χαρακτῆρ᾽ εἰσιδών, ᾧ πείσομαι;" (Euripides, *Electra*, 572).

60. On Penelope's sharpness towards Odysseus in this recognition scene, and early modern discomfort with it, see Tania Demetriou, "*Periphrōn* Penelope and her Early Modern Translations," in *The Culture of Translation in Early Modern England and France, 1500–1660*, ed. Tania Demetriou and Rowan Tomlinson (Basingstoke: Palgrave, 2015), 86–111.

61. "ἐμφανῆ τεκμήρια" (1109); "σαφῆ/ σημεῖ᾽" (885–6). On the theatrical ironies of this scene, see especially Mark Ringer, *Electra and the Empty Urn: Metatheater and Role Playing in Sophocles* (Chapel Hill: University of North Carolina Press, 1998), esp. 1–5 and 161–99. Earlier, Clytemnestra is persuaded that the Paedagogus comes "holding sure proofs of his [Orestes'] death" ("θανόντος πίστ᾽ ἔχων τεκμήρια," 774).

62. "ὦ Ζεῦ, τί δὴ χρυσοῦ μὲν ὃς κίβδηλος ᾖ/ τεκμήρι᾽ ἀνθρώποισιν ὤπασας σαφῆ,/ ἀνδρῶν δ᾽ ὅτῳ χρὴ τὸν κακὸν διειδέναι/ οὐδεὶς χαρακτὴρ ἐμπέφυκε σώματι;" (*Medea*, 516–19).

63. "Quid etiam impatientius uxores ferunt quam maritorum suorum adulteria et perfidiam?" Stiblinus, "In Medeam Praefatio," in *Evripides Poeta Tragicorum princeps*, 165.

64. Westminster schoolboys staged Euripides' *Orestes* in 1567; see APGRD for details of this and other performances. On early modern reception of the *Oresteia*, see Inga-Stina Ewbank, " 'Striking too short at Greeks': The Transmission of *Agamemnon* on the English Renaissance Stage," in Agamemnon *in Performance: 458 BC to AD 2004*, ed. Fiona Macintosh, Pantelis Michelakis, Edith Hall, and Oliver Taplin (Oxford: Oxford University Press, 2005), 37–52, and Louise Schleiner, "Latinized Greek Drama in Shakespeare's Writing of *Hamlet*," *Shakespeare Quarterly* 41:1 (1990), 29–48.

65. John Marston, *The Malcontent*, ed. G. K. Hunter, Revels Edition (Manchester: Manchester University Press, 1975, 1999), 1.5.13. I am grateful to Lucy Munro for calling this allusion to my attention.

66. *Orestes* and *Iphigenia in Aulis* date from 408 and 406 BCE; the latter was first staged in 405 BCE, after Euripides' death. On England's attraction to the generation after

Troy, see Pollard, "Encountering Homer through Greek Plays in Sixteenth-century Europe."

67. On signs and marks as proof in Greek fiction, see Montiglio, *Love and Providence*; on Shakespeare's debts to Greek romances for these identifying details, see Gesner, *Shakespeare and the Greek Romance*. As Tiffany Stern has argued, "miniaturizing" motifs such as birthmarks also lent themselves to the intimate size of the coterie theaters where these plays were staged; see Stern, "Actors and Audience on the Stage at Blackfriars," in *Inside Shakespeare: Essays on the Blackfriars Stage*, ed. Paul Menzer (Selinsgrove, PA: Susquehanna University Press, 2006), 35–53, 46.

68. *An AEthiopian historie*, 136v; Heliodorus, *Aethiopica*, 10.12.2.

69. After Donald and Elisabeth Martin make the astonishing discovery that they are married and share a daughter, the audience learns subsequently from the servant Mary that they have got it wrong: although they live at the same address and each has a daughter called Alice with one white eye and one red, one Alice has a white left eye and a red right eye, and the other the reverse: "Malgré les coïncidences extraordinaires qui semblent être des preuves définitives, Donald et Elisabeth n'étant pas les parents du même enfant, ne sont pas Donald et Elisabeth." *La Cantatrice Chauve*, in Eugéne Ionesco, *Théâtre*, ed. Jacques Lemarchand (Paris: Gallimard, 1954), 21–57, 33.

5

Bringing Back the Dead

Shakespeare's Alcestis

As we have seen, the bereaved mothers and sacrificial virgins linked with Greek theater offered new possibilities for responding to loss in comedy, as well as in their more familiar tragic contexts. Reversing tragedy's usual trajectory, *The Comedy of Errors* (*c.*1594) and *Twelfth Night* (1600–1) begin with mourning, and culminate in bringing back the dead. In increasingly tragicomic plots, Shakespeare merged these two structures, tracing the catastrophes that lead to death and mourning before reversing them by reanimating the dead. After the apparent death and climactic revival of Hero in *Much Ado About Nothing* (1598–99), he went on to revisit this plot device repeatedly, especially in *Pericles* (1607–8) and *The Winter's Tale* (1610–11). Each of these plays not only dramatizes a wife's miraculous return to life from apparent death, but also links this recovery with the performance of female lament, which elicits sympathies and melts audiences into supportive alliances. Just as Shakespeare absorbed Hecuba's tragic potential from George Peele, and began reuniting severed families by supplementing Plautus with Greek prose fictions, he developed the theatrical potential of reanimating dead wives through varying forms of collaborative conversations with authors including George Wilkins, Matteo Bandello, Robert Greene, Ovid, Plutarch, and especially Euripides. The resulting plays reconfigure tragedy with a happy ending, a hybrid genre that early moderns identified with Euripides. In particular, they recreate the ending of *Alcestis*, in which a grieving man encounters a veiled woman who is eventually revealed to be his lost wife, returned from death.

Reviving apparently dead women occupied Shakespeare from the beginning of his playwriting career. As Chapter 4 showed, in *The Comedy of Errors* he drew on a Greek-rooted prose fiction to rediscover a lost mother in a Greek goddess's temple. The possibility of women coming back to life also haunts his tragedies: *Romeo and Juliet* (1594–5), *Othello* (1603–4), *King Lear* (*c.*1606), and *Antony and Cleopatra* (1606–7) achieve some of their most terrible pathos when apparently dead women ignite hopes by reviving briefly before succumbing fully to death. More often, women return triumphantly from seeming death, as in *All's Well That Ends Well* (*c.*1604–5) and *Cymbeline* (1611), as well as the three plays explored in this chapter. The shock of apparent death in these plays, along with the even more startling return from it, jolts and mobilizes audiences both onstage and off. Critics have identified these moments with Christian resurrection, and intertextual readings have rooted many of their plots in Italian *novelle*.[1] Yet unlike Christ, Shakespeare's resurrected figures are almost invariably female, and Greek sources hover behind and alongside their better-known mediating texts. The plays that most fully explore these recovered women, moreover, feature conspicuously Greek settings, names, and details. Both *Much Ado* and *The Winter's Tale* take place in Sicily, a Greek province, while *Pericles* depicts a Greek king traveling in Mediterranean seas; Greek names such as Hero, Pericles, Hermione, and Autolycus evoke familiar Greek texts by Musaeus, Plutarch, and Homer, as well as Euripides; and Greek religious icons such as the Delphic Oracle and the Temple of Diana at Ephesus play pivotal roles in plots. These Hellenizing details call for explanation, especially because so many of them depart from Shakespeare's acknowledged sources.

Just as these plays perform a kind of theatrical necromancy, bringing back to life the ghostly specters of their recently expired mothers and daughters, I suggest that they also revive other literary ghosts hovering behind these figures. Most conspicuously, they call on ghosts summoned recently by English and Italian writers: Marlowe's Hero, Bandello's Fenicia, Gower's Thaise, and Greene's Bellaria and Fawnia. Behind these figures, none of whom embodies the pattern of death and resurrection, loom earlier classical prototypes—especially from Ovid, and *Apollonius of Tyre*—who in turn are shadowed by the potent figure of Euripides' Alcestis. Although the best-known archetypal heroes who return from death are men—Odysseus, Orpheus, and later Christ—Alcestis offers a female version of this motif, reflecting Euripides' characteristically counter-epic strategy of relocating heroism in women and domestic settings.[2] Drawing on the myth of Persephone's return from the under-world, Alcestis offered a new template for a hero's return from the dead, in a strange new genre hovering uneasily between tragedy, comedy, and satyr play.[3]

Proposing that Shakespeare responded to Alcestis is not itself new. In the nineteenth century, Israel Gollancz suggested that Shakespeare derived *The Winter's Tale*'s ending from *Alcestis*, and others have periodically echoed this idea.[4] Douglas B. Wilson argued for Shakespeare's possible familiarity with Buchanan's Latin translation of Euripides' play, Bruce Louden drew on this idea to trace larger preoccupations with Greek myth

in the play, Sarah Dewar-Watson pursued Buchanan's influence by proposing a specific verbal echo from his translation, and John Pitcher cited
Alcestis as one of the play's sources in his 2010 Arden edition of the play.[5]
In perhaps the most exhaustive study of Greek echoes in *The Winter's
Tale*, Earl Showerman argued that its detailed engagement with Greek
identifies the play's author as the Earl of Oxford, although his argument
hinges partly on inaccurate claims about the circulation of Euripides'
translations in early modern England.[6] Building on these studies, I argue
that Alcestis and her uncanny resurrection haunt Shakespeare's imagination
not only in *The Winter's Tale*, but also in the broader proliferation of revived
wives throughout his plays. By situating Alcestis in a previously invisible
early modern canon of Greek tragic models, moreover, I argue that her
meanings for Shakespeare have a privileged status that we have not yet
recognized. Just as Hecuba represents tragedy in the early modern imagination, and Iphigenia suggests the comic possibilities of youthful heroism,
Alcestis represents the hybrid possibility of tragicomic redemption, which
critics such as Helen Hackett and Helen Wilcox have suggested that
Shakespeare identified especially with maternity.[7] Unlike Hecuba, whom
Shakespeare's characters invoke directly by name, Alcestis presents an
indirect shadow, conjured especially by the figure of the veiled resurrected
wife offered to her grieving husband, yet this figure's recurrence suggests an
important sustained engagement. I suggest that Shakespeare's interest in
reviving apparently dead women takes inspiration not only from Alcestis,
but also from a broader fascination with the possibilities of theatrical
reanimation represented by long-dormant Greek dramatic icons. As Marvin
Carlson reminds us, the theater is a privileged site for necromancy; bringing
back the dead is not only possible but necessary.[8] In reviving Hero, Thaisa,
and Hermione, Shakespeare brings back the ghosts of Alcestis, Euripides,
and the tragic theater itself.

RECOVERING HERO

With few lines and a generally unobtrusive demeanor, Hero is often
relegated to the margins of *Much Ado About Nothing*, but her suffering
and feigned death provide the central catalyst for the play's transformations and eventual marriages. Her name also suggests her prominence by
identifying her with the protagonist of a Greek tragic legend. Self-
consciously recalling Marlowe's *Hero and Leander*, which Shakespeare
frequently cited in contexts of female suffering, Hero evokes a bereaved
Greek lover linked with veils, virginity, and sacrifice.[9] "Is Hero Greek to
us?," Diana Henderson has wondered about *Much Ado*, observing that her

allusive name separates her from the play's otherwise Italian contexts.[10] Although Marlowe, like Ovid and Musaeus, portrayed Hero in epyllion, her story was widely linked with tragedy; Marlowe cited the "tragedy divine Musaeus sung," and Julius Caesar Scaliger had earlier described the story as "quasi tragoedia."[11] It was also explicitly identified with its Greek origins; Marlowe referred to Leander as "the vent'rous youth of Greece," and his Leander asks Hero what "Greece will think" if she defies the goddess of love by remaining a virgin (I.57, 289). Taking seriously Hero's debt to a Greek tragic virgin highlights *Much Ado*'s other Greek literary ghosts. Critics have typically located the source of the play's false death plot in a story by Matteo Bandello, whose 1539 translation of Euripides' *Hecuba*, as previously noted, testifies to his own interest in Greek tragic women.[12] Yet Shakespeare's elaborate presentation of a veiled bride to the man responsible for her death does not appear in Bandello, or in any of the play's other acknowledged sources. Instead, this scene's close echoes of *Alcestis* suggest the similarly veiled presence of Euripides' play.[13]

Like other tragic female figures, Hero produces potent effects in her audiences. After gazing on her, Claudio startles both himself and Benedick by renouncing their shared homosocial world to turn husband: "I would scarce trust myself, though I had sworn the contrary, if Hero would be my wife" (1.1.184–5). Later, deceived into believing that Don Pedro wooed Hero for himself, he attributes to her the melting force so often associated with female dramatic performance: "Beauty is a witch/ Against whose charms faith melteth into blood" (1.2.164–65). Although his fears about his friend's susceptibility prove wrong, the play bears out his intuition about Hero's melting powers. Although Benedick insists "that fire cannot melt out of me" his hostility to the marriage (1.1.217–18), he too soon capitulates; Beatrice similarly finds her own bravado softening after hearing Hero recount Benedick's love, leading her to wonder, "What fire is in mine ears?" (3.1.107).

Hero's fiery impact emerges most forcefully when she is falsely accused. She speaks little, but her face is expressive: "in her eye," the Friar insists to Leonato, "there hath appeared a fire/ To burn the errors that these princes hold/ Against her maiden truth" (4.1.162–4). The resulting heat forges a crucial alliance: just as Hero's passionate response persuades the Friar of her innocence, he in turn persuades the raging Leonato to join in an elaborate project presenting Hero as dead. Hero's suffering also melts her closest intimate, Beatrice, into an uncharacteristic bout of tears.[14] In response to Benedick's concerned inquiry, "Lady Beatrice, have you wept all this while?," she replies, "Yea, and I will weep a while longer" (4.1.255–6). This exchange, in turn, moves Benedick to his bewildered confession of love, and his acceptance of a new alliance. "I do love nothing in the world so well as you," he reports: "is not that strange?" Beatrice, in turn, replies, "As strange as the thing I know not. It were as possible for me to say I loved nothing so well as you" (4.1.267–70). Hero's capacity to ignite, melt, and transfer sympathies brings about not only her own marriage, but that of her cousin as well.

Despite the comic pleasures of her own love story, Beatrice is moved by Hero's suffering not only to grief but also to violent rage. In commanding Benedick to "Kill Claudio" (4.1.288), she invokes the specter of revenge tragedy, albeit mingled with a black comedy that typically prompts startled laughter.[15] Her fury at Benedick's hesitation to challenge his friend darkens her cutting satire until it acquires tragic force. "Surely a princely testimony," she retorts,

> a goodly count! Count Comfit, a sweet gallant surely. O that I were a man for his sake! Or that I had any friend would be a man for my sake! But manhood is melted into curtsies, valour into compliment, and men are only turned into tongue, and trim ones too. He is now as valiant as Hercules that only tells a lie and swears it. I cannot be a man with wishing, therefore I will die a woman with grieving. (4.1.313–21)

In her earlier mockery of Benedick's military valor, Beatrice conjured the specter of the Plautine *miles gloriosus*, a braggart soldier with outsized appetites.[16] Here, however, this good-natured comic stereotype shifts towards that of Hercules—similarly linked with both fighting and gluttony—to produce a darker indictment. As half-man, half-god, linked simultaneously with heroic achievements, disabling madness, and sensual appetites, Hercules is a famously liminal figure noted for his generic ambiguity.[17] His frequent allusions throughout *Much Ado* also recall his prominent role in *Alcestis*, where he conveys the dead wife back to her grieving husband.[18] Beatrice invokes Hercules to challenge not only Benedick's capacity for heroic integrity, but reliance on male heroism more broadly. As manhood gives way to confectionary, the possibility of female heroism acquires an increased urgency: Beatrice wants to be Hercules herself, and the impossibility of this goal intensifies her grief. Paradoxically, however, in the act of lamenting her incapacity to be Hercules, she achieves his role; her grief moves Benedick to issue the challenge that begins to startle Claudio into understanding. It is fitting, then, that *Much Ado*'s Hercules allusions link Benedick and Beatrice, implicitly dividing the hero's role between them and attributing its success to their eventual partnership.[19]

Yet although both Beatrice and Benedick play crucial roles in defending Hero, Hero herself becomes the central agent in her own redemption. After witnessing the emotional impact of her collapse, the Friar suggests that she can most effectively press her case as a ghost. After death, he explains, she will exert a strangely invasive power:

> Th'idea of her life shall sweetly creep
> Into his study of imagination,
> And every lovely organ of her life
> Shall come apparelled in more precious habit,
> More moving, delicate, and full of life,
> Into the eye and prospect of his soul
> Than when she lived indeed.   (4.1.224–30)

Just as her death will be built of words, Hero's life will be reconstructed in the realm of the imagination, acquiring an intimate affinity with the internal realm of memory, thought, and emotion. In this reconceived life, she will have more power to move, both physically and affectively. Freed by her spectral status to penetrate study, eye, and soul, this ghostly Hero will intensify her impact through her unobstructed access to Claudio's increasingly interior spaces.

As Jonathan Bate has remarked, not only does the Friar's plan depart from Shakespeare's acknowledged sources, but this passage resonates with lines from *Alcestis* in which Admetus imagines his wife's return, after death, in image and dreams.[20] Bate stops short of exploring Euripides' actual language, which suggestively prefigures Hero's invasion of Claudio's imagination. Before her death, Admetus envisions Alcestis returning as a statue:

> Your form, made by the expert hand of craftsmen, will be stretched out on the bed, upon which I will fall, enfolding it in my hands, and calling your name, I will think, even though I'm not holding it, that I hold in my bent arms my dear wife: a cold pleasure, I think, but nevertheless I might diminish the heaviness of my soul. Coming in my dreams, you might cheer me: for it is sweet to look upon friends, even in the night.[21]

Admetus prefigures the Friar's emphasis on the curiously invasive force of the reconstituted dead wife: Alcestis' form will move unbidden into her husband's bed and dreams, just as Hero's image will creep into Claudio's soul. Admetus also suggests the image's aestheticized quality in his emphasis on the skilled hand (*sophē cheiri*, or *dextera artificis* in Buchanan's 1556 Latin translation), with both funerary and erotic overtones.[22] The Friar's sensually resonant image of Hero's "lovely organ" creeping in to Claudio's study in precious apparel suggestively recalls Euripides' deliberately erotic depiction of a man falling onto a simulacrum of his wife's body in bed.

If the Friar's vision of Hero as an invasive erotic phantom indirectly suggests Euripides' depiction of another temporarily dying wife, it also prefigures a closer echo. When Hero returns at the end of the play as a veiled enigma, Claudio asks, "Which is the lady I must seize upon?," and is told, "This same is she, and I do give you her."

CLAUDIO: Why, then she's mine. Sweet, let me see your face.
LEONATO: No, that you shall not, till you take her hand
Before this friar and swear to marry her. (5.4.53–7)

This drawn-out unveiling has no parallel in any of Shakespeare's acknowledged sources. Bandello's Timbreo marries an unveiled Fenicia without consciously recognizing her, and Ariosto's Ginevra, who never claimed to be dead, is defended and won in a duel. In *Alcestis*, on the other hand, Heracles leads in a veiled woman and instructs Admetus, "Take and keep this woman for me."[23] After lamenting the grief stirred by the figure's resemblance to his dead wife, Admetus instructs his servants to take her, only to be ordered to take her himself: "I trust only your right hand."[24] Claudio, like Admetus, is required to accept the hand of a veiled woman, against his instincts, before knowing her identity. If the Friar's mild rebuke responds to Heracles' sterner ones, it suggests Shakespeare's recognition and expansion of the marriage ceremony implicit in Heracles' insistent focus on Admetus' right hand.

If Hero's veiled return revisits this scene, Shakespeare's most striking revision lies with Hero's uncharacteristic boldness. Heracles reveals and announces a silent Alcestis, who does not speak for the duration of the play. Hero, on the other hand, reveals and announces herself. "And when I lived," she tells Claudio, "I was your other wife:/ And when you loved, you were my other husband" (5.4.60–1). These lines bear an uncanny similarity to words spoken by Admetus in his earlier farewell to Alcestis. In response to her request that he honor her memory by never remarrying, Admetus agrees: "And when I held you living," he tells her, "and in dying, my wife alone you will be called."[25] The parallelism of Hero's clauses ("And when I lived... And when you loved") closely echoes that of Admetus' *kai zōsan... kai thanous*: "and (when you were) living... and (in) dying." But where Admetus emphasizes both contrast and continuity between living and dying, Hero juxtaposes her previous state ("when I lived") with her husband's ("when you loved"). In doing so, she both indicts him for his failing, and offers the possibility of a return: just as she lives again, he can love again. This closeness to Euripides' language, in a structurally parallel scene, suggests the likelihood of Shakespeare's familiarity with *Alcestis*, which he could easily have read in a facing-page Greek–Latin edition.[26] In Buchanan's Latin, Euripides' parallel clauses, "*kai... kai...*" ("and... and...") emerge as a chiasmus—"*viva... sola/ sola mortua* (living... only/ only dying)."[27] Yet in his influential 1562 Greek–Latin Euripides edition, included in a 1582–3 inventory of texts for London's St. Paul's School, Gasparus Stiblinus offers the nearly word-for-word parallel clauses "Vivam habui, & mortua sola vocaberis,/ Mea mulier."[28]

If this exchange invokes *Alcestis*, Shakespeare's reassignment of these lines from a grieving husband to a triumphant bride provocatively rewrites the final scene. Alcestis returns in silence, reminding the audience that although her return delights Admetus, it nullifies the glory of her heroic self-sacrifice.[29] Hero, on the other hand, uses the moment of return to proclaim her heroism. In shaming her, Claudio had called her name into question: "O Hero," he laments, "what a Hero hadst thou been . . . !" (4.1.99). After her return, he returns her name to her—"Another Hero!"—which she insistently confirms: "Nothing certainer:/ One Hero died defiled, but I do live,/ And surely as I live, I am a maid" (5.4.62–4). As Bate has observed, Hero's name reverberates throughout the play, spoken sixty-three times—far more frequently than she herself speaks.[30] Yet in contrast to Alcestis, who earns heroism by dying, Hero earns heroism in the act of returning from death.

SHAKESPEARE'S *ALCESTIS*

If Shakespeare's revived wives gesture towards the specter of Alcestis, they implicitly raise the question of why this figure should loom so large in his tragicomic imagination. Though less visible than Hecuba in representing the Greek dramatic tradition, Alcestis—who volunteers to save her husband's life by dying in his place—featured especially prominently in Renaissance conversations about classical models for female heroism. Erasmus reminded readers that her virtues countered the women more typically presented in tragedy: "What do ye tragedes cum to your mynde? This adoulterous woman stroke in sunder her husbond with an axe. This poysoned him. . . . Why rather do nat Cornelia . . . cum to your remembraunce? Why do nat Alcestis so good a wyfe of nat so good an husbond?"[31] As a moral paradigm, she supported humanist defenses of a classical education; Thomas Elyot approvingly noted that "whan all men and women refused [to die for Admetus], only Alceste his wife consented therto, and willyngly dyed,"[32] and Philemon Holland's 1603 translation of Plutarch's *Moralia* (based on Amyot's 1572 French translation) described Alcestis' exceptional altruism in both "The Vertuous Deeds of Women" and "Of Love."[33]

As these writers suggest, Alcestis' absolute virtue distinguished her from vengeful figures such as Hecuba, Clytemnestra, and Medea; pity and sympathy for her suffering could not be contaminated by horror towards her subsequent misdeeds. Euripides repeatedly describes her as *aristé*, the best, and refers to her *kleos*, fame or glory.[34] In her heroic and voluntary death, she anticipates sacrificial virgins such as Iphigenia, Polyxena, and Antigone, but she merges their nobility with the passionate maternity so central to the affective power of Euripides' tragic mothers.[35] Although she earns fame for her devotion to her husband, she acquires particular poignance in her pre-dying declarations of love and sorrow, which she directs entirely to her children.[36] "Children, children," she laments, "your mother is no more, no more! Farewell, my children, be joyful as you look on the light!"[37] In particular, Alcestis turns her attention to the particular sorrows and challenges attendant on her daughter's motherless state: "And though a son has in his father a powerful defender, how will you, my daughter, grow to womanhood? . . . For your mother will never see you married, never stand by to encourage you in childbirth, my daughter, where nothing is better than a mother's kindness."[38] In her last words before death she tells Admetus, "Now become the mother, in my place, to these children."[39] The play also depicts her son's grief-stricken response, accentuating what Froma Zeitlin has described as "Euripides' concern with maternal affect, the closeness of emotional bonds between mother and child, and the pathos of separation and loss."[40] Yet along with combining crucial aspects of Euripides' iconic sacrificial daughters and bereaved mothers, *Alcestis* also offers perhaps his closest version of a happy ending: its protagonist earns not only reprieve from death, but also a return to her family, on celebrated terms.

These features offer context for Alcestis' unusual standing in the early modern tragic canon. Perhaps in part because of its challenges to audiences' expectations, the play spurred extensive literary responses; after the lost *Telephus*, which it followed in performance, it was Euripides' most-parodied play in antiquity, establishing an important foundation for its later reception.[41] *Alcestis* was among the most popular Greek plays in the sixteenth century; the play appeared in fourteen individual or partial editions before 1600, trailing only *Hecuba*, *Iphigenia in Aulis*, and *Medea*. Included in the first printed edition of Greek tragedies, a 1495 selection of four plays, it was subsequently translated into Latin by George Buchanan for performance at the Collège de Guyenne in Bourdeaux between 1539 and 1542.[42] Although we do not know which edition he read, in 1545 Roger Ascham attested to the play's visibility in England, when his Toxophilus discusses with Philologus the "Alcestis of Euripides, whiche tragidie you red openly not long ago."[43] Buchanan's translation was published in Paris in 1556, and reprinted in 1557, 1567 (in separate editions), 1568 (again in separate editions), and 1581; Italian translations appeared in 1525 and 1599; and additional translations of the play appeared in editions of Euripides' complete works.[44] After the 1539–42 Collège de Guyenne performance of Buchanan's translation, in Bourdeaux, there was at least one other documented performance in France, in 1606, of an adapted version titled *Alceste, ou la Fidelité*, by Alexandre Hardy.[45]

Perhaps even more than the sheer visibility and appeal of Alcestis herself, the play attracted early modern attention for its generic complexity, especially in its ability to generate affective intensity through unexpected swerves of plot. Marked by its curious status as the fourth play performed after a set of three tragedies—the position of the satyr play—the play hovers uneasily between genres.[46] Francesco Robortello cited *Alcestis* as a model for tragedy with a happy ending, as did Giraldi Cinthio.[47] "But if it displeases you," Giraldi wrote, "that it should have the name of Tragedy, to satisfy you it could be called Tragicomedy (since our language does use such a name), the outcome of which has conformed to Comedy—after troubles it is filled with gladness."[48] In his commentary on the play, Stiblinus similarly emphasized the dramatic excitement of the play's swerve from tragic beginning to comic ending: "This play has a happy, unexpected, and clearly comic ending: nevertheless its beginnings and scenes of intensification of tension are horrible and calamitous."[49] If Euripides offered an authoritative classical model for legitimizing the controversial genre of tragicomedy, *Alcestis* offered a crucial—and crucially female—site of origins for its authority.[50]

BRINGING BACK THE DEAD IN *PERICLES*

Although *Much Ado*'s recovered bride lacks the distinctively maternal focus of Alcestis' grief, in *Pericles* Shakespeare went on to pair the recuperation of a sacrificial virgin daughter with that of a bereaved mother, and underscored their centrality by opening the play with a return from the dead. The medieval poet Gower announces not only his own posthumous revival, but also his revival of an even more ancient story: "From ashes, ancient Gower is come,/ To sing a song that old was sung."[51] This haunting opening introduces a ghostly collaboration, complementing and expanding the play's mingling of Shakespeare's authorial voice with George Wilkins, and implicitly introducing the spectral author of *Apollonius of Tyre*, Gower's source.[52] Each of these ghosts makes a distinctive contribution to the play. Reanimating Gower becomes a synecdoche for a larger project of reanimating the dead, while his self-consciously archaized language, as Lucy Munro has shown, serves to jolt and reawaken the play's audiences.[53] And in turning to *Apollonius*, which had provided the frame narrative in *Comedy of Errors*, the play revives not only Gower and the classical story he ventriloquized, but also one of Shakespeare's own earliest plays, suggesting a nostalgic return to his theatrical beginnings. Yet unlike that earlier play, which turned its primary focus to the male twins of Plautus' *Menaechmi*, *Pericles* culminates in the mother–daughter reunion of its originally Greek source.[54]

The play's venture into the eerie project of animating the dead begins during Pericles' sea voyage with his pregnant wife, Thaisa. This storm-wrenched scene, generally seen as the beginning of Shakespeare's portion of the play, simultaneously brings Marina to life and Thaisa to death. Suspended between beginning and ending, comedy and tragedy, the scene spurs a newly dense, rich, and supernaturally infused language. Pericles' own similarly suspended emotional state focuses on Thaisa's labor. "How does my queen?," he asks;

> Lychorida!—Lucina, O,
> Divinest patroness and midwife gentle
> To those that cry by night, convey thy deity
> Aboard our dancing boat; make swift the pangs
> Of my queen's travails!   (3.1.7, 10–14)

After earlier addressing the storm, and then his wife's nurse, Pericles turns to the goddess of childbirth, whose invisible presence shapes the play's promises and perils. The invocation of Lucina echoes Antiochus' earlier praise of his daughter, "At whose conception . . . Lucina reigned" (1.1.9), and anticipates the presiding force of Diana, the classical goddess of both virginity and childbirth, of whom Lucina represents one aspect.[55] Yet although Diana will eventually fulfill her role as the play's patroness and midwife, belatedly delivering Thaisa's daughter to her temple in Ephesus, at this moment Pericles' prayer appears to be in vain.

When Lychorida appears, she greets Pericles with his child, instructing him to "Take in your arms this piece/ Of your dead queen" (16–19). Thaisa's death spurs imitations: as a "piece" of her dead mother, "all that is left living of your queen" (3.1.20), the child represents her mother's mortality. This terrible loss moves Pericles to curse the gods, and his blessings on his daughter are accordingly cautious. "Now, mild may be thy life!," he addresses her:

> For a more blusterous birth had never babe;
> Quiet and gentle thy conditions, for
> Thou art the rudeliest welcome to this world
> That ever was prince's child. Happy what follows!
> Thou hast as chiding a nativity
> As fire, air, water, earth and heaven can make
> To herald thee from the womb.   (3.1.27–34)

Pericles' wishes for his daughter encompass the turbulent mingling of emotions in which she emerges. Echoing his account of Lucina as "mid-wife gentle," he hopes her conditions will be "gentle," implicitly linking her high social status as a king's daughter with the quiet peace he hopes she'll attain despite her "rudeliest welcome." Her "chiding nativity" sug-gests an implicit parallel with Christ, whose birth (also in hostile environ-ments) had long represented the most conspicuous meaning of nativity. The word, which Shakespeare used rarely, echoes the ending of *Comedy of Errors*, when another shipwrecked wife and mother celebrates the figura-tive rebirth of her children with "the calendars of their nativity."[56] In this context, it might also conjure echoes of Tamburlaine's "Smile Stars that raign'd at my nativity," affectionately mocked in Glendower's boast in *1 Henry IV*, "At my nativity/ The front of heaven was full of fiery shapes."[57] If so, both associations would implicitly identify the infant, as well as her mother, with supernaturally tinged heroism, and the possibility of super-naturally tinged sacrifice.

These supernatural elements carry over into Thaisa's strange after-story. Although Marina's nativity prompts her mother's mortality, the magical phoenix-like restoration of Gower shadows Thaisa's apparent corpse. Her coffin washes up in Ephesus, famously the home of a storied temple to the goddess Diana.[58] The Ephesian setting follows the play's main source, *Apollonius of Tyre*, but also evokes another startling Shakespearean reunion in *The Comedy of Errors*, where it represented a determined break from the play's primary Plautine source. The implicit echoes of that play conjure a backdrop of magic, mystery, and unexpectedly central female roles, culmin-ating in miraculous recoveries and reunions. For the Syracusan Antipholus, this shadowy world suggested dark supernatural forces: "nimble jugglers," "[d]ark-working sorcerers," and "[s]oul-killing witches" (1.2.98–100). These same dark possibilities shadow the figure of *Pericles*' Cerimon, a physician whose study of "secret art" has acquainted him with "the blest infusions/ That dwell in vegetives, in metals, stones," and who suggests that the arts of "virtue and cunning" can verge on immortality, "Making a man a God" (3.2.32, 35–6, 27). Upon discovering Thaisa's apparently lifeless body, Cerimon suggests that his secret arts may yet be able to recover her. "Death may usurp on nature many hours," he tells his waiting gentlemen,

> And yet the fire of life kindle again
> The o'erpressed spirits. I heard of an Egyptian
> That had nine hours lain dead, who was
> By good appliance recovered. (3.2.81–5)

These lines are eerie, disturbing, and heretical. Egyptian magic suggested dark and pagan forces, and necromancy was an illicit art in Shakespeare's

Protestant England. Cerimon succeeds at reawakening Thaisa, however, through his medicine, his magic, and especially his music. The play's revival of Gower hovers as a fiction outside the story's frame, but Thaisa's revival, within the frame of the play, is real, and as unsettling as it is miraculous.

Thaisa reawakens in response to "rough and woeful music," on which Cerimon calls to "give her air," implicitly and metatheatrically evoking the musical airs central to the incantatory effects of the play's performance. "Gentlemen," he announces,

> this queen will live. Nature awakes;
> A warmth breathes out of her! She hath not been
> Entranced above five hours. See how she 'gins
> To blow into life's flower again.   (3.2.91–4)

Following his reference to music as producing air, Cerimon links Thaisa's awakening with warmth and breath, terms of animation that conjure up the vital fertility of "life's flower," and move his listeners to wonder.[59] Building on this language of vitality, he exclaims, "She is alive!... Live, and make/ Us weep to hear your fate, fair creature" (3.2.96, 100–1). But his eerie revival of Thaisa marks an unusual sort of recovery. Shakespeare's previously revived women were never actually dead—in *Comedy of Errors* we hear of the disappearance of Egeon's wife, but without any certainty of her fate, and in *Much Ado* we know that Hero's apparent death is a fiction. Thaisa's revival suggests a more substantive return; yet rather than being filled with joy, it marks her entrance into a hazy retreat of an afterlife, bereft of her husband and newborn infant.

As Thaisa recedes from the stage into the service of Diana, she seems magically to will Diana's virginal power into the service of her daughter, Marina. Sold into a brothel after surviving sensational attacks by assassin and pirates, Marina becomes a kind of sacrificial virgin, but hardly a passive one. Calling on Diana for support, she wields her chastity forcefully, as an invisible amulet to repel her would-be despoilers. "If fires be hot, knives sharp or waters deep," she insists, "Untried I still my virgin knot will keep./ Diana, aid my purpose!" (4.2.138–40). Her self-conscious invocation of Diana, whom Pericles and Gower had both earlier identified as her protector, suggests an invisible thread linking her to her mother, who was identified with Diana and virginity even before becoming her priestess in Ephesus.[60] Marina's new home in Mytilene, moreover, indirectly evokes that city's most eminent literary inhabitant, Sappho, already legendary in the early modern period as the pre-eminent poet of female passions, who would have been familiar to Shakespeare through Plutarch, one of his most intimately consulted sources.[61] Marina may appear to be cast alone on her own resources, but her strategies of self-defense rest on an invisible alliance of forceful female ghosts: supernatural, literary, virginal, and maternal.

Reinforced by Diana, Marina preaches the gospel of virginity with eloquence and persuasion, and her performances leave her audiences permanently reformed. "Come, I am for no more bawdy-houses," one tells another; "shall's go hear the vestals sing?" "I'll do any thing now that is virtuous," his interlocutor replies, "but I am out of the road of rutting for ever" (4.5.6–9). Her extraordinary ability to repel suitors alarms her bawd, who imagines her chilling effect in direct contrast to the melting typically linked with female tragic figures: "Fie, fie upon her. She's able to freeze the god Priapus and undo a whole generation" (4.5.12–13). Through her unflinching virtue, she earns the awe of Lysimachus, the governor of Mytilene, and the most eminent of her suitors. "For me/ That am a maid," she laments to him,

> though most ungentle Fortune
> Have placed me in this sty, where, since I came
> Diseases have been sold dearer than physic—
> O, that the gods
> Would set me free from this unhallowed place,
> Though they did change me to the meanest bird
> That flies i'th' purer air!   (4.5.99–106)

Marina's lament calls on supernatural forces to intervene and preserve her, but her appeal to sympathy persuades Lysimachus to do so in their stead. His resulting admiration and support respond not only to her beauty, but also to her intellectual acuity:

> I did not think
> Thou couldst have spoke so well, ne'er dreamt thou couldst.
> Had I brought hither a corrupted mind
> Thy speech had altered it.   (4.5.106–9)

Lysimachus offers a paradigmatic audience for Marina's performance of a sacrificial virgin's lament; his sympathies ignited, he pledges his support. As Elizabeth Archibald has noted, Shakespeare and Wilkins found a model for a learned heroine in *Apollonius of Tyre*, but most of the medieval versions of the story attributed the daughter's success to musical, rather than rhetorical, skill.[62] Shakespeare's depiction of Marina's virtuoso eloquence represents a concerted choice; like fellow ill-starred daughters Rosalind, Viola, and Imogen, she possesses a fierce intelligence and resourcefulness that allow her to transform tragic threats into tragicomic pleasures. Yet her success results especially from her ability to enlist sympathetic listeners into forming a supportive alliance. Calling on

Diana, Fortune, and the gods, she manages to escape the brothel by attracting the indirect support of her mother, and the direct support of Lysimachus.

Through her passionate laments, Marina melts and animates her audiences, reviving their faith and inspiring their allegiance. Yet her signal achievement lies in reawakening her father, who arrives at Mytilene barely alive, mourning his apparently dead daughter as well as his apparently dead wife. No longer speaking, and barely eating, he arrives in Mytilene needing recovery as desperately as Thaisa did in Ephesus—and like Thaisa, he experiences a miracle. Just as the play revives Gower from ashes, and Thaisa from the sea, the scene restores his daughter to him, and, in so doing, brings him back from his own deathlike state. More specifically, Marina herself brings him back from the dead, drawing on her "sacred physic" to use her "utmost skill in his recovery" (5.1.67, 69). Channeling her patron Diana and the uncanny physic of Cerimon, she becomes a midwife of sorts, easing her father's re-entrance into the world.

When the Mytileneans learn of Pericles' woes, their wishes to help are fruitless until a gentleman suggests, "we have a maid in Mytilene, I durst wager/ Would win some words of him," and is immediately seconded by Lysimachus:

> 'Tis well bethought.
> She questionless, with her sweet harmony
> And other choice attractions, would allure
> And make a battery through his deafened ports
> Which now are midway stopped.   (5.1.35–40)

Just as Cerimon called on "rough and woeful music" to awaken Thaisa, Lysimachus turns to Marina's "sweet harmony" to invade Pericles' "deafened ports," identifying the penetration of his ears with the ocean's siege of a city or harbor.[63] Yet Marina's liquid power lies less in her music than in her words, and especially in her self-conscious claim to tragic lament. Confronted by the stranger's incapacitating sorrow, she emphasizes that he is not alone: "She speaks,/ My lord, that, may be, hath endured a grief/ Might equal yours, if both were justly weigh'd" (5.1.77–9). Marina's insistence on the weightiness of her own grief establishes both her authority and a bond of identification between herself and the suffering figure she encounters. It also moves her to recount her own previously hidden history, which—combined with her newly registered appearance—stirs Pericles to the beginnings of recognition, and to speech.

As he absorbs the implications of Marina's story, Pericles gradually returns to life, not as a redeemed father but as a laboring mother. "I am great with woe," he announces as recognition dawns, "and shall deliver weeping" (5.1.97). Prompted to identification by Marina's claim that her grief could equal his, he imagines himself as female, adopting the vocabulary of fertility to present the emotions of reuniting with a lost child with the fullness and generativity specific to childbirth. Pregnant with affect, Pericles also turns his thoughts to Thaisa. "My dearest wife," he continues, "was like this maid, and such a one/ My daughter might have been" (5.1.98–9). Recognizing his resemblance to Marina through their equal grief, he expands this common bond to include his lost wife as well. As he presses further with questions, he returns insistently to her claim of equal suffering: "I think thou saidst...that thou thought'st thy griefs might equal mine/ If both were opened" (5.1.120–3). The authority of her grief even prompts him to understand their positions as reversed. After instructing her to "Tell thy story," he observes that her strength might be not only equal to his, but greater. "If thine considered prove the thousandth part/ Of my endurance," he proclaims, "thou art a man, and I/ Have suffered like a girl" (5.1.125–8). Through her capacity for moving audiences through lament to sympathetic participation in her grief, Marina awakens Pericles' sense of empathetic understanding, bringing him figuratively back to life.

In reanimating her father, Marina paradoxically becomes parent to her own parent: Pericles calls her "Thou that beget'st him that did thee beget" (5.1.185). Attributing maternal power to himself and his daughter, he imaginatively substitutes both for the lost Thaisa. Yet the play brings her back as well, through the specter of Diana, who invades Pericles' thoughts through a dream and summons him to the site of her power. "My temple stands in Ephesus," she intones; "Hie thee thither,/ And do upon mine altar sacrifice" (5.1.227–9). The direct invocation of sacrifice, in the context of a newly discovered virgin daughter and the goddess of virginity and childbirth, proclaims the play's most decisive shift into the allusive world of Greek tragic ghosts, which the play's culminating reunion intensifies. Upon Pericles' climactic announcement of his and Marina's identities, Thaisa faints, prompting Pericles to assume her death: "What means the nun? She dies" (5.3.15). "Noble sir," Cerimon explains, "If you have told Diana's altar true,/ This is your wife" (5.1.16–18). "I opened the coffin,/ Found there rich jewels, recovered her, and placed her/ Here in Diana's temple," he recounts, and observes her second return: "Look, Thaisa is/ Recovered" (5.3.23–5, 27–8). His repetition of "recover"—a word that recurs throughout the play—underscores the parallel between Thaisa's two returns from apparent death. In a nod to the significance of identifying signs explored in Chapter 4, Cerimon offers to show the jewels from Thaisa's coffin, but her words prompt recognition in themselves— "The voice of dead Thaisa!" (5.3.34). She, meanwhile, acknowledges his identifying sign. "Now I know you better," she observes; "When we with tears parted Pentapolis,/ The king my father gave you such a ring" (5.3.37–9).

Like Hero, Thaisa melts her audience: "on the touching of her lips," Pericles announces, "I may/ Melt and no more be seen" (5.3.42–3). And despite the greater critical and theatrical prominence given to the long father–daughter reunion, it is striking that the play reserves its final, most climactic reunion for the mother and daughter. Shakespeare presents this reunion as a profoundly physiological meeting of bodies. "My heart/ Leaps to be gone into my mother's bosom," Marina proclaims, imagining an arresting return to her mother's interior (5.3.44–5). Pericles echoes her uncanny image of bodily merging. "Look, who kneels here!," he exclaims: "Flesh of thy flesh, Thaisa;/ Thy burden at the sea, and called Marina/ For she was yielded there" (5.3.46–8). Repeating her husband's use of a possessive pronoun, Thaisa similarly emphasizes her identification with her daughter. "Blest," she replies, "and mine own!" (5.3.48).

Like *Much Ado About Nothing*, the play ends with a grieving man welcoming back his apparently dead wife. The play does not explicitly identify Thaisa as veiled in this final scene, but Pericles' inability to recognize her suggests the likelihood that she is veiled, which productions often stage.[64] Yet unlike *Much Ado*, *Pericles* stages the return of a dead wife in conjunction with her reunion with a sacrificial daughter, multiplying the play's Greek tragic icons. And just as the play depicts these figures transmitting sympathies to audiences, the play's project of reanimating the dead has metatheatrical resonances. Through the eerie forces of Diana, Cerimon, Gower, and Marina's laments, the play reanimates its own audiences, startling us out of habituated responses with strange, foreign, and moving elements. Shakespeare often describes audience members as sleeping and dreaming at plays. "If we shadows have offended," Puck famously advises, "Think but this, and all is mended,/ That you have but slumbered here/ While these visions did appear."[65] As an initially impenetrable audience to a sacrificial virgin's tragic lament, Pericles in particular evokes the figure of a sleeping auditor. His awakening by Marina serves to jolt and animate the play's audiences as well, suggesting that the moving force of iconic tragic laments can penetrate our deafened ports, bringing us back to life also.

MATERNAL BURDENS IN *THE WINTER'S TALE*

Just as *Pericles* alters *Much Ado*'s revived wife drama by transforming the lost wife into a mother, *The Winter's Tale* revisits this plot with a heightened focus on maternal investments. Shakespeare not only dwells extensively on Hermione's grief, but focuses the play's culminating revelation on the reunion between her and her daughter, rewriting the male–female recognition scenes in Shakespeare's earlier comedies and tragicomedies. This reunion also marks the play's most significant divergence from its primary source, Greene's *Pandosto* (1588), in which a jealous king commits suicide long after his innocent wife's death, stricken by the belated realization of his many sins. Other sources similarly fail to account for Hermione's revival; the statue scene recalls Ovid's Pygmalion, and the animated statue of *The Tryall of Chevalry* (1599–1601), but neither of these includes the return of a dead wife.[66] As observed, the play's implicit rewriting of *Alcestis* has drawn comments from a number of scholars, some of whom have suggested that it contains verbal echoes of Buchanan's translation.[67] I propose that *The Winter's Tale* deepens Shakespeare's longstanding engagement with the ghosts of Greek tragic women by turning concertedly to the power of maternal passions. When Hero dies, she mourns the loss of her reputation, and on awakening in Ephesus, Thaisa laments the loss of her husband. Both eventually recover what they have lost, but when Hermione collapses, her newborn daughter has been taken overseas to be abandoned, and her son has died, never to return. I argue that in shifting his revival plot's focus from abandoned bride to bereaved mother, Shakespeare extends his engagement with theatrical necromancy to develop even more fully an iconic type at the heart of the period's most avidly consumed Greek tragedies.

From its outset, *The Winter's Tale* is preoccupied by maternity.[68] Hermione is one of only a handful of pregnant female characters to appear onstage in Shakespeare's plays, and at the play's opening her fecundity is both conspicuous and threatening.[69] "Nine changes of the watery star," Polixenes observes early in the play, "hath been/ The shepherd's note since we have left our throne/ Without a burden" (1.2.1–3).[70] Scholars have observed the implicit reference to gestation in his stay's length, but not in his reference to leaving "without a burden." As discussed in Chapter 4, the word is etymologically linked with birth, and includes among its definitions, "That which is borne in the womb; a child."[71] Like the etymologically kindred "bear," which appears thirty-eight times throughout the play, and "born," which appears nineteen times, the word "burden" reverberates throughout the play.[72] Leontes reflects that, "While [Hermione] lives/ My heart will be a burden to me" (2.3.203–4), and later Autolycus' ballads wishfully transform the hazards of childbirth into "delicate burdens" (4.4.196) and comic accounts of a woman "brought to bed of twenty money-bags at a burden" (4.4.263–4). Although the word's ambivalent associations link childbirth with weightiness and trouble, the play presents these burdens as proving most painful in their absence.

Although Hermione insists on her loving fidelity towards her husband, the play, beginning as Leontes' suspicions are already erupting, does not portray their marriage as a source of pleasure whose loss threatens grief. Instead—in a departure from its recognized sources—it dwells on Hermione's affectionate and playful interactions with her son, and emphasizes her grief at losing him and her newborn daughter.[73] Before her apparent death, Hermione's most passionate words respond to her separation from her children. "My second joy," she tells Leontes,

> And first fruits of my body, from his presence
> I am barred, like one infectious. My third comfort,
> Starred most unluckily, is from my breast,
> The innocent milk in its most innocent mouth,
> Haled out to murder: myself on every post
> Proclaimed a strumpet: with immodest hatred
> The childbed privilege denied   (3.2.94–101)

As his mother's "first fruits," Mamilius embodies the play's pervasive language of planting and reaping, and prefigures the fertile botanical realm celebrated in the sheep-shearing scene. Hermione's insistent association of her daughter with breast and milk evokes female fertility even more forcefully. Similarly, the alliteration of milk, mouth, murder, and myself, alongside the cruel and unusual denial of the childbed privilege, emphasizes the urgency of Hermione's maternal suffering.[74]

After Hermione collapses under her burdens, the play shifts its focus from her maternal bereavement to her daughter. Separated from her mother, cast into overseas exile, and exposed to predatory elements and animals, Perdita becomes a kind of sacrificial virgin. Like Euripides' Iphigenia, however, she is rescued from death by a version of a *deus ex machina*. Her new life as shepherdess, tending flocks, family, and friends, suggests a pastoral equivalent to the priestess role taken by Iphigenia, as well as by Emilia in *Comedy of Errors*, and Thaisa in *Pericles*—especially when she reflects playfully on pagan gods, and becomes a version of one herself. She is "no shepherdess," Florizel tells her,

> but Flora
> Peering in April's front. This your sheep-shearing
> Is as a meeting of the petty gods,
> And you the queen on't.   (4.4.2–5)

Florizel imagines Perdita's encounters with the petty gods in terms of Ovidian seductions, modeling his own metamorphosis from prince to shepherd to woo her, but her own classical imagination takes a different direction. "O Proserpina," she exclaims, while imagining garlanding her visitors, "For the flowers now, that frighted thou let'st fall/ From Dis's wagon!" (4.4.116–18). In her odd apostrophe to Greek myth's original sacrificial virgin daughter, torn untimely from her mother into the under-world by male violence, Perdita implicitly reflects on her own kinship with this figure. And although this identification suggests a tragic backdrop, it also anticipates the partial restoration with which the play ends: Proser-pina is ultimately reunited with her bereaved mother, not permanently, but for part of every year.

Hermione's prominent maternity and Perdita's identification with Greek sacrificial virgins both resonate in the play's depiction of the Delphic Oracle. Critics have observed the play's interest in Apollo, to whom it alludes directly thirteen times—dramatically more than any other Shakespeare play—and some have linked his centrality with *Alcestis*, in which Apollo allows Admetus to escape death through his wife's willing-ness to sacrifice herself for him.[75] Yet Shakespeare's Apollo appears primarily through the form of the oracle, which defends Hermione rather than her husband. Readings of *Winter's Tale* rarely dwell on the Delphic oracle, despite its crucial role in the plot. Shakespeare inherited the oracle from Greene—whose 1570s education at St. John's College, Cambridge, exposed him to Greek—but he expanded its significance considerably: the word "oracle" appears fourteen times in *Winter's Tale*, double its seven instances in *Pandosto*.[76] Shakespeare's expanded attention to the oracle, alongside his relocation of Greene's romance to the Greek province of Sicilia, and his selection of names self-consciously associated with Greek literary origins, suggests a deliberate Hellenizing strategy. In the light of his extensive and well-documented interest in Plutarch, by 1611 he would almost certainly have known Plutarch's essays on the oracle in Philemon Holland's 1603 English translation of the *Moralia*.[77] His identification of the oracle's site as "Delphos" supports this possibility, since Holland refers to "Delphos" instead of "Delphi" throughout.[78] As discussed in this book's introduction, Plutarch explained that the oracle's knowledge was rooted in the purity of her body—"the said *Pythias* [Delphic oracle] keepeth her bodie pure and cleane from the company of man, and forbidden she is to converse or have commerce al her life time with any stranger"[79]—and Giulia Sissa has observed that this virginal purity allowed the god to penetrate the priestess's body through fumes pouring forth from a fissure in the earth.[80] As a result of this spiritual intercourse, the Pythia would contain the god himself: Plutarch explained, "it is knowen unto the God, when her bodie is prepared and disposed to receive (without danger of her person) this Enthusiasme."[81] The result was a metaphysical pregnancy; in his treatise *On the Sublime*, which also began circulating in the sixteenth century, Longinus wrote of the Pythia that, "by divine power set down in this way, she is impregnated, and delivers oracles through this inspiration."[82] Both pregnant and virginal, the oracle uncannily prefigured the Virgin Mary, a figure of uneasy nostalgic appeal in Reformation England.[83] She also suggests an intimate kinship with both the chastely pregnant Hermione and the virginal Perdita.

As a model for the embodied reproduction of the divine word, the oracle also represented collaborative poetic production. In *On the Sublime*, Longinus similarly described the transmission of literary power from one poet to another as a kind of pregnancy. After depicting the Pythia as impregnated by divine spirits, he likened her divine pregnancy to "the imitation (*mimēsis*) and emulation of previous great poets and writers." "In the same way," he went on,

> from the great natures of earlier men, to the souls of those who emulate them, as from sacred fissures, are carried along what we might call outpourings, so even those who seem little likely to be possessed, become inspired [*epipneomenoi*] with them, and become possessed [*sunenthousiōsi*] by others' greatness.[84]

The oracle, then, represented not only a paradoxical state of simultaneous pregnancy and chastity, but also a model for a distinctively female, embodied, and poetic form of creative reproduction. Characterized by both self-enclosure and permeability to another authorial source, this mode of production opposes independent authorship. The hollow-bodied oracle gains its potent mandate precisely from its uncanny combination of intact purity and openness.

Whether or not he was familiar with these newly visible Greek accounts of the oracle's pregnant chastity, Shakespeare depicts Hermione as aligning herself confidently with its authority. "Your honours all," she addresses the court at her trial, "I do refer me to the oracle" (3.2.112–13). Perhaps more surprisingly—because more of a departure from *Pandosto*—he repeatedly emphasizes the untouched purity of the oracle's scroll, which metonymically represents the Pythia's body. Dion refers to "the oracle,/ Thus by Apollo's great divine sealed up" (3.1.18–19), and during the trial, Leontes' Officer similarly calls attention to the intact state of the "sealed-up oracle" (3.2.125). "Swear upon this sword of justice," he instructs Cleomenes and Dion, ". . . that, since then/ You have not dared to break the holy seal" (3.2.122, 126–7). Leontes presents himself as the god who will penetrate the oracle and transmit his authority through its voice, ordering, at the pivotal moment in the trial, "Break up the seals and read" (3.2.129). Given the oracle's associations, his violent instructions suggest a kind of figurative rape. They do not, however, produce the offspring he expects.

Just as the oracle evokes virginity, it also explicitly invokes reproduction. In the play's first words about Delphos, Cleomenes identifies it with procreative power—"Fertile the isle" (3.1.2)—and Dion similarly identifies its opening not simply with knowledge, but also with birth. "When the oracle . . . / Shall the contents discover," he promises, "something rare/ Even then will rush to knowledge. Go. Fresh horses!/ And gracious be the issue" (3.1.18–19, 20–2). Like the play's previous childbirth scene, which produced Perdita, the oracle's "issue"—an affirmation of Hermione's chastity—confirms Leontes' paternity. Just as he did after the earlier scene, however, Leontes flouts the authority of this birth, prompting the immediate death of Mamilius and the apparent consequent death of Hermione. These disasters spur him, finally, to acknowledge the oracle's authority—"Apollo, pardon/ My great profaneness 'gainst thine oracle" (3.2.150–1)—but it is too late. His attempt to divert the fruition of the god's word results in a botched and abortive outcome.

Mediated by Leontes' defiance, the issue does not prove gracious, but the oracle's lingering authority continues to shape the play. Towards the end, when advisors urge Leontes to take a wife, Paulina reminds him of the oracle in order to enforce his continuing fidelity to his first marriage. "Besides," she tells him,

> the gods
> Will have fulfilled their secret purposes.
> For has not the divine Apollo said?
> Is't not the tenor of his oracle
> That King Leontes shall not have an heir
> Till his lost child be found?   (5.1.35–40)

In her insistent reminder of the oracle's implications for the kingdom's heir, Paulina echoes Dion's invocation of the "gracious issue" its opening promised to produce. The final scenes teem with references to "issue," a word that—like "oracle"—appears fourteen times in the play, far more than in any other work by Shakespeare.[85] Fittingly, the oracle regains centrality precisely when Perdita returns to Sicilia. The Second Gentleman observes, with awe that "the oracle is fulfilled" (5.2.22), and the third Gentleman describes Paulina with "one eye declined for the loss of her husband, another elevated that the oracle was fulfilled" (5.2.73–4). The culmination of the oracle's promises, however, arrives most directly with the return of the play's chaste mother, whose knowledge—both of her own innocence and of her daughter's survival—is finally vindicated.

Just as the Delphic Oracle's prominence suggests Greek literary ghosts behind the female alliances that lead to Hermione's return, Hermione's resurrection as a statue evokes not only Ovid's Pygmalion, but also *Alcestis*. Concealed at first by a curtain, Hermione's statue joins the veiled Hero and Thaisa in disconcerting a grieving husband.[86] When Leontes sees the statue, he is struck by its likeness to Hermione: "Her natural posture!/ Chide me, dear stone, that I may say indeed/ Thou art Hermione" (5.3.23–4). Sarah Dewar-Watson has argued that these lines respond to Admetus' alarm, in *Alcestis*, at the veiled woman's resemblance to his wife: "Woman, whoever you are, know that in shape you are like Alcestis and resemble her in appearance."[87] Dewar-Watson speculates that the term "statura" in Buchanan's Latin translation of these lines, technically referring to stature, hints at the idea of a statue, especially in the context of the moment's structural resonance.[88] I would add that the statue scene's pervasive language of softening stone indirectly evokes *Alcestis'* persistent stony vocabulary, as in Admetus' earlier vision of his wife returning as a statue that he will embrace in bed. Leontes fears that Hermione will turn her onlookers to stone. "I am ashamed," he tells Paulina upon first seeing the statue; "Does not the stone rebuke me/ For being more stone than it?" (5.3.37–8). He similarly worries about the statue petrifying Perdita: "There's magic in thy majesty, which has/ . . . From thy admiring daughter took the spirits,/ Standing like stone with thee" (5.3.39–42). Critics have suggested that this moment echoes antitheatrical concerns about the petrifying consequences of spectatorship; in *Playes Confuted in Five Actions*, Stephen Gosson asked, "Shall wee . . . so looke, so gaze, so gape upon plaies, that as men that stare on the head of Medusa and are turned into stones . . . ?"[89] Yet Medusa, a Greek figure, also features in Admetus' response to the veiled Alcestis. When Heracles orders, "Have the courage to stretch out your hand and touch the stranger," Admetus protests, "There, I stretch it out, as if I were cutting off a Gorgon's head."[90]

Instead of turning Admetus to stone, Alcestis' touch unexpectedly animates him, bringing the play back to life. Hermione's statue, similarly, not only comes to life, but melts her stony audiences, bringing her husband and daughter back to life as well. "'Tis time; descend," Paulina tells her; "be stone no more; approach./ Strike all that look upon with marvel" (5.3.99–100). With its near echo of marble, the marvel that Paulina invokes both matches and opposes the stony transformation that the statue originally seemed to promise; it will amaze and animate its onlookers.[91] Leontes, like Admetus, fears he is manipulated by an illusion, "mocked with art" (5.3.68). Yet, in keeping with the melting consequences of other female tragic performances, Hermione not only thaws her own apparent marble, but finally succeeds at melting Leontes' stony heart.

Although Leontes, like Admetus, narrates his silent wife's return in conversation with her conveyor, Hermione departs from Alcestis' silence by speaking—though not to her husband. While Alcestis' children have no part in her return, Hermione emphasizes that she returns to and for her daughter.[92] "Tell me, mine own," she addresses Perdita,

> Where hast thou been preserved? Where lived? How found
> Thy father's court? For thou shalt hear that I,
> Knowing by Paulina that the oracle
> Gave hope thou wast in being, have preserved
> Myself to see the issue.   (5.3.120–8)

Addressing her first words directly to her daughter, Hermione does not speak to her husband at all. Linking Perdita's experience to hers with the same verb, she presents their preservation as parallel and shared experiences. She also links their preservation to her knowledge of the oracle, mediated by the play's other fierce proponent of chaste pregnancy, Paulina.

Hermione's emergence into voice and motion echoes aspects of Hero's return in *Much Ado about Nothing*, and Thaisa's in *Pericles*. Just as Hero takes control of her return by appropriating Admetus' lines, here Hermione rewrites Alcestis' return to emphasize her own agency. And just as Paulina's call "Music, awake her; strike!" echoes the "rough and woeful music" (3.2.87) that Cerimon summons to awaken Thaisa, so Hermione's "mine own" echoes Thaisa's first words to her daughter: "Blest, and mine own!" (5.3.48). Yet even more than Thaisa, Hermione emphasizes the mobilizing power of her maternal bond. Unlike Alcestis, who is passively led back by Heracles, Hermione makes clear that she has self-consciously orchestrated both her disappearance and her return, with one goal: "to see the issue." Euripides presents Alcestis dying as a mother but returning as a wife; Shakespeare shows Hermione dying as a childless wife, but returning to life as a mother. Just as Leontes brought the play's early pastoral comedy into the fierce terrain of the tragic, here an alliance of female forces brings the play back towards a partially recovered tragicomic mode. The ending is bittersweet—Hermione is still bereaved of Mamilius, as well as of Perdita's early years, and her silence towards Leontes suggests an ambivalent reunion at best. Yet through the redemption, return, and reunion of a mother–daughter dyad, Sicilia becomes fruitful again.

In repeatedly staging women's apparent deaths and uncanny revivals, Shakespeare's tragicomedies reanimate a Euripidean motif transmitted through multiple authors and forms. Yet the particular recurring iconography of veiled women presented to grieving husbands argues for a self-conscious response to the figure of Alcestis, whom Shakespeare would have encountered in a range of textual forms. In *Much Ado About Nothing*,

Shakespeare engages with *Alcestis* alongside Italian romance models to examine and redeem the figure of the unjustly accused wife; in *Pericles* he approaches the same figure through ancient prose fiction, filtered through medieval romance, to yoke marital and maternal reunions; and in *Winter's Tale* he expands his romance source by juxtaposing Alcestis with Ovid's Pygmalion and Plutarch's Pythia, and shifts the trope's affective force by focusing especially on maternal passions. In all of these plays, acknowledging and recuperating female suffering proves crucial to the larger tragicomic project of redemption, and—in *Winter's Tale* especially—to the promise of futurity as a return on parental investment.[93] As Chapter 6 will argue, the reunion with a wife returning from the underworld became distinctively enough identified with Shakespeare that Ben Jonson went on to parody it in his reflections on Shakespeare's tragicomedies in his 1614 *Bartholomew Fair*. As this satire suggests, the theater's affinity with bringing back the dead became a signal feature of Shakespeare's responses to his dramatic predecessors.

NOTES

1. On Christian readings, see Sean Benson, *Shakespearean Resurrections* (Pittsburgh: Duquesne University Press, 2009); on Italian sources, see Martin Mueller, "Shakespeare's Sleeping Beauties: The Sources of *Much Ado about Nothing* and the Play of Their Repetitions," *MP* 91:3 (1994), 288–311.
2. On Euripides' female protagonists as modeling "a new heroism," see Marianne McDonald, "Cacoyannis and Euripides' *Iphigenia at Aulis*: A New Heroism," in *Euripides in Cinema: The Heart Made Visible* (Philadelphia: Centrum, 1983), 129–92; on Alcestis in particular as revising a male heroic motif, see Nicole Loraux, *Tragic Ways of Killing a Woman*, trans. Anthony Foster (Cambridge, MA: Harvard University Press, 1987), 29.
3. Responding to Jean-Pierre Guépin's formulation, Helene P. Foley has described plays of female revival as "*anodos* drama"; see Foley, "*Anodos* Dramas: Euripides' *Alcestis* and *Helen*," in *Innovations of Antiquity*, ed. Ralph Hexter and Daniel Selden (London: Routledge, 1992), 133–60 (also in Foley, *Female Acts in Greek Tragedy* [Princeton: Princeton University Press, 2001], 301–32), and Guépin, *The Tragic Paradox: Myth and Ritual in Greek Tragedy* (Adolf M. Hakkert, 1968).
4. Gollancz writes, "One cannot but think that, by some means or other, directly or indirectly, Shakespeare owed his *dénouement* to the Greek dramatist—certainly to the Greek story." Israel Gollancz, ed., *The Winter's Tale* (London: J. M. Dent, 1894), viii.
5. Douglas B. Wilson, "Euripides' *Alcestis* and the Ending of Shakespeare's *The Winter's Tale*," *Iowa State Journal of Research* 58 (1984), 345–55; Bruce

Louden, "Reading through The *Alcestis* to *The Winter's Tale*," *Classical and Modern Literature* 27:2 (2007), 7–30, 8; Sarah Dewar-Watson, "The *Alcestis* and the Statue Scene," *Shakespeare Quarterly* 60:1 (2009), 73–80; John Pitcher, ed., *The Winter's Tale*, Arden Shakespeare (London: Methuen, 2010); see also Tom F. Driver, "Release and Reconciliation: The *Alcestis* and *The Winter's Tale*," in *The Sense of History in Greek and Shakespearean Drama* (New York: Columbia University Press, 1960), 168–98.

6. Earl Showerman, "'Look Down and See What Death Is Doing': Gods and Greeks in *The Winter's Tale*," *The Oxfordian* 10 (2007), 55–74.

7. Helen Wilcox has suggested that tragicomedy "may be characterized as a maternal form"; see Wilcox, "Gender and Genre in Shakespeare's Tragicomedies," in *Reclamations of Shakespeare*, ed. A. J. Hoenselaars (Amsterdam: Rodopi, 1994), 129–38, 137. Helen Hackett has similarly described "tragicomedy as a maternal genre"; see Hackett, "'Gracious be the issue': Maternity and Narrative in Shakespeare's Late Plays," in *Shakespeare's Late Plays: New Readings*, ed. Jennifer Richards and James Knowles (Edinburgh: University of Edinburgh Press, 1999), 25–39, 29. On early modern responses to Greek tragic maternity, see Pollard, "Conceiving Tragedy," in *Shakespearean Sensations*, ed. Katharine Craik and Tanya Pollard (Cambridge: Cambridge University Press, 2013), 85–100.

8. See Marvin Carlson, *The Haunted Stage: The Theatre as Memory Machine* (Ann Arbor: University of Michigan Press, 2001, rpt. 2003).

9. Despite her robust sensuality, when Leander first sees Hero in Marlowe's poem she is "Vail'd to the ground, vailing her eyelids closed," and he harps repeatedly on her initial virginity; see *Hero and Leander*, in Christopher Marlowe, *The Poems*, ed. Millar Maclure (London: Methuen & Co, 1968), I.159, and I.262–4, 269–72, and 315–18. She is also identified four times with sacrifice, both to Venus and to Leander (I.158, 209, 310; II.48). On Marlovian echoes behind *Much Ado*'s Hero, see Mihoko Suzuki, "Gender, Class, and the Ideology of Comic Form: *Much Ado About Nothing* and *Twelfth Night*," *A Feminist Companion to Shakespeare* (Oxford: Blackwell, 2000), 121–43, 130–3, and Diana E. Henderson, "Mind the Gaps: The Ear, the Eye, and the Senses of a Woman in *Much Ado About Nothing*," in *Knowing Shakespeare*, ed. Lowell Gallagher and Shankar Raman (Basingstoke: Palgrave Macmillan, 2010), 192–215. On Shakespeare's tragicomic uses of *Hero and Leander* in *Two Gentlemen of Verona*, see Pollard, "Verona's Tragic Women," in *Theatre for a New Audience 360 Series* (2015), 10–12.

10. Henderson, "Mind the Gaps," 197.

11. *Hero and Leander*, I.52. Excusing Musaeus from the rules of epic, Scaliger writes, "Neque Musaeus in Leandri historia lepidissima damnandus est, quod eiusmodi legem non servavit. Est enim illa *quasi tragoedia*, ut rei et principium et finis suo utreumque loco recte sit" (emphasis mine)—"for that story is, as it were, a tragedy." Julius Caesar Scaliger, *Poetices Libri Septem*, ed. Luc Dietz (Stuttgart: Bad Cannstatt, 1995), vol. 3; p. 24, III.95.144b; see also Julius Caesar Scaliger, *Select Translations from Scaliger's Poetics*, trans. Frederick

Morgan Padelford (New York: Henry Holt, 1905), 56. I am grateful to Tania Demetriou for calling Scaliger's reference to my attention. Erich Segal held that in this period the lovers "were conceived as tales of heroic tragedy"; see Segal, "Hero and Leander: Góngora and Marlowe," *Comparative Literature* 15:4 (1963), 338–56, 340. On Renaissance responses to Hero and Leander, see especially Gordon Braden, *The Classics and English Renaissance Poetry* (New Haven, CT: Yale University Press, 1978), 55–153.

12. The false death plot does not appear in the play's other acknowledged source, Book Five of Ariosto's *Orlando Furioso*, in which a slandered heroine is proven innocent without dying. See Mueller, "Shakespeare's Sleeping Beauties"; Thomas E. Mussio "Bandello's 'Timbreo and Fenicia' and *The Winter's Tale*," *Comparative Drama* 34:2 (2000), 211–44; and Geoffrey Bullough, ed., *Narrative and Dramatic Sources of Shakespeare* (London: Routledge and Kegan Paul, 1963), vol. 2, 61–139. Bandello took this element of the story from a Greek prose romance, Chariton's *Chaereas and Callirho*; see also *Ecuba: Tragedia di Euripide; tradotta in verso Toscano da Matteo Bandello* (1539).

13. Jonathan Bate has proposed that the shadow of Alcestis offers "a powerful mythic prototype" behind the play, though "not a direct source for the Hero plot"; see Bate, "Dying to Live in *Much Ado about Nothing*," in *Surprised by Scenes: Essays in Honor of Professor Yasunai Takahashi*, ed. Yasunari Takada (Tokyo: Kenkyusha, 1994), 69–85, 81; also Claire McEachern, ed., *Much Ado about Nothing* (London: Bloomsbury, 2006), 21–2. Earl Showerman, "Shakespeare's Many Much Ado's: *Alcestis,* Hercules, and *Love's Labour's Wonne*," *Brief Chronicles* I (2009), 109–40, argues that the play's Euripidean debts identify the Earl of Oxford as author. Although I agree with Showerman's account of the play's debts to *Alcestis*, I do not support his conclusion, which hinges in large part on an erroneous claim that no Latin translation of *Alcestis* circulated in England during Shakespeare's lifetime.

14. On the intimate authority of Beatrice's position as Hero's bedmate, see Julie Crawford, "Women's Secretaries," in *Queer Renaissance Historiography*, ed. Vin Nardizzi, Stephen Guy-Bray, and Will Stockton (Burlington: Ashgate, 2008), 111–34, esp. 117–18.

15. On the affective tensions that this short, violent line elicits from audiences, see Philip Weller, "'Kill Claudio': A Laugh Almost Killed by the Critics," *Journal of Dramatic Theory and Criticism* 11.1 (1996), 101–10, and Sarah Antinora, "Please Let This Be Much Ado about Nothing: 'Kill Claudio' and the Laughter of Release," *Ceræ* 1 (2014), 1–21.

16. Robert Miola compares Benedick to Pyrgopolynices, the miles gloriosus of Plautus' play by that name; see *Shakespeare and Classical Comedy: The Influence of Plautus and Terence* (Oxford: Clarendon Press, 1994), 84.

17. On his generically ambivalent status, see Michael Silk, "Heracles and Greek tragedy," *Greece and Rome*, 2nd series, 32:1 (1985), 1–22; on his liminal mortal–immortal nature, see Elton Barker and Joel Christensen, "Even Heracles Had to Die: Homeric 'Heroism', Mortality and the Epic Tradition," *Trends in*

Classics, 6:2 (2014), 249–77. On Hercules' birth and the origins of tragicomedy, see Richard Hardin, "England's *Amphitruo* before Dryden: The Varied Pleasures of Plautus' Template," *Studies in Philology*, 109:1 (2012), 45–62.

18. On Hercules' roles in the two plays, see Showerman, "Shakespeare's Many Much Ado's," esp. 111–32.

19. In the play's first reference to the demigod, Benedick announces that Beatrice "would have made Hercules have turned spit, yea, and have cleft his club to make the fire too" (2.1.231–3), implicitly linking her with Omphale; shortly after, Don Pedro announces that he will "undertake one of Hercules' labors, which is to bring Signor Benedick and the Lady Beatrice into a mountain of affection th' one with th' other" (2.1.337–9).

20. Bate, "Dying to Live," 80.

21. "σοφῇ δὲ χειρὶ τεκτόνων δέμας τὸ σὸν/ εἰκασθὲν ἐν λέκτροισιν ἐκταθήσεται,/ ᾧ προσπεσοῦμαι καὶ περιπτύσσων χέρας/ ὄνομα καλῶν σὸν τὴν φίλην ἐν ἀγκάλαις/ δόξω γυναῖκα καίπερ οὐκ ἔχων ἔχειν:/ ψυχρὰν μέν, οἶμαι, τέρψιν, ἀλλ᾽ ὅμως βάρος/ ψυχῆς ἀπαντλοίην ἄν. ἐν δ᾽ ὀνείρασιν φοιτῶσά μ᾽ εὐφραίνοις ἄν: ἡδὺ γὰρ φίλους/ κἂν νυκτὶ λεύσσειν, ὅντιν᾽ ἂν παρῇ χρόνον." Euripides, *Alcestis*, 348–56. In his Latin version, Buchanan translates: "Quin et periti dextera artificis tua/ In lecto imago ficta collocabitur:/ Amplectar illam minibus, illi procidens/ Tuum vocabo nomen, ulnis conjugem/ Charam tenere, non tenens, fingam tamen:/ Este a voluptas frigida: at molestiam/ Animi levabit; umbre me per somnia/ Utinam reversa oblectet: etiam lurida/ Procidens"; *Euripidis Alcestis*, Latin trans. George Buchanan (Paris: Michel de Vascosan, 1556), 359–68.

22. Mary Stieber has pointed out that the verb *ekteinō*, to stretch out, was used primarily to describe the laying out of corpses; see Stieber, "Statuary in Euripides' *Alcestis*," *Arion*, Third Series, 5:3 (1998), 69–97, 71–2.

23. "γυναῖκα τήνδε μοι σῶσον λαβών" (1020).

24. "τῇ σῇ πέποιθα χειρὶ δεξιᾷ μόνῃ" (1115).

25. "ἐπεὶ σ᾽ ἐγὼ/ καὶ ζῶσαν εἶχον, καὶ θανοῦσ᾽ ἐμὴ γυνὴ/ μόνη κεκλήσῃ," 328–30.

26. On the circulation and uses of dual-language editions of Greek plays, see Pollard, "Greek Playbooks and Dramatic Forms in Early Modern England," in *Formal Matters: Reading the Materials of English Renaissance Literature*, ed. Allison Deutermann and Andras Kisery (Manchester: Manchester University Press, 2013), 99–123.

27. "nam mea,/ Viva ut fuisti sola, sola mortua/ Dicere conjux" ("For as when you were alive you were my only [wife], in death you are called my only wife"); Buchanan, 337–9.

28. *Evripides Poeta Tragicorum princeps* (Basel: Johannes Oporinus, 1562), 222. Aemilius Portus's facing-page edition similarly offers "Viventem habui, & mortua mea coniunx/ Sola vocaberis"; *Evripidis Tragoediae XIX* (Heidelbergae: H. Commelinus, 1597), 437. St. Paul's inventory includes "Euripides graeco-latin. Cum annotate. Stiblini et Brodaei"; see Baldwin, *William Shakspere's Small Latine and Lesse Greeke*, 2:648–9.

29. See Foley, "*Anodos* Dramas," and Victoria Wohl, *Intimate Commerce: Exchange, Gender, and Subjectivity in Greek Tragedy* (Austin: University of Texas Press, 1998), xvi.

30. Bate, "Dying to Live," 73–4.

31. Erasmus, *A Ryght Frutefull Epistle,* trans. Richard Tavernour (London: Robert Redman, 1536), Diiir.

32. Thomas Elyot, *The Dictionary of Syr Thomas Eliot Knyght* (London, 1538), Ggr.

33. Plutarch, *The Philosophie, Commonlie Called, the Morals,* trans. Philemon Holland (London, 1603), 483 and 1146. The 1603 English publication would make this text too late to have influenced *Much Ado about Nothing,* but Shakespeare could well have read it before writing *Pericles* and *Winter's Tale.*

34. See especially Foley, "Anodos Dramas."

35. On Alcestis' parallels with and distinctions from self-sacrificing virgins, see Michael Lloyd, "Euripides' *Alcestis,*" *Greece and Rome,* Second Series, 32:2 (1985), 119–31, 121. On the centrality of maternal lament to Greek tragedy, and especially Euripides, see Nicole Loraux, *Mothers in Mourning,* trans. Corinne Pache (Ithaca, NY: Cornell University Press, 1998), 27–8.

36. See Seth Schein, "*Philia* in Euripides' Alcestis," *Mètis* 3:1–2 (1988), 179–206, 194, and M. Dyson, "Alcestis' Children and the Character of Admetus," *Journal of Hellenic Studies* 108 (1988), 13–23. On the unusual prominence of Euripidean depiction of children more broadly, see Froma Zeitlin, "Intimate Relations: Children, Childbearing, and Parentage on the Euripidean Stage," in *Performance, Iconography, Reception: Studies in Honour of Oliver Taplin,* eds. Martin Revermann and Peter Wilson (Oxford: Oxford University Press, 2008), 318–32.

37. "τέκνα τέκν' οὐκέτ' οὐκέτ' ἔστι δὴ σφῷν μάτηρ./ χαίροντες, ὦ τέκνα, τόδε φάος ὁρῶτον." *Alcestis,* 270–1. Gasparus Stiblinus, in his translation, follows this structure closely: "O liberi, liberi, non amplius sane,/ Non amplius uestra mater est,/ Laeti & foelices hac luce fruamini" (Stiblinus, 221). Aemilius Portus follows Stiblinus almost exactly: "O liberi, liberi, non amplius iam,/ Non amplius iam vestra mater superes, Laeti, o filii, hoc lumen intueamini" (Portus, 434).

38. "καὶ παῖς μὲν ἄρσην πατέρ' ἔχει πύργον μέγαν/ [ὃν καὶ προσεῖπε καὶ προσερρήθη πάλιν]:/ σὺ δ', ὦ τέκνον μοι, πῶς κορευθήσῃ καλῶς;... οὐ γάρ σε μήτηρ οὔτε νυμφεύσει ποτέ/ οὔτ' ἐν τόκοισι σοῖσι θαρσυνεῖ, τέκνον,/ παροῦσ', ἵν' οὐδὲν μητρὸς εὐμενέστερον./ δεῖ γὰρ θανεῖν με: καὶ τόδ' οὐκ ἐς αὔριον" (*Alcestis,* 311–20). Stiblinus follows this order closely: "Et filius masculus quidem, magnum habet confugium/ In patre, cum quo mutuo miscere potest colloquia. Tu uero o filia quomodo annos floris uirginei/ Pulchre mihi exiges?... Non enim te mater unquam dabit nuptui,/ Nec in partu te confirmabit, o filia,/ Praesens, ubi nihil est matre beneuolentius: Mori enim me oportet" (Stiblinus, 222).

39. "σύ νυν γενοῦ τοῖσδ' ἀντ' ἐμοῦ μήτηρ τέκνοις" (*Alcestis,* 377). Stiblinus follows this word order closely: "Tu nunc his pro me mater sis liberis" (Stiblinus, 222).

40. See Zeitlin, "Intimate Relations," 329.
41. See Niall W. Slater, *Euripides: Alcestis* (London: Bloomsbury, 2013), 3.
42. See *Euripidou Medeia Hippolytos Alkestis Andromache* (Florence: Alopa, 1495). On Buchanan's performance, see http://www.apgrd.ox.ac.uk/produc tions/production/4880, accessed May 4, 2014.
43. Roger Ascham, *Toxophilus* (London, 1545), 12v.
44. See Appendices.
45. On Hardy's adaptation, see http://www.apgrd.ox.ac.uk/productions/produc tion/5465, accessed May 4, 2014.
46. On the generic implications of *Alcestis*'s status in the position of the satyr play, see especially Dana F. Sutton, "Satyric Elements in the *Alcestis*," *Rivista di Studi Classici* 21 (1973), 384–91, and Niall W. Slater, "Nothing To Do With Satyrs? *Alcestis* and the Concept of Prosatyric Drama," in *Satyr Drama: Tragedy at Play*, ed. George W. M. Harrison (Swansea: Classical Press of Wales, 2005), 83–101. Bernd Seidensticker identifies *Alcestis* with satyr play conventions especially in its use of Heracles; see Seidensticker, "Dithyramb, Comedy, and Satyr-Play," trans. Isabel Köster and Justina Gregory, in *A Companion to Greek Tragedy*, ed. Justina Gregory (Oxford: Blackwell, 2005), 38–54, 50–1. For an overview of critical debates about the play's genre, see Kiki Gounardiou, *Euripides and Alcestis: Speculations, Stimulations, and Stories of Love in the Athenian Culture* (Lanham, MD: University Press of America, 1998), 4–17.
47. Francesco Robortello, *In Librem Aristotelis* (Florence, 1548), 146, and Giovan Battista Giraldi [Cinthio], *Altile* (1583), 8–9.
48. See Giraldi, *Altile*, 8–9; translated by Frank Ristine, in *English Tragicomedy: Its Origin and History* (New York, 1963), 29, and discussed in Marvin T. Herrick, *Tragicomedy: Its Origin and Development in Italy, France, and England* (Illinois Studies in Language and Literature 39: Urbana, 1955), 67.
49. "Exitum autem haec fabula laetum, insperatum, et plane comicum habet: cuius protases tamen et epitases horribiles et funestae sunt." Stiblinus, "In Euripidis Alcestidem, Praefatio et Argumentum," in *Evripides Poeta Tragicorum princeps*, 239–44, 239.
50. See Pollard, "Tragicomedy," in *The Oxford History of Classical Reception in English Literature*, vol. 2: *The Renaissance*, eds. Patrick Cheney and Philip Hardie (Oxford: Oxford University Press, 2015), 419–32.
51. William Shakespeare and George Wilkins, *Pericles*, ed. Suzanne Gossett (London: Bloomsbury, 2004), 1.1.1–2. All citations of the play refer to this edition.
52. On the play's collaborative authorship, see especially Brian Vickers, *Shakespeare, Co-Author: A Historical Study of Five Collaborative Plays* (Oxford: Oxford University Press, 2002); Macdonald P. Jackson, *Defining Shakespeare: Pericles as Test Case* (Oxford: Oxford University Press, 2003); Gary Taylor and Macdonald P. Jackson, "Pericles," in *William Shakespeare: A Textual Companion*, ed. Stanley Wells and Gary Taylor (Oxford: Clarendon Press, 1987), 130–1, 556–92; and Gossett, "Introduction," *Pericles*, 49–70, 161–3.

On Wilkins' background and contributions, see Duncan Salkeld, "His collaborator George Wilkins," in *The Shakespeare Circle: An Alternative Biography*, ed. Paul Edmondson and Stanley Wells (Cambridge: Cambridge University Press, 2015), 289–96.

53. See Lucy Munro, *Archaic Style in English Literature, 1590–1674* (Cambridge: Cambridge University Press, 2014).

54. As discussed in Chapter 4, although *Apollonius of Tyre* reached the early modern period as a Latin text, scholars have identified its roots as Greek; see G. A. A Kortekaas, *The Story of Apollonius, King of Tyre: A Study of Its Greek Origin and an Edition of the Two Oldest Latin Recensions* (Leiden: Brill, 2004); Elizabeth Archbald, *Apollonius of Tyre: Medieval and Renaissance Themes and Variations* (Woodbridge: Boydell and Brewer, 1991).

55. See Gossett, "Introduction," 117–18, and Caroline Bicks, "Backsliding at Ephesus: Shakespeare's Diana and the Churching of Women," *Pericles: Critical Essays*, ed. David Skeele (Hove: Psychology Press, 2000), 205–27.

56. Shakespeare, *The Comedy of Errors*, ed. R. A. Foakes (London: Methuen, 1962), 5.1.404.

57. Marlowe, *Tamburlaine the Great, Part I*, ed. David Fuller, in *The Complete Works of Christopher Marlowe*, ed. Edward J. Esche (Oxford: Clarendon Press, 1998), 4.2.33; Shakespeare, *King Henry IV, Part 1*, ed. David Scott Kastan, Arden Shakespeare (London: Thomson, 2002), 3.1.12–13.

58. On the temple to Diana, see Chapter 4; also, Randall Martin, "Rediscovering Artemis in *The Comedy of Errors*," *Shakespeare and the Mediterranean*, ed. Tom Clayton, Susan Brock, and Vicente Fores (Newark: University of Delaware Press, 2004): 363–79, and Caroline Bicks, "Backsliding at Ephesus."

59. "The heavens," a listening gentleman replies, "Through you increase our wonder, and set up/ Your fame forever" (3.2.94–96).

60. Pericles invokes "bright Diana whom we honour all" (3.3.29) when instructing Cleon and Dionyza on her care, and Gower describes Marina's homage "to her mistress Dian" (4.Chorus.29). In deterring Thaisa's suitors before bestowing her on Pericles, Simonides had claimed, "One twelvemoons more she'll wear Diana's livery./ This by the eye of Cynthia hath she vowed/ And on her virgin honour will not break it" (2.5.10–12).

61. Significantly, some of Sappho's most famous lines appear in Plutarch's "Life of Demetrius," which was paired with his "Life of Pericles." Plutarch memorably transcribed the poem into his account of a Prince Antiochus, who fell into an incestuous passion: he bore "those signes in him, which *Sappho* wryteth to be in louers (to wit, that his words and speech did faile him, his colour became red, his eyes still rowled to and fro, and then a sodaine swet would take him, his pulse would beate fast and rise high, and in the end, that after the force and power of his hart had failed him, and shewed all these signes, he became like a man in an extasie & traunse, & white as a kearcher." See Plutarch, "The Life of Demetrius," *The Lives of the Noble Grecians and Romanes*, trans. Sir Thomas North (London: 1579), 960.

62. Elizabeth Archibald, "'Deep clerks she dumbs': The Learned Heroine in *Apollonius of Tyre* and *Pericles*," *Comparative Drama* 22:4 (1988–89), 289–303.

63. The Quarto text has "parts" instead of "ports"; see *Pericles*, ed. Gossett, n.5.1.39–40, p. 372.

64. Trevor Nunn's 2016 production of the play at Theatre for a New Audience, for instance, presented Thaisa veiled in this scene.

65. *Midsummer Night's Dream*, Epilogue, 1–4. On Shakespeare's recurring identification of theater-going with sleep, see Pollard, "'A Thing Like Death': Poisons and Sleeping Potions in *Romeo and Juliet* and *Antony and Cleopatra*," *Renaissance Drama* 32 (2003), 95–121.

66. On Pygmalion, see especially Kenneth Gross, *The Dream of the Moving Statue* (Ithaca, NY: Cornell University Press, 1992); Leonard Barkan, "'Living Sculptures': Ovid, Michelangelo, and *The Winter's Tale*," *ELH* 48:4 (1981), 639–67; and Lynn Enterline, "'You Speak a Language that I Understand Not': The Rhetoric of Animation in *The Winter's Tale*," *SQ* 48:1 (1997), 17–44. On *The Tryall of Chevalry*, see Bullough, *Narrative and Dramatic Sources*, VIII.133–134, and Catherine Belsey, *Shakespeare and the Loss of Eden* (Palgrave, 2001), 120.

67. See note 5, this chapter.

68. On links between the play's fascination with birth and its hybrid genre, see Beatrice Bradley and Tanya Pollard, "Tragicomic Conceptions: *The Winter's Tale* as response to *Amphitryo*," *English Literary Renaissance* 47:2 (forthcoming, 2017).

69. Others include Juliet in *Measure for Measure*, Helena in *All's Well that Ends Well*, and Thaisa in *Pericles*: all tragicomic plays featuring false deaths.

70. All citations to *The Winter's Tale* refer to Pitcher's Arden edition.

71. See OED, "burden": "from Old English *byrðen*. I. That which is borne. 1. A load. 2. *fig.* a. A load of labour, duty, responsibility, blame, sin, sorrow. . . . 4. a. That which is borne in the womb; a child" (www.oed.com, accessed February 18, 2014).

72. These counts include alternate forms of the words, such as "forbear" and "bearing." Maurice Hunt has explored the multivalent significance of the word "bear" in the play, though curiously he does not mention its crucial sense of "To bring forth, produce, give birth to"; see Maurice Hunt, "'Bearing Hence': Shakespeare's *The Winter's Tale*," *SEL: Studies in English Literature 1500–1900* 44:2 (2004), 333–46.

73. Greene's *Pandosto* mentions that the couple have a child, but does not provide any details about him or his relationship with his mother.

74. Admetus' unusual decision to bury Alcestis immediately, ignoring the usual three-days "lying in" period before burial, offers a suggestive parallel; see Stieber, "Statuary in Euripides' *Alcestis*," 77.

75. See David M. Bergeron, "The Apollo Mission in *The Winter's Tale*," in *The Winter's Tale: Critical Essays*, ed. Maurice Hunt (New York: Garland, 1995), 361–79. On the play's Apollo references as indicating echoes of *Alcestis*, see Showerman, "'Look Down and See What Death Is Doing.'"

76. See Robert Greene, *Pandosto* (London, 1588), in Bullough, *Narrative and Dramatic Sources*, VIII, 156–99. The word's fourteen instances in *Winter's Tale* represent more than half of its twenty-seven appearances in Shakespeare's works overall.

77. On Shakespeare's Plutarch, see Colin Burrow, *Shakespeare and Classical Antiquity* (Oxford: Oxford University Press, 2013), 202–39, and *Shakespeare's Plutarch*, ed. Mary Ann McGrail (*Poetica: An International Journal of Linguistic-Literary Studies*, 48 [1997]). On Plutarch as conveying Greek tragic material to Shakespeare, see Gordon Braden, "Classical Greek Drama and Shakespeare," in *Homer and Greek Tragedy in Early Modern England's Theatres*, ed. Tania Demetriou and Tanya Pollard, special issue of *Classical Receptions Journal* 9:1 (2017), 103–19 and Leah Whittington, "Shakespeare and the Greeks: Theatricality and Performance from Plutarch's *Lives* to *Coriolanus*," in *Homer and Greek Tragedy in Early Modern England's Theatres*, 120–43.

78. Shakespeare's conflation of Delphi, the home of Apollo's oracle, with the island of Delos, has prompted both mockery and questions. Terence Spencer observed that it reflects a widely held early modern belief, which he would have found in Greene's *Pandosto* as well as in contemporary cartographic writings; see Spencer, "Shakespeare's Isle of Delphos," *The Modern Language Review* (1952): 199–202. Spencer does not mention that Holland's Plutarch used the same spelling; his English translation would not have been available to Greene before his 1588 *Pandosto*, but Greene probably had access to Jacques Amyot's 1572 translation, which circulated in England, served as the model for Holland's English Plutarch, and located Apollo's oracle in "Delphes"; see Amyot, "Des oracles qui ont cessé et pourquoy," *Les Oeuvres morales et meslees* (Paris, 1572), vol. 3, 866–909.

79. Plutarch, "Of The Oracles That Have Ceased To Give Answere," in *The Philosophie, Commonlie Called, the Morals*, 1350.

80. Sissa writes, "The virginity of the prophetess is not merely an accessory quality, as it would be if it were merely a cultural precaution to ensure cleanliness: it is that which makes reception of the god possible"; Sissa, *Greek Virginity*, trans. Arthur Goldhammer (Harvard, 1990), 4.

81. Plutarch, "Of The Oracles That Have Ceased To Give Answere," 1350.

82. Longinus, *On the Sublime*, trans. William Rhys Roberts (Cambridge: Cambridge University Press, 1907), 13:2. On early editions and translations of Longinus in this period, see Bernard Weinberg, "Translations and Commentaries of Longinus, *On the Sublime*, to 1600: A Bibliography" in *Modern Philology*, 47 (1950), 145–51.

83. On the literary consequences of ambivalent Marian nostalgia in this period, see Katharine Goodland, *Female Mourning and Tragedy in Medieval and Renaissance English Drama* (Burlington: Ashgate, 2006), and Gary Waller, *The Virgin Mary in Late Medieval and Early Modern English Literature and Popular Culture* (Cambridge: Cambridge, University Press, 2011).

84. Longinus, "On the Sublime," 13.2.

85. *Richard III* follows, with half the number of uses at seven.
86. Although the play does not explicitly refer to a veil, the word "curtain" appears three times in the scene, as well as once in a stage direction; the statue's uncovering is a central element in the revelation that follows.
87. "σὺ δ᾽, ὦ γύναι,/ ἥτις ποτ᾽ εἶ σύ, ταῦτ᾽ ἔχουσ᾽ Ἀλκήστιδι/ μορφῆς μέτρ᾽ ἴσθι, καὶ προσήϊξαι δέμας" (*Alcestis*, 1061–3). See Dewar-Watson, "The *Alcestis* and the Statue Scene in *The Winter's Tale*."
88. "O femina,/ quaecumque tandem es, es profecto Alcestidi/ modo et statura corporis simillima" ("Woman, whoever you are, you are just like Alcestis, and the very image of her form"); Buchanan, 1137–9; see Dewar-Watson, "The *Alcestis* and the Statue Scene," 79.
89. Gosson, *Plays Confuted in Five Actions* (London, 1582), 180.
90. "τόλμα προτεῖναι χεῖρα καὶ θιγεῖν ξένης. / καὶ δὴ προτείνω, Γοργόν᾽ ὡς καρατομῶν" (*Alcestis*, 1117–18). Buchanan translates these lines extremely closely: "Protende promptus dexteram, tange hospitam./ Protendo, veluti Gorgonis sectum ad caput" (Buchanan, 1194–5).
91. See Abbe Blum, "'Strike all that look upon with mar[b]le': Monumentalizing Women in Shakespeare's Plays," *The Renaissance Englishwoman in Print: Counterbalancing the Canon*, ed. Anne M. Haselkorn and Betty S. Travitsky (Amherst: University of Massachusetts Press, 1990), 99–118.
92. Noting the incongruity between the prominence of Alcestis' children before her death, and their absence from her return, Dyson observes, "the woman who died as a wife and mother is reborn only as a wife" (Dyson, "Alcestis' Children," 18).
93. Valerie Forman identifies the redemption of tragicomic plotting especially with the promise of gain in growing global economic trade; see Forman, *Tragicomic Redemptions: Global Economics and the Early Modern English Stage* (Philadelphia: University of Pennsylvania Press, 2008). Children and maternal labor offer another kind of precarious and crucial investment.

6

Parodying Shakespeare's Euripides in *Bartholomew Fair*

Shakespeare's recurring fascination with Greek tragedy's female icons made an impression on his contemporaries, who identified him with the dramatic tradition these figures represented. As discussed in this book's introduction, in 1598 Francis Meres had already likened him to "these Tragicke Poets [who] flourished in Greece, Æschylus, Euripedes, Sophocles," and in 1646 the poet Samuel Sheppard similarly described "great Shakspeare" as "him,/ whose tragick scenes Euripides/ Doth equal."[1] Perhaps most significantly, Ben Jonson, Shakespeare's colleague, friend, and rival, wrote that to honor Shakespeare, he would "call forth thundering Aeschylus / Euripides, and Sophocles" into his company.[2] What did this kinship mean to Jonson? The most popular of the Greek tragic playwrights prompted both his mockery and his admiration. "Many things in Euripides hath Aristophanes wittily reprehended," Jonson wrote in *Discoveries*: "not out of art, but out of truth. For Euripides is sometimes peccant, as he is most times perfect."[3] This statement has been seen as reflecting negatively both on Euripides and on Jonson's own theatrical moment. Robert Miola has suggested that "[t]he Jonson who here appreciates Aristophanes' mockery of Euripides in *Frogs* and elsewhere likewise ridicules contemporary tragic plays and playwrights, especially Thomas Kyd, Christopher Marlowe and William Shakespeare." "Plays such as *The Spanish Tragedy*, *Tamburlaine* and *Titus Andronicus*," he adds, "continually evoke his scorn as old-fashioned and bombastic."[4] Like Miola, I see Jonson's interest in Aristophanes' tragic parodies as a telling reflection on his own satiric strategies. Yet it is striking that Jonson's praise of Euripides outweighs his criticism: although the tragic poet is "sometimes peccant," he is "most times perfect." This is not simple scorn. Just as Aristophanes' extensive attention to Euripides suggests preoccupation with a rival worth plundering, Jonson's own responses to the most popular of his contemporary tragic playwrights show a complex mix of competition, admiration, envy, and affection.[5]

This chapter argues that Jonson adopts an Aristophanic strategy to parody Shakespeare's versions of Euripidean heroines in *Bartholomew Fair* (1614). Critics including Miola, Matthew Steggle, and Helen Ostovich have documented Jonson's debts to Aristophanes.[6] Yet his emulation of Aristophanes' parodic responses to tragedy—sometimes termed "paratragedy"—has sparked little discussion.[7] With its self-conscious reflections on contemporary theater, and especially on Shakespeare's dramatic legacy, *Bartholomew Fair* offers a rich site for exploring Jonson's paratragic strategies.[8] Written the year after Shakespeare's retirement from the theater, the play explicitly invokes the specter of Shakespeare's late tragicomedies through references to "a servant-monster," "Tales, Tempests, and such like drolleries," a character named Mooncalf, and rival suitors who identify themselves as Palamon and Arcite (Ind.113, 115–16).[9] The fanciful realm of tragicomic romance served as lightning-rod for Jonson's complaints about Shakespeare; in 1629, he excoriated audiences who enjoyed "some mouldy tale/ Like *Pericles*."[10] Yet this attack, responding to audiences' hostility towards his own recently staged *New Inn*, reflects Jonson's characteristically ambivalent competitive envy towards his rival, and *Bartholomew Fair*'s debts to Shakespeare's tragicomic plots suggests more nuanced responses. I argue that the play simultaneously imitates, mocks, and pays homage to Shakespeare's tragicomic restorations, through parodic versions of the Greek female figures who loom behind their miraculous reversals. Joan Trash becomes "Ceres selling her daughter's picture," (2.5.8); Ursula is "Mother o'the Furies," known "by her firebrand" (2.5.56–8); and the play culminates with a modernized performance of *Hero and Leander*, which, as discussed in Chapter 5, evoked both Greece and tragedy.[11] As in *The Spanish Tragedy* and *Titus Andronicus*, which the play cites, suffering mothers and daughters mobilize the dramatic action with fierce performances of emotion, and as in *Much Ado About Nothing*, *Pericles*, and *The Winter's Tale*, the ending features reunions with veiled wives returning from a mock-underworld. Along the way, a suffering virgin—like *Twelfth Night*'s Viola, and *Pericles*'s Marina—employs resourcefulness and wit to escape the threat of sacrifice, by strategically negotiating an alternative to marrying an imbecile. Tracing the play's Euripidean underpinnings illuminates not only Jonson's complex relationship with Shakespeare, but also his own distinctive strategies for claiming the authority of Greek dramatic models. In his canny, tongue-in-cheek recreations of these quintessentially Shakespearean/Euripidean plots, Jonson recreates the pleasurable redemptions of his models while maintaining his wry skepticism towards their miraculous resolutions.

CERES SELLING HER DAUGHTER'S PICTURE: PARODYING TRAGIC WOMEN

In stark contrast to the predominantly male worlds typical of Jonson's earlier city comedies, *Bartholomew Fair* teems with female bodies, who both initiate the play's action and occupy its center. Getting to the fair requires the mobilizing force of mothers and daughters. "Win, long to eat of a pig, sweet Win, i' the Fair," John Littlewit implores his wife; "do you see? I' the heart of the Fair; not at Pie-corner. Your mother will do anything, Win, to satisfy your longing, you know; pray thee long, presently, and be sick o' the sudden, good Win" (1.5.141–5). Despite concerns about the fair's heathen temptations from Win's mother, Dame Purecraft, and the stringently puritan Zeal-of-the-Land-Busy, Win's pregnancy accords her a privileged license to solicit others' sympathies.[12] Win presents herself as an actress, whose looming maternity authorizes her performance. In response to her husband's urging, "play the hypocrite, sweet Win," she replies, "I can be hypocrite enough . . . I ha' somewhat o' the mother in me, you shall see" (1.5.126–34). But it is not only her own maternity that ensures her plan's success. Just as Busy reminds the Littlewits that "the disease of longing, it is a disease, a carnal disease, or appetite, incident to women" (1.6.39–40), Dame Purecraft presents her own maternal passions as overpowering her puritanism. "Truly, I do love my daughter dearly," she explains to Busy, "and I would not have her miscarry, or hazard her first fruits, if it might be otherwise" (1.6.53–4).

Performances of maternal instinct license the pleasures of appetite not only for Win and Purecraft, but also for Littlewit, and even the apparently skeptical Busy. "I will therefore eat," he announces in conceding, "yea I will eat exceedingly" (1.6.77–8). Littlewit describes his plan as a form of linguistic fertility, a "pretty conceit," which he experiences in bodily terms: "I do feel conceits coming upon me more than I am able to turn tongue to" (1.1.1, 24–5). Other characters similarly suggest that the fair's pleasures require surrendering to female authority. When Cokes's tutor Wasp explains that he has had to leave Cokes temporarily "in charge with a gentlewoman"—his sister, married to Justice Overdo—he notes ominously, "but what may happen under a woman's government, there's the doubt" (1.4.63, 65–6). In fact, Wasp has no doubt about the disorderliness that will result from even temporary female government, and the play bears out his fears. Female longing opens doors not only to the fair, but also within it. As Littlewit reminds Win, arriving is not enough: "we shall never see any sights i' the Fair, Win, except you long still, Win . . .

Now you ha' begun with pig, you may long for anything, Win" (3.6.3–7). Although Win's imagination turns to eating—"But we sha' not eat o' the bull and the hog, John: how shall I long, then?"—her husband points out that the fair's carnal offerings go beyond food: "O yes, Win! You may long to see as well as to taste, Win... good Win, go in, and long" (3.6.9–13). Licensed to long, Win becomes the portal through which others experience the tastes, sights, and other pleasures of the fair. The open and receptive nature of her pregnant body elicits sympathetic identification from her audiences, who access new liberties from following her example.

Although Littlewit urges Win to look further than pig, her starting point lies at the heart of the event. Just as the fair begins with maternal longings, its pleasures are identified especially with another maternal figure, "the fleshly woman... Urs'la" (3.6.26–7). "This is the very womb and bed of enormity!," Overdo observes of her stand, which he later labels "the sow of enormity" (2.2.87, 5.6.46). Ursula is the "Body o' the Fair!"; in reply to Quarlous's question, "What's this? Mother o'the bawds?," Knockem replies, "No, she's mother o'the pigs, sir, mother o'the pigs!" "Mother o'the Furies," Winwife rejoins, "I think, by her firebrand" (2.5.56–8). Noting Ursula's links with pigs, transformation, gluttony, and the dark retreat that Mooncalf describes as "my mistress' bower" (2.5.45), Gough has persuasively identified her with Circe, the sorceress who lures Odysseus' men to distraction.[13] I propose that Winwife's references to Furies and a firebrand also link her with Greek tragic women, including Hecuba, who, as previously discussed, famously dreamed of a firebrand while pregnant with Paris.[14] Like other early modern versions of Hecuba, Ursula evokes a liquid state of melting, albeit in tawdry form. Complaining about the heat of roasting pigs, she calls to an assistant, "quickly: a bottle of ale to quench me, rascal. I am all fire and fat, Nightingale; I shall e'en melt away to the first woman, a rib again, I am afraid. I do water the ground in knots as I go, like a great garden-pot: you may follow me by the S's I make" (2.2.43–5). As the first woman, Ursula is both Eve and a degraded Hecuba; she reigns over the fairground's comic Troy, whose satiric battles will result in Busy's destruction of mock homes, along with the loss of wives, and the performance of a Greek tragic poem. Nor is she the only female fairground figure linked derisively with Greek tragic loss. Quarlous, coming upon Ursula's colleague Joan Trash selling gingerbread, pronounces her "Ceres selling her daughter's picture, in ginger-work!" (2.5.8). The play reduces classical icons of grieving mothers and sacrificial daughters to lowbrow, commercial consumables, but it continues to invoke their presence as crucial to the fair's pleasures.

If Win and Ursula, as portal into the fair and the fair's heart, link its festivities with satiric versions of female longing and fertility, others offer up curious variations on their fruitfulness. The play's prologue advertises "such ware...As babies, hobby-horses, puppet-plays" (Prologue, 2, 5), and Leatherhead's ongoing refrain repeats this odd conjunction of childish objects: "What do you lack? What is't you buy? Rattles, drums, halberds, horses, babies o'the best?" (2.2.24–5). Babies feature conspicuously in the cornucopia of pleasures that the fair markets to its consumers.[15] Editions of the play rightly gloss "babies" as dolls, but in the context of the pregnancy that sets the play into motion, the word's pervasiveness also suggests the play's fascination with fertility. Critics who have observed the play's interest in pregnancy have typically derided it as superficial; Jonas Barish described the play's "procreative imagery" as limited to "the gratification of the senses, [and] physical release," and R. B. Parker argued that "The sex of the fair is infertile..., non-creative," claiming that "the pregnancy which Win uses as an excuse for visiting the fair is a lie; and the only 'babies' produced are dolls and puppets."[16] But both the fair and the play prove fertile in many senses, not least in their creative uses of popular dramatic materials to produce a witty and successful tragicomic plot that culminates in two marriages and a feast. Just as Littlewit's "pretty conceit" results in an original and influential reading of Hero and Leander, the play's parodic strategies produce a new response to popular dramatic models.[17]

While the play emphasizes female fertility, the women who mobilize its plots are not exclusively maternal figures. Grace Wellborn, Cokes's intended bride, offers a witty version of Shakespeare's resourceful sacrificial virgins. From the play's start, her betrothal to Cokes is marked out as a kind of tragedy. "What pity 'tis yonder wench should marry such a 'cokes'!" (1.5.41–2), Quarlous remarks, and Grace makes it clear that she shares his dismay. When Cokes remarks of Win, "A pretty little soul, this same Mistress Littlewit! Would I might marry her," Grace echoes in an aside, "So would I, or anybody else, so I might scape you" (1.5.66–7). Later, in response to Quarlous's inquiry into how she became Overdo's ward, she explains, "Faith, through a common calamity: he bought me, sir; and now he will marry me to his wife's brother, this wise gentleman that you see, or else I must pay value o'my land" (3.5.230–2). When Winwife comments on her stoic resignation to bad fortune, she explains, "Sir, they that cannot work their fetters off must wear 'em" (3.5.240).

Yet Grace in fact proves quite capable of working her fetters off once loosed in the freedom of the fair. "'Tis true (I have professed it to you ingenuously)," she tells Winwife and Quarlous, "that rather than to be yoked with this bridegroom is appointed me, I would take up any husband, almost upon any trust" (4.3.8–10). Through strategic savvy, she enlists both men to help her, flattering them into temporarily overcoming rivalry to work together to retrieve her marriage license. "For you are reasonable creatures," she tells them; "you have understanding and discourse. And if fate send me an understanding husband, I have no fear at all but mine own manners shall make him a good one" (4.3.28–31). Asking, "Will you consent to a notion of mine, gentlemen?" (4.3.33–4), Grace draws on a strategy from another recent tragicomedy, *Two Noble Kinsmen* (1613–14), collaboratively written by Shakespeare and Fletcher, and rooted in both medieval and classical sources.[18] Instructing her two suitors each to write a word or a name, she tells them that she will turn over the choice to the next person she meets, but she maintains control of the decision, and both men's allegiance, by withholding the answer. Despite sharp restrictions, Grace exploits the fair's freedoms to forge a creative escape from her hapless fate. In merging the roles of resourceful Shakespearean heroines such as Beatrice, Viola, and Marina with the typically male prototype of the city comedy wit, she joins the growing ranks of female tricksters, such as Maria in Fletcher's 1611 *The Tamer Tamed*, in establishing new possibilities for comic women.[19]

THE ART OF LOSING

The unregulated freedom that Grace discovers in the fair also proves especially susceptible to loss, a word that appears 34 times in the play.[20] The fair's consummate loser, Cokes, embraces the fair's risks as giddily as its freedoms. When Mistress Overdo, warning him about straying from his tutor Wasp, asks, "You will not let him go, brother, and lose him?," Cokes replies, "Who can hold that will away? I had rather lose him than the Fair" (1.5.86–7). Wasp is certain that Cokes cannot hold much: "If a leg or an arm on him did not grow on," he warns, "he would lose it i'the press" (1.5.90–1). "Pray you, take heed you lose not yourself," he similarly admonishes Cokes later; "Buy a token's worth of great pins to fasten yourself to my shoulder" (3.4.11–13). A caricature of the satirist onstage, sourly mocking the naivety of his wide-eyed charge, Wasp finds his primary cudgel in the threat of loss, which he facetiously imagines in terms that parody tragic dismemberment.[21]

Just as Wasp's vision of strewn limbs imbues Cokes's carelessness with dark undertones, the misadventures that follow prompt similarly mock-tragic laments. As Wasp predicts, Cokes begins losing immediately. "Stay, Numps," he interjects after the first bout of pickpocketing; "stay, set me down: I ha' lost my purse, Numps. Oh, my purse! One o'my fine purses is gone" (2.6.78–9). His losses quickly multiply. "Ha! humph! O God!," Cokes wails after another realization; "My purse is gone, my purse, my purse, etc." (3.5.149). As Wasp mocks him—"I pray you, seek some other gamester to play the fool with; you may lose it time enough, for all your Fair-wit" (3.5.153–4)—Cokes's distress escalates. "By this good hand, glove and all, I ha' lost it already, if thou hast it not—feel else—and Mistress Grace's handkerchief, too, out o' the t'other pocket" (3.5.155–6). After losing his cloak and hat as well, he summarizes his misadventures with a catalogue of losses: "I ha' lost myself, and my cloak and my hat, and my fine sword, and my sister, and Numps, and Mistress Grace (a gentlewoman that I should ha' married) and a cut-work handkerchief she ga' me, and two purses today. And my bargain o' hobby-horses and gingerbread, which grieves me worst of all" (4.2.65–9). While losing purses, garments, and goods simply accelerates the fair's consumption of Cokes's money, his loss of Grace's handkerchief foreshadows the more serious loss of Grace herself. As sites of intimate bodily exchange, handkerchiefs metonymically represent not only women's affections, but women themselves, lending this particular loss heightened meanings.[22] Having never possessed Grace's affections, Cokes's only claims to her lay in possessing her handkerchief and marriage license, both of which disappear at the fair. Like Celia's handkerchief in Jonson's earlier *Volpone* (1605–6), Grace's transitory handkerchief evokes tragic backdrops, especially *The Spanish Tragedy*, which Jonson cites directly in *Bartholomew Fair*'s Induction, as well as Shakespeare's *Othello* (c.1603).

If the handkerchief's disappearance reflects Cokes's carelessness, the more typically vigilant Wasp's inability to protect the license reflects other failings exacerbated by the fair. Wasp insists on holding the license out of confidence in his superiority to Cokes at safekeeping. "But gi' me this from you, i'the meantime," he tells Cokes; "I beseech you, see if I can look to this" (3.5.182–3). In response to the query, "Why, Numps?," Wasp explains irritably, "Why? Because you are an ass, sir—there's a reason the shortest way, and you will needs ha' it. Now you ha' got the trick of losing, you'd lose your breech an 'twere loose" (3.5.184–7). Yet although Wasp's skepticism towards Cokes is justified, he fails to recognize the weakness in his own cantankerous pride. When he fights with Knockem and Whit during the game of vapors, he becomes sufficiently consumed by his irate humors that he misses the pickpocket Edgworth stealing the license from the box he holds.

As the disappearance of handkerchief and license ultimately show, the most substantial losses at the fair are of wives, mislaid by a surprising number of the male fairgoers. Like Shakespeare, whose tragicomedies insistently dramatize the loss of wives to apparent death, Jonson offers his own versions of Alcestis descending to the underworld. Just as Cokes loses Grace, her handkerchief, and her marriage license, Justice Overdo's disguise antics leave him oblivious to his wife's disappearance into the clutches of the criminal underworld's prostitution ring, while Littlewit personally delivers his wife to Ursula and her men, little suspecting where she will end up. Zeal-of-the-Land-Busy and Winwife, meanwhile, lose their hopes of marrying the wealthy Dame Purecraft when she offers her hand to the madman Trouble-all—or rather, his canny impersonator, Quarlous. Although none of these women submit to the apparent deaths featured in Shakespeare's *Much Ado About Nothing, Pericles, The Winter's Tale*, or *Cymbeline*, they all disappear to the fair's dark underbelly before miraculously reappearing—albeit in some cases to different intended husbands than before—in the happy denouement of the tragic puppet show.

When Littlewit proposes to leave his wife "i'this good company, Win, for half an hour or so," her first reaction is concern: "Will you leave me alone with two men, John?" (4.5.2–6). Although Littlewit confidently reassures her that "they are honest gentlemen, Win" (4.2.7), as soon as he has left, Ursula laments that "we are undone for want of fowl i'the Fair," and instructs her helpers "Persuade this between you two to become a bird o'the game, while I work the velvet woman within" (5.4.11–12, 14–15). Win proves easily persuadable: when Whit pronounces, "De honesht woman's life is a scurvy dull life" (4.5.24–5), she is curious to learn more. "How, sir?," she asks; "Is an honest woman's life a scurvy life?" (4.5.26). She is delighted by the promise that she can "live like a lady... and be honest too" (4.5.28–30), especially when told that she can be in love with gallants, "and lie by twenty on 'em." "What, and be honest still?," she replies; "That were fine sport" (4.5.35–6). The carnal longings that she performed at the start of the play escalate, and prove susceptible to suggestion; when told, "it is the vapour of spirit in the wife to cuckold nowadays, as it is the vapour of fashion in the husband not to suspect," she cheerfully replies, "Lord, what a fool I have been!" (4.5.41–4). Although Dame Overdo's entrance into the trade is less smooth, chased and beaten as she is by a rival Bartholomew bird, Knockem assures her, "Come, brave woman, take a good heart: thou shalt be a lady, too," and Whit echoes, "Yes, fait, dey shall all both be ladies, and write 'Madam'" (4.5.73–5). With no objections from Dame Overdo, Jonson shows both wives entering their new lives in the fair's underworld voluntarily, and with enthusiasm.

JONSON'S ARISTOPHANIC PARATRAGEDY

Although *Bartholomew Fair*'s particular interest in Shakespeare's female figures suggest new territory for Jonson, the play's larger strategy of mining tragic materials for satirical uses recalls his long-running fascination with Kyd's *The Spanish Tragedy*, which the play also invokes deliberately. In prescribing rules for audience etiquette, the Induction's Scrivener explains, "He that will swear *Jeronimo* or *Andronicus* are the best plays yet shall pass unexpected at here, as a man whose judgement shows it is constant and hath stood still these five and twenty or thirty years" (Ind. 79–82). Although the reference mocks Kyd as outmoded, its nod to his lasting popularity also highlights Jonson's extensive debts to *The Spanish Tragedy*, which he revisited throughout his plays, and to which he—and/ or Shakespeare—may have contributed revisions.[23] In *Every Man In His Humour* (1598), the fops Bobadilla and Mattheo indulge in an extended panegyric to its pleasures: in response to Bobadilla's inquiry, "What new book have you there? What, 'Go by Hieronymo!',", Mattheo replies, "Ay, did you ever see it acted? Is't not well penned?" "Well penned?," Bobadilla echoes; "I would fain see all the poets of our time pen such another play as that was."[24] In *Poetaster* (1601), when Tucca, like Hamlet, calls for visiting players to perform a dramatic scene, Pyrgus obediently recites from Baltha- zar's famous lament for Bel-Imperia's love: "Oh, she is wilder and more hard withal/ Than beast or bird, or tree or stony wall."[25] In a more thorough and literal repurposing of the play's materials, *The Alchemist*'s Face advises Abel Drugger that to woo the Widow Pliant, "Thou must borrow/ A Spanish suit. Hast thou no credit with the players? . . . Hieronimo's old cloak, ruff, and hat will serve."[26] Improvising in response to Surly's Spanish disguise, Face presents the costume as offering exotic glamor, but his allusion implicitly suggests that Hieronimo's magnetic attraction for audiences will translate into erotic appeal, and Lovewit's eventual success at marrying Pliant in this guise seems to prove him right.

Bartholomew Fair makes similarly sustained use of *The Spanish Tragedy*'s characters and materials. As already observed, the transfer of a woman's handkerchief marks crucial shifting allegiances. More substantively, as in *The Alchemist*, winning the hand of a wealthy widow requires impersonat- ing a version of the mad Hieronimo. From among the many men who seek her hand, Dame Overdo proclaims herself in love with the madman Trouble-All, though in practice she ends up proposing to Quarlous, the man who play-acts this role, who aptly observes, "this madman's shape will prove a very fortunate one" (5.2.91–2). Similarly, the black box that Cokes believes holds his license to marry Grace Wellborn repurposes the black box that Pedringano mistakenly believes holds his pardon in *The Spanish Tragedy*.[27] Perhaps most significantly, the play imitates Kyd by culminat- ing in a metatheatrical performance.

Although Jonson's running fascination with the appeal of the mad Hieronimo differs from his Shakespearean borrowings in *Bartholomew Fair*, both strains represent the same underlying strategy of imitating popular tragedy for comic ends. As suggested above, this strategy, like Shakespeare's tragicomic women themselves, had a classical model. Jonson's satiric responses to popular tragedies and tragicomedies, I argue, channeled Aristophanes, whom he often cited as a model for comic power, and whose witty parodies of Euripides' tragicomic women formed an influential part of his legacy. The sheer scale of Aristophanes' allusions to Euripides indicates a substantial intellectual attraction; he quoted the tragedian more than one hundred times in his comedies, and presented him as a character in plays including *Acharnians, Thesmophoriazusae, Peace,* and *Frogs*.[28] Contemporaries linked the two writers; Cratinus, a rival comic playwright, coined the term "Euripidaristophanize" to describe their shared brand of wit.[29] Observing "a loosening of generic boundaries" in late fifth-century Athens, Helene Foley has argued for a reciprocal influence, suggesting not only that Aristophanes learned dramatic techniques from Euripides, but also that his satiric responses may have encouraged Euripides' own experiments with intertextual borrowing and generic hybridity.[30] Aristophanes used his characteristically self-conscious metatheater to critique a range of literary forms: exploring ways that his comedy "employs the self-reflexive discourse of genre," Emmanuella Bakola, Lucia Prauscello, and Mario Telò note that it "appropriates, manipulates and ridicules ancient discourse on literary criticism."[31] Euripidean tragedy, however, occupied a privileged place in his attention.

Some of Jonson's tragic borrowings are remarkably similar to Aristophanes' Euripides parodies. Quarlous's use of a madman disguise, for instance, recalls Aristophanes' repeated device of having a protagonist disguise himself as Telephus, a mad beggar from a lost Euripides' play who takes an infant hostage in order to successfully negotiate his way out of a dire situation.[32] Like Hieronimo, Telephus signaled the successful use of lament to appeal to listeners' pity; Rosemary Harriott argues that Aristophanes' recurring interest in Telephus "is a tribute to Euripides' power of evoking sympathy, not merely a jibe at his ragged heroes."[33] Yet the female characters who became Euripides' primary representatives in the early modern period also captured Aristophanes' attention; *Alcestis* is the most-cited tragedy after *Telephus,* and Harriott notes that "Euripides' studies of women are a favourite source of comedy."[34] *Thesmophoriazusae* features Euripides and Mnesilochus escaping from angry women by play-acting scenes from Euripides' *Helen* and *Andromeda,* which had been staged the previous year. Observing that the play "implicates comedy and tragedy in a . . . shared competitive game," Foley points out that "Aristophanes also appropriates . . . tragedy's expansive treatment of women on stage along with Euripides' signature theme of forcing men to learn from female experience by symbolically sharing in it."[35] As a model for Jonson, Aristophanes demonstrated productive ways to exploit the popular appeal not only of sympathetic suffering madmen, but also of sympathetic suffering women.

Aristophanes' paratragedy attracted interest from early modern commentators, and his Euripidean comedies *Frogs*, *Thesmophoriazusae*, and *Acharnians* enjoyed a disproportionately high level of visibility in sixteenth-century editions.[36] Jonson's account of Aristophanes' witty reprehension of Euripides shows his awareness of the comedian's successful commitment to parodying popular tragedy. Jonson's similar long-running parody of both Kyd and Shakespeare, moreover, suggest a similarly ambivalent combination of warmth and criticism. He famously wrote of Shakespeare, in *Discoveries*, "I loved the man, and do honour his memory on this side idolatry," though a few lines earlier he also wrote, "I remember the players have often mentioned it as an honour to Shakespeare, that in his writing, whatsoever he penned, he never blotted out line. My answer hath been, 'Would he had blotted a thousand.'"[37] Jonson's approach to Aristophanes suggests that *Bartholomew Fair*'s elaborate paratragic imitation found inspiration in the Greek playwright's response to another popular, witty, tragicomic poet for articulating his own vexed relationship—simultaneously admiring, competitive, and mocking—with Shakespeare. And by focusing especially on Shakespeare's versions of Greek tragic women for his parody, Jonson reflects not only on his friend and rival playwright, but also on the popular dramatic icons that found influential afterlives in Shakespeare's plays.

RECOVERING LOSSES AT THE THEATER

Like many of Euripides' tragedies, *Bartholomew Fair* culminates in revelations, recognitions, and reversals. And as in many of Shakespeare's comedies and tragicomedies, these events take place at a performance, and lead to reunions and restorations. The culminating puppet show proves a source of delight to Cokes, the first of the fairgoers to stumble across it. "How now?," he exclaims, "What's here to do?" In reply to the proffered explanation from Sharkwell, one of the fair's con-men—"'Tis a motion, an't please your worship"—he goes on to read a playbill:

A motion, what's that? (*He reads the bill.*) 'The Ancient Modern History of *Hero* and *Leander*, otherwise called *The Touchstone of True Love*, with as true a trial of friendship between Damon and Pythias, two faithful friends o'the Bankside.' Pretty, i' faith—what's the meaning on't? Is't an interlude? Or what is't? (5.3.1–9)

Cokes's confusion about the show is understandable: this motion, inter-
lude, or "ancient modern history" occupies a curiously ambiguous genre.
Yoking tragic lovers familiar from Christopher Marlowe's 1590s *Hero and
Leander* with legendary friends dramatized in Richard Edwards' 1564
Damon and Pythias, the title merges a story of loss with one of sacrifice
redeemed, suggesting the popular hybrid structure of tragedy with a happy
ending.[38] The performance joins contraries in other ways as well.
Although its tragic Greek figures suggest the literary prestige accorded to
grief and classical antiquity, its puppets, Bankside relocation, and fairgrounds setting identify it with contemporary popular entertainment. As
another of the fair's con-men, the aptly named Filcher, reminds Cokes,
the show's pleasures have an explicitly commercial purpose: "Yes, sir.
Please you come near; we'll take your money within" (5.3.10).

When the puppet show gets underway, its organizers explicitly invoke
the specter of tragedy before repudiating it. Lantern describes the play as a
"*tragical encounter*" (5.3.280), reminding us that although Hero and
Leander were best known from Marlowe's epyllion, they were widely
associated with tragedy, as discussed in Chapter 5. As Tom Harrison has
noted, the performance's presiding figure, Puppet Dionysius, evokes
not only the Sicilian tyrant of Edwards' *Damon and Pythias*, but also
Dionysus, the Greek god of theater.[39] Although the wider playgoing
public would have identified the allusion primarily with Marlowe, Jonson
himself would also have known Shakespeare's recurring comic uses of
Hero and Leander. In *Two Gentlemen of Verona* (1589–91), possibly
Shakespeare's first play, they loom behind the star-crossed lovers; Valen-
tine reflects on "some shallow story of deep love—/ How young Leander
cross'd the Hellespont," and later at court suggests that his rope ladder
"Would serve to scale another Hero's tower,/ So bold Leander would
adventure it."[40] In *Romeo and Juliet* (1594–6), Mercutio mocks Romeo's
adulation of Juliet by likening her to a catalogue of legendary mistresses:
"Laura to his lady was but a kitchen-wench; . . . Dido a dowdy; Cleopatra a
gipsy; Helen and Hero hildings and harlots."[41] When Benedick in *Much
Ado About Nothing* (1598–9) tries haplessly to compose a love poem for
Beatrice, he lists "Leander the good swimmer" as one of the lovers whose
suffering he exceeds, and more pervasively, if obliquely, Hero's ghost
looms behind that play's suffering bride.[42] Recounting to Orlando "the
patterns of love" in *As You Like It* (1599), Rosalind/ Ganymede insists that
"Leander, he would have lived many a fair year, though Hero had turned
nun, if it had not been for a hot midsummer night; for, good youth, he
went but forth to wash him in the Hellespont and, being taken with the
cramp, was drowned, and the foolish chroniclers of that age found it was
Hero of Sestos."[43]

Strikingly, all of these allusions feature in comic contexts—even in *Romeo and Juliet*, Mercutio's teasing of Romeo falls within the play's antic early acts—and all identify the lovers with oversexed melodramatic folly, anticipating Puppet Damon's accusation that *"Mistress Hero's a whore"* (5.4.262). Shakespeare, then, again offers a model for comic use of these particular tragic materials, and Jonson revises this model into sharper and more sardonic terms. The genre of puppet show offers a self-consciously lowbrow setting for Jonson's comic version of Greek tragic figures. As Leatherhead Lantern observes to Cokes, the subject matter proves inappropriate for a popular setting. "[T]hat is too learned and poetical for our audience," he explains; "what do they know what Helles-pont is, 'guilty of true love's blood'? Or what Abydos is, or 'the other, Sestos hight'?" "Thou'rt i'the right," Cokes concedes; "I do not know myself," to which Lantern continues, "No, I have entreated Master Littlewit to take a little pains to reduce it to a more familiar strain for our people" (5.3.84–9). In his explanation that audiences' lack of know-ledge required translating classical tragic material "to a more familiar strain for our people," Lantern Leatherhead offers a caricature of Jonson himself. As has been well documented, Jonson's own early experiments with classical tragedy were notable failures at the box office.[44] Tragic and classical models continued to loom behind his comedies, but the self-conscious classicism of earlier plays gave way to a more commercially successful light touch. Set in the conspicuously popular realm of the fairgrounds, and directing even its most hopeless characters to happy endings, *Bartholomew Fair* extends this trajectory, epitomized by the puppet show's exaggerated bowdlerization of Hero and Leander.

The puppet show's author, Littlewit, follows Lantern in offering Cokes a more detailed account of his revisions. "I have only made it a little easy and modern for the times, sir," he explains;

> that's all: as, for the Hellespont I imagine our Thames here; and then Leander, I make a dyer's son about Puddle Wharf and Hero a wench o'the Bankside, who, going over one morning to Old Fish Street, Leander spies her land at Trig Stairs, and falls in love with her: Now do I introduce Cupid, having metamorphosed himself into a drawer, and he strikes Hero in love, with a pint of sherry   (5.3.92–7)

As Roy Booth has pointed out, Littlewit was only the first of many adapters who could not resist building on the story's implicitly porno-graphic plot: "The joke seems to have taken root because, at a basic level, 'Hero and Leander' was a story about a young man who crossed to the other side of a waterway to get sex."[45] Cokes's reaction suggests that Littlewit has gauged his target audience well. In response to Littlewit's claim, "other pretty passages there are o' the friendship that will delight you, sir, and please you of judgement," he agrees emphatically: "I'll be sworn they shall: I am in love with the Actors already, and I'll be allied to them presently" (5.3.98–101).

As the puppet show gets underway, its irreverent depiction of Greek tragic icons as bawdy and belligerent commoners quickly descends into chaos and name-calling. As its presiding spirit, the ghost of Dionysius surfaces to ask Damon and Pythias

> *what harm*
> *Hath poor Dionysius done you in his grave*
> *That after his death, you should fall out thus, and rave,*
> *And call amorous Leander whoremaster knave?*   (5.4.285–8)

This invocation of Greek tragedy's ghost serves as the puppet show's breaking point, inciting Busy to his outraged interruption: "Down with Dagon, down with Dagon! 'Tis I, will no longer endure your profanations" (5.5.1–2). As critics have discussed, the ensuing attack and response re-enact antitheatrical debates about the theater's dangers, resulting in a triumphant victory for the puppets, whose claims to innocence are upheld in a parodic unveiling—"*The puppet takes up his garment*" (5.4.84)—refuting the charge of cross-dressing.[46] This moment of metatheatrical unveiling features centrally in many critical accounts of the play. Melinda Gough has shown that the puppet's gesture of mock-sexual exposure invokes the exposures of enchantresses throughout the romance epic tradition, from Homer's Circe through Spenser's Duessa.[47] I suggest that this unveiling, which results in other revelations and recognitions, also raises further implications, which we have not yet recognized.

The puppet's self-exposure prompts Overdo's own unveiling, in a stage direction—"*The Justice discovers himself*"—that parallels the puppet's self-discovery, and similarly meets with a round of wondering responses. Yet Overdo's self-revelation serves primarily as preamble to the play's final unveilings. In the context of the play's self-conscious response to Shakespeare's tragicomedies, I suggest that this cascade of unveilings gestures to the specter of the veiled Alcestis, who haunts the revived wives that *Bartholomew Fair* also revisits. In the wake of the unveilings of the puppet and Overdo, lost wives move to the center of the playgoers' attention. The puppet show coincides with a wave of anxiety about the fair's losses. When Cokes arrives, he is despondent: "I have lost all i'the Fair, and all my acquaintance too" (5.3.23–4). Others become aware of their losses as the show begins. Littlewit instructs Lantern, "make ready to begin, that I may fetch my wife" (5.4.7), and becomes concerned upon realizing that he cannot: "O Gentlemen! Did you not see a wife of mine? I ha' lost my little wife, as I shall be trusted—my little pretty Win" (5.6.11–12.). Justice Overdo similarly notices that things are awry as the crowd gathers: "My ward, Mistress Grace, in the company of a stranger!" (5.4.15). The lost wives attending the play, meanwhile, worry about their new status as they encounter husbands who do not recognize them in their unfamiliar guises. When Win sees her husband, she wonders, "Must I put off my mask to him?," leading Edgeworth to reply "Oh, by no means." (5.4.37–8).

Amid the unveilings prompted by the puppets' revelation, Justice Overdo responds to Littlewit's renewed expression of his plaint by offering to restore Win. "If this grave matron be your mother, sir," he announces, "stand by her, *et digito, compesce labellum*; I may perhaps spring a wife for you anon" (5.6.16–17). He similarly attempts to return another lost wife—"Mistress Grace, let me rescue you out of the hands of the stranger"—only to learn that the apparent stranger, Winwife, is in fact now her husband: "Master Winwife? I hope you have won no wife of her, sir" (5.6.20–1, 25). Following this unexpected discovery, he goes on to unveil Littlewit's wife. "Let me unmask your 'Ladyship,'" Overdo announces, to Littlewit's startled response: "O my wife, my wife, my wife!" (5.5.37–9). Throughout his mock-Herculean feats of returning lost wives, however, Overdo fails to notice that he has lost his own wife. It is fitting, then, that after the exposure of Quarlous as faux-madman—"I am mad, but from the gown outward"—the final and most eventful unveiling is that of Mistress Overdo. After another important stage direction—"*Mistress Overdo is sick, and her husband is silenced*"—Whit explains, "Dy very own wife, i' fait, worshipful Adam" (5.5.s.d.56, 59).

In its quasi-magical recuperation of loss, the scene parodically recalls the astonished recognitions attending the appearances of presumed-dead twins at the ending of *Comedy of Errors* and *Twelfth Night*. But the multiple exposures of puppets and wives, by drawing back skirts and veils, more specifically recall the unveilings of lost wives that end Shakespeare's tragicomic romances.[48] At the end of *Much Ado About Nothing*, the waiting bridegroom Claudio is presented with "*the women masked*"; in reply to his request, "Sweet, let me see your face," he is told to wait until after the exchange of vows, at which point Hero unmasks herself, explaining, "And when I lived I was your other wife" (5.4.s. d.51, 55, 60). Similarly, at the end of *Pericles*, a veiled Thaisa faints upon hearing Pericles' story of recovering Marina, and is uncovered by Cerimon—for the second time—to be returned to her husband. *The Winter's Tale* also opens its culminating revelation with a similar stage direction: "*Draws a curtain and reveals the figure of Hermione standing like a statue*."[49] If the ghost of Alcestis, as I have argued, lurks behind each of these unveilings, Jonson's parodic revisitation of these scenes presents a palimpsest showing the ghostly outlines of both Shakespeare's and Euripides' tragic heroines. And as in those precursors, the scene's unveilings of wives lead to revelations, recognitions, and the restoration of losses. Not only do Littlewit and Overdo retrieve their wives, but Cokes is reunited with his purses and possessions. Exposing Edgworth's pickpocketing, Quarlous tells Overdo, "If you have a mind to hang him now, and show him your magistrate's wit, you may—but I should think it were better recovering the goods, and to save your estimation in pardoning him" (5.5.64–7).

Although the play's discoveries bring humiliation—especially for Overdo, Wasp, and Busy, who lose the authority in which they revel—they also bring a new warmth, and an empathetic acceptance (uncharacteristic for Jonson, though characteristically Shakespearean) of shared human weakness. "And remember," Quarlous tells Overdo, "you are but Adam, flesh and blood!—you have your frailty. Forget your other name of Overdo, and invite us all to supper. There you and I will compare our 'discoveries,' and drown the memory of all enormity in your bigg'st bowl at home" (5.5.80–3). Just as Overdo's "bigg'st bowl" becomes part of the enormity of the fair, the vocabulary of "discovery"—versions of which feature eleven times in the play—brings Overdo's skeptical sleuthing into conversation not only with the uncovering of wives and puppets, but also with the title of Jonson's own eventual collection of literary criticism, suggesting an underlying commonality between fair-going and play-combing. In accepting his correction, Overdo seems also to accept this connection, and agrees to extend his hospitality: "I invite you home with me to my house to supper" (5.5.92). In Overdo's genial acceptance of those who have outdone him at the fair, and in Jonson's genial acceptance of the conventional comic ending he typically eschewed, we can see Jonson's own sardonic celebration of the popular theatrical models that he so frequently cites, mocks, and replays. Fittingly, it is Cokes—the eager consumer who shares his name with the fair—who reminds the gathering of the theatrical performance that prompts their happy ending. "Yes," he replies to Overdo, "and bring the actors along: we'll ha' the rest o' the play at home" (5.5.95). Rooted in Greek tragic legend, elegized by Musaeus, translated by Marlowe, repeatedly invoked by Shakespeare, and parodied by Littlewit, the ghosts of Hero and Leander bring their tragical encounter to the fairgoers, and to us, through the ventriloquists of the theater.

Jonson's invocations of Greek tragic women in *Bartholomew Fair* may appear to be merely cartoons, diminished versions of the mythic figures whose suffering authorizes their claims to audiences' sympathies. His Ceres has no daughters beyond the gingerbread wares and prostitutes that she sells; his Mother of the Furies directs her malevolence towards customers and fairgrounds regulations; and his Hero is a whore. Yet just as his plot, with its quasi-pastoral escape, losses, restorations, recognition, and reunions, brings his satiric comedy a new and unfamiliar kinship with the festive spirit of Shakespeare's popular tragicomedies, so too the play's forceful female figures lend a distinctive warmth to its theatrical pleasures. In the light of restored losses, returned wives, and forgiven behaviors, the play's closing invitation to celebrate at a communal meal offers a genuinely festive end: a long way from the comeuppances more typical to Jonson's earlier comic endings. In showcasing notable Euripidean/Shakespearean motifs whose popularity with audiences he recognized, Jonson shows their effectiveness even while lampooning them.

This book has argued that in the wake of emerging access to Greek plays, the female icons associated with tragedy's origins acquired a privileged authority for representing the genre. In particular, they came to embody the power of theatrical performance to transmit emotions sympathetically from speakers to audiences. This power attracted particular interest from Shakespeare, who explores it through versions of Greek tragedy's female figures throughout his plays. When Hamlet reflects on the theater's mysterious consequences, he turns to this tradition's primary prototype: "What's Hecuba to him, or he to Hecuba,/ That he should weep for her?" (2.2.494–5).[50] Yet if Hecuba and her followers highlight the tears that tragic performances can elicit from listeners, versions of the sacrificial daughters Iphigenia and Polyxena suggest the possibility of wresting glory out of defeat, and imitations of Alcestis show alternate approaches to redeeming and restoring apparently irrevocable losses.

Just as the original Greek models for these figures haunted Shakespeare's stages, Shakespeare's new responses to these figures went on to haunt his contemporaries and later imitators. As such, his plays offer an important bridge between the theater's Greek origins and new approaches for engaging audiences' sympathies. Identifying the prominence of iconic Greek tragic women in Shakespeare's plays offers a new understanding of the early modern theater's development, as well as a new model of theatrical influence, at the heart of England's tragic canon. When we weep with Hamlet, I suggest, we are also, always, weeping for Hecuba.

NOTES

1. Francis Meres, *Palladis Tamia* (London: Cuthbert Burbie, 1598), 283r; Samuel Sheppard, *The Times Displayed in Six Sestyads* (London: J. P., 1646); see Suzanne Gossett, "Introduction," *Pericles*, Arden Shakespeare (London: Thomson Learning, 2004), 1–164, 4.

2. Ben Jonson, "To the Memory of My Beloved, the Author, Mr. William Shakespeare,"in *Mr. William Shakespeares Comedies, Histories, & Tragedies* (London: Jaggard and Blount, 1623), A44–A4v.

3. *Discoveries*, ed. Lorna Hutson, in *The Cambridge Edition of the Works of Ben Jonson*, ed. David Bevington, Martin Butler, and Ian Donaldson (2012), vol. 7, pp. 481–596, ll.1827–9.

4. Robert Miola, "Aristophanes in England, 1500-1660," in *Ancient Comedy and Reception: Essays in Honor of Jeffrey Henderson*, ed. S. Douglas Olson (Berlin: De Gruyter, 2014), 479–502, 497.

5. See especially David Bevington, "Jonson and Shakespeare: A Spirited Friendship," *Ben Jonson Journal* 23:1 (2016), 1–23; Warren Chernaik, "The Dyer's Hand: Shakespeare and Jonson," *The Cambridge Companion to Shakespeare and Contemporary Dramatists*, ed. Ton Hoenselaars (Cambridge: Cambridge University Press, 2012), 54–69; Lynn S. Meskill, *Ben Jonson and Envy* (Cambridge: Cambridge University Press, 2009); and Richard Dutton, "Jonson and Shakespeare: Oedipal Revenge," *Ben Jonson Journal* 23:1 (2016), 24–51.

6. Jonson refers to Aristophanes in plays including *Every Man Out of his Humour* (1599) and *Poetaster* (1601), and cites him in Greek in *The Devil is an Ass* (1616). See Matthew Steggle, "Aristophanes in Early Modern England," in *Aristophanes in Performance, 421 BC–AD 2007: Peace, Birds and Frogs,* ed. Edith Hall and Amanda Wrigley (Oxford: Legenda, 2007), 52–65; Steggle, *Wars of the Theatres: The Poetics of Personation in the Age of Jonson* (Victoria: English Literary Studies, 1998); Helen Ostovich, "The Aristophanic Mode," in Ben Jonson, *Every Man Out of His Humour*, ed. Ostovich (Manchester: Manchester University Press, 2001), 18–28; and Miola, "Aristophanes in England." Earlier studies include Coburn Gum, *The Aristophanic Comedies of Ben Jonson* (The Hague: Mouton, 1969), and Aliki Lafkadiou Dick, *Paedeia Through Laughter: Jonson's Aristophanic Appeal to Human Intelligence* (The Hague: Mouton, 1974).

7. The term "paratragedy," fusing parody with tragedy, comes from discussions of Aristophanes' parodies of Euripides, which receive further discussion later in this chapter. See especially Michael Silk, "Aristophanic Paratragedy," in *Tragedy, Comedy, and the Polis*, ed. Alan Sommerstein (Bari: Levante, 1993), 477–504, and Ralph Rosen, "Aristophanes, Old Comedy and Greek Tragedy" in *A Companion to Tragedy*, ed. Rebecca Bushnell (Oxford: Blackwell, 2005), 251–68.

8. On the play's metatheatricality, see especially Melinda Gough, "Jonson's Siren Stage," *Studies in Philology* 96:1 (1999), 68–95; also Jonas Barish, "*Bartholomew Fair* and its Puppets," *MLQ* 20 (1959), 3–17. On its reflections on Shakespeare, see Thomas Cartelli, "*Bartholomew Fair* as Urban Arcadia: Jonson Responds to Shakespeare," *Renaissance Drama* 14 (1983), 151–72; John Scott Colley, "*Bartholomew Fair*: Ben Jonson's *A Midsummer Night's Dream*," *Comparative Drama* 11:1 (1977), 63–72; and Dutton, "Jonson and Shakespeare."

9. See Ben Jonson, *Bartholomew Fair*, ed. John Creaser, in *The Cambridge Edition of the Works of Ben Jonson*, ed. David Bevington, Martin Butler, and Ian Donaldson, vol. 4: *1611–1616* (Cambridge: Cambridge University Press, 2012), 271–428. Subsequent citations refer to this edition unless otherwise noted.

10. Jonson, "Ode to Himself," cited by Gossett in "Introduction," 1–164, 3.

11. As discussed in Chapter 5, Marlowe cited the "tragedy divine Musaeus sung" (*Hero and Leander*, I.52), and Scaliger described the story as "quasi tragoedia"; Julius Caesar Scaliger, *Poetices Libri Septem*, ed. Luc Dietz (Stuttgart: Frommann-Holzboog, 1995), vol. 3; p. 24, III.95.144b.

12. Lori Haslem has suggested that Win is not actually pregnant, but only feigning pregnancy in order to persuade her mother to let them attend the fair; see Lori Schroeder Haslem, "'Troubled with the Mother': Longings, Purgings, and the Maternal Body in *Bartholomew Fair* and *The Duchess of Malfi*," *Modern Philology* 92:4 (1995), 438–59. Most critics have assumed that Win is genuinely pregnant, and feigning only her craving for pork; see Suzanne Gossett, ed. *Bartholomew Fair* (Revels Plays, Manchester: Manchester University Press, 2000). On the "new stature" of women in the play, see Renu Juneja, "Eve's Flesh and Blood in Jonson's *Bartholomew Fair*," *Comparative Drama* 12:4 (1978–79), 340–55.

13. Gough, "Jonson's Siren Stage."

14. On Hecuba's firebrand dream, see Chapter 2, and Pollard, "Hecuba," *A Dictionary of Shakespeare's Classical Mythology* (2009–), ed. Yves Peyré, http://www.shakmyth.org/myth/107/hecuba

15. On the play's interest in the spirit of market capitalism, see Jean Christophe Agnew, *Worlds Apart: The Market and the Theater in Anglo-American Thought, 1550–1750* (Cambridge: Cambridge University Press, 1986), esp. 47, and Douglas Bruster, *Drama and the Market in the Age of Shakespeare* (Cambridge: Cambridge University Press, 1992), esp. 90–1.

16. See Barish, "*Bartholomew Fair* and its Puppets," 5; R. B. Parker, "Themes and Staging of *Bartholomew Fair*," *University of Toronto Quarterly* 39:4 (1970), 293–309, 297.

17. Roy Booth has observed that Jonson's puppet show was the first of many bawdy parodies of the myth; see Booth, "Hero's Afterlife: *Hero and Leander* and 'lewd unmannerly verse' in the late Seventeenth Century," *Early Modern Literary Studies* 12:3 (2007), 4.1–24.

18. See Dutton, "Jonson and Shakespeare."

19. On Maria as a female city comedy wit, see Lucy Munro, "Introduction," *The Tamer Tamed* (London: Bloomsbury, 2010), vii–xxix.

20. This count includes variant forms of the word: i.e., lose, lost, loser, and losing.

21. Tom Harrison has argued that the play dramatizes dismemberment in figurative terms, especially when the puppets dismantle Busy's beliefs; see Harrison, "'Thou art all licence, even licentiousness itself': Jonson, Euripides, and the Epistemological *Sparagmos* of *Bartholomew* Fair," conference paper presented at Renaissance Society of America, March 31, 2016.

22. See Bella Mirabella, "'Embellishing Herself with a Cloth': The Contradictory Life of the Handkerchief" in *Ornamentalism: The Art of Renaissance Accessories*, ed. Bella Mirabella (Ann Arbor: University of Michigan Press, 2011), 59–82.

23. See Rebekah Owens, "Parody and *The Spanish Tragedy*," *Cahiers Élisabéthains* 71 (2007), 27–36. Philip Henslowe's *Diary* records a payment to Jonson on September 25, 1601, for his "writtinge of his adicians in geronymo" and another on June 22, 1602, for "new adicyons for Jeronymo" (R.A. Foakes and R. T. Rickert, eds. *Henslowe's Diary* [Cambridge: Cambridge University Press, 1961], 182, 203). On recent suggestions that Shakespeare might have been the author of these additions, see especially Douglas Bruster, "Shakespearean Spellings and Handwriting in the Additional Passages Printed in the 1602 *Spanish Tragedy*," *Notes and Queries* (2013), 420–4; Brian Vickers, "Identifying Shakespeare's Additions to *The Spanish Tragedy* (1602): A new (er) approach," *Shakespeare* 8:1 (2012), 13–43; and José Manuel Rodríguez Herrera, "Much Ado About Whose Fingerprints? Shakespeare's Hand in the 1602 Additions to *The Spanish Tragedy*," *Neophilologus* 99:3 (2015), 505–20.

24. *Every Man In his Humor*, ed. David Bevington, in *The Cambridge Edition of the Works of Ben Jonson*, ed. David Bevington, Martin Butler, and Ian Donaldson, vol. 1: *1597–1601* (Cambridge: Cambridge University Press, 2012), 111–227, 1.3.101–4.

25. *Poetaster*, ed. Gabriele Bernhard Jackson, in *The Cambridge Edition of the Works of Ben Jonson*, ed. David Bevington, Martin Butler, and Ian Donaldson, vol. 2: *1601–1606* (Cambridge: Cambridge University Press, 2012), 1–181, 3.4.174–5.

26. *The Alchemist*, ed. Peter Holland and William Sherman, in *The Cambridge Edition of the Works of Ben Jonson*, ed. David Bevington, Martin Butler, and Ian Donaldson, vol. 3: *1606–1611* (Cambridge: Cambridge University Press, 2012), 541–710, 4.7.67–71. See Sean McEvoy, "Hieronimo's Old Cloak: Theatricality and Representation in Ben Jonson's Middle Comedies," *Ben Jonson Journal* 11 (2004), 67–87.

27. On Pedringano's black box, see Lynn Meskill, *Ben Jonson and Envy* (Cambridge: Cambridge University Press, 2009), 196.

28. Rosemary Harriott notes "Over a hundred quotations of Euripides in nine plays; nearly thirty references to characters or events; extensive paratragedy in *Acharnians* and *Peace*; two comedies largely concerned with Euripides"; Harriott, "Aristophanes' Audience and the plays of Euripides," *Bulletin of the Institute of Classical Studies* 9:1 (1962), 1–8, 1. See also Silk, "Aristophanic paratragedy," and Rosen, "Aristophanes, Old Comedy and Greek Tragedy."

29. See Cratinus, "Fragment 342 K," in *Fragments of Old Comedy*, vol. 1: *Alcaeus to Diocles*, ed. and trans. Ian C. Storey, Loeb Classical Library (Cambridge, MA: Havard University Press, 2011), 413. Observing that the coinage reflects "the symbiotic relationship of the two playwrights," Erich Segal writes that "This was not merely a joke. It was sound literary

observation"; see Segal, *The Death of Comedy* (Cambridge, MA: Harvard University Press, 2001, 2009), 124.

30. Helene Foley, "Generic Boundaries in Late Fifth-century Athens," in *Performance, Iconography, Reception: Studies in Honour of Oliver Taplin*, ed. Martin Revermann and Peter Wilson (Oxford: Oxford University Press, 2008), 15–36, 17.

31. Emmanuella Bakola, Lucia Prauscello, and Mario Telò, "Introduction: Greek Comedy as a Fabric of Generic Discourse," in *Greek Comedy and the Discourse of Genres*, ed. Bakola, Prauscello, and Telò (Cambridge: Cambridge University Press, 2013), 1–12, 2–3.

32. Dikaeopolis plays the role of Telephus in *Acharnians*, as does Mnesilochus in *Thesmophoriazusae*. On Aristophanes' use of *Telephus*, see Harriott, "Aristophanes' Audience and the plays of Euripides"; Harold W. Miller, "Euripides' *Telephus* and the *Thesmophoriazusae* of Aristophanes," *Classical Philology* 43:3 (1948), 174–83; and Malcolm Heath, "Euripides' *Telephus*," *Classical Quarterly*, n.s. 37:2 (1987), 272–80.

33. Harriott, "Aristophanes' Audience and the plays of Euripides," 4.

34. Harriott, "Aristophanes' Audience and the plays of Euripides," 5.

35. Foley, "Generic Boundaries in Late Fifth-century Athens," 22.

36. The Dutch humanist scholar Daniel Heinsius (1580–1655), whom Jonson cites frequently in *Discoveries*, discussed Aristophanes' responses to Euripides, and Scaliger discusses paratragedy in a chapter on parody. Individual or partial editions of Aristophanes' Euripidean plays before 1600 include *Komoidopoion aristu batrachoi. Inter comicos summi, ranae* (Basel: Froben, 1524); *Thesmophoriazousai: Scholia eis tēn kōmōdia* (Paris: Jean Loys, 1545); *Ranae* (Utrecht: Herman van Borculo, 1561); *Plutus, Knights, Clouds, Frogs, Acharniae* (Frankfurt: Johann Spiess, 1586); and *Comoediae quatuor: Plutus, Nebulae, Ranae, Equites in usum scholarum* (Leiden: Franciscus Raphelengius, 1596); see Appendices.

37. *Discoveries*, ll.473–4, 468–70.

38. *Hero and Leander* was published in 1598, though written before 1593.

39. See Harrison, "'Thou art all licence, even licentiousness itself.'"

40. Shakespeare, *Two Gentlemen of Verona*, ed. William Carroll, Arden Shakespeare (London: Thomson Learning, 2004), 1.1.21–2, and 3.1.119–20; see Pollard, "Verona's Tragic Women," in *Theatre for a New Audience 360 Series* (April 2015), 10–12.

41. Shakespeare, *Romeo and Juliet*, ed. René Weis, Arden Shakespeare (London: Bloomsbury, 2012), 2.4.42.

42. Shakespeare, *Much Ado about Nothing*, ed. Claire McEachern, Arden Shakespeare (London: Bloomsbury, 2006), 5.2.30–1.

43. Shakespeare, *As You Like It*, ed. Juliet Dusinberre, Arden Shakespeare (London: Thomson Learning, 2006), 4.1.91–7.

44. See Russ McDonald, "Jonsonian Comedy and the Value of *Sejanus*," *Studies in English Literature, 1500–1900* 21:2 (1981), 287–305; John G. Sweeney,

"*Sejanus* and the People's Beastly Rage," *ELH* 48:1 (1981), 61–82; and Blair Worden, "Ben Jonson among the Historians," in *Culture and Politics in Early Stuart England* (London: Macmillan, 1994), 67–89.

45. Booth, "Hero's Afterlife," 7.

46. See Gough, "Jonson's Siren Stage"; Barish, *The Antitheatrical Prejudice* (Berkeley: University of California Press, 1981); and Laura Levine, *Men in Women's Clothing: Anti-theatricality and Effeminization, 1579–1642* (Cambridge: Cambridge University Press, 1994).

47. See Gough, "Jonson's Siren Stage."

48. See Gough, "Jonson's Siren Stage." As Gough observes, the figure of the romance enchantress originates in Homer's Circe. Euripides' debts to Homer, and early modern conceptions of *The Odyssey* as the prototype for tragicomedy, suggest overlap between these traditions and prototypes. See Sarah Dewar-Watson, "Shakespeare's Dramatic Odysseys: Homer as a Tragicomic Model in *Pericles* and *The Tempest*," *Classical and Modern Literature* 25:1 (2005), 23–40, and Pollard, "Tragicomedy," in *The Oxford History of Classical Reception in English Literature*, vol. 2: *The Renaissance*, eds. Patrick Cheney and Philip Hardie (Oxford: Oxford University Press, 2015), 419–32.

49. Shakespeare, *The Winter's Tale*, ed. John Pitcher, Arden Shakespeare (London: Methuen, 2010), 5.3.s.d.20.

50. Citations are to William Shakespeare, *Hamlet*, ed. Ann Thompson and Neil Taylor, Arden Shakespeare (London: Thompson Learning, 2006). See Pollard, "What's Hecuba to Shakespeare?," *Renaissance Quarterly* 65:3 (2012), 1060–93.

APPENDICES

PREFATORY NOTE ON APPENDICES

In the course of exploring sixteenth-century responses to Greek plays, I set out to learn how accessible the plays were in the period, and which ones attracted attention. I soon realized that the answers to these questions were neither clear nor readily available. Accordingly, I set out to gather information on editions, translations, and performances of these plays, little knowing what a substantial project this would become in and of itself.

As I have come to learn, there are many challenges to establishing an accurate account of early modern editions of Greek plays. Some editions lack dates, cities, and/or printers on their title pages, leading to different labeling in different library catalogues, and ambiguities about which books constitute separate editions. Popular editions, such as those of Erasmus's Latin translations of *Hecuba* and *Iphigenia in Aulis*, were frequently reprinted—sometimes by the original press but often by others, both officially and unofficially, in editions that can be difficult to identify and differentiate. Because these books frequently involve more than one language, moreover, catalogue listings do not always reliably reflect the language(s) in which they are printed.

In order to arrive at as complete and accurate an accounting as possible, I have pored over copies of many of these books, primarily at the Bodleian Library of Oxford University, and have benefitted enormously from recently increasing access to digitized rare books, especially from the Münchener Digitalisierungszentrum/Digitale Bibliothek, of the Bayerische Staatsbibliothek in Munich; Bibliotheksverbund Bayern, the Bavarian Library Network; Gallica, of the Bibliothèque Nationale de France; and e-rara.ch, the platform for digitized rare books from Swiss libraries. During the final stage of this project, the Universal Short Title Catalogue established an online presence, which created a useful clearinghouse for comparing information on editions. For books that I have not been able to view either directly or digitally, I have compared multiple catalogue listings in order to verify details as reliably as possible, and in some cases contacted librarians with queries, though I may still be perpetuating errors. I have excluded references to editions for which I have not found enough evidence, and have noted questions about others.

For Appendices 1 and 2, on Greek and Latin editions of Greek plays, I have restricted my listings to extant printed editions. For Appendix 3, on vernacular translations, I have expanded my focus to include translations in manuscript— some of which are no longer extant, but are attested by earlier sources—in order to represent the fullest range of vernacular versions. Appendix 4, on performances of the plays, is necessarily the most speculative. Circulation in performance constitutes an important aspect of the plays' early modern reception, but productions are considerably more challenging to trace than the textual record, because of both the scarcity of references and their minimal details. Determining closeness to original texts is especially difficult, and so I have included records of performances of translations, imitations, and/or adaptations. This appendix draws especially heavily on the Productions Database of Oxford University's Archive of Performance of Greek and Roman Drama (APGRD), for which I am extremely grateful, but I have revised, excluded, and expanded upon some APGRD citations based on my assessment of the available evidence. There is considerable uncertainty around many of these records, and I look forward to seeing this information supplemented and revised in the light of future discoveries.

In keeping with this book's focus on early modern responses to the Greek dramatic tradition, these appendices primarily document the textual and theatrical afterlives of Greek plays. Because my claims about the associations of Greek tragedy in this period hinge in part on distinctions between these plays and those of Seneca, however, I have also included appendices on vernacular translations and performances of Seneca's tragedies. One of the most surprising findings of this project has been that Greek tragedies have turned up in higher numbers than Seneca's in both of these categories, contrary to typical claims about their relative standing in this period. To contextualize these numbers, I note that Seneca's tragedies were more typically read in their native Latin versions, so translating them into vernacular languages may not have seemed necessary, whereas the relative inaccessibility of Greek seems to have inspired more interest in translation. It is also the case that the thirty-three tragedies attributed to Greek playwrights in this period outweigh the ten attributed to Seneca. (For purposes of this study, I include *Octavia* as one of Seneca's tragedies, and *Rhesus* as one of Euripides', in keeping with early modern attribution.)

Even with this caveat, the apparent disparity in recorded performances may seem more surprising. As I have noted in this book's Introduction, in many cases we do not know whether a given performance was of a Greek or Senecan version; the titles *Medea*, *Hippolytus*, *Oedipus*, *Agamemnon*, and *Trojan Women* could refer to either Greek or Roman tragedies. Scholars have typically assumed that performances with these titles were by Seneca, despite occasional acknowledgments that we frequently lack evidence to draw this conclusion. In cases of uncertain attribution, including indirect adaptations, I have listed the performances in both the Greek and Roman appendices, and cited them as Euripides/Seneca, Sophocles/Seneca, or Aeschylus/Seneca, noting uncertainty of authorship. The decision to share attribution in cases that lack clear evidence one way or another has raised the number of Greek performances beyond those listed in the APGRD; I have also lowered the number of Seneca performances from those listed in the APGRD by excluding plays that can be described as Senecan only in style rather than in content, such as the neoclassical *Ricardus Tertius* or the Ovid-inspired *Progne*. Beyond these decisions, however, it is notable that many more performances could only be Greek (*Philoctetes*, *Antigone*, *Electra*, *Ajax*, *Iphigenia*, *Alcestis*, *Jocasta*, *Persians*) than could only be Senecan (*Thyestes*, *Octavia*). Even allowing for ambiguous cases, the information gathered in these appendices suggests that we have underestimated the performance traditions of Greek plays in this period.

Although I hope that these appendices are more complete and accurate than previously available information on Greek plays' early modern afterlives, I do not claim that they are fully complete or fully accurate. New information is continuing to emerge, especially as more books and catalogues become digitally available, and I look forward to learning about the additional materials and corrections that I am certain will emerge. Researching and compiling this material, however, has illuminated important patterns: that Euripides was disproportionately popular among the tragedians, that his female protagonists attracted strikingly more attention than males (in contrast to Seneca, who shows precisely the opposite pattern), and that *Hecuba* and *Iphigenia in Aulis* acquired a particular preeminence, especially (though not exclusively) in Erasmus's early and influential translations. These patterns form the underpinnings of the book's arguments.

These appendices represent extensive labor, from many people. For invaluable help with gathering and organizing information, I am grateful to Jennifer Alberghini, Alex Hajjar, Dan Jacobson, Patrick James, Ja Young Jeon, Melina Moore, and Rose Tomassi. For help with queries about editions, I am grateful to Lucy Evans at the Bodleian's Rare Books and Manuscripts Room; Jennifer Lee at Columbia's Rare Books and Manuscripts Library; and Anders Toftgaard at Københavns Universitetsbibliotek. The records of performances would not exist without the APGRD's Performance Database. For ongoing consultation on early modern publishers, editors, translators, title pages, colophons, and much more, I am especially grateful to my husband, Will Stenhouse.

Bibliographic Resources Consulted

INTERNET

The Universal Short Title Catalogue, http://ustc.ac.uk/
Worldcat, https://www.worldcat.org/
Bodleian Library Catalogue, http://www.bodleian.ox.ac.uk/
The British Library Catalogue, http://www.bl.uk/
Bayerischen Staatsbibliothek, https://www.bsb-muenchen.de/
Universitatsbibliothek Basel, http://www.ub.unibas.ch/ub-hauptbibliothek/
Bibliotheks Verbund Bayern, https://www.bib-bvb.de/
Martin-Luther-Universität Halle-Wittenberg, Universitäts-und Landesbibliothek
  Sachsen-Anhalt, http://bibliothek.uni-halle.de/
Bibliothèque Nationale de France, http://www.bnf.fr/fr/acc/x.accueil.html
Productions Database of Oxford University's Archive of Performance of Greek
  and Roman Drama (APGRD), http://www.apgrd.ox.ac.uk/research-collections/
  performance-database/productions

PRINT

Argelati, Filippo, ed. *Biblioteca degli volgarizzatori*. With additions and corrections
  by Angelo Teodoro. Milan: Federico Agnelli, 1767.
Boas, F. S. *University Drama in the Tudor Age*. Oxford: Clarendon Press, 1914.
Bolgar, R. R. *The Classical Heritage and its Beneficiaries*. Cambridge: Cambridge
  University Press, 1954.
Braticević, Irena, and Ivan Lupić. "Držićeva *Hekuba* Između Izvedbe I Knjige."
  Colloquia Maruliana XXII (2013), 77–116.
Delcourt, Marie. *Étude sur les traductions des tragiques grecs et latins en France
  depuis la Renaissance*. Bruxelles: Hayez, 1925.
Dudouyt, Cécile. "Aristophanes in Early-Modern Fragments: Le Loyer's *La
  Néphélococugie* (1579) and Racine's *Les Plaideurs* (1668)." In *Brill's Companion
  to the Reception of Aristophanes*, 175–94. Edited by Philip Walsh. Leiden: Brill,
  2016.
Erasmus, Desiderius. *The Poems of Desiderius Erasmus*. Edited by C. Reddijk.
  Leiden: Brill, 1956.
Highet, Gilbert. *The Classical Tradition: Greek and Roman Influences on Western
  Literature*. Oxford: Oxford University Press, 1949.
Hirsch, Rudolf. "The Printing Tradition of Aeschylus, Euripides, Sophocles and
  Aristophanes." *Gutenberg Jahrbuch* 39 (1964), 138–46.
Hoffman, S. F. G., ed. *Lexicon Bibliographicum sive Index Editionum et Inter-
  pretationum Scriptorum Graecorum*. Leipzig: J. A. G. Weigel, 1832.

Jacquot, Jean, ed. *Les Tragédies de Sénèque et le Théâtre de la Renaissance*. Paris: Editions du Centre National de la Recherche Scientifique, 1973.

Le Loyer, Pierre. *La Néphélococugie; ou, La Nuée des cocus*. Edited by Miriam Doe and Keith Cameron. Geneva: Droz, 2004.

Pettegree, Andrew, and Malcolm Walsby, eds. *French Books III & IV*. Leiden: Brill, 2011.

Pettegree, Andrew, and Malcolm Walsby, eds. *Netherlandish Books: Books Published in the Low Countries and Dutch Books Printed Abroad Before 1601*. Leiden: Brill, 2010.

Smith, Bruce. *Ancient Scripts and Modern Experience on the English Stage, 1500–1700*. Princeton: Princeton University Press, 1988.

Sturel, René. "Essai sur les traductions du théâtre grec en français avant 1550." *Revue d'Histoire littéraire de la France*. 20:2 (1913), 269–96.

Ticknor, George. *History of Spanish Literature, Vol 2*. Houghton Mifflin, 1891.

Wilkinson, Alexander S., ed. *Iberian Books: Books Published in Spanish or Portuguese or on the Iberian Peninsula Before 1601*. Leiden: Brill, 2010.

Wilson, F. P., and G. K. Hunter. *The English Drama, 1485–1585*. Oxford: Oxford University Press, 1969.

DIGITAL LIBRARY SITES FOR APPENDICES: NAMES, ABBREVIATIONS, AND BASIC URLS

Babel	Babel Hathi Trust Digital Library, http://babel.hathitrust.org
Berlin	Staatsbibliothek Berlin, http://digital.staatsbibliothek-berlin.de/
DFG	Deutsche Forschungsgemeinschaft, http://dfg-viewer.de/ueber-das-projekt/
EEBO	Early English Books Online, https://eebo.chadwyck.com/
E-rara	Digitized rare books from Swiss libraries, http://www.e-rara.ch/
Gallica	Gallica, gallica.bnf.fr/
Google Books	Google Books, books.google.com
MDZ	Münchener DigitalisierungsZentrum Digitale Bibliothek, https://www.digitale-sammlungen.de/
ONB	Österreichischen Nationalbibliothek, https://www.onb.ac.at/
OPAL	OPAL Libri antichi, http://www.opal.unito.it/psixsite/default.aspx
Raccolta	Raccolta Drammatica, http://www.braidense.it/risorse/raccoltadrammatica.php

APPENDIX 1

Editions of Greek Plays in Greek

Year	Playwright	Play(s)	Book Title
1495	Euripides	Medea, Hippolytus, Alcestis, Andromache	Tragoediae quattuor
1498	Aristophanes	Complete (9 plays)	Comoediae novem
1502	Sophocles	Complete	Tragodiai epta metexegeseon
1503	Euripides	Complete (17 plays)	Tragodiai eptaideka
1515	Aristophanes	Complete (9 plays)	Aristophanes Comoediae novem
1515	Aristophanes	Thesmophoriazusae and Lysistrata	Aristophanis Cereris sacra celebrantes. Eiusdem Lysistrate.
1517	Aristophanes	Plutus	Plutos. Plutus, Graeci sermonis.
1518	Aristophanes	Plutus	Ploutos
1518	Aeschylus	Complete (6 plays)	Tragoediae sex
1520	Euripides	Hecuba and Iphigenia in Aulis	Hecuba et Iphigenia in Aulide
1521	Aristophanes	Clouds	Nubes
1522	Sophocles	Complete	Tragodia epta
1524	Aristophanes	Frogs	Komoidopoion aristu batrachoi
1525	Aristophanes	Complete (9 plays)	Comoediae novem
1528	Aristophanes	Clouds and Plutus	Nephelai kai plutos
1528	Aristophanes	Complete (9 plays)	Komoidiae ennea
1528	Sophocles	Complete	Tragoediae septem
1528	Sophocles	Complete	Tragoediae septem
1528	Sophocles	Complete	Tragoediae septem
1530	Sophocles	Ajax	Aiax mastigophoros. Ajax flagellifer
1532	Aristophanes	Complete (11 plays)	Eutrapelotatu komodiai hendeka

City	Press	Editor	USTC	Verification
Florence	Laurentius de Alopa	Ioannis Lascaris	760837	Viewed at Bodleian
Venice	Aldus Manutius	Marcus Musurus	760249	Viewed at Bodleian
Venice	Aldus Manutius	Aldus Manutius	857020	Viewed at Bodleian; MDZ
Venice	Aldus Manutius	Aldus Manutius	828498	Viewed at Bodleian; Babel
Florence	Filippo Giunta	Filippo Giunta	810843	Viewed at Bodleian
Florence	Filippo Giunta	Filippo Giunta	810844	Viewed at Bodleian
Hagenau	Thomas Anshelm	Petrus Mosellanus	612855	Viewed at Bodleian; MDZ
Louvain	Thierry Martens	Thierry Martens	410123	Viewed at Bodleian
Venice	Aldus Manutius	Aldus Manutius and Andrea Torresano	807822	Viewed at Bodleian; MDZ
Louvain	Thierry Martens	Thierry Martens	437117	Viewed at Bodleian
Wittenberg	Melchior Lotter	Philip Melanchthon	612854	See Worldcat for details and libraries
Florence	Filippo Giunta	Filippo Giunta	857021	Viewed at Bodleian; Babel
Basel	Johann Froben	Johann Froben	612853	Viewed at Bodleian; MDZ
Florence	Filippo Giunta	Filippo Giunta	810845	Viewed at Bodleian
Hagenau	Johann Setzer	Philip Melanchthon	612849	MDZ
Paris	Pierre Vidoue Gilles de Gourmant	Jean Chéradame	145892	Viewed at Bodleian
Paris	Simon de Colines		146004	Viewed at Bodleian
Paris	Simon de Colines		186983	USTC lists as separate edition, but may be same as above
Paris	Simon de Colines		145998	USTC lists as separate edition, but may be same as above
Paris	Gerard Morrhy		185073	Google Books
Basel	Andreas Cratander & Johann Bebel		612851	MDZ

(*continued*)

Year	Playwright	Play(s)	Book Title
1534	Sophocles	Complete	Sophokleus tragodiai hepta
1534	Aristophanes	Frogs	Batrachoi
1535	Aristophanes	Complete (9 plays)	Comoediae novem
1536	Euripides	Orestes	Orestēs
1537	Euripides	Andromache	Andromachē
1537	Euripides	Complete (18 plays)	Euripidu tragodiai oktokaideka
1537	Aristophanes	Birds	Aves
1539	Euripides	Medea	Euripidis Medea
1540	Aristophanes	Complete (9 plays)	Comoedieae novem
1540	Aristophanes	Complete (11 plays)	Kōmōdiai endeka
1540	Aristophanes	Complete (11 plays)	Kōmōdiai endeka
1540	Aristophanes	Plutus, Clouds, Frogs	Plutus, Nebulae, Ranae
1540	Sophocles	Antigone	Antigone
1540	Sophocles	Ajax and Electra	Primae Sophoclis Tragoediae Duae Aiax et Electra
1542	Aristophanes	Complete (11 plays)	Comoediae undecim
1544	Aristophanes	Complete (11 plays)	Eutrapelotatu komodiai hendeka
1544	Euripides	Complete (18 plays)	Euripidu tragodiai oktokaideka
1544	Sophocles	Complete	Sophokleus tragodiai hepta
1545	Aristophanes	Thesmophoriazusae	Thesmophoriazousai
1545	Euripides	Medea	Mēdeia
1545	Euripides	Hecuba	Euripidou Hekabē
1545	Euripides	Electra	Elektra

City	Press	Editor	USTC	Verification
Hagenau	Johann Setzer	Joachim Camerarius	694171	Viewed at Bodleian; Babel, MDZ
Louvain	Rutgerus Rescius for Bartholomaeus Gravius		437720	See Worldcat for details and libraries
Paris	Pierre Vidoué; Jérome de Gourmont	Jean Chéradame	185511	See Worldcat for details and libraries
Paris	Jean Loys	Jean Loys	185701	See Worldcat for details and libraries
Louvain	Rutgerus Rescius		437877	See Worldcat for details and libraries
Basel	Johannes Herwagen	Johannes Oporinus	654573	Viewed at Bodleian; MDZ
Louvain	Rutgerus Rescius		437879	Also cited in Netherlandish Books
Paris	Jean Loys	Johannes Stracelius	186204	See Worldcat for details and libraries
Florence	Bernardo Giunta	Bernardo Giunta	810847	See Worldcat on details and libraries
Paris	Chrestien Wechel	Chrestien Wechel	160570	Viewed at Bodleian
Florence	Bernardo Giunta	Bernardo Giunta	810848	See Worldcat on details and libraries
Paris	Conrad Néobar	Jacques Toussain	182419	See Worldcat on details and libraries
Paris	Jean Loys	Jean Loys	186442	See Worldcat on details and libraries
Strasbourg	Wendelin Rihel	Claudius Theraeus	686553	Viewed at Bodleian; MDZ
Venice	Giovanni Farri	Giovanni Farri	810851	Viewed at Bodleian; Babel
Frankfurt	Peter Braubach	Simon Grynaeus	612850	Viewed at Bodleian; MDZ
Basel	Johannes Herwagen	Johannes Oporinus	654574	Viewed at Bodleian
Frankfurt	Peter Braubach	Peter Braubach	694180	MDZ, E-rara
Paris	Jean Loys	Gilles Bourdin	206705	Viewed at Bodleian
Paris	Jean Loys	Arsenios Apostolis	160187	See Worldcat on details and libraries
Paris	Jean Loys	Arsenios Apostolis	206707	Viewed at Bodleian
Rome	Antonio Blado	Pietro Vettori	828501	Viewed at Bodleian

(*continued*)

Year	Playwright	Play(s)	Book Title
1545	Sophocles	Ajax	Tragoediae Aias
1545	Sophocles	Complete	Tragōdiai epta
1546	Aristophanes	Complete (11 plays)	Kōmōdiai endeka
1547	Aristophanes	Complete (9 plays)	Komodiai ennea meta scholion
1547	Sophocles	Complete	Tragodiai hepta
1547	Aristophanes	Peace	Eirēnē
1548	Aeschylus	Prometheus	Promētheus desmōtēs
1548	Euripides	Orestes	Orestēs
1548	Aristophanes	Complete (11 plays)	Komodiai endeka
1549	Sophocles	Oedipus Coloneus	Sophoclis Oedipus Coloneus
1549	Sophocles	Complete	Sophokleus tragodiai hepta
1550	Aristophanes	Complete (11 plays)	Comoediae XI
1550	Aristophanes	Plutus	Ploutos
1550	Sophocles	Oedipus	Sophoclis Oedipus Tyrannus
1551	Euripides	Complete (18)	Euripidu tragodiai oktokaideka
1552	Aeschylus	Complete	Tragoediae septem
1552	Aeschylus	Complete	Promētheus desmōtēs, Epta epi Thēbais, Persai, Agamemnōn, Eumenides, Iketides
1552	Sophocles	Complete	Sophocles Hapanta
1552	Euripides	Hecuba	Hecuba
1553	Sophocles	Complete	Tragōdiai
1555	Euripides	Cyclops	Euripidou Kyklops
1555	Sophocles	Complete	Sophokleus tragodiai hepta

City	Press	Editor	USTC	Verification
Paris				See Worldcat for details and libraries
Paris	Jacques Bogard		116900	Viewed at Bodleian
Paris	Chrestien Wechel	Chrestien Wechel	160025	Viewed at Bodleian; Google Books
Basel	Johann Froben	Sigmund Gelen	612856	Viewed at Bodleian; MDZ
Florence	Bernardo Giunta	Bernardo Giunta	857025	Viewed at Bodleian; Google Books
Louvain	Servaes Sassenus		410486	See Worldcat for details and libraries
Paris	Christian Wechel	Jean Dorat	196107	See Worldcat for details
Paris	Jacques Bogard	Guillaume Morel	116975	Viewed at Bodleian
Venice	Johannes Gryphius	Angelus Caninius	810854	Viewed at Bodleian
Louvain	Servatius Sassenus			Viewed at Bodleian
Frankfurt	Peter Braubach	Peter Braubach	694175	Viewed at Bodleian
Paris	Chrestien Wechel	Chrestien Wechel	160026	Viewed images from Københavns Universitetsbibliotek
Paris	Guillaume Morel	Guillaume Morel	206860	See Worldcat on details and libraries
Louvain	Servaes Sassenus		410504	Viewed at Bodleian
Basel	Johannes Herwagen	Johannes Oporinus	654575	Viewed at Bodleian; MDZ
Venice	Gualtiero Scoto	Francesco Robortello	807823	Viewed at Bodleian
Paris	Adrianus Turnebus	Francesco Robortello	154188	Viewed at Bodleian; MDZ
Paris				Viewed at Bodleian; Google Books; title page does not specify publisher
Paris	Michel de Vascosan		196530	See Worldcat for details and libraries
Paris	Adrianus Turnebus	Demetrius Triklinius	154217	See Worldcat for details and libraries
Paris	Andreas Wechel			Worldcat. See also British Library Catalogue
Frankfurt	Peter Braubach		694181	Quarto edition; MDZ

(*continued*)

Year	Playwright	Play(s)	Book Title
1555	Sophocles	Complete	Sophokleus tragodiai hepta
1557	Aristophanes	Complete (11 plays)	Eutrapelotatou Komōdiai hendeka
1557	Aeschylus	Complete	Aeschyli Tragoediae VII
1558	Euripides	Complete (18 plays)	Euripidu tragodiai oktokaideka
1558	Aristophanes	Complete (11 plays)	Comoediae undecim
1560	Aristophanes	Complete (11 plays)	Comoediae undecim
1560	Euripides	Complete (18 plays)	Euripidu tragodiai oktokaideka
1562	Sophocles	Ajax and Electra	Primae Sophoclis Tragoediae Duae Aiax et Electra
1567	Aristophanes	Plutus	Ploutos
1567	Aristophanes	Plutus	Aristophanous Eutrapelotatou Ploutos
1567	Sophocles	Complete	Sophokleus tragodiai hepta
1567	Sophocles	Oedipus	Oedipus Tyrannus
1567	Sophocles	Oedipus	Oedipus Tyrannus
1568	Euripides	Phoenissae	Euripidis Phoenissae
1568	Sophocles	Complete	Sophokleous ai hepta tragoidiai
1570	Euripides	Alcestis	Poetae tragici alcestis
1571	Euripides	Complete (19 plays)	Tragodiai XIX
1575	Aeschylus	Prometheus	Promētheus desmōtēs
1575	Euripides	Trojan Women	Euripidou Troades
1577	Euripides	Orestes	Euripidu Orestes
1579	Sophocles	Complete	Tragōdiai Z

City	Press	Editor	USTC	Verification
Frankfurt	Peter Braubach		694178	Octavo edition; viewed at Bodleian; MDZ
Paris	Andreas Wechel		152208	See Worldcat for details and libraries
Geneva	Henri Estienne	Pietro Vettori	450455	Viewed at Bodleian
Frankfurt	Peter Braubach	Peter Braubach	654563	MDZ
Paris	Charles Périer		206046	See Worldcat for details and libraries
Paris	Andreas Wechel		198353	MDZ
Frankfurt	Peter Braubach		654562	See Worldcat for details and libraries
Strasbourg	Josias Rihelius	Claudius Theraeus	686554	Berlin
Paris	Jean Benenat		116587	See Lyon Bibliothèque municipale
Strasbourg	Christianus Mylius			Viewed at Bodleian
Frankfurt	Peter Braubach	Peter Braubach	694176	Viewed at Bodleian; MDZ
Strasbourg	Christianus Mylius	Ernestus Regius	708752	See Worldcat for details and libraries
Strasbourg	Christianus Mylius	Ernestus Regius	694192	USTC lists as separate edition, but may be same as above
Rostock	Stephan Möllemann	David Chytraus	654883	See Herzog August Bibliothek, Wolfenbüttel
Geneva	Henri Estienne	Joachim Camerarius	450242	Viewed at Bodleian; MDZ, E-rara
Strasbourg	Theodosius Rihel		654568	See Worldcat for details and libraries
Antwerp	Christopher Plantin	Giulielmus Canterus	411593	Viewed at Bodleian; MDZ
Paris	Jean Benenat		116666	See Worldcat for details and libraries
London	John Day		508002	EEBO
Wittenberg	Johann Kraft		654578	Viewed at Bodleian; MDZ
Antwerp	Christopher Plantin	Giulielmus Canterus	401806	Viewed at Bodleian; MDZ

(*continued*)

Year	Playwright	Play(s)	Book Title
1579	Sophocles	Complete	Tragōdiai Z
1580	Aeschylus	Complete	Tragōdiai
1584	Euripides	Orestes	Orestes
1585	Sophocles	Complete	Sophokleus tragodiai hepta
1585	Aeschylus	Seven at Thebes	Tragodia epta epi Thēbais
1585	Aristophanes	Plutus	Aristophanis Plutus
1586	Sophocles	Philoctetes	Philoktētēs
1586	Aristophanes	Peace	Eirēnē
1593	Aristophanes	Knights	Aristophanous Ippeis
1593	Sophocles	Complete	Tragoediae VII
1595	Euripides	Hecuba	Euripidis… Tragœdia Hecaba
1596	Aristophanes	Plutus, Knights, Clouds, Frogs	Comoediae quatuor: Plutus, Nebulae, Ranae, Equites

City	Press	Editor	USTC	Verification
Antwerp	Christopher Plantin	Giulielmus Canterus	415031	USTC lists as separate edition, but may be same as above
Antwerp	Christopher Plantin	Giulielmus Canterus	407834	MDZ
Paris	Fédéric Morel	Fédéric Morel		See Worldcat for details and libraries
Wittenberg	Matthaeus Welack		694177	See Worldcat for details and libraries
Paris	Fédéric Morel	Florent Chrestien	171844	Viewed at Bodleian
Wittenberg	Zacharias Lehmann		612832	See Gotha Forschungsbibliothek
Paris	Fédéric Morel	Florent Chrestien	170846	See Worldcat for details and libraries
Paris	Fédéric Morel		171949	See Worldcat for details and libraries
Oxford	Joseph Barnes		512311	Viewed at Bodleian; EEBO
Leiden	Christopher Plantin, Franciscus Raphelengius	Giulielmus Canterus	423131	Viewed at Bodleian; MDZ
Rostock	Stephan Möllemann	Johannes Possel	654880	See Worldcat for details and libraries
Leiden	Franciscus Raphelengius	Florent Chrestien	423544	See Worldcat for details and libraries

Editions of Greek Plays in Latin
(or Bilingual Greek–Latin)

Year	Playwright	Play	Book Title
1501	Aristophanes	Plutus	Plutus, antiqua comoedia
1505	Euripides	Hecuba	Euripidis tragici poete nobilissimi hecuba
1506	Euripides	Hecuba and Iphigenia in Aulis	Hecuba et Iphigenia
1506	Euripides	Hecuba and Iphigenia in Aulis	Hecuba et Iphigenia
1507	Euripides	Hecuba and Iphigenia in Aulis	Hecuba et Iphigenia
1508	Euripides	Hecuba and Iphigenia in Aulis	Hecuba et Iphigenia
1511	Euripides	Hecuba and Iphigenia in Aulis	Hecuba et Iphigenia
1512	Euripides	Hecuba and Iphigenia in Aulis	Hecuba et Iphigenia
1515	Euripides	Hecuba and Iphigenia in Aulis	Hecuba et Iphigenia
1515	Euripides	Hecuba	Hecuba tragedia
1518	Euripides	Hecuba and Iphigenia in Aulis	Hecuba et Iphigenia
1518	Euripides	Hecuba and Iphigenia in Aulis	Euripidis tragoediae duae
1519	Euripides	Hecuba and Iphigenia in Aulis	Euripidis tragoediae duae

City	Press	Translation	USTC	Other verification
Parma	Angelus Ugoleto	Fransciscus Passius	810842	Viewed at Bodleian
Leipzig	Jakob Thanner	Erasmus	654571	See Würzburg Universitätsbibliothek
Paris	Josse Bade	Erasmus	143156	Viewed at Bodleian; MDZ
Parma	Francisco Ugeleto	George Anselmus		See Worldcat for details and libraries
Venice	Aldus Manutius	Erasmus	828497	Viewed at Bodleian; MDZ
Lyons	Balthazar de Gabiano	Erasmus	143380	Viewed at Bodleian; Title page doesn't show date; Bodleian lists as 1507, USTC as 1508
Vienna	Hieronymi Vietoris & Ioannis Singrenii.	Erasmus	661856	Viewed at Bodleian; MDZ, Gallica
Paris	Josse Bade	Erasmus	183209	Google Books
Erfurt		Erasmus	654565	Worldcat lists a 1515 edition with same title but suggests it may have been published in Lyons
Erfurt	Hans Knappe	Erasmus	654569	See Bibliotheks Verbund Bayern
Florence	Filippo Giunta	Erasmus	828499	Viewed at Bodleian
Basel	Johannes Froben	Erasmus	654875	Viewed at Bodleian; MDZ
Cologne	Konrad Caesar	Erasmus	654873	See Worldcat; copy in British Library

(*continued*)

Year	Playwright	Play	Book Title
1520	Euripides	Hecuba and Iphigenia in Aulis	Euripidis tragoediae duae
1521	Aristophanes	Clouds	Nubes
1522	Euripides	Hecuba and Iphigenia in Aulis	Hecuba et Iphigenia
1524	Euripides	Hecuba and Iphigenia in Aulis	Euripidis tragoediae duae
1530	Euripides	Hecuba and Iphigenia in Aulis	Euripidis tragoediae duae
1531	Aristophanes	Plutus	Ploutos
1533	Aristophanes	Plutus	Plutus
1533	Aristophanes	Plutus	Plutus
1533	Sophocles	Ajax	Tragici aiax flagellifer
1534	Euripides	Hecuba and Iphigenia in Aulis	Hecuba et Iphigenia
1536	Euripides	Hecuba	Euripidis tragoedia Hecuba
1537	Euripides	Hecuba and Iphigenia in Aulis	Hecuba et Iphigenia in Aulide
1538	Aristophanes	Complete (11 plays)	Aristophanis comicorum principis
1538	Aristophanes	Complete (11 plays)	Aristophanis comicorum principis

City	Press	Translation	USTC	Other verification
Cologne	Konrad Caesar	Erasmus	654874	See Worldcat for details and libraries
Wittenberg	Melchior Lotter	Philip Melanchthon	612854	MDZ
Basel	Thomas Wolff	Erasmus	654876	USTC lists as only Iphigenia, but Worldcat lists as Hecuba and Iphigenia, and numerous library catalogues concur
Basel	Johannes Froben	Erasmus	654577	MDZ
Basel	Johannes Froben	Erasmus	654881	Viewed at Bodleian; MDZ
Nuremburg	Johann Petreius	Thomas Venatorious	612852	Viewed at Bodleian; MDZ
Antwerp	Michael Hillenius Hoochstratanus	Adrian Chilius	403870	Viewed at Bodleian
Antwerp	Michael Hillenius Hoochstratanus	Adrian Chilius	437670	USTC lists this and above as two separate imprints, but they may be the same
Basel	Johannes Herwagen	Ioannus Lonicerus	694174	E-rara
Hertogenbosch	Gerardus Hatardus	Erasmus	410773	Google Books; Both USTC and Netherlandish Books list the edition as including both Hecuba and Iphigenia; the digitized version on Google Books only includes Iphigenia.
Cracow	Mathias Scharffenberg	Erasmus		See Worldcat for details and libraries
Paris	Francois Gryphe	Erasmus	182202	See Worldcat for details and libraries
Venice	Giacomo Pocatela	Andrea Divo	810850	Babel
Venice	Bartolomeo Zenetti	Andrea Divo	810846	USTC lists this and above as two separate imprints, but they may be the same

(continued)

Year	Playwright	Play	Book Title
1539	Aristophanes	Complete (11 plays)	Aristophanis comicorum principis
1540	Euripides	Hecuba and Iphigenia in Aulis	Hecuba et Iphigenia
1540	Euripides	Hecuba and Iphigenia in Aulis	Omnia opera des. Erasmi roterodami
1540	Euripides	Hecuba and Iphigenia in Aulis	Hecuba et Iphigenia in Aulide
1541	Sophocles	Antigone	Sophoclis Antigone Tragoedia
1541	Euripides	Hecuba and Iphigenia in Aulis	Hecuba et Iphigenia in Aulide
1541	Euripides	Complete	Evripidis poetae antiquissimi
1542	Euripides	Medea	Medea fabula
1542	Aristophanes	Complete (11 plays)	Comoediae undecim
1542	Aristophanes	Complete (11 plays)	Comoediae undecim
1543	Euripides	Hecuba	Hecuba Euripidis latina
1543	Euripides	Medea	Medea
1543	Sophocles	Complete	Tragoediae omnes
1544	Euripides	Hecuba, Iphigenia in Aulis, and Medea	Hecuba et Iphigenia in Aulide, Medea
1545	Euripides	Hecuba and Iphigenia in Aulis	Hecuba et Iphigenia in Aulide

City	Press	Translation	USTC	Other verification
Basel	Andreas Cratander	Andrea Divus	612821	MDZ
Paris	Guillaume Morel	Erasmus		See The Poems of Desiderius Erasmus; no known extant copies
Basel	Johannes Froben	Erasmus	678376	See Worldcat for details and libraries
Lyons	Sebastian Gryphe	Erasmus	122491	Viewed at Bodleian
Lyons	Etienne Dolet	Gentian Hervet	140114	See Worldcat for details and libraries
Lyons	Sulpice Sabon for Antoine Constantin	Erasmus	204525	Viewed at Bodleian
Basel	Robert Winter	Dorotheus Camillus	654884	Viewed at Bodleian; E-rara
Antwerp	Matthias Crom	Petreius Tiara	408257	See Worldcat for details and libraries
Basel	Andreas Cratander	Andrea Divus	612820	MDZ
Venice	Giovanni Battista Pocatela	Andrea Divus	810852	Viewed at Bodleian
Paris	Archibald Hay	Erasmus	Worldcat	See Worldcat for details and libraries
Utrecht	Herman van Borculo	Petreius Tiara	425775	Viewed at Bodleian
Venice	Burgofrancho Papiensem	Giovanni Baptista Gabia	857023	Viewed at Bodleian; MDZ
Paris	Michel de Vascosan	Erasmus, Buchanan	149176	Viewed at Bodleian
Lyon	Sulpice Sabon for Antoine Constantin	Erasmus	200631	See also French Books III & IV; but note that date is uncertain, and might be same as the 1541 edition listed above.

(continued)

Year	Playwright	Play	Book Title
1545	Sophocles	Complete	Sophoclis tragici poetae
1546	Euripides	Hecuba and Iphigenia in Aulis	Hecuba et Iphigenia in Aulide
1546	Euripides	Electra	Euripidou Elektra
1546	Euripides	Electra	Euripidou Elektra
1546	Sophocles	Complete	Interpretatio tragoediarum sophoclis
1547	Aristophanes	Plutus	Plutus Aristophanis
1547	Aristophanes	Clouds	Nebulae
1547	Aristophanes	Complete (9 plays)	Komodiai ennea
1548	Aristophanes	Complete (11 plays)	Comoediae undecim
1549	Aristophanes	Plutus	Ploutos
1549	Sophocles	Complete	Interpretatio tragoediarum sophoclis
1550	Euripides	Complete	Euripidis tragicorum omnium principis
1550	Sophocles	Ajax, Antigone, and Electra	Aiax flagellifer, et Antigone. Electra
1551	Euripides	Orestes	Euripidis Orestes
1552	Aristophanes	Complete	Comoediae undecim
1552	Sophocles	Ajax, Philoctetes	Duae sophoclis tragoediae
1554	Euripides	Hecuba	Tragoedia Hecuba
1555	Euripides	Hecuba	Tragoedia Hecuba

City	Press	Translation	USTC	Other verification
Rome	Antonio Blado	Bartholomeo Marliano	857024	Viewed at Bodleian
Antwerp	Gillis Coppens van Diest	Erasmus	407435	See Worldcat for details and libraries
Basel	Johannes Oporinus	Pietro Vettori	654576	Viewed at Bodleian; MDZ
Tubingen	Ulrich Morhart	Pietro Vettori	Worldcat	See Worldcat for details and libraries
Frankfurt	Peter Braubach	Joachim Camerarius	666930	MDZ
Plutus	Michel de Vascosan	Michael Cabedius	149857	Viewed at Bodleian
Paris			153937	See also French Books III & IV
Basel	Johannes Froben	Sigmund Gelen	612856	See Worldcat for details and libraries
Venice	Melchiorre Sessa	Jean Gryphe	810849	Viewed at Bodleian
Paris	Christian Wechel and M. Dupuys	Charles Girard	150162	Viewed at Bodleian; Babel
Frankfurt	Peter Braubach	Joachim Camerarius	666929	See Worldcat for details and libraries
Basel	Johannes Oporinus	Dorotheus Camillus	654570	MDZ, E-rara
Lyon	Jean Gryphe	George Rataller	150404	Viewed at Bodleian; Gallica
Basel	Johannes Oporinus	Sigmund Gelen	654878	Viewed at Bodleian; E-rara
Basel	Andreas Cratander	Andreas Divus	612822	Viewed at Bodleian; E-rara
Strasbourg	Thomas Naogeorgus	Thomas Naogeorgus	668433	Google Books
Leipzig	Georg Hantschius	Joachim Camerarius	699283	MDZ
Leipzig	Georg Hantschius	Joachim Camerarius	699282	DFG

(continued)

Year	Playwright	Play	Book Title
1555	Aeschylus	Complete (6 plays)	Tragoediae sex
1556	Sophocles	Complete	Commentatio explicationum omnium tragoediarum sophoclis
1556	Euripides	Alcestis	Alcestis
1556	Aristophanes	Plutus	Plutus
1557	Aristophanes	Clouds	Nebulae
1557	Aeschylus	Complete	Tragœdiæ VII
1557	Euripides	Alcestis	Alcestis
1557	Sophocles	Complete	Tragoediae
1557	Sophocles	Complete	Tragoediae
1558	Euripides	Hecuba and Iphigenia in Aulis	Hecuba et Iphigenia in Aulide
1558	Euripides	Cyclops	Cyclops drama comicotragicum
1558	Euripides	Complete	Euripidis tragoediae
1558	Sophocles	Complete	Tragoediae
1558	Sophocles	Complete	Sophoclis tragoediae septem
1559	Aeschylus	Prometheus	Prometheus, cum interpretatione
1559	Euripides	Complete	Aristologia Euripidea Graecolatina
1560	Euripides	Hecuba	Ekabē

City	Press	Translation	USTC	Other verification
Basel	Johannes Oporinus	Johannes Sanravius	609466	MDZ
Basel	Johannes Oporinus	Joachim Camerarius	623389	MDZ
Paris	Michel de Vascosan	George Buchanan	204922	See Worldcat for details and libraries
Utrecht	Herman van Borculo	Hortensius Lambertus	421292	Viewed at Bodleian
Utrecht	Herman van Borculo	Hortensius Lambertus	421310	Viewed at Bodleian
Geneva	Henri Estienne	Pietro Vettori	450455	See Worldcat for details and libraries
Paris	Michel de Vascosan	George Buchanan	154348	MDZ
Paris	Fédéric Morel	Jean Lalamant	152363	See also French Books III & IV
Paris	Michel de Vascosan	Jean Lalamant	204978	Google Books
Venice	Aldus Manutius	Erasmus		Viewed at Bodleian; Not listed in USTC, but listed in Poems of Erasmus
Augsburg	Philipp Ulhart	Martin Balticus	641217	MDZ
Basel	Johannes Oporinus	Philip Melanchthon	654567	Viewed at Bodleian; Babel
Paris	Michel de Vascosan	Jean Lalamant	154411	Viewed at Bodleian
Basel	Johannes Oporinus	Thomas Naogeorgus	694173	See Universitatsbibliothek Basel
Basel	Johannes Oporinus	Matthias Garbitius	609465	MDZ
Basel	Johannes Oporinus	Michael Neander	612844	Viewed at Bodleian; MDZ
Paris	Guillaume Morel	Erasmus	152919	Viewed at Bodleian

(*continued*)

Year	Playwright	Play	Book Title
1561	Aristophanes	Frogs	Ranae
1561	Aristophanes	Knights	Equites
1562	Euripides	Complete	Euripides poeta tragicorum princeps
1562	Euripides	Complete	Euripides tragoediae
1566	Euripides	Hecuba	Hekabe
1567	Aeschylus	Prometheus	Tragoediae selectae Aeschyli, Sophoclis, Euripidis
1567	Euripides	Hecuba, Iphigenia, Medea, Alcestis	Tragoediae selectae Aeschyli, Sophoclis, Euripidis
1567	Euripides	Hecuba and Iphigenia in Aulis	Hecuba et Iphigenia in Aulide
1567	Euripides	Alcestis	Alcestis
1567	Sophocles	Ajax, Antigone, and Electra	Tragoediae selectae Aeschyli, Sophoclis, Euripidis
1567	Sophocles	Complete	Tragoediae
1568	Euripides	Alcestis and Medea	Georgii Buchanani Scoti poetae
1568	Euripides	Alcestis	Alcestis
1570	Sophocles	Complete	Tragoediae
1572	Euripides	Phoenician Women	Phoinissai Euripidu
1573	Sophocles	Ajax	Aias Mastigophoros

City	Press	Translation	USTC	Other verification
Utrecht	Herman van Borculo	Hortensius Lambertus	421418	Viewed at Bodleian
Utrecht	Herman van Borculo	Hortensius Lambertus	421419	Viewed at Bodleian
Basel	Johannes Oporinus	Gasparus Stablinus	654877	MDZ
Frankfurt	Ludovico Lucius	Philip Melanchthon	654564	MDZ
Venice	Domenico and Giovanni Batista Guerra	Gasparus Stablinus	828502	Perugia, Biblioteca Comunale Augusta
Geneva	Henri Estienne	Matthias Garbitius	450564	Viewed at Bodleian
Geneva	Henri Estienne	Erasmus, George Buchanan	450564	Viewed at Bodleian
Strasbourg	Josias Rihel	Erasmus	654822	DFG
Strasbourg	Josias Rihel	George Buchanan	654844	DFG
Geneva	Henri Estienne	George Rataller	450564	Viewed at Bodleian
Paris	Michel de Vascosan	Jean Lalamant	140511	See also French Books III & IV
Basel	Thomas Guarinus	George Buchanan	659392	MDZ, E-rara
Strasbourg	Josias Rihel	[George Buchanan]	708859	Listed in USTC and Worldcat, but no known copies; may be reprint of 1567 edition from same press, or may simply be same edition
Antwerp	G. Silvius	George Rataller	402664	MDZ
Wittenberg	Hans Lufft		683984	Viewed at Bodleian
Paris	Jean Benenat	Joseph Scaliger	116658	Viewed at Bodleian

(*continued*)

Year	Playwright	Play	Book Title
1574	Sophocles	Ajax	Ajax Lorarius
1576	Euripides	Medea	Medea Euripidis
1576	Sophocles	Complete	Tragœdiæ Sophoclis
1577	Euripides	Phoenissae	Phoenissae tragoedia
1577	Euripides	Alcestis	Alcestis
1578	Euripides	Trojan Women	Troades Euripidis
1579	Euripides	Phoenissae	Euripidis Phoenissae
1580	Euripides	Phoenician Women, Hippolytus, Andromache	Tres tragoediae
1581	Aeschylus	Seven at Thebes	Tragodia hepta epi thebais
1581	Euripides	Phoenician Women, Hippolytus, Andromache	Tres tragoediae
1581	Euripides	Alcestis	Alcestis
1581	Euripides	Alcestis	Alcestis Euripidis
1581	Sophocles	Antigone	Sophoclis Antigone
1582	Euripides	Cyclops	Cyclops Euripidis
1582	Aeschylus	Seven at Thebes	Septem ad Thebas
1583	Euripides	Medea	Medea
1584	Sophocles	Trachiniae	Trachiniae sophoclis

City	Press	Translation	USTC	Other verification
Geneva	Gaspard de Hus	Joseph Scaliger	450677	Viewed at Bodleian
Strasbourg	Nikolaus Wiriot	George Buchanan	675430	See Worldcat for details and libraries
Antwerp	Willem Silvius	George Rataller	406355	Viewed at Bodleian; MDZ
Strasbourg	Nikolaus Wiriot	George Calaminus	683978	Viewed at Bodleian; MDZ
Barcelona	Pedro Malo	George Buchanan	336163	See Iberian Books; in Biblioteca Nacional de España
Strasbourg	Nikolaus Wiriot	Philip Melanchthon	699542	MDZ
Rostock	Augustin Ferber	Janus Gulielmus	654879	See Worldcat for details and libraries
Antwerp	Christopher Plantins	George Rataller	414349	Viewed at Bodleian
Rostock	Stephanus Mylandrius	Johannes Caselius	610532	DFG
Antwerp	Christopher Plantins	George Rataller	401890	MDZ
Valencia	Pedro de Huete	George Buchanan	336164	See Biblioteca Pública Episcopal del Seminario de Barcelona
Wittenberg	Matthaeus Welack	George Buchanan	610652	MDZ
London	John Wolfe	Thomas Watson	509429	See Worldcat for details and libraries
Strasbourg	Nikolaus Wiriot	Philip Melanchthon	625827	See Worldcat for details and libraries
Rostock	Stephanus Mylandrius	Johannes Caselius		Viewed at Bodleian
Barcelona			351601	No known copies; see also Iberian Books.
Strasbourg	Anton Bertram	Johannes Cameraraius	698835	DFG

(*continued*)

Year	Playwright	Play	Book Title
1584	Sophocles	Complete	Tragoediae
1585	Aeschylus	Seven at Thebes	Septem Thebana tragoedia
1586	Aristophanes	Plutus, Knights, Clouds, Frogs, The Archarnians	Aristophanes veteris comoediae princeps
1586	Sophocles	Philoctetes	Philoctetes
1587	Sophocles	Ajax	Ajax Lorarius
1588	Sophocles	Trachiniae	Trachiniae sophoclis
1588	Aristophanes	Peace	In Aristophanis Irenam
1589	Aristophanes	Peace	In Aristophanis Irenam
1589	Aristophanes	Peace	In Aristophanis Irenam
1589	Aristophanes	Peace	In Aristophanis Irenam
1591	Sophocles	Ajax	Ajax Lorarius
1591	Sophocles	Ajax	Scaliger, Poemata in duas partes... Sophoclis aiax lorarius
1592	Euripides	Phoenician Women	Tragoedia Phoenissarum
1593	Euripides	Cyclops	Satyrus Cyclops

City	Press	Translation	USTC	Other verification
Antwerp	Jean Bellère	George Rataller	406681	MDZ
Paris	Fédéric Morel	Florent Chrestien	170795	Viewed at Bodleian
Frankfurt	Johann Spiess	Nicodemus Frischlin	677936	Viewed at Bodleian; Google Books
Paris	Fédéric Morel	Florent Chrestien	170842	Viewed at Bodleian
Strasbourg	Anton Bertram	Joseph Scaliger	694172	See Worldcat for details and libraries
Strasbourg	Anton Bertram	Thomas Naogeorgus	698834	MDZ
Paris	Fédéric Morel	Florent Chrestien	172136	See Worldcat for details and libraries
Paris	Fédéric Morel	Florent Chrestien	137987	Google Books
Paris	Fédéric Morel	Florent Chrestien	170947	USTC lists this and above as separate imprints, but they may be the same
Paris	Fédéric Morel	Florent Chrestien	170940	USTC lists this and above as separate imprints, but they may be the same
Geneva	Petrus Santandreanus	Joseph Scaliger	452092	See Worldcat for details and libraries
Heidelberg	Hieronymus Commelinus	Joseph Scaliger	668505	See Worldcat for details and libraries
Graz	Georg Widmanstetter	Nicolaus Gablmann	699290	MDZ
Barcelona	Sebastián de Cormellas	Dorotheus Camillus	336165	Copy in Biblioteca Pública Episcopal del Seminario de Barcelona

(*continued*)

Year	Playwright	Play	Book Title
1594	Aristophanes	Plutus	Aristophanis Plutus
1594	Euripides	Andromache	Andromacha tragoedia
1597	Aristophanes	Complete (11 plays)	Comoediae Aristophanis
1597	Aristophanes	Plutus, Knights, Clouds, Frogs, The Archarnians	Aristophanes veteris comoediae princeps
1597	Euripides	Complete	Euripidis tragoediae XIX
1597	Sophocles	Complete	Sophoclis tragoediae VII
1598	Euripides	Medea	Medea Euripidis
1599	Euripides	Hippolytus	Hippolytos Stephanephoros

City	Press	Translation	USTC	Other verification
Naples	Salviani		810856	See Worldcat for details and libraries; Translator not listed in any catalogues, but British Library entry specifies that text is in both Greek and Latin
Leiden	Franciscus Raphelengius	Florent Chrestien	423360	Google Books
Venice	Giovanni Battista & Giovanni Bernardo Sessa	Andrea Divus	810857	See Worldcat for details and libraries
Frankfurt	Johann Spiess	Nicodemus Frischlin	677935	Viewed at Bodleian; MDZ
Heidelberg	Hieronymus Commelinus	Aemilius Portus	654566	MDZ
Heidelberg	Hieronymus Commelinus	Giuelielmus Canterus	694179	MDZ
Strasbourg	Josias Rihel	George Buchanan	675431	Viewed at Bodleian
		Philip Melanchthon	662971	Viewed at Bodleian; MDZ

APPENDIX 3

Vernacular Translations of Greek Plays

Year	Playwright	Play	Book Title
1517	Euripides	Electra	La vengeanza de Agamenon, tragedia
1519	Euripides	Hecuba	Hecuba Tragedia
1525	Euripides	Alcestis	L'Alceste Tragedia di Euripide
1528	Sophocles	Electra	La vengança de Agamenon.
1531	Sophocles	Electra	La vengança de Agamenon.
1533	Sophocles	Antigone	L'Antigone, tragedia di Sophocle
1533	Sophocles	Antigone	Opere toscane di Luigi Alamanni
1533	Sophocles	Antigone	Opere toscane di Luigi Alamanni
1537	Sophocles	Electra	Tragedie De Sophocles Intitulée Electra
1539	Euripides	Hecuba	Ecuba: Tragedia di Euripide
1540	Euripides	not known	not known
1541	Sophocles	Electra	La vengança de Agamenon.

City	Press	Language	Translator	USTC		Notes
Alcalá de Henares	Arnao Guillén de Brocar	Spanish	Fernan Pérez de Oliva	347724		No known surviving copies; see Bolgar and Highet
Florence	Filippo Giunta	Italian	Giambattista Gelli	828500		See Biblioteca nazionale Marciana, Venezia
		Italian	Giovambattista Parisotti			Not printed until 1735; see Hoffman, Bolgar
Burgos	Juan de Junta	Spanish	Fernan Pérez de Oliva	341798		See Worldcat for libraries and details
Burgos	Juan de Junta	Spanish	Fernan Pérez de Oliva	340568		See Worldcat for libraries and details
Venice	Giovanni Antonio Nicolini da Sabbio	Italian	Luigi Alamanni	857022		See also Istituto Centrale per il Catalogo Unico
Lyon	Sébastien Gryphe	Italian	Luigi Alamanni	122146	Google Books	Translated between 1520–1527
Venice	Pietro Nicolini da Sabbio	Italian	Luigi Alamanni	808164	Google Books	
Paris	Louis Cyaneus	French	Lazare de Baïf	73599	Gallica	
		Italian	Matteo Bandello			In manuscript; not printed until 1813
		Spanish	Juan Boscan			Not printed; see Ticknor
Sevilla		Spanish	Fernan Pérez de Oliva	341799		Biblioteca Nacional de España, Madrid

(*continued*)

Year	Playwright	Play	Book Title
1542	Euripides	Trojan Women	
1542	Sophocles	Antigone	l'Antigone de Sophocles
1543	Euripides	Hecuba	La Hecuba tragedia
1544	Euripides	Hecuba	La tragedie nommée Hecuba
1545	Aristo-phanes	The Wasps	Les guespes attiques
1545	Aristo-phanes	Comoediae	Le comedie de'l facetissimo Aristofane, tradutte di greco in lingua commune d'Italia, per Bartolomio et Pietro Rositini de Prat'Alboino
1545–47	Euripides	Iphigenia in Aulis	
1549	Euripides	Iphigenia in Aulis	L'Iphigene
1549	Euripides	Phoenissae	Giocasta
1549	Euripides	Hecuba	La Hecuba tragedia
1549	Aristo-phanes	Plutus	Plutus
1549	Euripides	Iphigenia in Aulis	L'Iphigène d'Euripide
1550	Euripides	Hecuba	La tragedie nommee Hecuba
1550	Euripides	Hecuba	
1551	Euripides	Iphigenia in Aulis	Ifigenia

City	Press	Language	Translator	USTC		Notes
		French	Jacques Amyot			Not printed; see Bolgar
Paris		French	Calvy de la Fontaine			In manuscript; not printed until 2000
Venice	Gabriel Gioli di Ferrari	Italian	Lodovico Dolce	827058	MDZ	
Paris	Robert Estienne	French	Guillaume Bochetel	38543	ONB	
	Paris	French	Jean Vernou	27200		No known surviving copies
Venice	Vicenzo Vaugris	Italian	Bartolomeo and Pietro Rositini	810853	viewed at Bodleian, Babel	
		French	Jacques Amyot			See Bolgar; not printed
Paris	Gilles Corrozet	French	Thomas Sebillet	27262		See Worldcat for libraries and details
Venice	Aldi Filii	Italian	Lodovico Dolce	827069	OPAL	
Venice	Gabriele Giolito di Ferrari	Italian	Lodovico Dolce	827070	OPAL	
Paris		French	Pierre Ronsard			Not printed in full; fragments printed in 1617; see Highet
Paris	Gilles Corrozet	French	Thomas Sebillet	41493	Gallica	
Paris	Robert Estienne	French	Guillaume Bochetel	24313	MDZ, Gallica	
		Italian	Giorgio Trissino			See Bolgar
Venice	Gabriele Giolito di Ferrari	Italian	Lodovico Dolce	827073		See Worldcat for libraries and details

(continued)

Year	Playwright	Play	Book Title
1556	Sophocles	Antigone	Antigone tragedia di Luigi Alamanni
1556	Sophocles	Antigone	Een tragedie ghenaemt Antigone
1557	Euripides	Medea	La Medea
*c.*1557	Euripides	Iphigenia in Aulis	The Tragedie of Iphigenia
1558	Euripides	Medea	La Medea
1558	Sophocles	Electra	Tragoedia magyar nelvenn az Sophocles Electrajabol
1559	Euripides	Hecuba	Hekuba
1560	Aristophanes	Plutus	
1560	Euripides	Hecuba	La Hecuba
1560	Euripides	Iphigenia in Aulis	Ifigenia
1560	Euripides	Medea	La Medea
1560	Euripides	Phoenissae, Medea, Iphigenia, Hecuba	Tragedie

City	Press	Language	Translator	USTC		Notes
Florence		Italian	Luigi Alamanni	808175	MDZ	
Antwerp	Symon Cock	Dutch	Cornelis van Ghistele	408986		See Erfgoedbibliotheek Hendrik Conscience
Venice	Gabriele Giolito di Ferrari	Italian	Lodovico Dolce	827082		See Worldcat for libraries and details
		English	Jane, Lady Lumley			Manuscript in British Library; not printed until 1909
Venice	Gabriele Giolito di Ferrari	Italian	Lodovico Dolce	827083	OPAL	
Wien	Raphael Hoffhalter	Hungarian	Péter Bornemisza	305158		See Forschungsbibliothek Gotha, Universität Erfurt
Ragusa		Croatian	Marin Držić			Not printed until 1871; see Braticević and Lupić
		French	Jean Antoine de Baïf			See Bolgar; not printed
Venice	Gabriele Giolito di Ferrari	Italian	Lodovico Dolce	827095		See Worldcat for libraries and details
Venice	Gabriele Giolito di Ferrari	Italian	Lodovico Dolce	827096		See Worldcat for libraries and details
Venice	Gabriele Giolito di Ferrari	Italian	Lodovico Dolce	827097		See Worldcat for libraries and details
Venice	Gabriele Giolito di Ferrari	Italian	Lodovico Dolce	827102	OPAL	

(*continued*)

Year	Playwright	Play	Book Title
1565	Sophocles	Oedipus	Edippo
1565	Sophocles	Oedipus	Edippo
1565	Sophocles	Trachiniae	
1566	Euripides	Hecuba	Hecuba Tragedia
1566	Euripides	Iphigenia in Aulis	Ifigenia
1566	Euripides	Medea	La Medea
1566	Euripides	Phoenissae, Medea, Iphigenia, Hecuba	Tragedie
1570	Euripides	Medea	Medea
1570s	Euripides	Iphigenia in Aulis	Iphigenia
1573	Sophocles	Antigone	Euvres en rime
1573	Euripides	Phoenissae	Jocasta, in A hundredth sundrie flowers
1577	Aristophanes	Plutus	
1579	Aristophanes	Birds	Néphélococugie

City	Press	Language	Translator	USTC		Notes
Venice	Domenico Farri	Italian	Giovanni Andrea Dell'Anguillara	809532	OPAL	
Padua	Lorenzo Pasquato	Italian	Giovanni Andrea Dell'Anguillara	809533	Google Books, OPAL	
		French	Jean Antoine de Baïf			See Bolgar; not printed
Venice	Domenico Farri	Italian	Lodovico Dolce	827123	Raccolta	
Venice	Domenico Farri	Italian	Lodovico Dolce	827124	OPAL	
Venice	Domenico Farri	Italian	Lodovico Dolce	827125		See Worldcat for libraries and details
Venice	Domenico Farri	Italian	Lodovico Dolce	827128	Babel	
		French	Jean Antoine de Baïf			See Bolgar; not printed
Oxford		English	George Peele			Not published, and not extant, but cited by William Gager in contemporary poem
Paris	Lucas Breyer	French	Jean Antoine de Baïf	7492	Google Books	
London	Henrie Bynneman	English	George Gascoigne and Francis Kinwelmershe	507655	EEBO	Trans. 1566
		Spanish	Pedro Simón Abril			See Bolgar, Highet
Paris		French	Pierre Le Loyer	93574		Adaptation, see Le Loyer, Dudouyt

(continued)

Year	Playwright	Play	Book Title
1584	Euripides	Iphigenia in Aulis	Iphigenia in avlide
1585	Sophocles	Oedipus Rex	Edipo tiranno di Sofocle tragedia
1586	Sophocles	Electra	Las obras del Maestro Fernan Perez de Oliva
1586	Euripides	Hecuba	Las obras del Maestro Fernan Perez de Oliva
1587	Euripides	Phoenissae	Jocasta, in The vvhole woorkes of George Gascoigne Esquire
1588	Sophocles	Electra	Elettra tragedia di Sofocle
1589	Sophocles	Oedipus Rex	Edipo tiranno tragedia di Sofocle
1592	Euripides	Hecuba	L'Hecuba d'Euripide
1595	Euripides	Medea	Medea
1597	Euripides	Iphigenia in Aulis	Ifigenia
1599	Euripides	Alcestis	Alceste tragedia

City	Press	Language	Translator	USTC		Notes
	s.l.	German	Michael Bapst	668255		See Herzogin Anna Amalia Bibliothek, Weimar
Venice	Francesco Ziletti	Italian	Pietro Angelii Bargeo	857026	OPAL	
Cordoba	Gabriel Ramos Bejarano	Spanish	Fernan Pérez de Oliva	340711	Google Books	
Cordoba	Gabriel Ramos Bejarano	Spanish	Fernan Pérez de Oliva	340711	Google Books	
London	Abell Jeffes	English	George Gascoigne and Francis Kinwelmershe	510738	EEBO	
Venice	I Guarerra fratelli	Italian	Erasmo de Valvasone	857028	OPAL	
Florence	Bartolomeo Sermartelli	Italian	Pietro Angelii Bargeo	857027	Google Books	
Verona	Girolamo Discepolo	Italian	Giovanni Balcianelli	828503		See *Biblioteca degli volgarizzatori*; Copy in Biblioteca dell'Accademia dei Lincei e Corsiniana
Barcelona		Spanish	Pedro Simón Abril			See Bolgar, Highet, Pellicer.
Venice	Giovanni Battista & Giovanni Bernardo Sessa	Italian	Lodovico Dolce	827170		See Worldcat for libraries and details
Genoa	Giuseppe Pavoni	Italian	Hieronimo Giustiniano	828504		See Worldcat for libraries and details

APPENDIX 4

Performances of Plays by (or based on) Greek Playwrights

Date	Author	Play	Title	Country
1506–14	Euripides	Hecuba	Hecuba	Belgium
1512	Aristophanes	Plutus	Plutus	Italy
1517	Aristophanes	Plutus	Plutus	Germany
1521	Aristophanes	Plutus	Plutus	Germany
1521	Aristophanes	Plutus	Plutus	Germany
1525	Euripides	Hecuba	Hecuba	Germany
1531	Aristophanes	Plutus	Plutus	Switzerland
1533	Sophocles	Antigone	Antigone	Italy
1536	Aristophanes	Plutus	Plutus	England
1537	Sophocles	Electra	Electre	France
1539	Euripides	Medea	Medea	France
1539–42	Euripides	Alcestis	Alcestis	France
1540–49	Euripides	Medea	Medea	England
1540s	Sophocles	Philoctetes	Philoctetes	England
1546	Aristophanes	Peace	Peace	Greek
1549	Aristophanes	Clouds	Clouds	Czech Republic
1549–52	Aristophanes	Plutus	Plutus	France

Details	Language	Trans.	Source
Collège du Porc, Leuven	Greek	Dir. Melanchthon	APGRD
Florence		Adaptation	APGRD
Zwickau	Greek		APGRD
Zwickau	Greek	Dir. George Agricola	APGRD, Boas
Zwickau	Latin	Dir. George Agricola	APGRD, Boas
Wittenberg, students of Melanchthon	Latin	Trans. Erasmus, dir. Melanchthon	APGRD, Boas
Zurich; adherents of Zingli	Greek		APGRD, Boas
	Italian	Luigi Alamanni	Highet
St. John's College, Cambridge	Greek	Dir. Roger Ascham and John Cheke	APGRD, Boas
	French	Lazare de Baif	APGRD
Collège de Guyenne	Latin	George Buchanan	APGRD, Boas
Collège de Guyenne	Latin	George Buchanan	APGRD, Boas
status uncertain	Latin	George Buchanan	APGRD
Cambridge University; status uncertain	Latin	Roger Ascham	AGPRD
Trinity College, Cambridge	Greek	Dir. John Dee	APGRD, Boas
Jáchymov, Karlovarský kraj	Greek	Dir. Eberhardt	APGRD
Collège de Coquerel, Paris	French	Trans. Pierre Ronsard	APGRD, Highet

(continued)

Date	Author	Play	Title	Country
1551	Euripides/Seneca	Troas, Trojan Women	Troas	England
1550–67	Euripides/Pickering	Orestes	Horestes	England
1552–53	Euripides/Seneca	Hippolytus	Hippolytus	England
1553–54	Euripides/Seneca	Medea	La Médée	France
1554	Aeschylus	Agamemnon	Die mördisch königin Clitimestra	Germany
1555	Euripides	Iphigenia	Mordopffer der göttin Diane, mit der jungkfraw Ephigenie	Germany
1556	Sophocles	Oedipus	Edipo	Italy
1558	Sophocles	Electra	Electra	Hungary
1559	Euripides/Seneca	Hecuba	Hecuba or Troas	England
1559	Euripides/Seneca	Oedipus	Oedipus	England
1559	Euripides	Hecuba	Hecuba	Croatia
1560–61	Euripides/Seneca	Medea	Medea	England
1560–61	Euripides/Seneca	Troas, Trojan Women	Troas	England

Details	Language	Trans.	Source
Trinity College, Cambridge	Latin	Dir. Rudd	APGRD, Boas
London	English	Adapted by John Pickering	APGRD, Wilson
King's College, Cambridge; not clear which version	Unknown		APGRD
Paris; not clear which version	French	Adapted by Jean-Bastier de La Péruse and Scévole de Saint-Marie	APGRD, Delcourt
Nuremberg	German	Indirect adaptation	AGPRD
Nuremberg	German	Adaptation by Hans Sach	APGRD
		Lodovico Dolce	APGRD
	Hungarian	Adaptation by Peter Bornemisza	APGRD
Trinity College, Cambridge; not clear which version	Latin		APGRD, Boas, Smith
Trinity College, Cambridge; usually assumed to be Seneca's, but not certain	English	Probably Alexander Neville	APGRD, Boas, Smith
Ragusa	Croatian	Trans. Marin Držić	Lupic
Trinity College, Cambridge; not clear which version	Latin		APGRD, Boas, Smith
Trinity College, Cambridge; not clear which version	Latin		APGRD, Boas, Smith

(*continued*)

Date	Author	Play	Title	Country
1563	Euripides/Seneca	Medea	Medea	England
1564	Sophocles	Ajax	Ajax Flagallifer (planned)	England
1565	Sophocles	Oedipus	Edippo	Italy
1566	Euripides	Phoenician Women	Jocasta	England
1567	Euripides	Orestes	Orestes	England
1571	Sophocles	Ajax	Ajax and Ulysses	England
1571	Aeschylus	Persians	Persai	Greece
1573	Euripides/Seneca	Hippolytus	Hippolyte	France
1575	Euripides	Iphigenia	Iphigenie	France
1575	Sophocles	Ajax	Aias	France
1576–82	Euripides	Iphigenia	Iphigenia	England
1577–92	Euripides/Seneca	Oedipus	Oedipus	England
1578	Aristophanes	Birds	Néphélococugie	France
1579	Euripides/Seneca	Trojan Women	La Troade	France
1583	Sophocles	Antigone	Antigone	England

Details	Language	Trans.	Source
Queens College, Cambridge; not clear which version	Latin		APGRD, Boas
King's College, Cambridge	Latin		APGRD, Boas
Padua	Italian	Trans. Giovanni Andrea dell'Anguillara	APGRD
Gray's Inn, London	English	Gascoigne and Kinwelmersh	APGRD, Wilson
Performed for Queen Elizabeth, probably by Westminster School boys	Latin		APGRD, Smith
Children of the Chapel Royal	English	Adaptation; dir. William Hunnis	APGRD, Wilson
Zakynthos	Probably Italian		APGRD
Performance details uncertain	French	adapted by Robert Garnier	APGRD
Schultheater, Strasbourg	Greek		APGRD
Schultheater, Strasbourg	Greek		APGRD
Children of St. Paul's, dir Sebastian Westcott	English	Unknown; possibly Lumley or Peele	APGRD, Wilson
Adaptation by William Gager	Latin	adapted by William Gager	APGRD, Boas
Free adaptation	French	adapted by Pierre Le Loyer	APGRD, Dudouyt
Free adaptation	French	adaptation	APGRD
Either Inns of Court or St. John's College, Cambridge	Latin	Thomas Watson	APGRD, Smith

(continued)

Date	Author	Play	Title	Country
1584	Aeschylus/Seneca	Agamemnon	Agamemnon and Ulysses	England
1584	Euripides/Seneca	Hecuba, Trojan Women	Polyxène	France
1585	Sophocles	Oedipus	Edipo Tiranno	Italy
1587	Sophocles	Ajax	Aias	France
1588	Aristophanes	Plutus	Plutus	England
1589	Euripides	Andromache	Astianatte	Italy
1598	Euripides	Medea	Medea	France
1599	Euripides/ Aeschylus	Orestes, Agamemnon	Agamemnon	England
1599	Euripides/ Aeschylus	Orestes, Agamemnon	Orestes' Furies	England

Details	Language	Trans.	Source
"Presented and enacted before her maiestie by the Earle of Oxenford his boyes on St Iohns daie at night at Grenewich"	English	Adaptation	APGRD
Adaptation	French	Adaptation	APGRD
Vicenza	Italian	Trans. Orsatto Giustiniani	APGRD
Schultheater, Strasbourg	Latin	Trans. Joseph Scaliger	APGRD
Cambridge, details unknown	Greek		APGRD
Venice	Italian	Bongianni Gratarolo	APGRD
Schultheater, Strasbourg	Greek		APGRD
Rose Theater	English	Indirect adaptation by Dekker and Chettle	APGRD
Rose Theater	English	Indirect adaptation by Dekker and Chettle; may be same play as 1599 Agamemnon	APGRD

Vernacular Translations of Seneca's Plays

Year	Playwright	Play(s)	Language	Book Title
1388	Seneca	Medea; Thyestes; Troades; Hercules Furens	Catalan	Les Tragedies de Seneca
1497	Seneca	Hippolytus	Italian	Hippolytus
1497–8	Seneca	Agamemnon	Italian	Agamemnon
1534	Seneca	Complete	French	Les Tragedies
1543	Seneca	Thyestes	Italian	Thyeste
1547	Seneca	Thyestes	Italian	Thyeste
1556	Seneca	Agamemnon	French	La tragedie d'Agamemnon
1557	Seneca	Agamemnon	French	La tragedie d'Agamemnon
1559	Seneca	Troas	English	The sixt tragedie entituled Troas
1560	Seneca	Thyestes	English	The seconde tragedie entituled Thyestes
1560	Seneca	Thyestes	Italian	Thieste
1560	Seneca	Complete	Italian	Le tragedie
1560	Seneca	Thyestes	Italian	In Le tragedie di m. Lodovico Dolce

City	Press	Translation	USTC	Notes
		Antoni de Vilaragut		Manuscript; not Manuscript; not published until 1914
Venice	Christophorus de Pensis	Picio da Montevarchi	991130	
Venice	Petrus de Quarengiis	Evangelista Fossa	991132	
Paris	Denis Janot	Pierre Grognet	88772	
Venice	Gabriele Giolito De Ferrari	Lodovico Dolce	827059	OPAL
Venice	Gabriele Giolito De Ferrari	Lodovico Dolce	827067	OPAL
Paris	Martin Le Jeune	Charles Toustain	83398	
Paris	Martin Le Jeune	Charles Toustain	37700	MDZ
London	Richard Tottell	Jasper Heywood	505645	EEBO
London	Thomas Berthelet	Jasper Heywood	505785	EEBO
Venice	Gabriele Giolito De Ferrari	Lodovico Dolce	827101	
Venice	Giovanni Battista & Melchiorre Sessa	Lodovico Dolce	855888	MDZ
Venice	Gabriele Giolito De Ferrari	Lodovico Dolce	827102	OPAL

(*continued*)

Year	Playwright	Play(s)	Language	Book Title
1561	Seneca	Hercules Furens	English	The first tragedie intituled Hercules furens
1561	Seneca	Agamemnon	French	La tragedie d'Agamemnon
1562	Seneca	Troas	English	The sixt tragedie entituled Troas
1563	Seneca	Oedipus	English	The lamentable tragedie of Oedipus
1566	Seneca	Medea	English	The seventh tragedie entituled Medea
1566	Seneca	Agamemnon	English	The eyght tragedie. Entituled Agamemnon
1566	Seneca	Thyestes	Italian	Thyeste
1566	Seneca	Thyestes	Italian	In Le tragedie di m. Lodovico Dolce
1581	Seneca	Complete	English	Seneca his tenne tragedies
1589	Seneca	Agamemnon, Thyestes	French	Le premier livre du théâtre tragique
1590	Seneca	Agamemnon, Thyestes	French	Le premier livre du théâtre tragique

City	Press	Translation	USTC	Notes
London	Henry Sutton	Jasper Heywood	505903	EEBO
Paris	Jean Le Preux	Le Duchat?	94605	No known surviving copy
London	Thomas Powell	Jasper Heywood	506058	EEBO
London	Rowland Hall	Alexander Neville	506179	EEBO
London	Thomas Colwell	John Studely	506577	EEBO
London	Thomas Colwell	John Studely	506576	EEBO
Venice	Domenico Farri	Lodovico Dolce	827127	OPAL
Venice	Domenico Farri	Lodovico Dolce	827128	Babel
London	Thomas Marsh	Jasper Heywood et al	509428	EEBO
Paris	Claude de Montroeil et Jean Richer	Roland Brisset	20290	
Paris	Claude de Montroeil et Jean Richer	Roland Brisset	19173	Gallica

Pre-1600 Performances of Plays by (or Based on) Seneca in England and Continental Europe

Date	Author	Original Play	Title	Country
1474	Seneca	Hippolytus	Phaedra	France
1485	Seneca	Hippolytus	Hippolytus	Italy
1486	Seneca	unknown	unknown	Germany
1509	Seneca	Hippolytus	Phaedra	Italy
1526	Seneca	Thyestes	Thyestes	Germany
1543–47	Seneca	Hippolytus	Hippolytus	England
1551	Euripides/Seneca	Troas, Trojan Women	Troas	England
1552–53	Euripides/Seneca	Hippolytus	Hippolytus	England
1553–54	Euripides/Seneca	Medea	La Médée	France
1554	Seneca	Hippolytus	Hippolytus	Germany
1556	Seneca	Agamemnon	Agamemnon	France
1559	Euripides/Seneca	Hecuba	Hecuba or Troas	England
1559	Euripides/Seneca	Oedipus	Oedipus	England

Details	Language	Trans./Dir.	Source
Palais de Cardinal Saint Georges	Latin		APGRD
Performed in Rome by students of Pomponius Laetus	Latin	Dir. Pomponius Laetus	APGRD, Boas, Smith
Universität Leipzig	Latin		APGRD
Ferrara, under auspices of Cardinal Riario	Latin		APGRD, Jacquot
Wittenberg, students of Melanchthon	Latin	Prologue by Melanchthon	APGRD, Boas
Westminster School, London	Latin	Dir. Alexander Nowell	APGRD, Smith
Trinity College, Cambridge	Latin	Dir. Rudd	APGRD, Boas
King's College, Cambridge; not clear which version	unknown		APGRD
Paris; not clear which version	French	Adapted by Jean-Bastier de La Péruse and Scévole de Saint-Marie	APGRD, Delcourt
Wittenberg, university students	Latin	Prologue by Paul Eber	APGRD, Boas
Performance details uncertain	French	Charles Toustain	APGRD, Highet
Trinity College, Cambridge; not clear which version	Latin		APGRD, Boas, Smith
Trinity College, Cambridge; usually assumed to be Seneca's, but not certain	English	Probably Alexander Neville	APGRD, Boas, Smith

(continued)

Date	Author	Original Play	Title	Country
1560–61	Euripides/Seneca	Medea	Medea	England
1560–61	Euripides/Seneca	Troas, Trojan Women	Troas	England
1563	Euripides/Seneca	Medea	Medea	England
1566	Seneca	Agamemnon	Agamemnon	England
1572	Seneca	Medea	La Médée	France
1573	Euripides/Seneca	Hippolytus	Hippolyte	France
1577–92	Euripides/Seneca	Oedipus	Oedipus	England
1578	Seneca	Medea	Medea	France
1579	Euripides/Seneca	Troas, Trojan Women	La Troade	France
1584	Aeschylus	Agamemnon	Agamemnon and Ulysses	England
1584	Euripides/Seneca	Hecuba, Trojan Women	Polyxène	France
1588–90	Seneca	Octavia	Octavia	England
1592	Seneca	Hippolytus	Hippolytus	England

Details	Language	Trans./Dir.	Source
Trinity College, Cambridge; not clear which version	Latin		APGRD, Boas, Smith
Trinity College, Cambridge; not clear which version	Latin		APGRD, Boas, Smith
Queens College, Cambridge; not clear which version	Latin		APGRD, Boas
Performance details uncertain	English	Trans. John Studely	APGRD
Performance details uncertain	French	Trans. Jean Bastier de La Péruse	APGRD
Performance details uncertain	French	Adapted by Robert Garnier	APGRD
Adaptation by William Gager	Latin	Adapted by William Gager	APGRD, Boas
Strasbourg	Latin		APGRD
Performance details uncertain	French	Adapted by Robert Garnier	APGRD
"Presented and enacted before her maiestie by the Earle of Oxenford his boyes on St Iohns daie at night at Grenewich"	English	Adaptation	APGRD
Adaptation	French	Adaptation	APGRD
Christ Church College, Oxford	English		APGRD, Boas
Christ Church College, Oxford	English	Trans. Alexander Nowell, Dir. William Gager	APGRD, Boas

APPENDIX 7

Extant Greek Plays

Author	Play	Date (BCE)
Aeschylus	The Persians	472
Aeschylus	Seven Against Thebes	467
Aeschylus	The Suppliants	c.463
Aeschylus	Agamemnon	458
Aeschylus	Libation Bearers	458
Aeschylus	Eumenides	458
Aeschylus	Prometheus Bound	Uncertain
Sophocles	Trachiniae	Uncertain
Sophocles	Ajax	c.450–445
Sophocles	Antigone	c.441
Sophocles	Oedipus Tyrannus	c.429
Sophocles	Electra	c.410–406
Sophocles	Philoctetes	409
Sophocles	Oedipus at Colonus	c.406
Euripides	Alcestis	438
Euripides	Medea	431
Euripides	Heracleidae	c.430
Euripides	Hippolytus	428
Euripides	Andromache	c.425
Euripides	Hecuba	c.424
Euripides	The Suppliants	c.423
Euripides	Electra	c.420
Euripides	Heracles	c.416
Euripides	The Trojan Women	415
Euripides	Iphigenia in Tauris	c.414
Euripides	Ion	c.414

Author	Play	Date (BCE)
Euripides	Helen	412
Euripides	Phoenician Women	c.410
Euripides	Orestes	408
Euripides	Bacchae	405
Euripides	Iphigenia in Aulis	405
Euripides	Rhesus	Authorship disputed
Euripides	Cyclops	Date uncertain
Aristophanes	Acharnians	425
Aristophanes	Knights	424
Aristophanes	Clouds	423, revised 420–417
Aristophanes	Wasps	422
Aristophanes	Peace	421
Aristophanes	Birds	414
Aristophanes	Lysistrata	411
Aristophanes	Thesmophoriazusae	411
Aristophanes	Frogs	405
Aristophanes	Ecclesiazusae	c.392
Aristophanes	Plutus	408, revised 388

Bibliography

Abbott, D. M. "Buchanan, George (1506–1582)." *Oxford Dictionary of National Biography*. Oxford: Oxford University Press, 2004. Online edition, May 2006. Accessed Aug 18, 2016. http://www.oxforddnb.com/view/article/3837.

Adams, Barry. "The Audiences of *The Spanish Tragedy*." *Journal of English and Germanic Philology* 68 (1969), 221–36.

Adelman, Janet. *Suffocating Mothers*. New York and London: Routledge, 1992.

Aeschylus. *Choephoroi*. In *Septum Quae Supersunt Tragoedias*. Edited by Denys Page. 199–244. Oxford: Clarendon Press, 1972, 1975.

Agnew, Jean Christophe. *Worlds Apart: The Market and the Theater in Anglo-American Thought, 1550–1750*. Cambridge: Cambridge University Press, 1986.

Alexander, Michael Van Cleave. *The Growth of English Education, 1348–1648: A Social and Cultural History*. University Park: Pennsylvania State University Press, 1990.

Antinora, Sarah. "Please Let This be Much Ado About Nothing: 'Kill Claudio' and the Laughter of Release." *Cerae* 1 (2014), 1–21.

APGRD: The Archive of Performances of Greek and Roman Drama. http://www.apgrd.ox.ac.uk.

Archibald, Elizabeth. "'Deep clerks she dumbs': The Learned Heroine in *Apollonius of Tyre* and *Pericles*." *Comparative Drama* 22:4 (1988–89), 289–303.

Archibald, Elizabeth. *Apollonius of Tyre: Medieval and Renaissance Themes and Variations*. Woodbridge: Boydell and Brewer, 1991.

Archibald, Elizabeth. "Ancient Romance," in *A Companion to Romance from Classical to Contemporary*. Edited by Corinne Saunders. 10–25. Oxford: Wiley-Blackwell, 2004.

Aristophanes. *Komoidopoion aristu batrachoi. Inter comicos summi, ranae*. Basel: Johannes Froben, 1524.

Armstrong, Elizabeth. "English Purchases of Printed Books from the Continent, 1465–1526." *English Historical Review* 94 (1979), 268–90.

Ascham, Roger. *Toxophilus*. London: Edward Whitechurch, 1545.

Ascham, Roger. *The Scholemaster*. London: John Day, 1570.

Ascham, Roger. *The Whole Works of Roger Ascham*. Edited by J. A. Giles. 3 vols, vol. 1. London: J.R. Smith, 1864.

Ascham, Roger. "Roger Ascham to John Brandesby, Cambridge." In *English Historical Documents, 1458–1558*. Edited by C. H. Williams. 1070–1. Oxford: Oxford University Press, 1967.

Athenaeus, *The Deipnosophists*, ed. Charles Burton Gulick. 7 vols, vol. 4. London: William Heinemann, 1930.

Austen, Gillian. *George Gascoigne*. Cambridge: D. S. Brewer, 2008.

Axton, Marie. *The Queen's Two Bodies: Drama and the Elizabethan Succession.* London: Royal Historical Society, 1977.

Bakola, Emmanuella, Lucia Prauscello and Mario Telò. "Introduction: Greek Comedy as a Fabric of Generic Discourse." In *Greek Comedy and the Discourse of Genres.* Edited by Emmanuella Bakola, Lucia Prauscello and Mario Telò. 1–12. Cambridge: Cambridge University Press, 2013.

Baldwin, T. W. *William Shakspere's Small Latine and Lesse Greeke.* 2 vols. Urbana: University of Illinois Press, 1944.

Ballaster, Ros. "The First Female Dramatists." In *Women and Literature in Britain, 1500–1700.* Edited by Helen Wilcox. 267–73. Cambridge: Cambridge University Press, 1996.

Bamber, Linda. *Comic Women, Tragic Men: A Study of Gender and Genre in Shakespeare.* Palo Alto: Stanford University Press, 1982.

Bandello, Matteo, trans. *Ecuba: Tragedia di Euripide, Tradotta in verso Toscano da Matteo Bandello.* Rome: Nella stamperia De Romanis, 1813.

Bandello, Matteo. *Certaine Tragicall Discourses.* Translated by Geoffrey Fenton. London: Thomas Marshe, 1567.

Barish, Jonas. "*Bartholomew Fair* and its Puppets." *MLQ* 20 (1959), 3–17.

Barish, Jonas. *The Antitheatrical Prejudice.* Berkeley: University of California Press, 1981.

Barkan, Leonard. "'Living Sculptures': Ovid, Michelangelo, and *The Winter's Tale.*" *ELH* 48:4 (1981), 639–67.

Barker, Elton and Joel Christensen. "Even Heracles Had to Die: Homeric 'Heroism', Mortality and the Epic Tradition," *Trends in Classics* 6:2 (2014), 249–77.

Barker, Nicholas. *Aldus Manutius and the Development of Greek Script Type in the Fifteenth Century.* New York: Fordham University Press, 1992.

Barton, Anne. *Shakespeare and the Idea of the Play.* London: Chatto and Windus, 1962.

Bate, Jonathan. "The Performance of Revenge: *Titus Andronicus* and *The Spanish Tragedy.*" In *The Show Within: Dramatic and Other Insets: English Renaissance Drama (1550–1642).* Edited by Francois Laroque. 267–83. Montpellier: Paul-Valery University Press, 1990.

Bate, Jonathan. "Dying to Live in *Much Ado about Nothing.*" In *Surprised by Scenes: Essays in Honor of Professor Yasunai Takahashi.* Edited by Yasunari Takada. 69–85. Tokyo: Kenkyusha, 1994.

Bate, Jonathan. *Shakespeare and Ovid.* Oxford: Clarendon Press, 1994.

Bate, Jonathan. "In the Script Factory." *TLS,* 15 April 2003. 3–4.

Belle, Marie-Alice. "Locating Early Modern Women's Translations: Critical and Historiographical Issues." In *Women's Translations in Early Modern England and France.* Edited by Marie-Alice Belle. Special issue of *Renaissance & Reformation/Renaissance et Réforme* 34:5 (2012), 5–23.

Belsey, Catherine. *Shakespeare and the Loss of Eden.* Basingstoke: Palgrave, 2001.

Belsey, Catherine. "The Elephants' Graveyard Revisited: Shakespeare at Work in *Antony and Cleopatra, Romeo and Juliet* and *All's Well That Ends Well*." *Shakespeare Survey* 68 (2015), 62–72.

Benson, Sean. *Shakespearean Resurrections*. Pittsburgh: Duquesne University Press, 2009.

Bergeron, David M. "The Apollo Mission in *The Winter's Tale*." In *The Winter's Tale: Critical Essays*. Edited by Maurice Hunt. 361–79. New York: Garland, 1995.

Bevington, David. *From Mankind to Marlowe*. Cambridge, MA: Harvard University Press, 1962.

Bevington, David. "Jonson and Shakespeare: A Spirited Friendship." *Ben Jonson Journal* 23:1 (2016), 1–23.

Bicks, Caroline. "Backsliding at Ephesus: Shakespeare's Diana and the Churching of Women." In *Pericles: Critical Essays*. Edited by David Skeele. 205–27. Hove: Psychology Press, 2000.

Biggie, Roya. "Ecologies of the Passions in Early Modern English Tragedies." PhD diss., CUNY Graduate Center, 2016.

Billing, Christian M. "Lament and Revenge in the *Hekabe* of Euripides." *New Theatre Quarterly* 23:1 (2007), 49–57.

Bistué, Belén. *Collaborative Translation and Multi-Version Texts in Early Modern Europe*. Aldershot: Ashgate, 2013.

Bloom, Harold. *The Anxiety of Influence: A Theory of Poetry*. Oxford: Oxford University Press, 1973, 1997.

Blum, Abbe. "'Strike all that look upon with mar[b]le': Monumentalizing Women in Shakespeare's Plays." In *The Renaissance Englishwoman in Print: Counterbalancing the Canon*. Edited by Anne M. Haselkorn and Betty S. Travitsky. 99–118. Amherst: University of Massachusetts Press, 1990.

Blundell, Mary Whitlock. *Helping Friends and Harming Enemies*. Cambridge: Cambridge University Press, 1991.

Boas, Frederick S. *University Drama in the Tudor Age*. Oxford: Clarendon Press, 1914.

Bolgar, R. R. *The Classical Heritage and its Beneficiaries*. Cambridge: Cambridge University Press, 1954.

Bolgar, R. R. "Classical Reading in Renaissance Schools." *Durham Research Review* 6 (1955), 18–26.

Booth, Roy. "Hero's Afterlife: *Hero and Leander* and 'lewd unmannerly verse' in the late Seventeenth Century." *Early Modern Literary Studies* 12:3 (2007), 4.1–24.

Botley, Paul. *Learning Greek in Western Europe, 1396–1529: Grammars, Lexica, and Classroom Texts*. Philadelphia: American Philosophical Society, 2010.

Boyd, Brian. "Mutius: An Obstacle Removed in *Titus Andronicus*." *The Review of English Studies* 55:219 (2004), 196–209.

Braden, Gordon. *The Classics and English Renaissance Poetry*. New Haven, CT: Yale University Press, 1978.

Braden, Gordon. *Renaissance Tragedy and the Senecan Tradition*. New Haven, CT: Yale University Press, 1985.

Braden, Gordon. "Classical Greek Tragedy and Shakespeare." *Homer and Greek Tragedy in Early Modern England's Theatres*. Edited by Tania Demetriou and Tanya Pollard. Special issue of *Classical Receptions Journal* 9:1 (2017), 103–19.

Bradley, Beatrice, and Tanya Pollard, "Tragicomic Conceptions: *The Winter's Tale* as response to *Amphitryo*." *English Literary Renaissance* 47:2 (forthcoming, 2017).

Braun, Georg and Franz Mogenberg, ed. *Civitates Orbis Terrarum*, vol. 2. Cologne, 1575.

Bremer, J. M. "The popularity of Euripides' *Phoenissae* in Late Antiquity." In *Actes du VIIe Congrès de la Federation Internationale des Associations d'Études Classiques* 1 (1983), 281–8.

Brown, Allen Pamela. "The Counterfeit *Innamorata*, or, The Diva Vanishes." *Shakespeare Yearbook* 10 (1999), 402–26.

Brown, J. Howard. *Elizabethan Schooldays*. Oxford: Blackwell, 1933.

Brown, Pamela Allen. "'Cattle of this Colour': Boying the Diva in *As You Like It*." *Early Theatre* 15:1 (2012), 145–66.

Brown, Pamela Allen. "Dido, Boy Diva of Carthage." In *Transnational Mobilities in Early Modern Theater*. Edited by Robert Henke and Eric Nicholson. 113–30. Aldershot, Ashgate, 2014.

Brown, Pamela Allen. "Anatomy of an Actress: Bel-imperia as Tragic Diva." *Shakespeare Bulletin* 33:1 (2015), 49–65.

Bruce, John. *Liber Famelicus of Sir James Whitelocke*, vol. LXX. Camden Society, 1858.

Bruster, Douglas. *Drama and the Market in the Age of Shakespeare*. Cambridge: Cambridge University Press, 1992.

Bruster, Douglas. "Shakespearean Spellings and Handwriting in the Additional Passages Printed in the 1602 *Spanish Tragedy*." *Notes and Queries* 60:3 (2013), 420–4.

Bullough, Geoffrey, ed. *Narrative and Dramatic Sources of Shakespeare*. 8 vols. London: Routledge and Kegan Paul, 1961–1975.

Burrow, Colin. *Shakespeare and Classical Antiquity*. Oxford: Oxford University Press, 2013.

Bush, Douglas. *English Literature in the Earlier Seventeenth Century*. Oxford: Oxford University Press, 1945.

Bushnell, Rebecca. *A Culture of Teaching: Early Modern Humanism in Theory and Practice*. Ithaca, NY: Cornell University Press, 1996.

Butler, Martin. "The Auspices of Thomas Randolph's *Hey for Honesty, Down with Knavery*." *Notes and Queries*, n.s. 35 (1988), 491–2.

Bywater, Ingram. *Four Centuries of Greek Learning in England*. Oxford: Clarendon Press, 1919.

Calabresi, Bianca. "'Red Incke': Reading the Bleeding on the Early Modern Page." In *Printing and Parenting in Early Modern England*. Edited by Douglas A. Brooks. 237–64. Aldershot: Ashgate, 2005.

Calvo, Clara. "Thomas Kyd and the Elizabethan Blockbuster: *The Spanish Tragedy.*" In *The Cambridge Companion to Shakespeare and Contemporary Dramatists.* Edited by Ton Hoenselaars. 19–33. Cambridge: Cambridge University Press, 2012.

Carlson, Marvin. *The Haunted Stage: The Theatre as Memory Machine.* Ann Arbor: University of Michigan Press, 2001, 2003.

Cartelli, Thomas. "*Bartholomew Fair* as Urban Arcadia: Jonson Responds to Shakespeare." *Renaissance Drama* 14 (1983), 151–72.

Carter, Sarah. "*Titus Andronicus* and Myths Of Maternal Revenge." *Cahiers Élisabéthains* 77 (2010), 37–49.

Cartwright, Kent. *Theatre and Humanism: English Drama in the Sixteenth Century.* Cambridge: Cambridge University Press, 1999.

Castelvetro, Lodovico. *Castelvetro on the Art of Poetry.* Edited and translated by Andrew Bongiorno. Binghamton, NY: Medieval and Renaissance Texts & Studies, 1984.

Cerasano, S.P. and Marion Wynne-Davies, eds. *Readings in Renaissance Women's Drama: Criticism, History, and Performance 1594–1998.* London and New York: Routledge, 1998.

Chalk, Darryl. "'To Creep In At Mine Eyes': Theatre and Secret Contagion in *Twelfth Night.*" In *Rapt in Secret Studies: Emerging Shakespeares.* Edited by Darryl Chalk and Laurie Johnson. 171–94. Newcastle: Cambridge Scholars Publishing, 2010.

Chambers, E. K. *The Elizabethan Stage.* Oxford: Clarendon Press, 1923.

Chapman, George. *The Revenge of Bussy D'Ambois.* Edited by Robert J. Lordi. In *The Plays of George Chapman.* Edited by Allan Holaday. Cambridge: D. S. Brewer, 1987.

Charlton, Kenneth. *Education in Renaissance England.* London: Routledge, 1965.

Chatterley, Albert. "Watson, Thomas (1555/6–1592)." *Oxford Dictionary of National Biography.* Oxford: Oxford University Press, 2004. Online edition, Jan 2008. Accessed Aug 18, 2016. http://www.oxforddnb.com/view/article/28866.

Chaudhuri, Pramit. "Classical Quotation in *Titus Andronicus.*" *ELH* 81:3 (2014), 787–810.

Chernaik, Warren. "The Dyer's Hand: Shakespeare and Jonson." *The Cambridge Companion to Shakespeare and Contemporary Dramatists.* Edited by Ton Hoenselaars. 54–69. Cambridge: Cambridge University Press, 2012.

Chetwood, William. *The British Theater.* London: R. Baldwin, 1752.

Chetwood, William. *A General History of the Stage: From Its Origin in Greece Down to the Present Time.* London: W. Owen, 1749.

Ciccolella, Federica. *Donati Graeci: Learning Greek in the Renaissance.* Leiden: Brill, 2008.

Cicero, Marcus Tullius. *De Oratore.* Edited by E. W. Sutton and H. Rackham. 2 vols. Cambridge, MA: Harvard University Press, 1942, 1976–77.

Clare, Janet. *Shakespeare's Stage Traffic.* Cambridge: Cambridge University Press, 2014.

Clark, Donald Lemen. *John Milton at St. Paul's School: A Study of Ancient Rhetoric in English Renaissance Education.* New York: Columbia University Press, 1954.

Clarke, M. L. *Classical Education in Britain.* Cambridge: Cambridge University Press, 1959.

Clubb, Louise. *Italian Drama in Shakespeare's Time.* New Haven, CT: Yale University Press, 1992.

Clubb, Louise. "Intertextualities: Some Questions." In *The Italian World of English Renaissance Drama: Cultural Exchange and Intertextuality.* Edited by Michele Marrapodi and A. J. Hoenselaars. 179–89. Newark: University of Delaware Press, 1998.

Clubb, Louise. "Italian Stories on the Stage." In *The Cambridge Companion to Shakespearean Comedy.* Edited by Alexander Leggatt. 32–46. Cambridge: Cambridge University Press, 2001.

Clubb, Louise, ed. *Pollastra and the Origins of Twelfth Night.* Aldershot: Ashgate, 2010.

Coffin, Charlotte. "Théorie et pratique des mythes: les paradoxes de Thomas Heywood." *Revue de la Société d'Études Anglo-Américaines des XVIIe et XVIIIe Siècles* 60 (2005), 63–76.

Coffin, Charlotte. "The Gods' Lasciviousness, Or How to Deal With It? The Plight of Early Modern Mythographers." *Cahiers Élisabéthains* 81 (2012), 1–14.

Coffin, Charlotte. "Heywood's *Ages* and Chapman's Homer: Nothing in Common?" In *Homer and Greek Tragedy in Early Modern England's Theatres.* Edited by Tania Demetriou and Tanya Pollard. Special issue of *Classical Receptions Journal* 9:1 (2017), 55–78.

Collections of Statutes for the University and the Colleges of Cambridge. London: William Clowes, 1840.

Colley, John Scott. "*Bartholomew Fair*: Ben Jonson's *A Midsummer Night's Dream.*" *Comparative Drama* 11:1 (1977), 63–72.

Cook, Amy. "For Hecuba or for Hamlet: Rethinking Emotion and Empathy in the Theatre." *Journal of Dramatic Theory and Criticism* 25:2 (2011), 71–87.

Cooper, Lane. *The Poetics of Aristotle.* Ithaca, NY: Cornell University Press, 1923.

Craik, Katharine. *Reading Sensations in Early Modern England.* Basingstoke: Palgrave, 2007.

Craik, Katharine and Tanya Pollard, eds. *Shakespearean Sensations: Experiencing Literature in Early Modern England.* Cambridge: Cambridge University Press, 2013.

Crane, Frank D. "Euripides, Erasmus, and Lady Lumley." *The Classical Journal* 39:4 (1944), 223–8.

Crane, Mary Thomas. "Male Pregnancy and Cognitive Permeability in *Measure for Measure.*" *Shakespeare Quarterly* 49:3 (1998), 269–92.

Cratinus. "Fragment 342 K." In *Fragments of Old Comedy,* vol. 1: *Alcaeus to Diocles.* Edited and translated by Ian C. Storey, Loeb Classical Library. 413. Cambridge, MA: Havard University Press, 2011.

Crawford, Julie. "Women's Secretaries." In *Queer Renaissance Historiography.* Edited by Vin Nardizzi. Stephen Guy-Bray, and Will Stockton. 111–34. Burlington: Ashgate, 2008.

Crawford, Julie. *Mediatrix: Women, Politics, and Literary Production in Early Modern England.* Oxford: Oxford University Press, 2014.

Cressy, David. *Education in Tudor and Stuart England.* London: St. Martin's, 1976.

Cribiore, Raffaella. "The Grammarian's Choice: The Popularity of Euripides' *Phoenissae* in Hellenistic and Roman Education." In *Education in Greek and Roman Antiquity.* Edited by Yun Lee Too. 241–59. Leiden: Brill, 2001.

Croke, Richard. *Orationes.* Paris: Simon de Colines, 1520.

Cronk, Nicholas. "Aristotle, Horace, and Longinus: The Conception of Reader Response." In *The Cambridge History of Literary Criticism*, vol. 3: *The Renaissance.* Edited by Glyn Norton. 199–204. Cambridge: Cambridge University Press, 1999.

Csapo, Eric and Margaret Christina Miller. *The Origins of Theater in Ancient Greece and Beyond.* Cambridge: Cambridge University Press, 2007.

Cunliffe, John W. *Early English Classical Tragedies.* Oxford: Clarendon Press, 1912.

Cunliffe, John W. *The Influence of Seneca on Elizabethan Tragedy.* New York: G. E. Stechert & Co., 1925.

Curley, Dan. *Tragedy in Ovid: Theater, Metatheater, and the Transformation of a Genre.* Cambridge: Cambridge University Press, 2013.

"De tragoedia et comoedia," in *Tragoediae selectae AESCHYLI, SOPHOCLIS, EURIPIDIS.* 118–28. Geneva: Henricus Stephanus, 1567.

DEEP, Database of Early English Playbooks. http://deep.sas.upenn.edu.

Demers, Patricia. "On First Looking into Lumley's Euripides." *Renaissance and Reformation/Renaissance et Réforme* 23:1 (1999), 25–42.

Demers, Patricia. "'God may open more than man maye vnderstande': Lady Margaret Beaufort's Translation of the *De Imitatione Christi.*" *Renaissance & Reformation/Renaissance et Réforme* 35:4 (2012), 45–61.

Demetriou, Tania. "'Essentially Circe': Spenser, Homer and the Homeric Tradition." *Translation and Literature* 15:2 (2006), 151–76.

Demetriou, Tania. "'Strange appearance': The Reception of Homer in Renaissance England." PhD diss., University of Cambridge, 2008.

Demetriou, Tania. "Chapman's *Odysses* (1614-1615): Translation and Allegory." In *Homère à la Renaissance: Le Mythe et Ses Transfigurations.* Edited by Luisa Capodieci and Philip Ford. 245–60. Rome: Somogy/Académie de France à Rome, 2011.

Demetriou, Tania. "Periphrōn Penelope and her Early Modern Translations." In *The Culture of Translation in Early Modern England and France, 1500–1660.* Edited by Tania Demetriou and Rowan Tomlinson. 86–111. Basingstoke: Palgrave, 2015.

Demetriou, Tania and Tanya Pollard. "Homer and Greek Tragedy in Early Modern English Theatres: An Introduction." *Homer and Greek Tragedy in*

Early Modern England's Theatres. Edited by Tania Demetriou and Tanya Pollard. Special issue of *Classical Receptions Journal* 9:1 (2017), 1–35.

DeMolen, Richard L. "Richard Mulcaster and the Elizabethan Theatre." *Theatre Survey* 13 (1972), 28–41.

Dewar-Watson, Sarah. "Shakespeare's Dramatic Odysseys: Homer as a Tragicomic Model in *Pericles* and *The Tempest.*" *Classical and Modern Literature* 25:1 (2005), 23–40.

Dewar-Watson, Sarah. "Aristotle and Tragicomedy." In *Early Modern Tragicomedy.* Edited by Subha Mukherji and Raphael Lyne. 15–27. Suffolk: Boydell and Brewer, 2007.

Dewar-Watson, Sarah. "The *Alcestis* and the Statue Scene in *The Winter's Tale.*" *Shakespeare Quarterly* 60:1 (2009), 73–80.

Dewar-Watson, Sarah. "Jocasta: 'A Tragedie Written in Greek.'" *International Journal of the Classical Tradition* 17:1 (2010), 22–32.

Di Maria, Salvatore. "Italian Reception of Greek Tragedy." In *A Companion to Greek Tragedy.* Edited by Justina Gregory. 428–43. Oxford: Wiley-Blackwell, 2005.

Dick, Aliki Lafkadiou. *Paedeia Through Laughter: Jonson's Aristophanic Appeal to Human Intelligence.* The Hague: Mouton, 1974.

Dolce, Lodovico. *La Hecuba Tragedia di M. Lodovico Dolce, Tratta da Euripide.* Venetia: Gabriel Gioli di Ferrari, 1543.

Dolce, Lodovico. *Giocasta.* Venice: Aldi Filii, 1549.

Dolven, Jeff. *Scenes of Instruction in Renaissance Romance.* Chicago: University of Chicago Press, 2007.

Donald, Roslyn Lander. "Formulas and Their Imitations: *The Spanish Tragedy* and *Titus Andronicus.*" *Publications of the Arkansas Philological Association* 4:2 (1978), 13–18.

Draper, F. W. M. *Four Centuries of Merchant Taylors' School, 1561–1961.* London: Oxford University Press, 1962.

Driver, Tom F. "Release and Reconciliation: The *Alcestis* and *The Winter's Tale.*" In *The Sense of History in Greek and Shakespearean Drama.* 168–98. New York: Columbia University Press, 1960.

Duckworth, George E. "The Influence of Plautus and Terence upon English Comedy." In *The Nature of Roman Comedy: A Study in Popular Entertainment.* 396–441. Princeton: Princeton University Press, 1952.

Dunn, Leslie C. "Ophelia's Songs in Hamlet: Music, Madness, and the Feminine." In *Embodied Voices: Representing Female Vocality in Western Culture.* Edited by Leslie C. Dunn and Nancy A. Jones. 50–64. Cambridge: Cambridge University Press, 1994.

Dunworth, Felicity. *Mothers and Meaning on the Early Modern English Stage.* Manchester: Manchester University Press, 2010.

Dutton, Richard. "Jonson and Shakespeare: Oedipal Revenge." *Ben Jonson Journal* 23:1 (2016), 24–51.

Dyson, M. "Alcestis' Children and the Character of Admetus." *Journal of Hellenic Studies* 108 (1988), 13–23.

Elam, Keir. "The Fertile Eunuch: *Twelfth Night*, Early Modern Intercourse, and the Fruits of Castration." *Shakespeare Quarterly* 47:1 (1996), 1–36.

Elliott, Jr., John R. "Plays, Players, and Playwrights in Renaissance England." In *From Page to Performance: Essays in Early English Drama*. Edited by John A. Alford. 179–94. East Lansing: Michigan State University Press, 1995.

Elyot, Thomas. *The Boke Named the Governour*. London: Thomas Bertelet, 1531.

Elyot, Thomas. *The Dictionary of Syr Thomas Eliot Knyght*. London: Thomas Bertelet, 1538.

Enterline, Lynn. "'You Speak a Language that I Understand Not': The Rhetoric of Animation in *The Winter's Tale*." *Shakespeare Quarterly* 48:1 (1997), 17–44.

Enterline, Lynn. *The Rhetoric of the Body from Ovid to Shakespeare*. Cambridge: Cambridge University Press 2000.

Enterline, Lynn. *Shakespeare's Schoolroom: Rhetoric, Discipline, Emotion*. Philadelphia: University of Pennsylvania Press, 2011.

Erasmus. *A Ryght Frutefull Epistle*. Translated by Richard Tavernour. London: Robert Redman, 1536.

Erasmus. *Collected Works of Erasmus*, vol. 1. Translated by R. A. B. Mynors and D. F. S Thomson. Toronto: University of Toronto Press, 1974.

Erasmus. *Collected Works of Erasmus*, vol. 2. Translated by R. A. B. Mynors and D. F. S. Thomson. Toronto: University of Toronto Press, 1975.

Erasmus. *De Ratione Studii*. Translated by Brian McGregor. In *Collected Works of Erasmus*, vol. 24. Edited by Craig R. Thompson. 666–91. Toronto: University of Toronto Press, 1978.

Erasmus. *Collected Works of Erasmus*, vol. 6. Translated by R. A. B. Mynors and D. F. S Thomson. Toronto: University of Toronto Press, 1982.

Erne, Lukas. *Beyond The Spanish Tragedy: A Study of the Works of Thomas Kyd*. Manchester: Manchester University Press, 2001.

Erne, Lukas. *Shakespeare as Literary Dramatist*. Cambridge: Cambridge University Press, 2003.

Euripides. *Euripidou Medeia Hippolytos Alkestis Andromache*. Edited by J. Lascaris. Florence: Alopa, 1495.

Euripides. *Hecuba, & Iphigenia in Aulide Euripidis tragoediae in Latinum tralatae Erasmo*. Translated by Erasmus. Venice: Aldus, 1507.

Euripides. *Evripidis tragoediae dvae, Hercuba & Iphigenia in Aulide*. Translated by Erasmus. Basel: Joannes Froben, 1524.

Euripides. *Euripidis Alcestis*. Translated by George Buchanan. Paris: Michel de Vascosan, 1556.

Euripides. *Euripides Tragoediae XIX*. Translated by Aemilius Portus. Heidelberg: Commelinus, 1597.

Euripides. *Hecuba*. In *Euripidis Fabulae*, vol. 1. Edited by James Diggle. 333–98. Oxford: Oxford University Press, 1984.

Euripides. *Iphigenia in Aulis*. In *Euripidis Fabulae*, vol. 2. Edited by James Diggle 357–425. Oxford: Oxford University Press, 1984.

Euripides. *Medea*. In *Euripidis Fabulae*, vol. 1. Edited by James Diggle. 85–155. Oxford: Oxford University Press, 1984.

Euripides. *Phoenician Women*. Edited by E. M. Craik. Warminster: Aris & Phillips, 1988.

Euripides. *Phoenissae*. In *Euripidis Fabulae*, vol. 2. Edited by James Diggle. 71–179. Oxford: Clarendon Press, 1994.

Euripides. *Phoenissae*. Edited by Donald J. Mastronarde. Cambridge: Cambridge University Press, 1994.

Ewbank, Inga-Stina. "'Striking too short at Greeks': The Transmission of *Agamemnon* on the English Renaissance Stage." In Agamemnon *in Performance: 458 BC to AD 2004*. Edited by Fiona Macintosh, Pantelis Michelakis, Edith Hall, and Oliver Taplin. 37–52. Oxford: Oxford University Press, 2005.

Farley-Hills, David. *Shakespeare and the Rival Playwrights 1600–1606*. London and New York: Routledge, 1990.

Farmer, Alan B. "Cosmopolitanism and Foreign Books in Early Modern England." *Shakespeare Studies* 35 (2007), 58–65.

Farnham, Willard. *The Medieval Heritage of Elizabethan Tragedy*. Berkeley: University of California Press, 1936.

Feeney, Denis. *Beyond Greek: The Beginnings of Latin Literature*. Cambridge, MA: Harvard University Press, 2016.

Fehrenbach, Robert J., Elisabeth Leedham-Green, and Joseph L. Black, *Private Libraries in Renaissance England*. 9 vols. Binghamton, NY: Medieval & Renaissance Texts & Studies, 1992–2009.

Fenton, Geoffrey. "To the righte honorable and vertuous *Ladie, the Ladye Marye Sydney*." In Bandello, *Certaine Tragicall Discourses*, trans. Geoffrey Fenton (London: Thomas Marshe, 1567), ir–v.

Fienberg, Nona. "Jephthah's Daughter: The Part Ophelia Plays." In *Old Testament Women in Western Literature*. Edited by Raymond-Jean Frontain and Jon Wojcik. 128–43. Conway, AR: UCA Press, 1991.

Findlay, Alison. *Playing Spaces in Early Women's Drama*. Cambridge: Cambridge University Press, 2006.

Findlay, Alison and Stephanie Hodgson-Wright. "Introduction." In *Women and Dramatic Production, 1550–1700*. Edited by Alison Findlay and Stephanie Hodgson-Wright with Gweno Williams. 1–14. London: Routledge, 2000.

Floyd-Wilson, Mary. *Occult Knowledge, Science, and Gender on the Shakespearean Stage*. Cambridge: Cambridge University Press, 2013.

Foakes, R. A. "Tragedy at the Children's Theatres after 1600: A Challenge to the Adult Stage." In *The Elizabethan Theatre II*. Edited by David Galloway. 37–59. Toronto: Macmillan, 1970.

Foakes, R. A. and R. T. Rickert, eds. *Henslowe's Diary*. Cambridge: Cambridge University Press, 1961.

Foley, Helene P. "Marriage and Sacrifice in Euripides' *Iphigeneia in Aulis*." *Arethusa* 15:1/2 (1982), 159–80.

Foley, Helene P. "*Anodos* Dramas: Euripides' *Alcestis* and *Helen*." In *Innovations of Antiquity*. Edited by Ralph Hexter and Daniel Selden. 133–60. London: Routledge, 1992.

Foley, Helene P. *Female Acts in Greek Tragedy*. Princeton: Princeton University Press, 2001.

Foley, Helene P. "Generic Boundaries in Late Fifth-century Athens." In *Performance, Iconography, Reception: Studies in Honour of Oliver Taplin*. Edited by Martin Revermann and Peter Wilson, 15–36. Oxford: Oxford University Press, 2008.

Foley, Helene P. *Reimagining Greek Tragedy on the American Stage*. Berkeley: University of California Press, 2012.

Foley, Helene P. *Euripides: Hecuba*. London: Bloomsbury, 2014.

Forman, Valerie. *Tragicomic Redemptions: Global Economics and the Early Modern English Stage*. Philadelphia: University of Pennsylvania Press, 2008.

Förster, Max Th. W. "Gascoigne's Jocasta: A Translation from the Italian." *Modern Philology* 2:1 (1904), 147–50.

Fox, Cora. "Grief and Ovidian Politics of Revenge in *Titus Andronicus*." In *Ovid and the Politics of Emotion in Elizabethan England*. 105–24. Basingstoke: Palgrave Macmillan, 2009.

Fox-Good, Jacquelyn. "Ophelia's Mad Songs: Music, Gender, Power." In *Subjects on the World's Stage: Essays on British Literature of the Middle Ages and the Renaissance*. Edited by David C. Allen and Robert A. White. 217–38. Newark: University of Delaware Press, 1995.

Freeman, Arthur. *Thomas Kyd: Facts and Problems*. Oxford: Clarendon Press, 1967.

Freeman, James. "Hamlet, Hecuba, and Plutarch." *Shakespeare Studies* 7 (1974), 197–202.

Frischlinus, Nicodemus. "De Veteri Comoedia Eiusque Partibus." In *Aristophanes Veteris Comoediae Princeps*. 15v–19v. Frankfurt: Johann Spiess, 1586.

Gager, William. "In Iphigenia[m] Georgij Peeli Anglicanis Versibus Reddita[m]." In *The Life and Works of George Peele*. Edited by David H Horne. Vol. 1, 43. New Haven, CT: Yale University Press, 1952.

Gair, Reavley. *The Children of Paul's: The Story of a Theatre Company, 1553–1608*. Cambridge: Cambridge University Press, 1982.

Garland, Robert. *Surviving Tragedy*. London: Duckworth, 2004.

Gascoigne, George and Francis Kinwelmersh. *Jocasta: A Tragedie vvritten in Greke by Euripides*, in George Gascoigne, *A hundreth sundrie flowres bounde vp in one small poesie* London: Henrie Bynneman, 1573.

Gascoigne, George and Francis Kinwelmersh. *Jocasta*. In *Early English Classical Tragedies*. Edited by John W. Cunliffe. Oxford: Clarendon Press, 1912.

Gaunt, D. M. "Hamlet and Hecuba." *Notes and Queries* 16 (1969), 136–7.

Geanakoplos, Deno John. *Greek Scholars in Venice*. Cambridge, MA: Harvard University Press, 1962.

Gesner, Carol. *Shakespeare and the Greek Romance*. Lexington: University of Kentucky Press, 1970.

Ghose, Indira. *Shakespeare and Laughter: A Cultural History*. Manchester: Manchester University Press, 2008.

Gibson, Anthony. *A Womans Woorth, Defended Against all the Men in the World.* London, 1599.

Gibson, Strickland. *Abstracts from the Wills and Testamentary Documents of Binders, Printers, and Stationers of Oxford, from 1493 to 1638.* London, 1907.

Gibson, Strickland, ed. *Statuta Antiqua Universitatis Oxoniensis.* Oxford: Clarendon Press, 1931.

Gildenhard, Ingo and Martin Revermann, ed. *Beyond the Fifth Century: Interactions with Greek Tragedy from the Fourth Century BCE to the Middle Ages.* Berlin and New York: de Gruyter, 2010.

Giraldi Cinthio, Giovan Battista. *Discorsi di M. Giovambattista Giraldi Cinthio.* Ferrarra, 1554.

Giraldi Cinthio, Giovan Battista. *Altile Tragedia.* Venetia: Giulio Cesare Cagnacini, 1583.

Giraldi Cinthio, Giovan Battista. *Discourse or Letter on the Composition of Comedies and Tragedies.* Translated by Daniel Javitch. *Renaissance Drama* 39 (2011), 207–55.

Glasgow, Eric. "Greek in the Elizabethan Renaissance." *Salzburg Studies in English Literature* 71:2 (1981), 18–31.

Glasgow, Eric. "Some Early Greek Scholars in England." *Salzburg Studies in English Literature* 71:2 (1981), 3–17.

Goldhill, Simon. "Learning Greek is Heresy! Resisting Erasmus." In *Who Needs Greek?: Contests in the Cultural History of Hellenism.* 14–59. Cambridge: Cambridge University Press, 2002.

Goodland, Katharine. *Female Mourning in Medieval and Renaissance English Drama:From the Raising of Lazarus to King Lear.* Aldershot: Ashgate, 2006.

Goodrich, Jaime. "Returning to Lady Lumley's Schoolroom: Euripides, Isocrates, and the Paradox of Women's Learning." *Renaissance & Reformation/Renaissance et Réforme* 35:4 (2012), 97–117.

Gosson, Stephen. *Playes Confuted in Five Actions.* London: Thomas Gosson, 1582.

Gough, Melinda. "Jonson's Siren Stage." *Studies in Philology* 96:1 (1999), 68–95.

Gould, John. "Tragedy and Collective Experience." In *Tragedy and the Tragic: Greek Theatre and Beyond.* Edited by M. S. Silk. 217–43. Oxford: Clarendon Press, 1996.

Gounardiou, Kiki. *Euripides and Alcestis: Speculations, Stimulations, and Stories of Love in the Athenian Culture.* Lanham, MD: University Press of America, 1998.

Gourlay, Patricia. "Guilty Creatures Sitting at a Play: A Note on *Hamlet,* Act II, Scene 2." *Renaissance Quarterly* 24:2 (1971), 221–5.

Gower, John. *Confessio Amantis.* Edited by Russell A Peck. New York: Holt, Rinehart and Winston, 1968.

Grafton, Anthony and Lisa Jardine. *From Humanism to the Humanities: Education and the Liberal Arts in Fifteenth and Sixteenth-Century Europe.* London: Duckworth, 1986.

Grantley, Darryll. *Wit's Pilgrimage: Drama and the Social Impact of Education in Early Modern England.* Aldershot: Ashgate, 2000.

Green, A. Wigfall. *The Inns of Court and Early English Drama*. New Haven, CT: Yale University Press, 1931.

Green, Douglas E. "Interpreting 'Her Martyr'd Signs': Gender and Tragedy in *Titus Andronicus*." *Shakespeare Quarterly* 40:3 (1989), 317–26.

Greenblatt, Stephen. "Shakespeare and the Exorcists." In *Shakespeare and the Question of Theory*. Edited by Patricia Parker and Geoffrey Hartman. New York: Methuen, 1985.

Greene, Robert. *Pandosto*. London, 1588.

Greene, Robert. *Greenes Orpharion*. London: Edward White, 1599.

Greene, Thomas M. *The Light in Troy: Imitation and Discovery in Renaissance Poetry*. New Haven, CT: Yale University Press, 1982.

Gregory, Justina. "Comic Elements in Euripides." *Illinois Classical Studies* 24–5 (1999–2000), 59–74.

Grogan, Jane. "'Headless Rome' and Hungry Goths: Herodotus and *Titus Andronicus*." *English Literary Renaissance* 43:1 (2013), 30–60.

Gross, Kenneth. *The Dream of the Moving Statue*. Ithaca, NY: Cornell University Press, 1992.

Gross, Kenneth. *Shakespeare's Noise*. Chicago: University of Chicago Press, 2001.

Guépin, J. P. *The Tragic Paradox: Myth and Ritual in Greek Tragedy*. Amsterdam: Adolf M. Hakkert, 1968.

Gum, Coburn. *The Aristophanic Comedies of Ben Jonson*. The Hague: Mouton, 1969.

Hackett, Helen. "'Gracious be the issue': Maternity and Narrative in Shakespeare's Late Plays." In *Shakespeare's Late Plays: New Readings*. Edited by Jennifer Richards and James Knowles. 25–39. Edinburgh: University of Edinburgh Press, 1999.

Hagen, Tanya. "An English Renaissance Understanding of the Word 'Tragedy.'" In *Early Modern Literary Studies* 1 (1997), 5.1–30. Accessed September 1, 2014. http://purl.oclc.org/emls/si-01/si-01hagen.html.

Hall, Edith. "Greek Tragedy and the British Stage, 1566–1997." *Cahiers du Gita*, 12 (1999), 113–34.

Hall, Edith. "Towards a theory of performance reception." *Arion* 12:1 (2004), 51–89.

Hall, Edith and Stephe Harrop, eds. *Theorising Performance: Greek Drama, Cultural History, and Critical Practice*. London: Duckworth, 2010.

Hall, Edith and Fiona Macintosh. *Greek Tragedy and the British Theatre, 1660–1914*. Oxford: Oxford University Press, 2005.

Hall, Joseph. "The Honour of the Married Clergy Maintained." In *The Works of the Right Reverend Father in God, Joseph Hall*. Edited by Josiah Pratt. 10 vols. Vol. 9, 97–213. London: C. Whitingham, 1808.

Hanna, Sara. "From Illyria to Elysium: Geographical Fantasy in *Twelfth Night*." *Litteraria Pragensia* 12:23 (2002), 21–45.

Hanna, Sara. "Shakespeare's Greek World: The Temptations of the Sea." In *Playing the Globe: Genre and Geography in English Renaissance Drama*. Edited by John Gillies and Virginia Mason Vaughan. 107–28. Madison, NJ: Fairleigh Dickinson University Press, 1998.

Happe, Peter. *English Drama before Shakespeare*. London: Longman, 1999.

Harbage, Alfred, ed. *Annals of English Drama, 975–1700*. Revised. S. Schoenbaum. 3rd edn. Revised by Sylvia Stoler Wagonheim. London and New York: Routledge, 1989.

Hardin, Richard F. "*Menaechmi* and the Renaissance of Comedy." *Comparative Drama* 37:3,4 (2003–4), 255–74.

Hardin, Richard F. "Encountering Plautus in the Renaissance: A Humanist Debate on Comedy." *Renaissance Quarterly* 60:3 (2007), 789–818.

Hardin, Richard F. "England's *Amphitruo* before Dryden: The Varied Pleasures of Plautus's Template." *Studies in Philology*, 109:1 (2012), 45–62.

Hardwick, Lorna and Christopher Stray, eds. *A Companion to Classical Receptions*. Oxford: Blackwell, 2008.

Harriott, Rosemary. "Aristophanes' Audience and the plays of Euripides." *Bulletin of the Institute of Classical Studies* 9:1 (1962), 1–8.

Harrison, Tom. "'Thou art all licence, even licentiousness itself': Jonson, Euripides, and the Epistemological *Sparagmos* of *Bartholomew Fair*." Paper presented at Renaissance Society of America, March 31, 2016.

Hartman, Geoffrey. "Shakespeare's Poetical Character." In *Twelfth Night: New Casebooks*. Edited by R. S. White. New York: St. Martin's Press, 1996.

Harvey, Elizabeth D. *Ventriloquized Voices: Feminist Theory and English Renaissance Texts*. London: Routledge, 1992.

Haslem, Lori Schroeder. "'Troubled with the Mother': Longings, Purgings, and the Maternal Body in *Bartholomew Fair* and *The Duchess of Malfi*." *Modern Philology* 92:4 (1995), 438–59.

Haynes, Katharine. *Fashioning the Feminine in the Greek Novel*. London: Routledge, 2003.

Heavey, Katherine. The *Early Modern Medea*. London: Palgrave, 2015.

Heath, Malcolm. "Euripides' *Telephus*." *Classical Quarterly*, n.s. 37:2 (1987), 272–80.

Heath, Malcolm. "'Jure principem locum tenet': Euripides' *Hecuba*." *Bulletin of the Institute of Classical Studies* 34 (1987), 40–68.

Henderson, Diana E. "Mind the Gaps: The Ear, the Eye, and the Senses of a Woman in *Much Ado About Nothing*." In *Knowing Shakespeare*. Edited by Lowell Gallagher and Shankar Raman. 192–215. Basingstoke: Palgrave, 2010.

Henke, Robert. *Pastoral Transformations: Italian Tragicomedy and Shakespeare's Late Plays*. Newark: University of Delaware Press, 1997.

Henke, Robert and Eric Nicholson, eds. *Transnational Exchange in Early Modern Theater*. Aldershot: Ashgate, 2008.

Henke, Robert and Eric Nicholson, eds. *Transnational Mobilities in Early Modern Theater*. Aldershot: Ashgate, 2014.

Herendeen, Wyman H. *William Camden: A Life in Context*. Woodbridge: Boydell, 2007.

Herington, C. John. *Aeschylus*. New Haven, CT: Yale University Press, 1986.

Herodotus. *The Famous Hystory of Herodotus*. London: Thomas Marshe, 1584.

Herrick, Marvin T. *Tragicomedy: Its Origin and Development in Italy, France, and England*. Urbana: University of Illinois Press, 1955.

Heywood, Thomas. *Apology for Actors*. London: Nicholas Okes, 1612.

Hill, E. D. "Senecan and Vergilian Perspectives in *The Spanish Tragedy.*" *English Literary Renaissance* 15 (1985), 143–65.

Hillman, David. *Shakespeare's Entrails*. Basingstoke: Palgrave, 2007.

Hippocrates. "Diseases of Women 1." Translated by Ann Ellis Hanson. *Signs* 1:2 (1975), 567–84.

Hirsch, Rudolf. "The Printing Tradition of Aeschylus, Euripides, Sophocles and Aristophanes." *Gutenberg Jahrbuch* 39 (1964), 138–46.

Hirschfeld, Heather. *Joint Enterprises: Collaborative Drama and the Institutionalization of the English Renaissance Theater*. Amherst: University of Massachusetts Press, 2004.

Hobgood, Allison. *Passionate Playgoing in Early Modern England*. Cambridge: Cambridge University Press, 2014.

Hodgson-Wright, Stephanie. "Jane Lumley's *Iphigenia at Aulis*: Multum in parvo, or less is more." In *Readings in Renaissance Women's Drama: Criticism, History, and Performance 1594–1998*. Edited by S.P. Cerasano and Marion Wynne-Davies. 129–41. London and New York: Routledge, 1998.

Hoenselaars, Ton, ed. *The Cambridge Companion to Shakespeare and Contemporary Dramatists*. Cambridge: Cambridge University Press, 2012.

Homer, *Iliad*. Cambridge, MA: Harvard University Press, 1924.

Honig, Bonnie. *Antigone, Interrupted*. Cambridge: Cambridge University Press, 2013.

Holland, Peter. "Coasting in the Mediterranean: The Journeyings of *Pericles.*" In *Charting Shakespearean Waters: Text and Theatre*. Edited by Niels Bugge Hansen and Søs Haugaard. 11–30. Copenhagen: Museum Tusculanum Press, 2005.

Houlahan, Mark. "'Like To Th'Egyptian Thief': Shakespeare Sampling Heliodorus in *Twelfth Night.*" In *Rapt in Secret Studies: Emerging Shakespeares*. Edited by Darryl Chalk and Laurie Johnson. 305–17. Newcastle upon Tyne: Cambridge Scholars, 2010.

Howard, Tony. *Women as Hamlet: Performance and Interpretation in Theatre, Film and Fiction*. Cambridge: Cambridge University Press, 2007.

Hoxby, Blair. "The Doleful Airs of Euripides: The Origins of Opera and the Spirit of Tragedy Reconsidered." *Cambridge Opera Journal* 17:3 (2005), 253–69.

Huet, Marie-Hélène. *Monstrous Imagination*. Cambridge, MA: Harvard University Press, 1993.

Hughes, Dennis D. *Human Sacrifice in Ancient Greece*. London: Routledge, 1991.

Hunt, Cameron. "Jephthah's Daughter's Daughter: Ophelia." *ANQ* 22:4 (2009), 13–16.

Hunt, Maurice. "'Bearing Hence': Shakespeare's *The Winter's Tale.*" *SEL: Studies in English Literature 1500–1900* 44:2 (2004), 333–46.

Hunt, Maurice. "Shakespeare's *Twelfth Night* and 'The Pregnant Enemy': The Devil in *What You Will.*" *The Upstart Crow: A Shakespeare Journal* 30 (2011), 5–17.

Hunter, G. K. "Elizabethan Theatrical Genres and Literary Theory." In *The Cambridge History of Literary Criticism*, vol. 3: *The Renaissance*. Edited by Glyn Norton. 248–58. Cambridge: Cambridge University Press, 1999.

Ionesco, Eugene. *La Cantatrice Chauve*. In Eugéne Ionesco, *Théâtre*. Edited by Jacques Lemarchand. 21–57. Paris: Gallimard, 1954.

Irish, Bradley, J. "Vengeance, Variously: Revenge before Kyd in Early Elizabethan Drama." *Early Theatre* 12:2 (2009), 117–34.

Jackson, Macdonald P. "Stage Directions and Speech Headings in Act 1 of *Titus Andronicus* Q (1594): Shakespeare or Peele?." *Studies in Bibliography* 49 (1996), 134–48.

James, Heather. *Shakespeare's Troy*. Cambridge: Cambridge University Press, 1997.

James, Heather. "Dido's Ear: Tragedy and the Politics of Response." *Shakespeare Quarterly* 52:3 (2001), 360–82.

James, Heather. "Shakespeare, the Classics, and the Forms of Authorship." *Shakespeare Studies* 36 (2008), 80–9.

Jardine, Lisa. "Humanism and the Sixteenth Century Cambridge Arts Course." *History of Education* 4:1 (1975), 16–31.

Jauss, Hans. *Toward an Aesthetic of Reception*. Translated by Timothy Bahti. Minneapolis: University of Minnesota Press, 1982.

Javitch, Daniel. "Introduction to Giovan Battista Giraldi Cinthio's *Discourse or Letter on The Composition of Comedies and Tragedies*." *Renaissance Drama* 39 (2011), 197–206.

Jayne, Sears and Francis R. Johnson, eds. *The Lumley Library: The Catalogue of 1609*. London: Trustees of the British Museum, 1956.

Jenkyns, Richard. "United Kingdom." In *A Companion to the Classical Tradition*. Edited by Craig W. Kallendorf. 265–78. Oxford: Blackwell, 2007.

Jervis, Swynfen. *A Dictionary of the Language of Shakspeare*. London: John Russell Smith, 1868.

Jones, Emrys. *The Origins of Shakespeare*. Oxford: Clarendon Press, 1977.

Jones, John. *A Briefe, Excellent, and Profitable Discourse, of the Naturall Beginning of all Growing and Liuing Things*. London: William Iones, 1574.

Jones, John. *The Arte and Science of Preseruing Bodie and Soule*. London: Henrie Bynneman, 1579.

Jones, Michael K. and Malcolm G. Underwood. *The King's Mother: Lady Margaret Beaufort, Countess of Richmond and Derby*. Cambridge: Cambridge University Press, 1993.

Jonson, Ben. "To the Memory of My Beloved, the Author, Mr. William Shakespeare." In *Mr. William Shakespeares Comedies, Histories, & Tragedies*. A44–A4v. London: Jaggard and Blount, 1623.

Jonson, Ben. *Bartholomew Fair*. Edited by Suzanne Gossett, Revels Plays. Manchester: Manchester University Press, 2000.

Jonson, Ben. *The Alchemist*. Edited by Peter Holland and William Sherman. In *The Cambridge Edition of the Works of Ben Jonson*. Edited by David Bevington, Martin Butler, and Ian Donaldson, vol. 3: *1606–1611*. 541–710. Cambridge: Cambridge University Press, 2012.

Jonson, Ben. *Bartholomew Fair*. Edited by John Creaser. In *The Cambridge Edition of the Works of Ben Jonson*. Edited by David Bevington, Martin Butler, and Ian Donaldson, vol. 4: *1611–1616* 271–428. Cambridge: Cambridge University Press, 2012.

Jonson, Ben. *Discoveries*. Edited by Lorna Hutson. In *The Cambridge Edition of the Works of Ben Jonson*, vol. 7. Edited by David Bevington, Martin Butler, and Ian Donaldson. 481–596. Cambridge: Cambridge University Press, 2012.

Jonson, Ben. *Every Man In his Humor*. Edited by David Bevington. In *The Cambridge Edition of the Works of Ben Jonson*. Edited by David Bevington, Martin Butler, and Ian Donaldson, vol. 1: *1597–1601* 111–227. Cambridge: Cambridge University Press, 2012.

Jonson, Ben. *Poetaster*. Edited by Gabriele Bernhard Jackson, in *The Cambridge Edition of the Works of Ben Jonson*. Edited by David Bevington, Martin Butler, and Ian Donaldson, vol. 2: 1601–1606 1–181. Cambridge: Cambridge University Press, 2012.

Juneja, Renu. "Eve's Flesh and Blood in Jonson's *Bartholomew Fair*." *Comparative Drama* 12:4 (1978–79), 340–55.

Juric, Lea Puljcan. "Illyrians in *Cymbeline*." *English Literary Renaissance* 42:3 (2012), 425–51.

Kahn, Coppelia. *Roman Shakespeare: Warriors, Wounds, and Women*. London: Routledge, 1997.

Keith, Alison. "Dionysiac Theme and Dramatic Allusion in Ovid's *Metamorphoses* 4." In *Beyond the Fifth Century: Interactions with Greek Tragedy from the Fourth Century BCE to the Middle Ages*. Edited by Ingo Gildenhard and Martin Revermann. 187–217. Berlin and New York: de Gruyter, 2010.

Kelliher, Hilton. "Francis Beaumont and Nathan Field: New Records of their Early Years." *English Manuscript Studies 1100–1700*, 8 (2000), 1–42.

Kenward, Claire. "Sights to make an Alexander? Reading Homer on the Early Modern Stage." In *Homer and Greek Tragedy in Early Modern England's Theatres*. Edited by Tania Demetriou and Tanya Pollard. Special issue of *Classical Receptions Journal* 9:1 (2017), 79–102.

Kerrigan, John. *Revenge Tragedy: Aeschylus to Armageddon*. Oxford: Clarendon Press, 1996.

Kietzman, Mary Jo. " 'What Is Hecuba to Him or [S]he to Hecuba?' Lucrece's Complaint and Shakespearean Poetic Agency." *Modern Philology* 97:1 (1999), 21–45.

Kinney, Arthur F. "Shakespeare's *Comedy of Errors* and the Nature of Kinds." *Studies in Philology* 85:1 (1988), 29–52.

Knapp, Robert S. "The Academic Drama." In *A Companion to Renaissance Drama*. Edited by Arthur F. Kinney. 257–65. Oxford: Blackwell, 2002.

Knight, Sarah. " 'Goodlie anticke apparrell?': Sophocles' *Ajax* at Early Modern Oxford and Cambridge." *Shakespeare Studies* 38 (2009), 25–42.

Knight, Sarah et al., eds. *The Intellectual and Cultural World of the Early Modern Inns of Court*. Manchester: Manchester University Press, 2011.

Knox, B. M. W. "Euripidean Comedy." In *The Rarer Action: Essays in Honor of Francis Fergusson*. Edited by Alan Cheuse and Richard Koffler. 68–96. New Brunswick, NJ: Rutgers University Press, 1970.

Knox, B. M. W. "The *Medea* of Euripides." *Yale Classical Studies* 25 (1977), 197–202.

Korda, Natasha. *Labors Lost: Women's Work and the Early Modern English Stage.* Philadelphia: University of Pennsylvania Press, 2011.

Kortekaas, G. A. A. *The Story of Apollonius, King of Tyre: A Study of Its Greek Origin and an Edition of the Two Oldest Latin Recensions.* Leiden: Brill, 2004.

Kos, Marjeta Šašel. "Cadmus and Harmonia in Illyria." *Arheološki vestnik* 44 (1993), 113–36.

Kos, Marjeta Šašel. "Mythological stories concerning Illyria and its name." In *L'Illyrie Méridionale et l'Épire dans l'Antiquité* IV. Edited by Pierre Cabanes and Jean-Luc Lamboley. 493–504. Paris: De Baccard, 2004.

Kott, Jan. "Hamlet and Orestes." Translated by Boleslaw Taborski. *PMLA* 82:5 (1967), 303–13.

Krappe, Alexander Haggerty. "Euripides' *Alcmaeon* and the *Apollonius Romance.*" *Classical Quarterly* 18:2 (1924), 57–8.

Kyd, Thomas. *The Works of Thomas Kyd.* Edited by Frederick S. Boas. Oxford: Clarendon Press, 1901, 1962.

Kyd, Thomas. *The Spanish Tragedy.* Edited by Clara Calvo and Jesús Tronch. Arden Early Modern Drama. London: Bloomsbury, 2013.

Larmour, David. "Tragic *Contaminatio* in Ovid's *Metamorphoses.*" *ICS* 15:1 (1990), 131–41.

Lazarus, Micha. "Greek Literacy in Sixteenth-Century England." *Renaissance Studies* 20:3 (2015), 433–58.

Lazarus, Micha. "Sidney's Greek Poetics." *Studies in Philology* 112:3 (2015), 504–36.

Leach, Arthur F. *Educational Charters and Documents 598–1909.* Cambridge: Cambridge University Press, 1911.

Leedham-Green, Elisabeth. *Books in Cambridge Inventories.* Cambridge: Cambridge University Press, 1986.

Lefkowitz, Mary R. *Women in Greek Myth.* Baltimore: Johns Hopkins University Press, 1986.

Lefteratou, Anna. "Myth and Narrative in the Greek Novel." PhD diss., University of Oxford, 2010.

Lefteratou, Anna, "Iphigenia revisited: Heliodorus' *Aethiopica and* the 'Der Tod und das Mädchen' pattern." In *Intende, Lector—Echoes of Myth, Religion and Ritual in the Ancient Novel.* Edited by Marília P. Futre Pinheiro, Anton Bierl, and Roger Beck, 200–22. Berlin: de Gruyter, 2013.

Levin, Richard. "Gertrude's Elusive Libido and Shakespeare's Unreliable Narrators." *SEL* 48:2 (2008), 305–26.

Levine, Laura. *Men in Women's Clothing: Anti-theatricality and Effeminization, 1579–1642.* Cambridge: Cambridge University Press, 1994.

Liebler, Naomi Conn. "Getting it all Right: *Titus Andronicus* and Roman History." *Shakespeare Quarterly* 45:3 (1994), 263–78.

Liebler, Naomi Conn, ed. *The Female Tragic Hero in English Renaissance Drama.* Basingstoke: Palgrave, 2002.

Lodge, Thomas. *A Reply to Stephen Gosson's School of Abuse, in Defence of Poetry, Music, and Stage Plays*. London, 1579.

Logan, F. Donald. "The Origins of the So-called Regius Professorships: An Aspect of the Renaissance in Oxford and Cambridge." In *Renaissance and Renewal in Christian History*. Edited by Derek Baker. 271–8. Oxford: Oxford University Press, 1977.

Logan, F. Donald. "The First Royal Visitation of the English Universities, 1535." In *English Historical Review* 106 (1991), 861–88.

Longinus. *On the Sublime*. Edited by William Rhys Roberts. Cambridge: Cambridge University Press, 1907.

Longo, Odonne. "The Theater of *Polis*." In *Nothing to Do with Dionysos?: Athenian Drama in Its Social Context*. Edited by John Winkler and Froma Zeitlin. 12–19. Princeton: Princeton University Press, 1990.

Loraux, Nicole. *Tragic Ways of Killing a Woman*. Translated by Antony Foster. Cambridge: Cambridge University Press, 1987.

Loraux, Nicole. *Mothers in Mourning*. Translated by Corinne Pache. Ithaca, NY: Cornell University Press, 1998.

Louden, Bruce. "Reading through *The Alcestis* to *The Winter's Tale*." *Classical and Modern Literature* 27:2 (2007), 7–30.

Louden, Bruce. "Telemachos, The *Odyssey* and *Hamlet*." *Text & Presentation* 11 (2014), 33–50.

Lumley, Jane. *Iphigenia in Aulis*. Edited by Harold Child. London: Malone Society Reprints, 1909.

Machiavelli, Niccolò. "Niccolo Machiavelli to Francesco Vettori, Florence, December 10, 1513." In *Machiavelli and His Friends: Their Personal Correspondence*. Translated by James B. Atkinson and David Sices. 262–5. DeKalb: Northern Illinois University Press, 1996.

McConica, James. "The Rise of the Undergraduate College." In *The History of the University of Oxford*. Vol. 3 of *The Collegiate University*. Edited by James McConica. 1–68. Oxford: Oxford University Press, 1986.

McDonald, Marianne. "Cacoyannis and Euripides' *Iphigenia at Aulis*: A New Heroism." In *Euripides in Cinema: The Heart Made Visible*. 129–92. Philadelphia: Centrum, 1983.

McDonald, Marianne. "Iphigenia's '*Philia*': Motivation in Euripides' *Iphigenia at Aulis*." *Quaderni Urbinati di Cultura Classica* 34:1 (1990), 69–84.

McDonald, Russ. "Jonsonian Comedy and the Value of *Sejanus*." *Studies in English Literature, 1500–1900* 21:2 (1981), 287–305.

McDonnell, Michael. *The Annals of St. Paul's School*. Cambridge: Cambridge University Press, 1959.

McEvoy, Sean. "Hieronimo's Old Cloak: Theatricality and Representation in Ben Jonson's Middle Comedies." *Ben Jonson Journal* 11 (2004), 67–87.

McGrail, Mary Ann, ed. *Shakespeare's Plutarch. Poetica: An International Journal of Linguistic-Literary Studies* 48 (1997).

McJannet, Linda. "Genre and Geography: The Eastern Mediterranean in *Pericles* and *The Comedy of Errors*." In *Playing the Globe: Genre and Geography in English*

Renaissance Drama. Edited by John Gillies and Virginia Mason Vaughan. 86–106. Madison, NJ: Fairleigh Dickinson University Press, 1998.

McManaway, James G. "Ophelia and Jephtha's Daughter." *Shakespeare Quarterly* 21:2 (1970), 198–200.

McManus, Clare. *Women on the Renaissance Stage: Anna of Denmark and Female Masquing in the Stuart Court (1590–1619)*. Manchester: Manchester University Press, 2002.

McMillin, Scott. "The Book of Seneca in The Spanish Tragedy." *Studies in English Literature, 1500–1900* 14:2 (1974), 201–8.

Macintosh, Fiona. *Dying Acts: Death in Ancient Greek and Modern Irish Tragic Drama*. Cork: Cork University Press, 1994.

Macintosh, Fiona. "Performance Histories." In *A Companion to Classical Receptions*. Edited by Lorna Hardwick and Christopher Stray. 247–58. Oxford: Blackwell, 2008.

Macintosh, Fiona, and Amanda Wrigley, eds. *Dionysus Since 69: Greek Tragedy at the Dawn of the Third Millenium*. Oxford: Oxford University Press, 2004.

Maguire, Laurie. "The Girls from Ephesus." In *The Comedy of Errors: Critical Essays*. Edited by Robert S. Miola. 355–91. New York: Routledge, 1997.

Maguire, Laurie. *Shakespeare's Names*. Oxford: Oxford University Press, 2007.

Maguire, Laurie and Emma Smith. "What Is A Source? Or, How Shakespeare Read His Marlowe." *Shakespeare Survey* 68 (2015), 15–31.

Mahaffy, J. P. *Euripides*. London, 1879.

Manutius, Aldus. "Epistolam ad Catherina Piam." In *Musarum Panegyris*. Venice: Baptista de Tortis, 1487–91.

Marcus, Leah S. *Puzzling Shakespeare*. Berkeley and Los Angeles: University of California Press, 1988.

Marlowe, Christopher. *Hero and Leander*. In *The Poems*. Edited by Millar Maclure. 1–103. London: Methuen & Co, 1968.

Marlowe, Christopher. *The Jew of Malta*. In *The Complete Works of Christopher Marlowe*. Vol. 4. Edited by Roma Gill. 3–85. Oxford: Clarendon Press, 1995.

Marlowe, Christopher. *Tamburlaine the Great, Part I*. Edited by David Fuller. In *The Complete Works of Christopher Marlowe*. Vol 5. 3–77. Edited by Edward J. Esche. Oxford: Clarendon Press, 1998.

Marrapodi, Michele, ed. *Italian Culture in the Drama of Shakespeare and His Contemporaries*. Aldershot: Ashgate, 2007.

Marston, John. *The Malcontent*. Edited by G. K. Hunter. Revels Edition. Manchester: Manchester University Press, 1975, 1999.

Martin, Randall. "Rediscovering Artemis in *The Comedy of Errors*." *Shakespeare and the Mediterranean*. Edited by Tom Clayton, Susan Brock, and Vicente Fores. 363–79. Newark: University of Delaware Press, 2004.

Martindale, Charles. *Redeeming the Text: Latin Poetry and the Hermeneutics of Reception*. Cambridge: Cambridge University Press, 1993.

Martindale, Charles and Richard Thomas, eds. *Classics and the Uses of Reception*. Oxford: Blackwell, 2006.

Mastronarde, Donald J. *The Art of Euripides: Dramatic Technique and Social Context*. Cambridge: Cambridge University Press, 2010.

Mastronarde, Donald J, ed. "Stiblinus' Prefaces and Arguments on Euripides (1562)." http://ucbclassics.dreamhosters.com/djm/stiblinus/stiblinusMain.html. Accessed August 7, 2015.

Maus, Katharine Eisaman. "A Womb of His Own: Male Renaissance Poets in the Female Body." In *Sexuality and Gender in Early Modern Europe*. Edited by James Grantham Turner. 266–88. Cambridge: Cambridge University Press, 1993.

Meek, Richard. "'O, what a sympathy of woe is this': Passionate Sympathy in *Titus Andronicus*." *Shakespeare Survey* 66 (2013), 287–97.

Mellows, William Thomas, ed. *Peterborough Local Administration, The Foundation of Peterborough Cathedral, A.D. 1541. The Publications of the Northamptonshire Record Society*. 13 (1941).

Mentz, Steve. *Romance for Sale in Early Modern England: The Rise of Prose Fiction*. Aldershot: Ashgate, 2006.

Mentz, Steve. *At the Bottom of Shakespeare's Ocean*. London: Continuum, 2009.

Meres, Francis. *Palladis Tamia*. London: Cuthbert Burbie, 1598.

Meskill, Lynn S. *Ben Jonson and Envy*. Cambridge: Cambridge University Press, 2009.

Micyllus, Jacobus. "De Tragoedia et Eivs Partibus προλεγομενα." In *Evripides Poeta Tragicorum princeps*. 671–9. Basel: Johannes Oporinus, 1562.

Miller, Harold W. "Euripides' *Telephus* and the *Thesmophoriazusae* of Aristophanes." *Classical Philology* 43:3 (1948), 174–83.

Milne, Kirsty. "The Forgotten Greek Books of Elizabethan England." *Literature Compass* 4:3 (2007), 677–87.

Miola, Robert S. "*Titus Andronicus* and the Mythos of Shakespeare's Rome." *Shakespeare Studies* 14 (1981), 85–98.

Miola, Robert S. "Aeneas and Hamlet." *Classical and Modern Literature* 8:4 (1988), 275–90.

Miola, Robert S. *Shakespeare and Classical Tragedy: The Influence of Seneca*. Oxford: Clarendon Press, 1992.

Miola, Robert S. *Shakespeare and Classical Comedy: The Influence of Plautus and Terence*. Oxford: Clarendon Press, 1994.

Miola, Robert S. *Shakespeare's Reading*. Oxford: Oxford University Press, 2000.

Miola, Robert S. "Euripides at Gray's Inn: Gascoigne and Kinwelmersh's *Jocasta*." In *The Female Tragic Hero in English Renaissance Drama*. Edited by Naomi Liebler. 33–50. Basingstoke: Palgrave, 2002.

Miola, Robert S. "Aristophanes in England, 1500–1660." In *Ancient Comedy and Reception: Essays in Honor of Jeffrey Henderson*. Edited by S. Douglas Olson. 479–502. Berlin: De Gruyter, 2014.

Miola, Robert S. "Early Modern Antigones: Receptions, Refractions, Replays." *Classical Receptions Journal* 6:2 (2014), 221–44.

Mirabella, Bella. "'Embellishing Herself with a Cloth': The Contradictory Life of the Handkerchief." In *Ornamentalism: The Art of Renaissance Accessories*. Edited by Bella Mirabella. 59–82. Ann Arbor: University of Michigan Press, 2011.

Montiglio, Silvia. "The Call Of Blood: Greek Origins Of A Motif, From Euripides To Heliodorus." *Syllecta Classica* 22 (2011), 113–29.

Montiglio, Silvia. *Love and Providence: Recognition in the Ancient Novel.* Oxford: Oxford University Press, 2013.

More, Thomas. "To Oxford University." In *Sir Thomas More: Selected Letters.* Edited by Elizabeth Frances Rogers. 94–103. New Haven, CT: Yale University Press, 1961.

Mosley, Charles, ed. *Burke's Peerage, Baronetage & Knightage.* 107th edition. 3 vols. Wilmington, Delaware: Genealogical Books Ltd, 2003.

Mossman, Judith. *Wild Justice: A Study of Euripides'* Hecuba. Oxford: Clarendon Press, 1995.

Motter, T. H. Vail. *The School Drama in England.* London: Longmans, 1929.

Mueller, Martin. *Children of Oedipus and Other Essays on the Imitation of Greek Tragedy 1550–1800.* Toronto: University of Toronto Press, 1980.

Mueller, Martin. "Shakespeare's Sleeping Beauties: The Sources of *Much Ado about Nothing* and the Play of Their Repetitions." *MP* 91:3 (1994): 288–311.

Mueller, Martin. "*Hamlet* and the World of Ancient Tragedy." *Arion* 5:1 (1997), 22–45.

Mulcaster, Richard. *Positions.* London: Thomas Vautrollier, 1581.

Mullaney, Steven. "Mourning and Misogyny: *Hamlet, The Revenger's Tragedy,* and the Final Progress of Elizabeth I, 1600–1607." *Shakespeare Quarterly* 45:2 (1994), 139–62.

Munro, Lucy. *Children of the Queen's Revels: A Jacobean Theatre Repertory.* Cambridge: Cambridge University Press, 2005.

Munro, Lucy. "Shakespeare and the Uses of the Past: Critical Approaches and Current Debates." *Shakespeare* 7:1 (2011), 102–25.

Munro, Lucy. *Archaic Style in English Literature, 1590–1674.* Cambridge: Cambridge University Press, 2013.

Murray, Gilbert. *Hamlet and Orestes: A Study in Traditional Types.* Oxford: Oxford University Press, 1914.

Nardizzi, Vin. "'No Wood, No Kingdom': Planting Genealogy, Felling Trees, and the Additions to *The Spanish Tragedy.*" *Modern Philology* 110:2 (2012), 202–25.

Nashe, Thomas. *The Works of Thomas Nashe.* Edited by R. B. McKerrow. Revised by. F. P. Wilson. 5 vols. Oxford: Blackwell, 1958.

Nelson, Alan H., ed. *Records of Early English Drama:Cambridge.* Toronto: University of Toronto Press, 1989.

Nelson, Alan H. "The Universities and the Inns of Court." In *The Oxford Handbook to Early Modern Theatre.* Edited by Richard Dutton. 280–91. Oxford: Oxford University Press, 2009.

Nelson, Alan H. "New Light on Drama, Music, and Dancing at the Inns of Court to 1642." In *The Intellectual and Cultural World of the Early Modern Inns of Court.* Edited by Jayne Archer, Elizabeth Goldring, and Sarah Knight. 302–14. Manchester: Manchester University Press, 2011.

Newman, J. K. "Small Latine and Lesse Greeke? Shakespeare and the Classical Tradition." *Illinois Classical Studies* 9:2 (1984), 309–30.

Nicholson, Eric. "Ophelia Sings Like a *Prima Donna Innamorata*: Ophelia's Mad Scene and the Italian Female Performer." In *Transnational Exchange in Early Modern Theater*. Edited by Robert Henke and Eric Nicholson. 81–98. Aldershot: Ashgate, 2008.

Norland, Howard. *Neoclassical Tragedy in Elizabethan England*. Newark: University of Delaware Press, 2009.

Norton, Thomas and Thomas Sackville. *Gorboduc* (1561). In *Early English Classical Tragedies*, ed. John W. Cunliffe. Oxford: Clarendon Press, 1912.

Nuttall, A. D. "Action at a Distance: Shakespeare and the Greeks." In *Shakespeare and the Classics*. Edited by Charles Martindale and A. B. Taylor. 209–22. Cambridge: Cambridge University Press, 2004.

Ostovich, Helen. "The Aristophanic Mode." In Ben Jonson, *Every Man Out of His Humour*. Edited by Helen Ostovich. 18–28. Manchester: Manchester University Press, 2001.

Ovid. *The XV books of P. Ovidius Naso, Entitled Metamorphoses*. Translated by Arthur Golding. London: William Seres, 1567.

Owens, Rebekah. "Parody and *The Spanish Tragedy*." *Cahiers Élisabéthains* 71 (2007), 27–36.

Pache, Corinne. "Theban Walls in Homeric Epic." *Trends in Classics* 6:2 (2014), 278–96.

Padel, Ruth. "Women: Model for Possession by Greek Daemons." In *Images of Women in Antiquity*. Edited by Averil Cameron and Amélie Kuhrt. 3–19. London: Routledge, 1983.

Panoussi, Vassiliki. "Polis and Empire: Greek Tragedy in Rome." In *A Companion to Greek Tragedy*. Edited by Justina Gregory. 413–27. Oxford: Blackwell, 2005.

Papadopolou, Thalia. *Euripides: Phoenician Women*. London: Bloomsbury, 2014.

Park, Katharine and Lorraine J. Daston. "Unnatural Conceptions: The Study of Monsters in Sixteenth- and Seventeenth-Century France and England." *Past and Present* 92:1 (1981), 20–54.

Parker, Patricia. *Shakespeare from the Margins: Language, Culture, Context*. Chicago: University of Chicago Press, 1996.

Parker, Patricia. "Was Illyria as Mysterious and Foreign as We Think?" In *The Mysterious and the Foreign in Early Modern England*. Edited by Helen Ostovich, Mary V. Silcox, and Graham Roebuck. 209–34. Newark: University of Delaware Press, 2008.

Parker, R. B. "Themes and Staging of *Bartholomew Fair*." *University of Toronto Quarterly* 39:4 (1970), 293–309.

Paster, Gail Kern. *The Body Embarrassed: Drama and the Disciplines of Shame in Early Modern England*. Ithaca, NY: Cornell University Press, 1993.

Paster, Gail Kern. *Humoring the Body: Emotions and the Shakespearean Stage*. Chicago: University of Chicago Press, 2004.

Peele, George. *The Life and Works of George Peele*, vol. 1. Edited by David H. Horne. New Haven, CT: Yale University Press, 1952.

Peele, George. *Battle of Alcazar*. Edited by John Yoklavich. In *The Dramatic Works of George Peele*, vol. 4. New Haven, CT: Yale University Press, 1961.

Pelling, Christopher. "The Shaping of *Coriolanus*: Dionysius, Plutarch, and Shakespeare." *Poetica* 48 (1997), 3–32.

Pelling, Christopher. "Seeing a Roman Tragedy through Greek Eyes: Shakespeare's *Julius Caesar*." In *Sophocles and the Greek Tragic Tradition*. Edited by Simon Goldhill and Edith Hall. 264–88. Cambridge: Cambridge University Press, 2009.

Pentland, Elizabeth. "Beyond the 'Lyric' in Illyricum: Some Early Modern Backgrounds to *Twelfth Night*." In *Twelfth Night: New Critical Essays*. Edited by James Schiffer. 149–66. London: Routledge, 2011.

Pertusi, Agostino. "Il Ritorno alle fonti del teatro Greco classico: Euripide nell'Umanesimo e nel Rinascimento." In *Venezia e l'Oriente fra tardo Medioevo e Rinascimento*. 205–24. Firenze: Sansoni, 1966.

Peterson, Kaara L. and Deanne Williams, eds. *The Afterlife of Ophelia*. Basingstoke: Palgrave Macmillan, 2012.

Peyré, Yves. "Heywood's Library." In Thomas Heywood, *Troia Britanica*. Edited by Yves Peyré et al. Early English Mythological Texts Series. Accessed August 7, 2015. http://www.shakmyth.org/page/Early+Modern+Mythological+Texts%3A+Troia+Britanica%2C+Library.

Philologus, Benedictus. "De Tragoedia." In *Senecae Tragoediae*. Edited by Benedictus Philologus. Aiiiir-aiiiiv. Florence: Filippo Giunta, 1506.

Pigman, G. W. "Versions of Imitation in the Renaissance." *Renaissance Quarterly* 33:1 (1980), 1–32.

Pincombe, Michael. *The Plays of John Lyly: Eros and Eliza*. Manchester: Manchester University Press, 1996.

Pletcher, James. "Euripides in Heliodorus' *Aethiopiaka* 7–8." *GCN* 9 (1998), 17–27.

Plutarch. *Les Oeuvres morales et meslees de Plutarque*. Translated by Jacques Amyot. Vol. 3. Paris: Michel de Vascosan, 1572.

Plutarch. *The Lives of the Noble Grecians and Romanes*. Translated by Thomas North. London: Thomas Vautroullier and John Wight, 1579.

Plutarch. *The Philosophie, Commonlie Called, the Morals*. Translated by Philemon Holland. London: Arnold Hatfield, 1603.

Pollard, Tanya. "'A Thing Like Death': Poisons and Sleeping Potions in *Romeo and Juliet* and *Antony and Cleopatra*." *Renaissance Drama* 32 (2003), 95–121.

Pollard, Tanya. "A Kind of Wild Medicine: Revenge as Remedy in Early Modern England." *Revista Canaria de Estudios Ingleses* 50 (2005), 57–69.

Pollard, Tanya. *Drugs and Theater in Early Modern England*. Oxford: Oxford University Press, 2005.

Pollard, Tanya. "Romancing the Greeks: A Look at *Cymbeline*'s Generic Models." In *How To Do Things With Shakespeare*. Edited by Laurie Maguire. 34–53. Oxford: Blackwell, 2007.

Pollard, Tanya. "Hecuba." In *A Dictionary of Shakespeare's Classical Mythology*. Edited by Yves Peyré (2009–). http://www.shakmyth.org/myth/107/hecuba/analysis.

Pollard, Tanya. "Audience Reception." In *The Oxford Handbook to Shakespeare*. Edited by Arthur Kinney. 452–67. Oxford University Press, 2011.

Pollard, Tanya. "What's Hecuba to Shakespeare?" *Renaissance Quarterly* 65:4 (2012), 1060–93.

Pollard, Tanya. "Conceiving Tragedy." In *Shakespearean Sensations: Experiencing Literature in Early Modern England*. Edited by Katharine Craik and Tanya Pollard. 85–100. Cambridge: Cambridge University Press, 2013.

Pollard, Tanya. "Greek Playbooks and Dramatic Forms in Early Modern England." In *Forms of Early Modern Writing*. Edited by Allison Deutermann and Andras Kisery. 99–123. Manchester: Manchester University Press, 2013.

Pollard, Tanya. "Tragicomedy." In *The Oxford History of Classical Reception in English Literature*, vol. 2: *The Renaissance*. Edited by Patrick Cheney and Philip Hardie. 419–32. Oxford: Oxford University Press, 2015.

Pollard, Tanya. "Verona's Tragic Women." *Theatre for a New Audience 360 Series* (2015), 10–12.

Pollard, Tanya. "Encountering Homer through Greek Plays in Sixteenth-Century Europe." In *Epic Performances: From the Middle Ages into the Twenty-First Century*. Edited by Fiona Macintosh, Justine McConnell, Stephen Harrison, and Claire Kenward. Oxford: Oxford University Press, forthcoming.

Pontani, Filippomaria. "Ancient Greek." In *The Classical Tradition*. Edited by Anthony Grafton, Glenn W. Most, and Salvatore Settis. 405–9. Cambridge, MA: Harvard University Press, 2010.

Poole, Adrian. "Euripides." In *The Classical Tradition*. Edited by Anthony Grafton, Glenn W. Most, and Salvatore Settis. 346–7. Cambridge, MA: Harvard University Press, 2010.

Porter, Enid. *Cambridgeshire Customs and Folklore*. London: Routledge & Kegan Paul, 1969.

Purkiss, Diane. "Introduction." *Three Tragedies by Renaissance Women*. Edited by Diane Purkiss. xi–xliii. London and New York: Penguin, 1998.

Purkiss, Diane. "Blood, Sacrifice, Marriage and Death: Why Iphigeneia and Mariam have to die." *Women and Writing* 6:1 (1999), 27–45.

Purkiss, Diane. "Medea in the English Renaissance." In *Medea in Performance, 1500–2000*. Edited by Edith Hall, Fiona Macintosh, and Oliver Taplin. 32–48. Oxford: Legenda, 2000.

Puttenham, George. *The Art of English Poesy*. London: Richard Field, 1589.

Quintilian, *Institutio Oratoria*. Edited by Donald Russell. 5 vols, vol. 3. Cambridge, MA: Harvard University Press, 2002.

Quint, David. *Origin and Originality in Renaissance Literature*. New Haven, CT: Yale University Press, 1983.

Rainolds, John. *Th'Overthrow of Stage Plays*. Middelburg: Richard Schilders, 1599.

Raven, James. "Selling Books Across Europe, c. 1450–1800: An Overview." *Publishing History* 34 (1993), 5–19.

REED, Records of Early English Drama. http://reed.utoronto.ca.

Rehm, Rush. "Performing the Chorus: Choral Action, Interaction and Absence in Euripides." *Arion* 3rd series 4:1 (1996), 45–60.

Reiss, Timothy. "Renaissance Theatre and the Theory of Tragedy." In *The Cambridge History of Literary Criticism*, vol. 3: *The Renaissance*. Edited by Glyn Norton. 229–47. Cambridge: Cambridge University Press, 1999.

Reynolds, L. D. and N. G. Wilson. *Scribes and Scholars: A Guide to the Transmission of Greek and Latin Literature*. Oxford: Clarendon Press, 1968, 1991.

Rhodes, Neil. "Marlowe and the Greeks." *Renaissance Studies* 27:2 (2013), 199–218.

Riehle, Wolfgang. *Shakespeare, Plautus, and the Humanist Tradition*. Cambridge: Boydell and Brewer, 1990.

Ringer, Mark. *Electra and the Empty Urn: Metatheater and Role Playing in Sophocles*. Chapel Hill: University of North Carolina Press, 1998.

Ringler, William. "The Immediate Source of Euphuism." *PMLA* 53:3 (1938), 678–86.

Ristine, Frank. *English Tragicomedy: Its Origin and History*. New York: Columbia University Press, 1963.

Roach, Joseph. *Cities of the Dead: Circum-Atlantic Performance*. New York: Columbia University Press, 1996.

Robortello, Francesco. *In Librem Aristotelis*. Florence, 1548.

Rodríguez Herrera, José Manuel. "Much Ado About Whose Fingerprints? Shakespeare's Hand in the 1602 Additions to *The Spanish Tragedy*." *Neophilologus* 99:3 (2015), 505–20.

Rose, Mary Beth. "Where are the Mothers in Shakespeare?: Options for Gender Representation in the English Renaissance." *Shakespeare Quarterly* 42:3 (1991), 291–314.

Rosen, Ralph. "Aristophanes, Old Comedy and Greek Tragedy." In *A Companion to Tragedy*. Edited by Rebecca Bushnell. 251–68. Oxford: Blackwell, 2005.

Royster, Francesca. "White-limed walls: Whiteness and Gothic Extremism in Shakespeare's *Titus Andronicus*." *Shakespeare Quarterly* 51: 4 (2000), 432–55.

Rummel, Erika. *Erasmus as a Translator of the Classics*. Toronto: University of Toronto Press, 1985.

Rummel, Erika. *Erasmus on Women*. Toronto: Toronto University Press, 1996.

Rummel, Erika. "Fertile Ground: Erasmus' Travels in England." In *Travel and Translation in the Early Modern Period*. Edited by Carmine di Biase. 45–52. Amsterdam: Rodopi, 2006.

Saladin, Jean Christophe. "Euripide Luthérien?" In *Mélanges de l'Ecole Française de Rome* 108:1 (1996), 155–70.

Salkeld, Duncan. "His Collaborator George Wilkins." In *The Shakespeare Circle: An Alternative Biography*. Edited by Paul Edmondson and Stanley Wells. 289–96. Cambridge: Cambridge University Press, 2015.

Saxonhouse, Arlene W. "Another Antigone: The Emergence of the Female Political Actor in Euripides' *Phoenician Women*." *Political Theory* 33:4 (2005), 472–94.

Scaliger, Julius Caesar. *Select Translations from Scaliger's Poetics*. Edited and translated by Frederick Morgan Padelford. New York: Henry Holt, 1905.

Scaliger, Julius Caesar. *Poetices Libri Septem*. Edited by Luc Dietz. 5 vols. Stuttgart: Frommann-Holzboog, 1995.

Scharffenberger, Elizabeth W. "A Tragic Lysistrata? Jocasta in the 'Reconciliation Scene' of the *Phoenician Women*." *Rheinisches Museum für Philologie* 138:3/4 (1995), 312–36.

Scharffenberger, Elizabeth W. "Euripidean 'Paracomedy': A Reconsideration of the *Antiope*." *Text and Presentation* 17 (1996), 65–72.

Schein, Seth. "*Philia* in Euripides' *Alcestis*." *Metis* 3:1–2 (1988), 179–206.

Schleiner, Louise. "Latinized Greek Drama in Shakespeare's Writing of *Hamlet*." *Shakespeare* Quarterly 41:1 (1990), 29–48.

Schoenfeldt, Michael. *Bodies and Selves in Early Modern England: Physiology and Inwardness in Spenser, Shakespeare, Herbert, and Milton*. Cambridge: Cambridge University Press, 1999.

Scott, William. *The Model of Poesy*. Edited by Gavin Alexander. Cambridge: Cambridge University Press, 2013.

Segal, Erich. "Hero and Leander: Góngora and Marlowe." *Comparative Literature* 15:4 (1963), 338–56.

Segal, Erich. *Roman Laughter: The Comedy of Plautus*. Oxford: Oxford University Press, 1968.

Segal, Erich. "'The comic catastrophe': An Essay on Euripidean Comedy." *Bulletin of the Institute of Classical Studies* 40:66 (1995), 46–55.

Segal, Erich. *The Death of Comedy*. Cambridge, MA: Harvard University Press, 2009.

Seidensticker, Bernd. "Dithyramb, Comedy, and Satyr-Play." Translated by Isabel Köster and Justina Gregory. In *A Companion to Greek Tragedy*. Edited by Justina Gregory. 38–54. Oxford: Blackwell, 2005.

Selden, John. *Titles of Honour* (London: William Stansby, 1614).

Selleck, Nancy. *The Interpersonal Idiom in Shakespeare, Donne and Early Modern Culture*. New York: Palgrave MacMillan, 2008.

Semenza, Gregory M. Colón. "*The Spanish Tragedy* and Metatheatre." In *The Cambridge Companion to English Renaissance Tragedy*. Edited by Emma Smith and Garrett Sullivan. 153–62. Cambridge: Cambridge University Press, 2010.

Seneca. *Troas*. Translated by Jasper Heywood. London, 1560.

Shakespeare, William. *The Winter's Tale*. Edited by Israel Gollancz. London: J. M. Dent, 1894.

Shakespeare, William. *The Comedy of Errors*. Edited by R. A. Foakes. Arden Shakespeare. London: Methuen, 1962.

Shakespeare, William. *The Complete Works*, ed. Stanley Wells and Gary Taylor. Oxford: Clarendon Press, 1986.

Shakespeare, William. *The Rape of Lucrece*, in *Shakespeare, The Poems*. Edited by John Roe. 147–238. Cambridge: Cambridge University Press, 1992, 2006.

Shakespeare, William. *Titus Andronicus*. Edited by Jonathan Bate. Arden Shakespeare. London: Routledge, 1995, 2005.

Shakespeare, William. *Julius Caesar*. Edited by David Daniell. Arden Shakespeare. London: Thomson Learning, 1998, 2003.

Shakespeare, William. *The Tragical History of Hamlet Prince of Denmark*. Edited by A. R. Braunmuller. The Pelican Shakespeare. New York: Penguin Classics, 2001.

Shakespeare, William. *King Henry IV, Part 1*. Edited by David Scott Kastan. Arden Shakespeare. London: Thomson Learning, 2002.

Shakespeare, William. *Hamlet, Prince of Denmark*. Edited by Philip Edwards. Cambridge: Cambridge University Press, 2003.

Shakespeare, William. *Two Gentlemen of Verona*. Edited by William Carroll. Arden Shakespeare. London: Thomson Learning, 2004.

Shakespeare, William. *As You Like It*. Edited by Juliet Dusinberre. Arden Shakespeare. London: Thomson Learning, 2006.

Shakespeare, William. *Hamlet*. Edited by Ann Thompson and Neil Taylor. Arden Shakespeare. London: Thompson Learning, 2006.

Shakespeare, William. *Much Ado about Nothing*. Edited by Claire McEachern. Arden Shakespeare. London: Bloomsbury, 2006.

Shakespeare, William. *Hamlet*. Edited by Jonathan Bate and Eric Rasmussen, The RSC Shakespeare. New York: Modern Library, 2008.

Shakespeare, William. *Twelfth Night*. Edited by Keir Elam. Arden Shakespeare. London: Bloomsbury, 2008.

Shakespeare, William. *The Winter's Tale*. Edited by John Pitcher. Arden Shakespeare. London: Methuen, 2010.

Shakespeare, William. *Romeo and Juliet*. Edited by René Weis. Arden Shakespeare. London: Bloomsbury, 2012.

Shakespeare, William. *Coriolanus*. Edited by Peter Holland. Arden Shakespeare. London: Bloomsbury, 2013.

Shakespeare, William. *Henry IV Part Two*. Edited by James Bulman. Arden Shakespeare. London: Bloomsbury, 2016.

Shakespeare, William and George Wilkins. *Pericles*. Edited by Suzanne Gossett. Arden Shakespeare. London: Bloomsbury, 2004.

Shannon, Laurie. "Nature's Bias: Renaissance Homonormativity and Elizabethan Comic Likeness." *Modern Philology* 98:2 (2000), 183–210.

Shapiro, James. *Rival Playwrights: Marlowe, Jonson, Shakespeare*. New York: Columbia University Press, 1991.

Sheppard, Samuel. *The Times Displayed in Six Sestyads*. London: J. P., 1646.

Showalter, Elaine. "Representing Ophelia: Women, Madness, and the Responsibility of Female Criticism." In *Shakespeare and the Question of Theory*. Edited by Patricia Parker and Geoffrey Hartman. 77–94. London: Methuen, 1985.

Showerman, Earl. "Orestes and Hamlet: From Myth to Masterpiece, Part I." *The Oxfordian* 7 (2004), 89–114.

Showerman, Earl. "'Look Down and See What Death Is Doing': Gods and Greeks in *The Winter's Tale*." *The Oxfordian* 10 (2007), 55–74.

Showerman, Earl. "Shakespeare's Many Much Ado's: *Alcestis*, Hercules, and *Love's Labour's Wonne*." *Brief Chronicles* I (2009), 109–40.

Shuger, Deborah. *The Renaissance Bible: Scholarship, Sacrifice, and Subjectivity*. Berkeley: University of California Press, 1998.

Sidney, Philip. *The Defence of Poesie*. London: William Ponsonby, 1595.

Silk, Michael. "Heracles and Greek Tragedy." *Greece and Rome*, 2nd series, 32:1 (1985), 1–22.

Silk, Michael. "Aristophanic Paratragedy." In *Tragedy, Comedy, and the Polis*. Edited by Alan Sommerstein. 477–504. Bari: Levante, 1993.

Silk, Michael. "Shakespeare and Greek Tragedy: Strange Relationship'." In *Shakespeare and the Classics*. 241–57. Edited by Charles Martindale and A. B. Taylor. Cambridge: Cambridge University Press, 2004.

Sissa, Giulia. *Greek Virginity*. Translated by Arthur Goldhammer. Cambridge, MA: Harvard University Press, 1990.

Skretkowicz, Victor. *European Erotic Romance: Philhellene Protestantism, Renaissance Translation and English Literary Politics*. Manchester: Manchester University Press, 2010.

Slater, Niall W. "Dead Again: (En)gendering Praise in Euripides' *Alcestis*." *Helios* 27:2 (2000), 105–21.

Slater, Niall W. "Nothing To Do With Satyrs? *Alcestis* and the Concept of Prosatyric Drama." In *Satyr Drama: Tragedy at Play*. Edited by George W. M. Harrison. 83–101. Swansea: Classical Press of Wales, 2005.

Slater, Niall W. *Euripides: Alcestis*. London: Bloomsbury, 2013.

Smith, Bruce R. *Ancient Scripts and Modern Experience on the English Stage 1500–1700*. Princeton: Princeton University Press, 1988.

Smith, Emma. "Hieronimo's Afterlives." In *The Spanish Tragedie with the First Part of Jeronimo*. Edited by Emma Smith. 133–59. London: Penguin, 1998.

Smith, Emma. "Ghost Writing: *Hamlet* and the *Ur-Hamlet*." In *The Renaissance Text*. Edited by Andrew Murphy. 177–90. Manchester: Manchester University Press, 2000.

Smith, Emma. "Shakespeare and Early Modern Tragedy." In *The Cambridge Companion to English Renaissance Tragedy*. Edited by Emma Smith and Garrett Sullivan. 132–50. Cambridge: Cambridge University Press, 2010.

Smith, G. C. Moore. *College Plays Performed in the University of Cambridge*. Cambridge: Cambridge University Press, 1923.

Smith, Rebecca. "A Heart Cleft in Twain: The Dilemma of Shakespeare's Gertrude." In *The Woman's Part: Feminist Criticism of Shakespeare*. Edited by Carolyn Ruth Swift Lenz, Gayle Greene, and Carol Thomas Neely. 194–210. Urbana: University of Illinois Press, 1980.

Solinus, Julius. "Of the Lesser Asia: of the Temple of Diana at Ephesus." In *The Excellent and Pleasant Worke of Iulius Solinus Polyhistor*. Translated by Arthur Golding. London: J. Charlewoode for Thomas Hacket, 1587.

Solmsen, Friedrich. *Electra And Orestes: Three Recognitions in Greek Tragedy*. Amsterdam: N.V. Noord Hollandsche Uitgevers Maa Tschappij, 1967.

Soone, William. "Letter to George Braun." In *Civitates Orbis Terrarum*, vol. 2. Edited by Braun and Hogenberg. Cologne, 1575.

Spencer, Terence. "Shakespeare's Isle of Delphos." *The Modern Language Review* 47 (1952), 199–202.

Stanivukovic, Goran. "'What country, friends, is this?': The Geographies of Illyria in Early Modern England." *Litteraria Pragensia* 12:23 (2002): 5–21.

Stanivukovic, Goran. "Illyria Revisited: Shakespeare and the Eastern Adriatic." In *Shakespeare and the Mediterranean*. Edited by Tom Clayton, Susan Brock, and Vicente Fores. 401–15. Newark: University of Delaware Press, 2004.

Steggle, Matthew. *Wars of the Theatres: The Poetics of Personation in the Age of Jonson*. Victoria: English Literary Studies, 1998.

Steggle, Matthew. "Aristophanes in Early Modern England." In *Aristophanes in Performance, 421 BC–AD 2007: Peace, Birds and Frogs*. Edited by Edith Hall and Amanda Wrigley. 52–65. Oxford: Legenda, 2007.

Steggle, Matthew. *Laughing and Weeping in Early Modern Theatres*. Aldershot: Ashgate, 2007.

Stern, Tiffany. "Actors and Audience on the Stage at Blackfriars." In *Inside Shakespeare: Essays on the Blackfriars Stage*. Edited by Paul Menzer. 35–53. Selinsgrove, PA: Susquehanna University Press, 2006.

Stern, Tiffany and Simon Palfrey. *Shakespeare in Parts*. Oxford: Oxford University Press, 2007.

Stevenson, Jane. "Greek Learning and Women." In *Encyclopedia of Women in the Renaissance: Italy, France, and England*. 122–4. Edited by Diana Maury Robin, Anne R. Larsen, and Carole Levin. Santa Barbara: ABC-Clio, 2007.

Stiblinus, Gasparus. "Argumentum Et Praefatio Gaspari Stiblini In Iphigeniam Tauricam." In *Evripides Poeta Tragicorum princeps*. 381. Basel: Johannes Oporinus, 1562.

Stiblinus, Gasparus. "In Hecabam Euripidis Praefatio." In *Evripides Poeta Tragicorum Princeps*. 38–9. Basel: Johannes Oporinus, 1562.

Stiblinus, Gasparus. "Praefatio in *Phoenissas*." In *Evripides Poeta Tragicorum Princeps*. 124–6. Basel: Johannes Oporinus, 1562.

Stieber, Mary. "Statuary in Euripides' *Alcestis*." *Arion*, Third Series, 5:3 (1998), 69–97.

Straznicky, Marta. *Privacy, Playreading, and Women's Closet Drama, 1500–1700*. Cambridge: Cambridge University Press, 2004.

Streufert, Paul. "Christopherson at Cambridge: Greco-Catholic Ethics in the Protestant University." In *Early Modern Academic Drama*. 45–63. Edited by Jonathan Walker and Paul Streufert. Burlington: Ashgate, 2008.

Sutton, Dana F. "Satyric Elements in the *Alcestis*." *Rivista di Studi Classici* 21 (1973), 384–91.

Suzuki, Mihoko. "Gender, Class, and the Ideology of Comic Form: *Much Ado About Nothing* and *Twelfth Night*." In *A Feminist Companion to Shakespeare*. Edited by Dympna Callaghan. 121–43. Oxford: Blackwell, 2000.

Sweeney, John G. "*Sejanus* and the People's Beastly Rage." *ELH* 48:1 (1981), 61–82.

Sypherd, Wilbur. *Jephthah and his Daughter*. Newark: University of Delaware Press, 1948.

Taplin, Oliver. "Fifth-Century Tragedy and Comedy: A Synkrisis." *Journal of Hellenic Studies* 106 (1986), 163–74.

Taplin, Oliver. "Comedy and the Tragic." In *Tragedy and the Tragic: Greek Theatre and Beyond*. Edited by M. S. Silk. 188–202. Oxford: Clarendon Press, 1996.

Tarrant, R. J. "Senecan Drama and its Antecedents." *Harvard Studies in Classical Philology* 82 (1978), 213–63.

Tassi, Marguerite. *Women and Revenge in Shakespeare*. Selinsgrove, PA: Susquehanna University Press, 2011.

Tatlock, John S. P. "The Siege of Troy in Elizabethan Literature, Especially in Shakespeare and Heywood." *PMLA* 30:4 (1915), 673–770.

Taylor, Gary and Macdonald P. Jackson. "Pericles." In *William Shakespeare: A Textual Companion*. Edited by Stanley Wells and Gary Taylor. 130–1, 556–92. Oxford: Clarendon Press, 1987.

Teramura, Misha. "Brute Parts: From Troy to Britain at the Rose, 1595–1600." In *Lost Plays in Shakespeare's England*. Edited by David McInnis and Matthew Steggle. 127–47. New York: Palgrave Macmillan, 2014.

The Lost Plays Database. Edited by Roslyn L. Knutson, David McInnis, and Matthew Steggle. Melbourne: University of Melbourne, 2009. www.lostplays.org

Thomson, J. A. K. *Shakespeare and the Classics*. London: George Allen & Unwin, 1952.

Tilley, Arthur. "Greek Studies in Early Sixteenth-Century England." *English Historical Review* 53 (1938), 221–39 & 438–56.

Traub, Valerie. *The Renaissance of Lesbianism in Early Modern England*. Cambridge: Cambridge University Press, 2002.

Uman, Deborah. "Wonderfully Astonied at the Stoutenes of her Mind: Translating Rhetoric and Education in Jane Lumley's *The Tragedie of Iphigenia*." In *Performing Pedagogy in Early Modern England: Gender, Instruction and Performance*. Edited by Kathryn M. Moncrief and Kathryn R. McPherson. 53–64. Aldershot: Ashgate, 2011.

Uman, Deborah. *Women as Translators in Early Modern England*. Newark: University of Delaware Press, 2012.

Uman, Deborah and Belén Bistué. "Translation as Collaborative Authorship: Margaret Tyler's *The Mirrour of Princely Deedes and Knighthood*." *Comparative Literature Studies* 44:3 (2007), 298–323.

Underdowne, Thomas, trans. *An AEthiopian Historie Written in Greeke by Heliodorus*. London: Frances Coldock, 1569.

Urry, William. *Christopher Marlowe and Canterbury*. Edited by Andrew Butcher. London: Faber and Faber, 1988.

Usher, Penelope Meyers. "Greek Sacrifice in Shakespeare's Rome: Titus Andronicus and Iphigenia in Aulis." In *Rethinking Shakespeare Source Study: Audiences, Authors, and Digital Technologies*. Edited by Dennis Britton and Melissa Walter. Abingdon: Routledge, forthcoming 2017.

Usher, Phillip John. "Tragedy and Translation." *A Companion to Translation Studies.* Edited by Sandra Bermann and Catherine Porter. 467–78. Oxford: Wiley-Blackwell, 2014.

van Elk, Martine. "'This sympathizèd one day's error': Genre, Representation, and Subjectivity in *The Comedy of Errors.*" *Shakespeare Quarterly* 60:1 (2009), 47–72.

van Elk, Martine. "'Thou Shalt Present Me as an Eunuch To Him': Terence in Early Modern England." In *A Companion to Terence.* Edited by Antony Augoustakis and Ariana Trill. 410–28. Oxford: Wiley-Blackwell, 2013.

Van Es, Bart. *Shakespeare in Company.* Oxford: Oxford University Press, 2013.

Vernant, Jean-Pierre and Pierre Vidal-Naquet. *Myth and Tragedy in Ancient Greece,* trans. Janet Lloyd. New York: Zone Books, 1990.

Vickers, Brian. *Shakespeare, Co-Author: A Historical Study of Five Collaborative Plays.* Oxford: Oxford University Press, 2002.

Vickers, Brian. "Identifying Shakespeare's Additions to *The Spanish Tragedy* (1602): A new(er) approach." *Shakespeare* 8:1 (2012), 13–43.

Vine, Angus. "Myth and Legend." In *The Ashgate Research Companion to Popular Culture in Early Modern England.* Edited by Abigail Shinn, Matthew Dimmock, Andrew Hadfield. 103–18. Aldershot: Ashgate, 2014.

Walden, J. W. H. "Stage-Terms in Heliodorus's *Aethiopica.*" *Harvard Studies in Classical Philology* 5 (1894), 1–43.

Walker, Jonathan and Paul D. Streufert, eds. *Early Modern Academic Drama.* Burlington: Ashgate, 2008.

Wallace, Andrew. *Virgil's Schoolboys: The Poetics of Pedagogy in Renaissance England.* Oxford: Oxford University Press, 2010.

Ward, Allyna. *Women and Tudor Tragedy: Feminizing Counsel and Representing Genre.* Madison: Fairleigh Dickinson Press, 2013.

Warner, Marina. "'Come to Hecuba': Theatrical Empathy and Memories of Troy." *The Shakespearean International Yearbook* 11 (2011), 61–87.

Watson, Thomas. *Sophoclis Antigone.* London: John Wolf, 1581.

Watson, Thomas. *Sophocles' Antigone.* Translated by Dana Sutton. http://www.philological.bham.ac.uk/watson/antigone/index.html. Accessed August 15, 2014.

Webbe, William. *A Discourse of English Poetrie.* London: John Charlewood, 1586.

Weber, Clifford. "The Dionysus in Aeneas." *Classical Philology* 97:4 (2002), 322–43.

Webster, John. *The White Devil.* In *The Works of John Webster,* vol. 1. Edited by David Gunby, David Carnegie, Antony Hammond, and Doreen DelVecchio. Cambridge: Cambridge University Press, 1995.

Weil, Judith. "Visible Hecubas." In *The Female Tragic Hero in English Renaissance Drama.* Edited by Naomi Conn Liebler, 51–69. Basingstoke: Palgrave, 2002.

Weinberg, Bernard. "Translations and Commentaries of Longinus, *On the Sublime,* to 1600: A Bibliography." *Modern Philology* 47 (1950), 145–51.

Weller, Philip. "'Kill Claudio': A Laugh Almost Killed by the Critics." *Journal of Dramatic Theory and Criticism* 11:1 (1996), 101–10.

Werth, Andrew. "Shakespeare's 'Lesse Greek.'" *The Oxfordian* 5 (2002), 11–29.

Westney, Lizette. "Hecuba in Sixteenth-Century English Literature." *College Language Association Journal* 27:4 (1984), 436–9.

Whittington, Leah. "Shakespeare and the Greeks: Theatricality and Performance from Plutarch's *Lives* to *Coriolanus*." In *Homer and Greek Tragedy in Early Modern England's Theatres*. Edited by Tania Demetriou and Tanya Pollard. Special issue of *Classical Receptions Journal* 9:1 (2017), 120–43.

Whitworth, Charles. "Rectifying Shakespeare's Errors: Romance and Farce in Bardeditry." In *The Theory and Practice of Text-editing: Essays in Honour of James T. Boulton*. Edited by Ian Small and Marcus Welsh. 107–41. Cambridge: Cambridge University Press, 1991.

Wiersma, Stanley. "The Ancient Greek Novel and its Heroines: A Female Paradox." *Mnemosyne* 43 (1990), 109–23.

Wiggins, Martin. *Shakespeare and the Drama of his Time*. Oxford: Oxford University Press, 2000.

Wiggins, Martin, with Catherine Richardson, eds. *British Drama 1533–1642*. 4 vols, vol. 4, 1598–1602. Oxford: Oxford University Press, 2014.

Wilcox, Helen. "Gender and Genre in Shakespeare's Tragicomedies." In *Reclamations of Shakespeare*. Edited by A. J. Hoeneslaars. 129–38. Amsterdam: Rodopi, 1994.

Williams, Gweno. "Translating the Self, Performing the Self." In *Women and Dramatic Production, 1550–1700*. Edited by Alison Findlay and Stephanie Hodgson-Wright with Gweno Williams. 15–41. London: Routledge, 2000.

Williams, Wes. *Monsters and Their Meanings in Early Modern Culture: Mighty Magic*. Oxford: Oxford University Press, 2011.

Wilson, Douglas B. "Euripides' *Alcestis* and the Ending of Shakespeare's *The Winter's Tale*." *Iowa State Journal of Research* 58 (1984), 345–55.

Wilson, Emily. *Mocked with Death: Tragic Overliving from Sophocles to Milton*. Baltimore: Johns Hopkins Press, 2004.

Wilson, F. P. *The English Drama, 1485–1585*. Oxford: Clarendon Press, 1968.

Wilson, H. B. *The History of Merchant-Taylors' School*. London, 1814.

Wilson, Mary Floyd. *Occult Knowledge, Science, and Gender on the Shakespearean Stage*. Cambridge: Cambridge University Press, 2013.

Wilson, N. G. *From Byzantium to Italy: Greek Studies in the Italian Renaissance*. London: Duckworth, 1992.

Winston, Jessica. "Expanding the Political Nation: *Gorboduc* at the Inns of Court and Succession Revisited." *Early Theatre* 8:1 (2005), 11–34.

Winston, Jessica. "Seneca in Early Elizabethan England." *Renaissance Quarterly* 59:1 (2006), 29–58.

Winston, Jessica. "Early 'English Seneca': From 'Coterie' Translations to the Popular Stage." In *Brill's Companion to the Reception of Senecan Tragedy*. Edited by Eric Dodson-Robinson. 174–202. Leiden: Brill, 2016.

Wofford, Susanne. "Foreign Emotions on the Stage in *Twelfth Night.*" In *Transnational Exchange in Early Modern Theater.* Edited by Robert Henke and Eric Nicholson. 141–58. Aldershot: Ashgate, 2008.

Wohl, Victoria. *Intimate Commerce: Exchange, Gender, and Subjectivity in Greek Tragedy.* Austin: University of Texas Press, 1998.

Wohl, Victoria. "Tragedy and Feminism." In *A Companion to Tragedy.* Edited by Rebecca Bushnell. 145–60. Oxford: Blackwell Publishing, 2009.

Wolff, Samuel. *The Greek Romances in Elizabethan Prose Fiction.* New York: Columbia, 1902.

Worden, Blair. "Ben Jonson among the Historians." In *Culture and Politics in Early Stuart England.* 67–89. London: Macmillan, 1994.

Wright, Matthew. "*Orestes*, a Euripidean Sequel," *Classical Quarterly* 56:1 (2006), 33–47.

Wright, Matthew. *Euripides: Orestes.* London: Bloomsbury, 2008.

Wynne-Davies, Marion. "The Good Lady Lumley's Desire: Iphigeneia and the Nonsuch Banqueting House." In *Heroines of the Golden StAge: Women and Drama in Spain and England 1500–1700.* Edited by Rina Walthaus and Marguérite Corporaal. 111–28. Kassel: Reichenberger, 2008.

Xenophon. *An Ephesian Tale.* Translated by Graham Anderson. In *Collected Ancient Greek Novels.* Edited by B. P. Reardon. 125–69. Berkeley: University of California Press, 1989.

Zamir, Tzachi. "Wooden Subjects." *New Literary History* 39:2 (2008), 277–300.

Zeitlin, Froma. "The Closet of Masks: Role-playing and Myth-making in the *Orestes* of Euripides." *Ramus: Critical Studies in Greek and Roman Literature* 9 (1980), 51–77.

Zeitlin, Froma. "Art, Memory, and *Kleos* in Euripides' *Iphigenia in Aulis*." In *History, Tragedy, Theory: Dialogues on Athenian Drama.* Edited by Barbara E. Goff. 174–201. Austin: University of Texas Press, 1995.

Zeitlin, Froma. *Playing the Other: Gender and Society in Classical Greek Literature*: Chicago: University of Chicago Press, 1996.

Zeitlin, Froma. "Intimate Relations: Children, Childbearing, and Parentage on the Euripidean Stage." In *Performance, Iconography, Reception: Studies in Honour of Oliver Taplin.* Edited by Martin Revermann and Peter Wilson. 318–32. Oxford: Oxford University Press, 2008.

Zeitlin, Froma. "A Study in Form: Recognition Scenes in the Three Electra Plays." *Lexis* 30 (2012), 361–78.

Index